THE COMPARATIVE DEVELOPMENT OF ADAPTIVE SKILLS:
Evolutionary Implications

Edited by

Eugene S. Gollin
University of Colorado, Boulder

LEA LAWRENCE ERLBAUM ASSOCIATES, PUBLISHERS
1985 Hillsdale, New Jersey London

Lawrence Erlbaum Associates, Inc., Publishers
365 Broadway
Hillsdale, New Jersey 07642

Library of Congress Cataloging in Publication Data

Main entry under title:

The Comparative development of adaptive skills.

Includes bibliographies and indexes.
1. Adaptability (Psychology) 2. Adaptation
(Biology) 3. Psychology, Comparative. 4. Developmental
psychology. 5. Nature and nurture. I. Gollin,
Eugene S.
BF335.C574 1985   156   84–24667
ISBN 0-89859-519-3

47,393

Printed in the United States of America
10 9 8 7 6 5 4 3 2 1

Contents

iii

Contributors

JEFFREY R. ALBERTS, Department of Psychology, Indiana University, Bloomington, Indiana 47405.

ANNE BEKOFF, Department of Environmental, Population, and Organismic Biology, University of Colorado, Boulder, Colorado 80309.

JERRAM BROWN, Department of Biological Sciences, State University of New York, Albany, New York 12207.

DAVID CHISZAR, Department of Psychology, University of Colorado, Boulder, Colorado 80309.

EUGENE S. GOLLIN, Department of Psychology, University of Colorado, Boulder, Colorado 80309.

ANDREW LOCK, Department of Psychology, Fylde College, University of Lancaster, Bailrigg, Lancaster, England LAI 4YF.

CELIA L. MOORE, Department of Psychology, Harbor Campus, University of Massachusetts, Boston, Massachusetts 02125.

W. JOHN SMITH, Department of Biology, University of Pennsylvania, Philadelphia, Pennsylvania 19174.

Preface

The aim of this book is to examine the development of adaptive skills in a comparative context. Comparative explorations have evolutionary implications. Thus it is inevitable that the contributors to this volume, all of whom come to the study of development with a comparative perspective, manifest concern with the relationships between ontogeny and phylogeny. Historically, attempts to deal with this set of relationships have produced brilliant insights as well as obscurant nonsense and socially malevolent doctrines. In our day these qualities of thought persist but increasing sophistication about the intricate and complex web of relationships that bind individual development to the history of life forms should contribute to the clarification of some of the perplexing problems that confront students of biobehavioral development. In this volume both field and laboratory approaches are presented. It is quite clear that the laboratory studies are increasingly informed by ecological considerations that derive from field excursions. It is also the case that laboratory findings are becoming an essential source in directing field inquiries.

The problems explored are theoretically rich and methodologically significant and the comparative scope of the contributions range widely among vertebrate species. It is our conviction that without comparative analysis information is of very limited value, and without mutual contributions from field and laboratory the story will remain only half told.

E. S. Gollin

1 Ontogeny, Phylogeny, and Causality

Eugene S. Gollin
University of Colorado, Boulder

INTRODUCTION

There are fundamental conceptual differences that divide students of development. These differences are prominent in the fields of developmental psychology, developmental psychobiology, and developmental biology. The differences are centered in conceptions of living systems, particularly with respect to the role they are thought to play in their own development. The conceptual issues affect the ways in which development is studied, how developmental outcomes are explained, what influences are assigned to the genetic substrate and to environmental events in the drama of development. An additional problem, and one addressed particularly by the contributors to this volume, is the relationship between developmental plasticity and evolutionary change.

The diverse attitudes toward the study of development are expressed in the following quotations:

> My main purpose, however, is to begin a reconceptualization of evolutionary theory in terms of energy. This is evolution considered as a process: what evolves however, is the phenotype and its variation *and the phenotype is development* (italics added). Evolution is the control of development by ecology. (Van Valen, 1976 p. 179)

A sharply different view is expressed by Cooke (1982):

> But what has been eclipsed, in the erosion of the organism from contemporary biology, is a science of those dynamic properties distinctive to the developmental

1

process, which place themselves between the repository of genetic information and the demands of the selective environment so as to constitute a shaping force in their own right during the emergence of novelty. It is doubtful whether evolution *can* really be understood without postulating and studying these, the deep transformational as opposed to the surface phenotypic aspects of organisms. The conception of the phenotype as a flat, passive interface at which the results of a particular genome are tested for adequacy against an environment is a further harmful abstraction due to neo-Darwinism. It goes hand in hand with the preoccupation of the organism as a set of achieved, "surface" structures and behavioural competences which can be scanned by a human observer for their adaptive value, to the neglect of theory concerning those levels of organization of matter and sets of transformations which underlie the coherence of the individual seen *as a development*. Since organisms *are* developments evolution is the change and diversification, with time, of developments, rather than of phenotypes in the flat surface sense of that term. (p. 122)

In this last statement the constructive contribution of the organism to development is asserted. This view is closely allied to the epigenetic ideas of Kuo (1976) and of Mayr (1963). Kuo emphasized that morphogenetic structures and their functional properties actively constrain the directions of development. In his view organismic patterns are affected by effective environmental patterns and in turn modify the effective character of the environment.

Consistent with this position is Mayr's assertion that the state of an organism at any particular time during ontogenesis is the product of a complex interacting system, the total epigenotype. The integration of genotypes, Mayr (1963) wrote, "occurs at a different level (from chromosomal architecture) with natural selection as its agent and the developmental level its locale" (p. 278).

If the idea of epigenesis is not to be reduced to jargon (Alberch, 1983) then it must be recognized that in the course of development the living system plays a crucial role in directing environment-organism transactions. As Lehrman (1953) made clear, the transactions are between an organism and an environment, not between heredity and environment, or genes and environment. The process is not one of unfolding, but of building. The building is guided by a dynamic scaffold that provides both opportunities for change and constraints upon its direction.

The constraints on the developing system are those that inhere in any collective moving from simplified to elaborated organization (Gollin, 1984b; Gottlieb, 1973; Gould, 1977; Koffka, 1959; Kuo, 1976; Weiss, 1970). The constraints are not absolute with respect to behavior or morphology since neither gene organization, environmental matrix, nor organismic history are constant for either individuals or populations (Gollin, 1981). Thus, the phrase *probabilistic epigenesis* is preferred by many (see Gottlieb, 1973, 1984) to the term *deterministic epigenesis* to describe the succession of organismic changes in behavior and morphology that constitute development.

This viewpoint is also held by Alberch (1983) who has written that even if the complete DNA sequence of an organism were known, its morphology could not be reconstructed without knowledge of the epigenetic interactions that generate the phenotype. Alberch and others who present this argument (see, for example, Jaffe, 1982; Lindenmayer, 1982) are not dismissive of genetics. Rather, they have concluded that reductive explanations are insufficient to account for the complex patterning involved in morphogenesis. As developmentalists, they are concerned with organizing principles. These principles do not appear to be reducible to physicochemical interactions (in this regard see also Stebbins, 1966, 1969).

The course of psychobiological development, like the course of morphogenesis, is not to be explained by reductionist principles. Nor is the issue of causality resolved by assigning causal functions to sets of events or properties because of temporal priority. This is tantamount to confusing development with history. Rather, what appears to be involved at every period in development is a configuration or pattern of structural and functional components constrained by organismic and experiential transactions.

Gould (1981) has dealt with this issue by pointing out that a complete theory of evolution must acknowledge a balance between "external" forces of environment that impose selection pressures and "internal" hereditary and developmental constraints. Developmental constraints, as manifested in the early stages of ontogeny, are refractory to evolutionary change, possibly because their organizational quality is so intimately related to the integrity of the developing organism (Gould & Lewontin, 1979).

However, developmental plasticity enables organisms to achieve considerable adaptive change without selection. Examples include human adaptation to high altitude environments (Gould & Lewontin, 1979) and general organismic malleability to rearing circumstances (Gollin, 1981; Gottlieb, 1983). The enormous transmissable impact of culture observable in human societies, and the intergenerational transmission of changed patterns of behavior observed in other primate groups (Harding & Strumm, 1976; Kawai, 1965; Rowell, 1972), are also illustrations of adaptive change without selection.

Only extensive comparative analysis of biobehavioral development will make it possible to distinguish, eventually, those features of structure and function that represent evolutionary change from those features that are adaptive without selection. To a considerable extent the contributors to this volume provide such an analysis of complex adaptive skills. In general the contributors are sensitive to Kummer's observation (1971) that:

> Discussions of adaptation sometimes leave us with the impression that every trait observed in a species must by definition be ideally adaptive, whereas all we can say with certainty is that it must be tolerable since it did not lead to extinction. Evolution, after all, is not sorcery. (p. 90)

COMPARATIVE ANALYSIS AND DEVELOPMENTAL PLASTICITY

While much comparative analysis is devoted to establishing ancestral relations between groups of organisms, it can have other objectives. These analyses, whether they are carried out interspecifically or intraspecifically between different ecological or cultural settings, can have as their objective the description of multiple exemplars of how living creatures make their way in the world. The value of such an approach is that all instances are treated as variants without recourse to normative judgments that are based often on the frequency of occurrence of the observed form, on moral or political models that are all too often implicit, or on the availability or convenience of the specimens observed. Examples of the last named are the laboratory rat and certain ecological settings in which primate behavior is detailed.

Knowledge of many exemplars will provide a broader basis for comprehending how any exemplar comes to pass and will also afford insight into how novel developments might occur. This is a much sounder way of approaching these issues than the anthropomorphizing and reductionist strategies that underlie much sociobiological explanatory work (for critiques of sociobiological explanatory efforts see Barnett, 1983; Coe, 1981).

A comparative-developmental approach permits us to distinguish between those aspects of development that are formal and general and those features that are substantive and particular. The division is not absolute but convenient in that it helps to delineate principles that have the appearance of universality from those that are reflective of specialized ecological conditions, unique developmental histories, and/or pathogenic agencies.

Development should be thought of as a succession of qualitative reorganizations, each of which is likely to manifest properties relevant to the contemporaneous circumstances in which the organism is functioning, and also to contain precursal properties (Gollin, 1984b; Lehrman, 1953; Sameroff & Chandler, 1975; Weiss, 1971). Examples of each kind of property are provided by several chapters in this volume (Alberts, Chapter 4; Smith, Chapter 6; Chiszar, Chapter 7).

Each qualitative reorganization contains a conservative array of measurable properties as well as transitional dynamics (Weiss, 1971). Some time ago Lehrman (1953) defined the problem in a way that has value for both theory and research design. He wrote:

> The problem for the investigator who wishes to make a causal analysis of behavior is: How did this behavior come about? . . . The problem of development is the problem of the development of new structures and activity patterns from the resolution of the interactions of *existing* structures and patterns within the organism and its internal environment, and between the organism and its outer environment . . .

The interaction out of which the organism develops . . . is between *organism* and environment! And the organism is different at each stage of its development. (p. 345)

The only change in emphasis from the Lehrman formulation required for current definitions of the problem would be a de-emphasis of the implied dichotomy between organism and environment. That entails replacing the interactionist model with a transactionist model that would be more consonant with a systems approach. The advantage of a systems approach is that it mandates a research strategy that systematically varies within the research context both organismic state and environmental circumstance, recognizing that behavior is best understood contextually. In a systems analysis the assumption is avoided that an organism is definable by a particular set of experimental operations or habitat conditions. In a systems analysis it is assumed that organismic qualities, including behavior, are a co-function of organismic state and presently acting circumstance.

If development is to be studied comparatively, in terms of intraspecific individual and group differences, as well as in terms of interspecific differences, then it becomes necessary to define a concept of developmental time (Gollin, 1984a, 1984b). *Developmental time* is to be distinguished from chronology and from ontogenetic markers such as conceptual age, birth, and weaning. Individual differences in organismic state remain even when there is identity of chronological course. There are, of course, radical variations in the state of the central nervous system, the sensory systems, and the motor system in different species at the time of birth. Additionally, there are individual differences as well as group and species differences in the configural character of the successively reorganized states that constitute the developmental course. Three distinct sets of factors must be taken into account (for a more detailed discussion see Gollin, 1984a):

1. Individual differences in the time course of sequential reorganizations characterize development.

2. Interspecific differences in the timing of sequential events during ontogenesis, including differences in the timing and ordering of sensitive periods, and in the relationships between the sensitive periods and markers such as birth, characterize development. For example, in guinea pigs, sheep, and monkeys the brain growth spurt occurs prenatally; in humans it commences during the fetal period, reaches a peak about term, and continues for at least 2 or 3 years postnatally. In the rat, it is coextensive with the suckling period from birth to 21 days (Dobbing & Sands, 1979). Obviously, an informed comparative-developmental analysis will take such patterns of difference into account.

3. Subsystem development is asynchronous. Periods of rapid change in one subsystem are not necessarily accompanied by comparable acceleration in other

subsystems. Therefore, an ecological event or a laboratory-generated agent that is facilitative or disruptive to one subsystem may have no effect on other systems, or it may have delayed effects, or opposite effects (Gollin, 1984a, 1984b; Rodier, 1984). In general, the qualitative state of the organism at any period is the configured pattern of relationships of the subsystems.

The central concept of developmental time, therefore, requires recognition that biological and behavioral systems and subsystems are components of a configuration of greater or lesser durability. Each successive configuration constitutes an organismic state with certain definable properties and characteristics. These properties and characteristics are stipulated by appropriate research. They are constituted by the relationships across and within levels of functioning, and their configural organization is the developmental status of the organism. It is this configuration that tempers extrinsically defined stimulus events and determines, in most instances, whether an organism/environment transaction will be inductive, facilitative, or maintaining (see Gottlieb, 1976, for a more elaborate discussion of this distinction). The only kind of instance that might violate this extrinsic tempering model would be a catastrophic event, a gross somatic insult, to use Kurt Lewin's term, such as a brick falling on your head from the roof of a building.

FIELD AND LABORATORY

The basic question to be considered in this section is, "How are the data relevant to understanding psychobiological development to be generated?" This issue, as has been noted above, is involved intimately with notions about causality and explanation, and was partly delineated in the Lorenz-Lehrman polemic. Lorenz preferred to study behavior as it was observed in so-called natural settings (1965). He regarded behavioral variations from normative expectations as evidence of pathology and believed that such variations were of little value to the understanding of how adaptive behavior developed. Lehrman advocated the introduction of intrusions into the developmental course and the careful analysis of the consequences of intrusion. In that way, he believed, "we gain the most illuminating insights into the normal processes of development" (Lehrman, 1970, p. 39). Lehrman concentrated on experimentally controlled variations of rearing environments, a position also advocated by Gottlieb (1983), who regards the experimental demonstration of new phenotypes as a way of exhibiting the limits of developmental plasticity and providing indicators of possible evolutionary directions.

Gottlieb (1984) is also sensitive to the need to integrate laboratory and field work as was Tinbergen (1975) in his classic studies of eggshell removal by black-headed gulls. In those studies, field observations led to laboratory confirmations and discomfirmations of field-generated hypotheses. In Gottlieb's work the reciprocation between field and laboratory has also been demonstrated. The task, as Gottlieb defined it, was to achieve understanding of the acoustic mediation of the attachment of young birds and human infants to the vocalizations of their mothers. The natural calls of the birds were brought into the laboratory to see if the effects produced in the field could be duplicated. Once this was accomplished the experimental analysis of the calls was undertaken. The two calls studied were the "assembly" call (the young bird approaches the mother) and the "alarm" call (the duckling freezes and ceases vocalizing). Following laboratory duplication the calls were systematically degraded so that critical acoustic features could be identified.

The analysis demonstrated that effective auditory stimulation is multidimensional and that the dimensions are hierarchically organized and synergistic. Those features of the call that effectively direct behavior were identified by precise experimental manipulations.

In one species of ground-nesting mallard ducks it was found that the rate of acoustic emissions was of the greatest importance in affecting behavior whereas frequency modulation played a much lesser role. By contrast, among hole-nesting wood ducks frequency modulation was of the greatest importance and repetition rate had little consequence for duckling activity patterns.

Without the systematic experimental degradation of the acoustic signal the difference between species with regard to feature salience would not be known. Once such a difference is understood, the laboratory studies can be employed to direct field inquiries. For example, are the differences between nesting ecologies related to the differences in the potency of acoustic features to direct behavior? Second, the obvious need for comparative work is illustrated. Without it the understanding of acoustic effects on behavior would be distorted.

A comparable hierarchy of acoustic features exists in human vocalizing and the FM component appears to be responsible for the human infant's attraction to baby talk. The comparative animal research provides a model for the exploration of the human infant's acoustic skills.

Thus, it is clear that so-called naturalistic observations yield essentially descriptive data and only indirectly provide high confidence information about process. This information is not very helpful in revealing causal sequences since it is essentially correlational. Field-derived information may, as has been indicated above, point to problems suitable for laboratory analysis. This is no small contribution but it should not be confused with the kind of power that resides in well-thought-out experimental analyses.

"Naturalistic" observations are not unbiased as some advocates of that methodology seem to assert (McCall, 1977, 1981). The observational tools, perceptions, expectations, preconceived parameters, checklists, and methodologies are contrivances in much the same way as are laboratory arrangements. Examples would include Goodall's placing stocks of bananas in bins for the chimpanzees in the neighborhood, Altmann sitting down in the midst of the baboon group she was scrutinizing (1980), and Sir Solly Zuckerman's reporting baboon behavior through Freudian spectacles (Kelso & Trevathan, 1984).

"Naturalistic" observers, whether they operate in schoolyards, home settings, game reserves, or other confines appear to be easily deceived by their instrumentalities since they assume frequently that the adjective "natural" endows their observations with a purer kind of objectivity. They tend to believe that they avoid the artificiality of the experimental setting and come to the field setting with blank minds. They may be right, in some respects, but they should be reminded of the Kantian warning that there is no warrant for a doctrine of immaculate perception.

To some extent the delusion of factual immanence is associated with the Lorenzian notion of natural settings discussed earlier. Yet many organisms occupy a wide variety of ecological niches and often manifest extensive differences in biology, behavior, and social organization, differences that can frequently be demonstrated to be niche appropriate. Traits like aggression, sociality, dominance, cooperation may or may not typify behavior. Coyotes who enjoy the fare provided by suburban Angelenos function rather differently than those who dwell in deserts, and both are rather different from occupiers of still other niches.

A very nice illustration of this is provided by the work of Harding and Strumm (1976) who observed the behavior of olive baboons on Kekopey ranch in Kenya. Over the years the predatory tactics of adult males changed significantly. Fortuitous capture of prey began to be supplemented by more systematic hunting behaviors. Initially there was no cooperation between animals. What emerged was a relay system in which baboons took turns in chasing a gazelle, chasing it in the direction of a nearby male. The prey-capturing behavior of young mothers also increased and provided a scenario for the transmission of newly acquired behaviors to the next generation in a manner reminiscent of the more directly induced behaviors of the Japanses macaques on Koshima Islet (Kawai, 1965).

In the Kekopey baboons, additional tactical hunting patterns emerged. Harding and Strumm speculate that these changes may have been triggered by an explosion of the antelope population subsequent to the destruction of the major predators in the region (lions and leopards) by cattlemen. Other habitat-behavior variations are reported by Jolly (1972) and by Rowell (1972).

It is clear that there are many "natural" settings and that the descriptions of the behaviors that emerge are a function of the creatures under observation, the ecological conditions, and the objectives rather than the objectivities of the observers. These constraints apply to all observational efforts, laboratory and field, and in all disciplines (see, for example, the extent to which Freudian ideas influenced cultural anthropologists during the first half of this century, as typified by the work of Ruth Benedict and Margaret Mead, and the extent to which the formulation of learning theories was based on the performance of albino rats in the t-maze).

SUMMARY

In this chapter a rationale is presented for the comparative analysis of adaptive skills. The relationship between field and laboratory investigations is examined and the quality of contribution from each approach is evaluated. Two prevalent but contrasting views of ontogeny are considered. The first is the idea that evolution is the control of development by ecology. The second emphasizes the constructive role played by the organism in its own development. The latter viewpoint is held to be more appropriate since the transactions of interest are between the organism and its environment, rather than between genes and the environment.

Although organismic constraints are shown to exert a powerful effect on development, they are not absolute. A probabilistic epigenetic model as contrasted with a deterministic model is to be preferred since there are intraspecific as well as interspecific differences in genes, environments, developmental histories, and qualities of developmental organization.

Reductionist and organismic theories of psychobiological development are reviewed and the relationship between evolution and developmental plasticity is explored. It is pointed out that adaptive changes need not reflect selection processes in the evolutionary sense.

Development is represented as a succession of qualitative reorganizations, each of which generally is geared to niche conditions operative at that phase of development. A discussion of the notion of *developmental time* is provided, together with the necessity for such a formulation.

SYNOPSIS OF THE BOOK

Chapter 2

In Moore's chapter the comparative-developmental approach is employed to generate an in-depth analysis of the development of sexual behavior. Moore concentrates on sexual, as contrasted with asexual, reproductive behaviors. While it is possible to deal with asexual reproduction in largely bioecological terms, the analysis of behaviors associated with sexual reproductivity requires the consideration of complex social contexts.

Social behaviors are closely tied to each individual's developmental history of social experiences. This is the grand theme of Moore's contribution. Adequate sexual behavior and its reproductive concomitants are to a considerable extent dependent upon the acquisition of skills described in Chapter 4 (Alberts), Chapter 3 (Bekoff), and Chapters 6 and 7 (Smith, and Chiszar).

In the course of her comparative analysis Moore makes the point that while the problems of reproduction may be general, the solutions entail a great deal of variability across species. Only by intensive comparative-developmental analysis will knowledge of the various solution modes and their ontogenetic courses become available.

Consistent with the social-contextual theme of her chapter Moore describes an ontogenetic succession of social relationships that includes mother-litter, sibling, and male-female groups. Ignoring these groupings and their dynamic qualities is responsible for the incomplete picture of sexual functioning that has characterized much of the literature on this topic.

Underlining these points is the observation that social restriction during ontogenesis not only has differential interspecific effects on adult sexual functioning but also affects the males and females differently within a species. The timing of the restriction during ontogenesis is important in terms of prospective consequences for adult sexual adequacy. The understanding of the role of timing entails a careful species by species analysis of *developmental time* as discussed earlier in this chapter.

Moore also deals with the relationships between behavior patterns and the presence or absence of gonadal hormones. The synergistic effects of several other physiological and social factors are subjected to detailed review.

An argument is presented against attempts to account for the acquisition of complex social behaviors, including sexual behavior, by reductionist explanations. Moore takes the position that the understanding of complex socialization must be vested in an analysis of supraindividual units that change in the course of ontogenesis. Attention to these social units is likely to reveal a new set of proximate causal concepts that will have value for evolutionary theorizing.

In her chapter Moore has provided a comparative analysis of sexual development. She has emphasized the differential consequences for different species of various kinds of physiological and social deprivation and has related explicitly her comparative-developmental perspective to evolutionary considerations.

Chapter 3

Bekoff provides an in-depth analysis of the development of locomotor systems from comparative and evolutionary perspectives. The comparative perspective, as employed by Bekoff, generates a picture of those aspects of locomotion that are consistent across species. These are the conservative, phylogenetically stable features of locomotion that are likely to have general adaptive value. Comparative analysis also makes it possible to delineate properties of locomotion that are confined to particular groups and appear to represent special adaptations.

Taken together, the stable, and the particular characteristics of locomotion constitute a pattern that provides a clear basis for evolutionary speculations.

Illustrative of the above described relationships is the observation that although early stages of motor behavior, regardless of timing, appear to be similar in all vertebrates, the chronology and morphology of first movements vary widely in different species. These differences have not as yet been related to the ecological conditions that prevail in post-natal life.

One set of factors observable during embryological development that may relate to adult life-styles is that of the spontaneous movement of embryos. Bekoff suggests a line of research that should help to clarify whether the quality of embryonic spontaneous activity is, indeed, ecologically significant.

An additional point, stressed by Bekoff, is that the same neural circuitry may subserve different movements at different periods in the course of ontogenesis. A principle of considerable developmental significance may emerge if this observation is generally true and not solely characteristic of the developing locomotor system.

Chapter 4

Alberts, in his chapter, breaks recognition into five functional categories. He deals with these categories within the framework of a comparative-developmental perspective. For him the development of recognitory behavior is a social and a biological occurrence. He is concerned with both the adaptive and the evolutionary implications of the emergence of recognition systems. There is a discussion of the heuristic utility of metaphors in the study of recognition as well as some cautionary advice regarding the misuse of metaphors.

An evolutionary perspective is provided by relating Hamilton's theory of kin selection with the topic of kin recognition. Alberts is quite explicit about the speculative nature of this link-up.

An analysis of the developmental basis of the recognitory processes by which social interaction is mediated is also presented. In consonance with Chiszar's formulation (Chapter 7) Alberts defines development as a progression through a series of developmental niches, each of which has a contemporary significance for the developing organism as well as possible prospective significance.

There is a detailed discussion of predetermined recognition that is clearly influenced by Arnold's treatment of the concept of the innate (1981). The criteria for designating a recognitory act as predetermined are described.

Experimental procedures that relate uterine and embryonic experiences to postnatal recognitory behavior are presented and comparative illustrations of these phenomena are provided. Additionally, the roles of genetic, experiential, and maturational factors that contribute to recognitory behavior are analyzed.

The value of the experimental method for exploring mechanism-outcome relationships is underlined. A particularly telling example is given of the way in which phenotypic continuities can mask substrate discontinuities in ontogenesis. This focuses attention on the issue of the contributions of field and laboratory studies to the disciplines of developmental psychology, developmental biology, and developmental psychobiology discussed earlier. The current disproportionate valuation of field studies advocated in many quarters and the denigration of experimental procedures (see for example, McCall, 1977, 1981) for the exploration of the processes of development is put in proper perspective by the example given by Alberts, who demonstrates conclusively the essential value of experimental analysis for the stipulation of the processes that mediate developmental change.

The relevance of the development of recognition systems to evolutionary change is considered. The ways in which the coordinated interdependence of such systems might play an evolutionary role are discussed. There is also a discussion of rates of change, and of evolutionarily fixed and evolutionarily plastic systems (see also Bekoff, Chapter 3). A particularly valuable illustration of the genetic coupling of signal-recognition systems stresses the notion of the evolution of supraindividual units, a theme also dealt with by Moore (Chapter 2).

Chapter 5

Brown's chapter is devoted to an analysis of helping behavior and kin selection. These complex social functions are approached from an ecological perspective with a heavy emphasis on sociobiological explanations.

Although the chapter concentrates upon helping behavior in birds the general orientation is comparative as well as developmental. Thus several patterns of the ontogeny of helping behavior are described. As might be expected in a sociobiological analysis a good deal of attention is directed at hypothesized "payoffs," largely in terms of delayed breeding success, to the "helping" animals.

The skills required for successful reproductive behaviors are described. They include learning to forage efficiently, learning to build nests, and achieving territorial dominance. With regard to these skills, variations between species as well as individual differences within species are described.

The significance of prolonged immaturity for behavioral role determinations in complex social systems is analyzed. The impact of variability in the duration, termination, and permanence of juvenile traits on social behaviors is discussed.

Three theoretical accounts of the origin and evolution of helping behavior are presented and evaluated. Additionally, a decision-making model is set up with regard to helping and breeding activities. The model is cast in terms of a logical implicational system that relates decision making to ecological factors. Brown provides a simple mathematical system to deal with these relationships.

The chapter concludes with a review of the concepts of mutualism (reciprocal benefits between individuals), helping, and inclusive fitness. The relationship of these concepts to a theory of natural selection is considered.

Chapter 6

Smith's chapter deals with the development of communication systems. A broad sketch is provided of the transspecific similarities and differences in communicative modes. The general principle that not only is diversity inevitable but that it is also limited is stressed. This principle applies to individuals and to species.

Communication is defined as the sharing of information. Ethologists have preferred to study communication in natural settings but the importance of research conducted under controlled conditions is not to be discounted.

A detailed, comparatively oriented account of the characteristics of communication systems is presented including a description of formalized signaling behavior. Formalized signaling not only provides information about organismic states but also plays a central role in the identification of individuals (see also Chapter 7, Chiszar, in this regard). Special attention is devoted to those aspects of signaling that change in the course of ontogenesis as a function of maturational and experiential influences. The context-dependent nature of responding to signals is described and the role communication plays in weaving the complex web of social structure is elaborated. Included in the social structure are activities related to mating, feeding, location, and so forth. Thus communication is a facilitator of social organization and a derivative of it at the same time. This point is particularly clear when a developmental perspective is brought to bear. The perspective, in this instance, as in the other contributions to this book, generates a picture of development as a sequence of adaptations to a succession of ecological niches. It should be emphasized that this employment of the term ecology includes not just physical-geographic and resource contexts but also social contexts provided largely but not necessarily exclusively by conspecifics.

A suitable conceptual framework, Smith asserts, in concert with the other contributors to this volume, must deal with the two central facets of development discussed earlier (Chapter 1, Gollin), being and becoming. An organism is always involved in both aspects. It has the current business of existence to transact, and simultaneously it is on the way to the construction and occupation of new niches and new activity patterns.

Chapter 7

In his chapter on the ontogeny of communicative systems Chiszar treats communication in its broadest sense, as a system for the transmission of information. He is sensitive to a number of issues that are frequently ignored or dealt with in cursory fashion in the comparative literature. Central to these issues is the need to stress the context for the emission of informative signaling, typically, the presence of another organism. The emergence of communication systems is a social phenomenon and must be understood as such. In Chapter 2, Celia Moore makes the same point with respect to the development of adult sexual patterns, and in Chapter 4 (Alberts) the social nature of recognitory development is similarly emphasized.

Chiszar also calls attention to the being-becoming issue by pointing out that the niche occupied by young organisms is not the same as that typically described for older organisms. Needs and adaptive demands are appropriate to current developmental status. While some characteristics of morphology and behavior may contain prospecitve or precursory features, they also may have predominantly contemporaneous functional roles to fulfill. Thus, signaling patterns may have current instrumental purposes as well as proactive or "perfecting" functions.

Consistent with the theme of this volume, there is an exploration of the evolutionary implications of the ontogeny of communication systems, including the rather novel suggestion that associative learning may have preceded canalized song acquisition in birds in the course of evolution rather than the sequential converse. A scenario is also provided for the possible relationships between ontogenetic events and evolutionary events.

Other issues dealt with by Chiszar are the multimodal character of developing communicative systems, the theoretical developmental character of the notion of *prospective resource value,* the relationships between natural selection and the ontogenetic timing of signal detection, and the dyadic reciprocity of infant-mother behaviors. In dealing with these issues Chiszar stresses the need to retain the orginism as a central focus of study and to concentrate on its contribution to the developmental course. This theme is also stressed by Lock (Chapter 8).

Finally, Chiszar reviews the hydraulic model of instinctive behavior as proposed by Lorenz and introduces Baerend's updated use of the concept of innate releasing mechanisms. He concludes that the released behavior is not best thought of as fixed and rigid but rather as variable and reflective of the experiential history of the organism.

Chapter 8

Lock's contribution, while avowedly speculative, is argued with commendable logic. In it he offers a tentative account of the evolution of human language systems. Before dealing with language per se, he presents a set of axioms or principles that describe the way in which the evolutionary "game" is played. There are, within the "game" plan, sets of constraints that fix the order of evolutionary events, that set the relationships between organisms and occupied niches, and that create a probabilistic base for structure-function-niche possibilities.

The theme of organism-environment interdefinition, as discussed earlier in this chapter, is also dealt with by Lock, who discusses the relationships between emerging organismic systems and evolving ecological niches. The constructive role played by organic forms in the creation or modification of environments is emphasized. The framework for this thesis is a hierarchy of constrained probabilistic relationships that are governed by logically necessary implications.

This same implicational hierarchic device is then used to analyze early communicative development in human infants, and also to supply a model for the development of systems of written language. It is Lock's contention that the changes observed in vocal and written communication systems exhibit formal properties similar to those that characterize evolutionary changes.

There follows a critique of recapitulation theory in both its strong and weak forms. He argues, as does Gould (1977), that the similarities observed between ontogeny and phylogeny are analogous rather than homologous because each follows the only course available, not because there is a causal linkage between the sets of events. He adapts this critique to the speculative description of language evolution.

A detailed description of what Lock calls the nonverbal prelude to a linguistic system is presented. He hypothesizes how the transformation from the prelinguistic communication system to vocalization and then to word naming and symbolic representation is accomplished. The shift to reflective, propositional self-consciousness is asserted to have developed continuously from the earlier gestural system. Since the former system occupies a different realm of cognition it is also to be regarded as functionally discontinuous from the ontogenetically precedent system.

The processes that mediate these developmental transformations have a distinctly Wernerian cast in that they entail a shift from a holistic (global), to a differentiated, to an autonomous-constructive state. This last quality is said, in the Gibsonian sense, to ''afford'' its own development.

The above-described developmental theme is asserted, by Lock, to characterize also the evolution of language. It does so, not in the sense of Haeckel's recapitulation theory, but rather in the sense that all developmental systems reflect the same formal dynamisms. This is very similar to the position espoused by Koffka (1959) who advocated a correspondence theory rather than a recapitulation theory to account for the similarities observed between ontogenesis and phylogenesis.

Governed by these considerations Lock presents an evolutionary scenario for the emergence of modern language from its hypothesized primeval gestural base. For evidential support he relies heavily on morphological changes in the location of the larynx, as well as upon other anatomical modifications. Additional support is derived from an analysis of the record of progressively complicated tool making and tool use, which is asserted to indicate clearly a shift in cognitive capacities. The question of whether cognitive elaboration led to linguistic elaboration or vice versa is left open.

REFERENCES

Alberch, P. (1983). Mapping genes to phenotypes, or the rules that generate form. *Evolution, 37,* 861–863.

Arnold, S. J. (1981) The microevolution of feeding behavior. In A. C. Kamil & T. D. Sargent

(Eds.), *Foraging behavior: Ecological, ethological, and psychological approaches.* New York: Garland STPM Press.

Altmann, J. (1980). *Baboon mothers and infants.* Cambridge: Harvard University Press.

Barnett, S. A. (1983). Humanity and natural selection. *Ethology and Sociobiology, 4,* 35–51.

Coe, S. P. (1981). Sociobiology: some general considerations. *American Psychologist, 36,* 1462–1464.

Cooke, J. (1982). Neo-Darwinism and developmental biology. In S. Rose (Ed.), *Towards a liberatory biology.* London: Allison & Busby.

Dobbing, J., & Sands, J. (1979). Comparative aspects of the brain growth spurt. *Early Human Development, 3,* 79–83.

Gollin, E. S. (1981). Development and plasticity. In E. S. Gollin (Ed.), *Developmental plasticity: Behavioral and biological aspects of variations in development.* New York: Academic Press.

Gollin, E. S. (1984a). Developmental malfunctions: Issues and problems. In E. S. Gollin (Ed.), *Malformations of development: Biological and psychological sources and consequences.* New York: Academic Press.

Gollin, E. S. (1984b). Early experience and developmental plasticity. *Annals of Child Development. 1,* 239–261.

Gottlieb, G. (1973). Introduction to behavioral embryology. In G. Gottlieb (Ed.), *Behavioral embryology,* (Vol. 1). New York: Academic Press.

Gottlieb, G. (1976). The roles of experience in the development of behavior and the nervous system. In G. Gottlieb (Ed.), *Neuronal and behavioral specificity: Studies on the development of behavior and the nervous system* (Vol. 3). New York: Academic Press.

Gottlieb, G. (1983). The psychobiological approach to developmental issues. In M. Haith & J. Campos (Eds.), *The handbook of child psychology. Vol. 2, Biology and infancy.* New York: Wiley.

Gottlieb, G. (1984). On discovering significant acoustic dimensions of auditory stimulation for infants. In G. Gottlieb & N. A. Krasnegor (Eds.), *Measurement of audition and vision in the first year of life: A methodological overview.* Norwood, NJ: Ablex.

Gould, S. J. (1977). *Ontogeny and phylogeny.* Cambridge: Harvard University Press.

Gould, S. J. (1981, April). This view of life. *Natural History,* 14–21.

Gould, S. J., & Lewontin, R. C. (1979). The spandrels of San Marco and the Panglossian paradigm: A critique of the adaptationist programme. *Proceedings of the Royal Society of London, 205,* 581–598.

Harding, R. S. O., & Strumm, S. C. (1976, March). The predatory baboons of Kekopey. *Natural History,* 46–53.

Jaffe, L. F. (1982). Developmental currents, voltages, and gradients. In S. Subtelny & P. B. Green (Eds.), *Developmental order: Its origin and regulation.* New York: Alan R. Liss.

Jolly, A. (1972). *The evolution of primate behavior.* New York: Macmillan.

Kawai, M. (1965). Newly acquired pre-cultural behavior of the natural troop of Japanese monkeys on Koshima Islet. *Primates, 6,* 1–30.

Kelso, A. J., & Trevathan, W. R. (1984). *Physical anthropology.* Englewood, NJ: Prentice-Hall.

Koffka, K. (1959). *The growth of the mind: An introduction to child psychology.* Littlefield, Adams. Paterson, NJ.

Kummer, H. (1971). *Primate societies: Group techniques of ecological adaptation.* New York: Aldine.

Kuo, Z. Y. (1976). *The dynamics of behavior development: An epigenetic view.* New York: Plenum Press.

Lehrman, D. S. (1953). A critique of Konrad Lorenz's theory of instinctive behavior. *The Quarterly Review of Biology, 28,* 337–363.

Lehrman, D. S. (1970). Semantic and conceptual issues in the nature-nurture problem. In L. R. Aronson, E. Tobach, D. S. Lehrman, & J. S. Rosenblatt (Eds.), *Development and evolution of behavior.* San Francisco: Freeman.

Lindemayer, A. (1982). Developmental algorithms: lineage versus interactive control mechanisms. In S. Subtelny & P. B. Green (Eds.), *Developmental order: Its origin and regulation.* New York: Alan R. Liss.

Lorenz, K. Z. (1965). *Evolution and modification of behavior.* Chicago: University of Chicago Press.

Lorenz, K. Z. (1981). *The foundations of ethology.* New York: Springer-Verlag.

Mayr, E. (1963). *Animal species and evolution.* Cambridge, MA: Belknap Press.

Mayr, E. (1983). How to carry out the adaptationist program? *American Naturalist, 121,* 324–334.

McCall, R. B. (1977). Challenges to a science of developmental psychology. *Child Development, 48,* 333–344.

McCall, R. B. (1981). Nature-nurture and the two realms of development: A proposed integration with respect to mental development. *Child Development, 52,* 1–12.

Rodier, P. M. (1984). Exogenous sources of malformations in development: CNS malformations and developmental repair processes. In E. S. Gollin (Ed.), *Malformations of development: Biological and psychological sources and consequences.* New York: Academic Press.

Rowell, T. (1972). *The social behavior of monkeys.* Baltimore: Penguin Books.

Sameroff, A. J., & Chandler, M. J. (1975). Reproductive risk and the continuum of caretaker causality. In F. D. Horowitz, M. Heatherington, S. Scarr-Salapatek, & G. Siegel (Eds.), *Review of child development research,* (Vol. 4). Chicago: University of Chicago Press.

Stebbins, G. L. (1966). *Processes of organic evolution.* Englewood Cliffs, NJ: Prentice-Hall.

Stebbins, G. L. (1969). *The basis of progressive evolution.* Chapel Hill: University of North Carolina Press.

Tinbergen, N. (1975). *The animal in its world: Explorations of an ethologist* (2 Vols.) Cambridge: Harvard University Press.

Van Valen, L. (1976). Energy and evolution. *Evolutionary Theory, 1,* 179–229.

Weiss, P. A. (1970). *Life, order, and understanding: A theme in three variations.* In Volume III Supplement, The Graduate Journal, the University of Texas.

Weiss, P. A. (1971). The living system: Determinism stratified. In A. Koestler & J. R. Smythies (Eds.), *Beyond reductionism: New perspectives in the life sciences.* Boston: Beacon Press.

2 Development of Mammalian Sexual Behavior

Celia L. Moore
University of Massachusetts at Boston

INTRODUCTION

The fundamental meaning of sex in evolutionary biology derives from the distinction between sexual and asexual reproduction (Mayr, 1963). In sexual reproduction, haploid gametes from two separate diploid individuals fuse as the first stage in the development of a new diploid individual. The selective advantage of sexual reproduction is thought to derive from genetic recombination of parental chromosomes, an efficient way to produce new genetic variants. In changing environments, it may be advantageous to produce numerous variants, some of which may meet the demands of new conditions. Support for this idea has been found in some invertebrates that can elect to reproduce either sexually or asexually: They adopt the sexual mode when environmental conditions change to be less favorable (Williams, 1966). With only a few interesting exceptions of parthenogenesis, vertebrates reproduce sexually.

In keeping with the distinction between modes of reproduction, sexual behavior may be defined as any behavior that increases the likelihood of sexual reproduction, and many behavioral scientists so use the term (Beach, 1965). However, this meaning casts a wide net and may include, depending on the species, migration, territoriality, courtship, copulation, nest building, care of young, weaning, and various other behavioral patterns that have a reproductive function. Although this is justified on functional grounds, it is often more manageable to restrict the category of sexual behavior to only a portion of the larger category of reproductive behavior. Bermant and Davidson (1974) have done this by defining sexual behavior as "behavior that increases the likelihood of gametic union" (p. 9), thus restricting its scope to courtship and copulation. Developmental studies within this restricted functional domain are reviewed in the present chapter. This

19

is an arbitrary choice made in the interest of coherence and brevity. General principles can be applied by extension to other aspects of reproductive behavior.

The formation of two sex classes is not an inevitable concomitant of sexual reproduction, but it is typical. The relation between the sexes has been of great interest to all who study reproduction. It is instructive to note that the relation is viewed rather differently by scientists who focus on the consequences of sexual reproduction and those who focus on the mechanisms underlying its achievement. Bermant and Davidson (1974), who are primarily concerned with mechanisms of reproduction, view the sexes in terms of a cooperative division of labor. "The sexes of a species are the classes of reproductively incomplete individuals. In order for a sex member to . . . reproduce part of itself into the next generation, it must remedy its incompleteness" (p. 9). To sociobiologists, who are interested in identifying the units on which natural selection acts, the most salient aspect of sexual reproduction is the incompleteness with which individuals are able to reproduce themselves: a parent can reproduce only half of its genes in an offspring. Both perspectives identify incompleteness as an aspect of sexual reproduction, but differ in the implications drawn from this observation.

Sexual behavior is not seen by sociobiologists as a process to remedy incompleteness: The incomplete reproduction is seen as a source of social conflict. Individuals in sexually reproducing species are genetically more variable—unlike one another—than those in asexually reproducing species. Wilson (1975) points out that societies of asexually reproducing insects are more harmonious than societies of sexually reproducing animals. He argues that "social evolution is constrained and shaped by the necessities of sexual reproduction and not promoted by it. Courtship and sexual bonding are devices for overriding the antagonism that arises automatically from genetic differences induced by sexual reproduction" (p. 315). This position is derived by Wilson from the principle that fitness is determined by the relative number of genes contributed to future generations. Even though a male and female must mate before reproduction is possible, they are, because of the genetic differences between them, in competition for numbers in the next generation. This point of view has stimulated a search for differences in selective pressures on the reproductive behavior of males and females (Daly & Wilson, 1978; Wilson, 1975). Because the sexes are different, if in no other way than in the size of their gametes, they may very well be subjected to different selective pressures. For example, maximal genetic contribution to future generations may require a different optimal number of offspring for male and female parents. At this stage of our understanding of the evolution of reproductive behavior, metaphors of cooperation, competition, and exploitation all seem apt to describe the relations between the sexes, but how useful any of these metaphors will ultimately prove to be is another question.

Sexual behavior is an inherently functional category. While no functional analysis can help to identify underlying mechanisms or developmental processes (Michel & Moore, 1978), they may help to identify problems which, to speak metaphorically, have to be solved by individual animals and for which there must, then, be mechanisms. The evolution of sexual reproduction certainly has set complex problems for which a great deal of animal behavior functions to solve. Some of these problems can be described rather generally as follows: (1) If gametic union is to occur, individuals must develop the means to identify, locate, attract, and select an appropriate mate. (2) Individuals must develop the ability to coordinate their movements with a potential mate so that gametic union is possible. (3) Individuals must also become able to release and to have the mate release eggs or sperm in the right place at the right time so that fertilization is possible. (4) On a longer time scale, it is also necessary for individuals to produce gametes that mature at the right time, in coordination with the mate and with environmental conditions appropriate for continued development of the offspring. (5) In some species, adaptations for reproduction include social organization that extends beyond mating, in which social behavior is often far more extensive than sexual behavior. Individuals in these species have the new behavioral problem of developing the means of appropriately selecting specifically sexual behavior from the general social behavioral repertoire.

From the functional perspective, these problems and their solutions may be identical across many different species; from the perspective of underlying processes, the problems and their solutions will vary greatly.

This chapter addresses the development of sexual behavior in vertebrates. Although sexual behavior as a functional unit is used as a focus, it becomes apparent that many underlying abilities, mechanisms, or processes that function toward sexual ends cannot be categorized as uniquely sexual. Therefore, a developmental analysis of sexual behavior must often include phenomena that contribute to behavior that appropriately functions in other contexts as well, or to behavior that may not be immediately recognized as relevant to sexual function. To keep the length manageable, the review will be limited to those aspects of sexual behavior that might be construed as adaptive skills, in keeping with the theme of this book, and will rather arbitrarily exclude nonmammalian species and the large literature on identification and attraction of mates.

COORDINATION OF SEXUAL BEHAVIORAL PATTERNS WITH A MATE

To achieve fertilization, sexually reproducing organisms must be able to coordinate with the mate so that it is possible for eggs and sperm to unite. For self-fertilizing species, like some hydra, the problem is solved anatomically, with appropriate placement of egg- and sperm-shedding organs, but for the vast majority of sexually reproducing species in which gametes from different individuals are fused, the processes leading up to fertilization must include behavioral adjustment to a partner. There is much variety in how this adjustment is achieved throughout the animal kingdom (Bastock, 1967; Bermant & Davidson, 1974).

Among mammals, sexual behavior culminates in copulation during which the male's penis is inserted into the female's vagina so that fertilization can take place within the female's reproductive tract. Before this can occur, male and female must engage in precopulatory behavioral adjustments so that appropriately oriented physical contact is achieved. There are many species differences in exactly how this is achieved, but the well-studied laboratory rat can be used to illustrate many general features of mammalian copulation.

Copulation in rats is preceded by active locomotion during which a male pursues a female and sniffs her, particularly her anogenital region; thus, the typical orientation of a moving pair is male head to female rear. The female moves in front of the male, alternating rapid darts or hops with sudden stops. The abrupt stops facilitate contact of the male with the female's hindquarters. If copulation is to occur, the male will then reach over the female's rump to clasp her flanks with his forepaws and orient his erect penis toward her vagina. While clasping the female, he palpates rapidly with his forepaws while simultaneously thrusting with his hindquarters. Whether he succeeds in effecting intromission depends on the behavior of the female. She may move away from the male, kick at him with her hind feet, throw him off by rolling over on her back, or she may assume a lordosis posture. The lordosis posture includes fairly rigid extension of all limbs, dorsoflexion of the vertebral column so that the head and rear are elevated, and lateral deflection of the tail, all of which provide the male with a stationary partner and an exposed vagina. The lordosis posture is essential for intromission. It is a response to the flank and perineal stimulation provided by the mounting male, but its occurrence requires the presence of estrogen in the female's system. Rats exhibit multiple intromissions before an ejaculation and multiple ejaculations before satiety; thus, a sexual episode as described behaviorally consists of a series of pursuits and mounts/lordoses.

While copulation clearly involves a number of specialized behavioral patterns, many elements of a copulatory sequence are common to other social contexts, including responses of mobile young to their mothers. I argue that the development of mammalian sexual behavior includes development of some rather general socially directed perceptual and motor skills that are mastered rather early in life. In rats, for example, the final stage of maternal lactation is characterized by pup-initiated feeding during which the pups must often follow their mother and stimulate her to remain stationary and allow them to suckle (Rosenblatt & Lehrman, 1963). Because the abilities to orient toward, approach, and follow the mother are essential for nursing one can be sure that in the absence of experimental intervention, they have been achieved in all rats who survive to mate. While details vary, a similar relationship between sexual and more generally social behavior can be described in a number of other mammals.

Effects of Social Restriction

There have been several experiments designed to determine whether juvenile social experience contributes to the development of male sexual behavior in mammals. These studies have used deprivation methods, in which an animal is isolated from companions of a particular sort, during prepubertal periods. When male rats are reared alone in cages, from 2 weeks of age or from weaning (Duffy & Hendricks, 1973; Folman & Drori, 1965; Gerall, Ward, & Gerall, 1967; Gruendel & Arnold, 1974; Hård & Larsson, 1968; Zimbardo, 1958), their subsequent sexual behavior is deficient. The deficiencies result from problems they have in orienting to a partner. Previously isolated rats have no lack of interest in the receptive female; they approach her frequently, climb on her, and attempt to mount her. However, the climbs or mount attempts are often oriented toward the side or head of the female. If sufficient opportunities are provided, a climb will eventually be oriented properly and may be completed as a mount. It is unknown to what extent the normally experienced female partner contributes to this adjustment. Only properly oriented mounts stimulate lordosis, which provides a stationary target for, and tactile stimuli to, the penis and surrounding regions of the male. It is this tactile stimulation that leads to a successful intromission (Adler & Bermant, 1966). Once social isolates perform a properly oriented mount and intromission, they have no further problems with sexual behavior. They continue to mount at a high rate and their climbing behavior declines. These results have been interpreted to mean that prepubertal social isolation interferes with sexual behavior because it eliminates the opportunity to practice climbing (Gerall et al., 1967; Hård & Larsson, 1968).

The relevant isolation does seem to be social and not some nonspecific stimulation or nonsocial play. When rats were reared alone in enriched environments that included objects for play, they were not superior in their sexual behavior to rats reared alone in ordinary cages (Gruendel & Arnold, 1974). The lack of opportunity to climb may be only the most obvious component of a lack of opportunity to engage in a more general perceptual-motor learning to coordinate movement with another moving animal. This learning begins early on, with mother and littermates, and continues during the intensive play of juveniles. Isolation is more detrimental the earlier it is imposed (Larsson, 1978), and rats reared artificially without mother or littermates were extremely deficient in sexual behavior, never performing correctly oriented mounts during four weekly tests (Gruendel & Arnold, 1969). At least for rats that have had some previous social experience, postpubertal experience can compensate for prepubertal social isolation (Hård & Larsson, 1968).

Guinea pigs (Valenstein, Riss, & Young, 1955), cats (Rosenblatt, 1965), dogs (Beach, 1968), and rhesus monkeys (Harlow, 1965; Mason, 1960) also have difficulty with orienting to copulate after prepubertal social isolation. In guinea pigs, neither physical contact nor practice of copulatory responses are important. If visual and olfactory contact with conspecifics was allowed through a wire-mesh screen during prepubertal periods, male guinea pigs would mount appropriately during postpubertal tests (Gerall, 1963). This suggests that guinea pigs may be able to learn to orient their movements to partners through the use of distance cues. Experience of conspecifics through a wire screen is not sufficient in male rats (Gerall et al., 1967). Within mammals, species may differ not so much in whether or not experience is important, but in the nature of the underlying perceptual-motor patterns with a mate. Although some practice of movement relative to a partner may be essential before copulation is possible in both guinea pigs and rats, guinea pigs may be better able than rats to engage in this at a distance, while separated by a wire screen for example.

Social isolation interferes with the ability of female rats to perform male sexual behavior (Duffy & Hendricks, 1973), which indicates that females undergo similar if not as extensive development as males. Since androgenized females play like males (Olioff & Stewart, 1978), they get equivalent prepubertal social experience that may contribute to the enhancement, originated by perinatal androgen, of their performance of male sexual behavior. Although prepubertal social isolation does not interfere with the lordosis reflex in female rats, no one has looked for possible effects on other more active elements of female sexual behavior.

Rhesus monkeys reared in complete social isolation from birth or shortly thereafter exhibit a number of deficiencies in their subsequent sexual behavior, including inappropriate mounting (Harlow, 1965; Mason, 1960; Missakian, 1969). Mounts performed by these isolated monkeys are often directed to the side of the partner and lack footclasp components; thrusts may be shown without a prior mount. These deficiencies cannot be remedied simply by leaving the previously isolated males with females (Harlow, 1965). It is likely that previously isolated monkeys have major deficiencies in many aspects of their social behavior. Many factors, including interference from competing fear-based responses or inability to recognize or respond appropriately to mount invitations or other gestures of the female, may conspire to make it unlikely that copulatory skills will be learned during cohabitation with adult females (Goy & Goldfoot, 1974). The isolates do not seem to lack sexual interest; further, when male isolates that had been reared on cloth-covered, vaguely monkey-shaped surrogates were tested as adults with these surrogates, they were able to mount with "appropriate" orientation and even to footclasp (Deutsch & Larsson, 1974).

The nature of the missing social experience has been investigated by partial social isolation. If rhesus monkeys are isolated from mothers but given daily access to peers, some males will develop rear-oriented footclasp mounting (Goy & Goldfoot, 1974). However, this behavior is not performed by all males, and it is shown far less frequently than simple (immature) mounts without footclasps. Likewise, isolation from peers while reared with the mother results in less frequent and less complete mounts (Harlow, Joslyn, Senko, & Dopp, 1966). When reared in groups made up of five mothers and their same-aged infants, subsequent sexual behavior was far superior. Footclasp mounting by males was observed at an earlier age, and was performed more frequently than mounts without footclasps (Goy & Goodfoot, 1974; Goy, Wallen, & Goldfoot, 1974). However, even this relatively enriched laboratory social group was not as effective as a complex, mixed-age and -sex troop in facilitating early footclasp mounting; further, unlike what has been observed in free-ranging troops, young laboratory-reared females very rarely perform footclasp mounting (Goy, 1978; Hanby, 1976).

Monkeys reared only with peers are deprived of the opportunity to climb around on the bodies of adults or to be carried dorsally. In the absence of these opportunities, mounting develops later, most probably in the context of social play. Male rhesus monkeys exhibit much higher levels of all categories of social play than females, especially during the first 2 years of life (Goy, 1968, 1970), and therefore have increased opportunities for social interactions that may lead to mounting. Prenatally androgenized females play at levels intermediate to male and female age-mates; they also mount more frequently than females and perform footclasp mounts (Goy, 1968, 1970, 1978).

Play per se does not account for the development of normal levels of rear-oriented footclasp mounting. Peer-reared and mother-plus-peer-reared monkeys play at equivalent levels, but footclasp mounting is far less frequent and occurs at later ages in monkeys reared without adults (Goy & Goldfoot, 1974). If it is the case that fully coordinated mounting normally develops through interaction with adults, play with peers may be a species-typical vehicle through which the motor skill is maintained and, perhaps more importantly, through which the social ramifications of performing the behavioral pattern are learned. In monkeys that are reared without adults, play may also become an alternative route through which mounting as a perceptual-motor skill is acquired. If so, conditions that promote participation in social play ought also to promote the acquisition of this skill. One such condition results from prenatal androgens, and the facilitating effect of prenatal androgens on the development of footclasp mounting may be mediated through increased opportunities for play.

Sex differences in mounting may also result from differences in the behavior of the partner upon being mounted by males and females. Goy (1970) has suggested that prenatally androgenized females may be more effective than untreated females in stimulating the partner to stand still, thus increasing the likelihood that a mount may be completed. Females reared in all-female peer groups are more likely to mount than are females reared in mixed-sex groups (Goldfoot & Wallen, 1978), suggesting that female partners are better elicitors of this behavior or that male partners somehow inhibit the behavior. Males reared in mixed-sex peer groups do not exhibit a sex of partner preference, but when reared in mixed mother and peer groups prefer to mount female partners (Goy & Goldfoot, 1974).

One difficulty in interpreting the studies on controlled rearing of monkeys is created by the confounding of developmental and situational factors. The behavior of the mounted animal may make a great difference since it must cooperate if footclasp mounting is to occur. Some rearing conditions can interfere with cooperation by the mounted partner as well as with the behavior of the mounter. For example, the high level of aggression observed in peer-only groups has been hypothesized to interfere with the frequency of footclasp mounts (Goy et al., 1974). Interpretation of the effects of social experience in controlled rearing studies would be clarified if in future studies more standardized testing procedures could be used or if the details of social interactions were described in such a way that the contribution of each partner could be identified.

There have been no experimental investigations of the development of "presenting," but it may be inferred that relatively complex social rearing conditions are required for its development since it is performed by both male and female infants reared in troops, but not by those reared in laboratories (Hanby, 1976). Although presenting is an essential element of sexual behavior, the same variable motor pattern is found in a wide range of other social contexts. It is, for example, used by both males and females in what Rowell (1972) describes as a gesture of politeness. The rules governing its appropriate use may be complex and require a rich social context to be acquired.

Social restriction studies have identified several contributions of social stimulation to the development of sexual behavior. The specific contributions in any given instance will vary with the stage of social development achieved by the animal when exposed to the socially provided stimulus and with the nature of the organization of sexual behavior in that particular sex and species. Thus, there are sex and species differences in response to social restriction, and social restriction has different effects when imposed at different developmental periods. The next section examines the course of development in species-typical environments of social skills necessary for the performance of sexual behavior. Particular attention is paid to laboratory rats and rhesus monkeys.

Development of Oriented Sexual Behavior
in Laboratory Rats

To behave sexually, an animal must be able to identify, locate, approach, and orient its behavior toward a conspecific. These abilities are common to many social contexts. In rats, they develop in coaction with emerging sensory and motor abilities during preweaning periods. Specifically sexual patterns build on these general abilities, but add new characteristics related to changing hormonal conditions in each partner. These developmental processes are described in the next two sections.

Ontogeny of Responsiveness to Social Stimuli in the Mother-Litter Context.
The preweaning ontogeny of altricial mammals is usefully divided into three broad stages, described by the sensory processes that predominate and by the young's developing ability to differentiate its environment (Rosenblatt, 1976). In the first stage, behavior is based on thermotactile stimulation and is characterized by both general orienting responses, like forward crawling and turning, and

specialized motor patterns, like suckling and huddling. The young show little discrimination among the features of their environment at this time and insofar as mother, nest, and littermates share similar thermotactile properties, they will be responded to similarly.

During the second stage, olfactory and thermotactile cues are used not only to arouse and motivate behavior, but also to guide and direct movement. Olfaction allows effective discrimination between familiar and unfamiliar objects and identification of and orientation toward stimuli at a greater distance than is possible through use only of thermotactile cues. The home nest or the mother may be identified on the basis of olfaction (Gregory & Pfaff, 1971; Leon & Moltz, 1972), and olfactory cues may be used in combination with exploratory sniffing patterns to orient to the source of the stimulus (Welker, 1964).

In rats, olfaction is involved in some behavioral responses in very early neonatal stages. Experimentally induced olfactory deficits greatly interfere with nursing in rat pups as young as 2 days (Alberts, 1976), perhaps by interfering with nipple identification and attachment (Hofer, Shair, & Singh, 1976; Teicher & Blass, 1976). However, young rats only begin to use olfaction to orient toward and make contact with the nest site at 9 days (Gregory & Pfaff, 1971) and with the mother at 14 days (Leon & Moltz, 1972). Olfaction is also important for the maintenance of contact with littermates in the huddling of 10-day-old rat pups, but apparently not that of 5-day olds (Alberts, 1978). Therefore, the development of the ability to orient toward social stimuli through the use of olfactory cues develops later than orientation based on either tactile or thermal cues. There is some evidence that with increasing age thermal cues become less important for orienting (Alberts, 1978), perhaps related to the development of internal thermoregulation.

The third stage of development, as described by Rosenblatt, is characterized by use of visual stimuli and by advances in central organization. The addition of vision greatly increases the information about its environment that is available to the young animal. An animal that can see is better able to locate its mother and siblings and to make distinctions about their behavior. The role of auditory cues has not been studied in the context of social development of these mammals, but they are likely to be important along with other distance cues.

The experience of visual cues in combination with familiar olfactory and thermotactile cues allows their integration, enabling the young to use visual cues for direct orientation and for rapid behavioral adjustments to their mother, other companions, and the physical environment. The eyes open in rat pups at around 14 days of age, the age when pups begin to approach and follow their mother as she moves outside the nest and when maternal rats begin to emit a characteristic odor which the pups find attractive (Leon & Moltz, 1972). Apparently, both smell and vision are used to approach and follow the mother at this age, and for approaching other rats during general exploration outside the nest, often leading to social attraction to solid food sources (Alberts & Leimbach, 1980; Galef & Clark, 1972).

By the time they are weaned, young rats and other mammals have developed behavioral capacities for approaching and following a moving species-mate from a distance and for directing toward it specific behavioral patterns appropriate for the context. These oriented movements are controlled through multiple sensory modalities. Their gradual development, in which the different modalities emerge successively and build upon behavioral organization achieved through previously active modalities, ensures that the functioning of different sensory systems will be well integrated. The continued simultaneous availability of visual, olfactory, tactile, and thermal cues in social objects reinforces this integration.

These general mechanisms and social skills carry over to the next ontogenetic stage where they are used and further developed during play with siblings.

Ontogeny of Sexual Responsiveness in the Sibling Context.   The social behavior of juvenile rats, with particular emphasis on play, has been described by Meaney and Stewart (1981). Their description covers the age period of 21–55 days (weaning through sexual maturity) for both males and females reared in mixed-sex sibling groups. Playing juveniles frequently pounce on one another, wrestle, box, and chase one another about. Approach and contact are elements common to the various play patterns. Two specialized contact behaviors described by Meaney and Stewart are particularly interesting in the present context. These are the "on-top posture," in which the forepaws of one animal are placed upon a second animal, and "anogenital sniff," in which one animal brings its snout very near the anogenital region of a second animal. Both of these patterns are motorically similar to elements of sexual behavior. Anogenital sniffing is performed frequently by mature males and relatively less frequently by mature females during sexual behavior. The on-top posture is apparently equivalent to what has been labeled "climbing" in sexual behavior studies. A "climb" is described by Larsson (1978) as similar to a mount, but there are no clasp or thrust components and it is less well oriented. Some climbs are from the rear, like a mount, whereas others are oriented to the head or side of the partner.

Meaney and Stewart (1981) reported that the frequency with which males assumed the on-top posture increased rapidly from 21 to 30 days. This behavior was maintained at a high level until 40 days, at which time it began to drop sharply. It was at this time that the females in the group began to show lordosis behavior and the males greatly increased mounting behavior. Very few mounts were observed before 41 days of age; therefore, "on-top posture" precedes mounting ontogenetically and once mounting begins to be performed, on-top contacts begin to decline. A similar ontogenetic pattern of increase and decrease of the climbing response (= on-top posture) was observed by Hård and Larsson (1971), who tested developing male rats repeatedly with receptive females. Hård and Larsson (1968) also reported that after males successfully performed intromission behavior, they rarely climbed on the female.

Anogenital sniffing by males begins to appear with some frequency around 35 days of age (Meaney & Stewart, 1981), which is several days before the onset of mounting behavior (Meaney & Stewart, 1981; Sachs & Meisel, 1979; Södersten, Damassa, & Smith, 1977). It remains at a high level after copulatory behavior becomes well established; indeed, it becomes an integral component of copulatory behavior (e.g., Sachs & Barfield, 1976).

Chasing behavior exhibits both a prepubertal and a pubertal increase in frequency of performance by males (Meaney & Stewart, 1981). There is a substantial increase from 21 to 30 days which parallels increases in other play patterns, like pouncing, and there is a secondary increase between 35 and 45 days which might be related to the onset of mounting. This secondary increase is associated with a sex of partner preference: chasing females increases while chasing other males decreases. Mounting and anogenital sniffing by males are also directed more frequently toward females than toward other males.

Based on these data, it can be argued that mature, properly oriented mounting responses, which set the necessary stimulus conditions for intromission and ejaculation, develop during three general stages. During early interactions with mother, littermates, and their olfactory and thermal deposits in the nest, the young rat first develops the general ability to orient toward, approach, and direct responses to another rat. Building on this foundation, rats next develop the ability to use specialized orienting and contact responses, like chasing and climbing, in coordinated play with moving companions during the later preweaning and postweaning juvenile period. Finally, previously established social behavior patterns (chasing, climbing) are integrated with newly emerging patterns (anogenital sniffing, clasping, and thrusting), and the orientation of these patterns toward particular body regions of a female partner is achieved during puberty. Testicular androgens are essential for the final stage.

Very little is known about the development of female sexual behavior, other than that ovarian hormones are essential for its expression and that prenatal and neonatal androgens can interfere with its development (Harris & Levine, 1962). However, the female is not passive in interactions with the male either during the juvenile period or after puberty. Her behavior and odors provide stimuli that focus the male's approaches and contacts. Larsson (1978) tested young males with receptive females, some of which were immobilized with tetrabenazine, or with nonreceptive females. When with moving, receptive females, 57% of climbs were oriented to the rear while only 4% of climbs on immobile receptive females were rear-oriented. Immobile females were climbed on as frequently as nonsedated ones, but climbs were oriented to the head or side. In fact, there were significantly more rear climbs of nonestrous, moving females (28%) than of estrous, sedated females. This suggests that the behavior of the female plays a significant role in appropriately orienting mounts of males even when she is not in estrus. The effectiveness of her behavior may be enhanced by the attractiveness of odors from her anogenital region. In mixed-sex groups, developing males are more attracted to the anogenital regions even of juvenile prepubertal females (Meaney & Stewart, 1981). Further, males reared in isosexual groups of other males are less likely to mount receptive females than are males reared in mixed-sex groups (Hård & Larsson, 1968).

Descriptions of social behavior, like those in the above accounts, have traditionally relied on categories defined in terms of postures or actions of individual animals. Although these categories are useful, it is also illuminating to describe the social behavior of moving mammals in terms that treat the two interactants as a single unit (Golani, 1976). This descriptive technique has been applied to the sexual behavior of Tasmanian devils to reveal interesting stabilities in the relative movement of male and female (Eisenberg & Golani, 1977).

The social behavior of mammals often has extraordinary variability when it is described in terms of movement patterns. It may, however, be seen as highly invariant when described in terms of the goal the movements achieve: maintenance of a particular stimulus input from the partner, a stimulus source that usually is also in motion. When both interactants behave in this fashion with respect to the other, a joint is said to be formed at the point around which movements pivot. Sometimes there is physical contact, and sometimes there is an intervening space (Golani, 1976). In view of the contributions of the partner to the development of mounting, only a limited account of the development of this behavior can be achieved by focusing only on the performing individual.

The development of sex differences in social behavior may be particularly illuminated by simultaneous attention to both partners. Males are more likely than females to develop mounting behavior. They are also more likely than females to perform many of the juvenile social behavior patterns described here. Before puberty, they are more likely to perform on-top posture or climbing and, to a lesser extent, chasing. After 41 days and the onset of sexual behavior in both sexes, males are more likely than females to mount, anogenital sniff, and chase (Meaney & Stewart, 1981). These sex differences both set intriguing questions for developmental analyses and support some of the developmental precursors of mature sexual patterns.

A large part of the sex difference in mounting is explained by differences in circulating hormones. The onset of sexual behavior is correlated with increased testosterone secretion in males (Sachs & Meisel, 1979; Södersten et al., 1977), and it has been known for some time that castration eliminates and testosterone reinstates male sexual behavior. When female rats are ovariectomized and given testosterone, they exhibit high levels of mounting (Beach, 1942). There is some evidence that testosterone secreted prenatally and/or neonatally by male rats increases the probability that males will later exhibit mounting in response to testosterone (Gerall & Ward, 1966; Harris & Levine, 1965). The mechanism for this potentiation is unclear. One hypothesis is that the early testosterone increases sensitivity to testosterone encountered later in life; another possibility, not antithetical to the first, is that the sex difference develops out of differences in social experience during the juvenile period.

Sex differences in prepubertal play patterns are not dependent on differences in circulating gonadal hormones, because gonadectomized juveniles exhibit the same sex differences as intact animals. However, there is an effect of neonatal hormones on these differences. Female rats injected with androgens on the day of birth will play as frequently as their male siblings, and neonatally castrated juvenile males will show reduced levels of vigorous play (Meaney & Stewart, 1981; Olioff & Stewart, 1978). Therefore, while there are no qualitative play differences there are quantitative differences, with rats treated neonatally with androgen substantially more active than nonandrogenized siblings. The mechanisms through which early hormones increase juvenile play are unknown; they may very well involve a nonspecific effect of testosterone on gross motor activity. However, these nonspecific effects may serve as the foundation for more articulated differences in later stages.

Development of Coordinated Sexual Behavior in Rhesus Monkeys

Infant monkeys have well-developed motor capacities, and all sensory systems are functional at birth. Thus, the sequential sensory development that underlies the social orientation of altricial mammals probably does not apply to these precocial primates. However, the development of perceptual-motor skills essential for the performance of correctly oriented sexual behavior does depend on stimulation provided by the mother and other social companions. Like most mammals, the mother is the most important source of stimulation at the earliest stages.

Hanby (1976) has provided a thought-provoking review and description of the ontogeny of sociosexual behavior in male and female primates reared in complex, species-typical groups. "Sociosexual" is a carefully chosen label: despite the clearly sexual function that such patterns as mounting, thrusting, and presenting have, they also appear in other contexts. Hanby proposes that the social environment of young monkeys provides the means for developing these sociosexual patterns.

Newborn monkeys spend all of their time on the mother's ventrum, but within a few days begin to move around on her body and to take brief trips away from her. As the infant climbs and slides around on the mother, it can gain information about her body and its own as well. The infant gains additional experience by its frequent departures from and returns to the mother. She may be boarded from many different angles and in many different regions, not all of which provide equivalent stimulation to the infant, particularly to its genitals (Simpson, 1978). Tactile stimulation of the genital region may lead the infant to repeat actions, such as thrusting, that provide further stimulation.

Dorsal mounting may be encouraged in some species by dorsal carrying of infants. Adults often signal for dorsal mounts from infants with gestures and "present" postures. As Hanby (1976) argues, the adult's behavior may facilitate in the infant both correctly oriented mounting and genital exploration through thrusting. Infants also explore the genitalia of adults through touch, vision, olfaction, and taste. Little is known of the relative roles of these modalities in the development of sexual behavior, but the colorful, conspicuous genitalia do seem to attract both young and adult animals. Odor is important for attracting adult male rhesus monkeys to females (Keverne & Michael, 1971) and may also be an important source of attraction for infants. These various stimuli may all act to orient mounting behavior to the rear of a partner.

Both male and female infants of various monkey species show rear-oriented mounts with thrusting. These patterns have been observed in a number of separate studies as early as 9–12 weeks of age (reviewed by Hanby, 1976). Although the mount with double footclasp has been characterized as a mature, sexual form of mounting (Goy & Goldfoot, 1974; Harlow, 1965), it is found in young infants of both sexes reared under relatively natural social conditions (Hanby, 1976). The footclasp refers to gripping the ankles or legs of the mounted animal with the hind feet; in the double footclasp, all the weight of the mounter is supported by the mounted animal. Because of the way monkeys are built, intromission is not possible without a double footclasp, so it is reasonable to categorize it as a necessary component of mature sexual behavior. To understand its development, however, it may be best to think of this form of mounting in infants and adults as agility in the service of genital stimulation.

Two additional factors encourage a continued high level of mounting and the integration of mounting with intromission. These are the possession of a penis and the availability of appropriate partners. Hanby (1976) reports that females decline in the frequency with which they mount and thrust during the first year of life while males increase their frequency of mounting and thrusting during this time span. Intromission with adult females has been observed to occur in some males toward the end of the first year, and may be temporally associated with increased mounting activity. This suggests that the discovery of intromission may be important for maintaining performance of mounting as a frequent behavioral event and for its continued development as a sexual behavioral pattern. The presence of partners that will allow male infants to mount and that will stimulate thrusting once mounted is an important element in the maintenance of mounting by developing males. Therefore, the sexual behavior of young males is most effectively promoted by having a variety of adult females in the group, but mounting is also directed to the mother and to age-mates of both sexes (Hanby, 1976).

Both male and female infants also develop the "present" posture. Hanby (1976) hypothesizes that this behavioral pattern may develop from the extensive genital inspection and grooming provided to infants by adults (Rowell, 1972). Initially, young infants are held for these activities, but they soon actively engage in behavior that orients their rears close to the face of an adult. Adults respond to these advances by grooming. Presenting while at a distance from a partner may develop from these early interactions as the behavior comes under the control of visual cues.

Early in the first year of life, mounting, thrusting, and presenting develop into fully coordinated behavioral patterns, essentially equivalent in form to those shown by copulating adults. Unlike the case in most mammals, these patterns appear during a period of gonadal quiescence, long before pubertal increases in gonadal hormones. They may also be shown by castrated juvenile rhesus monkeys (Goy & Goldfoot, 1974). Since both males and females perform mounting, thrusting, and presenting, the prenatal androgen that is specific to male embryos plays no essential role in their development. However, prenatal androgen may set the conditions for maintaining mounting in males and for its integration with intromission. Androgen-dependent male genitalia may be an important element of this maintenance (Herbert, 1973).

A clear sex difference in the mounting behavior of rhesus monkeys reared in a laboratory with only peers or with peers and mothers has been well established. Females are less likely to mount and will very rarely perform footclasp mounting. These sex differences originate with prenatal androgen; when prenatally treated with testosterone, females are more likely to mount and to mount with footclasp (Goy, 1970, 1978; Goy & McEwen, 1980). Because males begin to show footclasp mounting at a later age under these laboratory conditions than is the case for males reared in more complex species-typical groups, it can be inferred that the relatively restricted rearing provides a less than optimal environment for the development of mounting behavior (Hanby, 1976). Although it may not be the case for monkeys reared in species-typical groups where both male and female infants frequently mount with footclasp, prenatal androgen plays an important role in the initial, later appearing development of footclasp mounting of peer-reared monkeys. It may be that characteristics such as increased body size and enlarged phallus that originate from prenatally secreted or injected androgen may allow the prospective young mounter to succeed more frequently, either by eliciting more cooperative behavior from a partner or by compensating more effectively for inadequate size or behavior of a partner.

THE DEVELOPMENT OF COPULATION

Males and females must become able to coordinate their behavior so that sperm are released into the female reproductive tract at approximately the time of ovulation. Although females of many species can store sperm for long periods, thereby having sperm available whenever eggs are produced, storage is possible for only a few hours in mammals. Therefore, ovulation must be closely linked with copulation for gametic union to occur. Except for humans and some other primates that also copulate at other times (Rowell, 1972), mammals accomplish this temporal coordination by copulating only during the preovulatory estrous stage of the ovarian cycle.

Copulatory behavior functions in mammals to coordinate gametic release. It also serves to facilitate related physiological processes in some species. For example, the performance of characteristic copulatory patterns in a characteristic temporal sequence is necessary to stimulate physiological changes in the female rat that underlie sperm transport or the initiation of pregnancy (Adler, 1978). This temporal sequence is also required before males will ejaculate (Sachs & Barfield, 1976). The pattern of male copulation is species-typical and diverse among mammals, with temporal and sequential features that correlate with species-typical requirements for these physiological changes (Dewsbury, 1978).

Studies of copulatory behavior frequently distinguish sexual interest from performance. Sexual interest refers to those elements that initiate copulation (e.g., following and attempts to mount). Performance consists of the motor elements of copulation (e.g., mounts, intromission patterns, and ejaculatory patterns) and their temporal and sequential organization. Of course, measures of performance presuppose sexual interest; for example, intromissions cannot occur unless a rat is willing to mount. Therefore, a failure to copulate may indicate lack of interest rather than an inability to perform. Performance deficits are identified by incomplete sequences (e.g., mounting but no ejaculatory pattern) or by atypical temporal characteristics (e.g., lengthened inter-intromission intervals).

The largely intuitive distinction between interest and performance may not be the best way to divide copulatory behavior, but both conceptual and empirical analyses have shown that male copulatory behavior is not a unitary phenomenon and must be divided before it can be explained. Beach (1956) argued that at least two conceptually distinct mechanisms were required to explain male sexual behavior. These were a sexual arousal mechanism and a copulatory mechanism. Recent factor analysis of male rat copulation has revealed that even further distinctions are needed and that a minimum of four separate conceptual mechanisms are required to account for the behavior (Sachs, 1978). Dissociation by physiological means of various components of sexual behavior has also been accomplished. For example, mounting, intromission pattern, and ejaculatory pattern can be differentially affected by some neuroendocrine manipulations (Bermant & Davidson, 1974; Goy & McEwen, 1980).

Similar analyses of female copulatory behavior have not been carried out, perhaps because most studies of female sexual behavior have measured only lordosis (Doty, 1974), which is generally considered to measure receptivity. Beach (1976) has urged that attention must also be paid to attractivity and proceptivity. Attractivity refers to those characteristics that stimulate the initiation of sexual behavior in a partner, and proceptivity refers to active precopulatory behavior, like sniffing the male and darting, performed by the female.

Some of the developmental factors that affect the likelihood and the nature of the performance of various components of male and female copulatory behavior are considered in the following sections.

Effects of Sensory and Social Restriction

As described above, social restriction leads to deficient male sexual behavior, but most deficiencies have been found to reside in the behavior preliminary to copulation (e.g., orientation) rather than in the copulatory components (e.g., intromission) that lead up to ejaculation. Of course, ejaculation cannot ordinarily occur in the absence of adequate precopulatory behavior, but there is some evidence to suggest that the ability to ejaculate and the ability to orient and mount develop separately. Rats reared in social isolation from 2 weeks of age or from weaning will initially be unable to mount as adults, but with sufficient experience can do so. Once mounting is achieved by these isolates, normal intromission and ejaculatory behavior follow rather quickly (Larsson, 1978, and above). Monkeys that are reared in social isolation have great difficulty in copulating with a partner but they frequently masturbate; they may also masturbate during misoriented or incomplete mounts of a partner (Goy & Goldfoot, 1974).

In this section, evidence from social restriction, sensory restriction, and combined social and sensory restriction studies are reviewed to show that stimuli normally encountered during development can contribute to the likelihood and to the temporal structure of components of copulatory behavior.

Total social isolation from birth leads to a failure to develop male sexual behavior in rats (Gruendel & Arnold, 1969). Male rats that were reared singly in incubators subsequently failed to mount or to engage in other sexual behavior. Although the possibility that these isolates would develop sexual behavior as adults was not sufficiently tested by giving them extensive experience with females in adulthood, there was no evidence of improvement during the four separate tests used in this study. The lack of mounting in total social isolates suggests either that they were not attracted to the test female as an object for sexual behavior or that they had not developed the ability to copulate. Rats reared in groups in the incubator with no mother did subsequently exhibit sexual interest as measured by clasping the female, but they did not show pelvic thrusting, intromission, or ejaculatory responses. The mother evidently plays a role in the development of male copulatory behavior in rats. Her presence provides the means to become familiar with olfactory and other stimuli that later elicit and direct mounting and contribute to the arousal necessary for ejaculation. Maternal licking and handling also provides stimulation important to developing copulatory mechanisms (Moore, 1984; next section).

Olfactory stimuli are generally important for copulation in male mammals and are essential in some species. Mice and hamsters will not mate at all if they cannot smell (Murphy & Schneider, 1970; Powers & Winans, 1975). Thus, it is not surprising that neonatal bulbectomy eliminates copulatory behavior in male hamsters (Murphy & Schneider, 1970). Anosmic rats and cats remain able to copulate, although there are changes in some performance measures (Aronson & Cooper, 1974; Larsson, 1971).

The age at which olfactory bulbectomy is performed makes a great deal of difference in the nature of subsequent behavioral effects in rats. Bulbectomy at 30 days of age followed by either group rearing with females through sexual maturity or rearing alone led to severe deficits in sexual behavior of male rats (Wilhelmsson & Larsson, 1973). Bulbectomized isolates did not mount, intromit, or ejaculate, although they did approach the female and engage in some climbing. Climbing was, however, less frequent than in intact isolates. As in other studies, intact isolates eventually developed complete male sexual behavior. Group rearing after bulbectomy resulted in the development of mounting by some animals, but less than that observed in intact group-reared males. Further, while half of the bulbectomized, group-reared males achieved ejaculation, the pacing of intromissions and ejaculation in these ejaculating bulbectomized rats was slower than in intact controls. A similar slowing of copulation has been reported for male rats bulbectomized as adults (Larsson, 1971). It is thus apparent that the effects of social isolation on the development of sexual behavior are far more deleterious in male rats that are deprived of olfactory input; conversely, eliminating olfactory input interferes less in the performance of sexual behavior if sexual or at least social experience will be or has been provided.

If olfactory bulbectomy is performed at 6 days of age in male rat pups that are then reared with mother and littermates until weaning at 21 days of age, no deficits in normal male sexual behavior are observed (Pollak & Sachs, 1975). One possible explanation for these apparently discrepant results is that males made anosmic early in life will make use of other sensory routes to develop their sexual behavior (Pollak & Sachs, 1975) whereas juvenile males, which have come to rely on olfaction in their social interactions, are less able to switch to a new modality. Once the perceptual-motor skills underlying mounting have been well developed, as they are in adult males, the behavior can continue to be performed even though some of the relevant information is missing. Although vision is apparently not important for sexual behavior in otherwise intact male rats (Hård & Larsson, 1968), it may be that pups with impaired olfactory functioning come to depend on vision for socially oriented movement and that this experience provides the foundation for sexual behavior.

Tactile stimulation of genital and surrounding regions contributes importantly to the performance of intromission and ejaculation patterns in rats (Adler & Bermant, 1966; Carlsson & Larsson, 1964; Larsson & Södersten, 1973; Lodder & Zeilmaker, 1976), cats (Aronson & Cooper, 1968; Cooper & Aronson, 1962), and rhesus monkeys (Herbert, 1973). From the available data, it seems as though penile stimulation is essential for intromission in cats, is of major importance in rats, and is less important in rhesus monkeys. Ejaculation is eliminated by genital desensitization in cats and rhesus monkeys, but is retained in some rats that continue to intromit (Larsson & Södersten, 1973). Further, genital desensitization leads to a slow decline in sexual interest of adult male cats (Aronson & Cooper, 1968) and to a more rapid decline in rhesus monkeys (Herbert, 1973).

To examine the role of penile stimulation in the development of sexual behavior, Spaulding and Peck (1974) removed the glans penis of 20-day-old male rats and found that the various components of copulatory behavior, including ejaculation, could still be performed when the rats were sexually mature. However, some temporal aspects of the copulatory pattern were altered; notably, the latency to ejaculate was longer. These rats were housed in mixed-sex groups from weaning at 20 days until testing and therefore were socially and possibly also sexually experienced. Although removal of the glans penis reduces tactile input, it does not eliminate all input to the genital region, so it is possible that the remaining tactile stimulation may have played a role.

A similar experiment was conducted by Dahlof and Larsson (1976), but instead of removing the glans penis, they sectioned the pudendal nerve to desensitize the penis. Age of nerve transection and social experience were varied. Social experience consisted of rearing in mixed-sex groups either before or after transection and may have included sexual experience. Pudendal nerve transection decreased the probability of ejaculation and lowered the frequency of intromission patterns, but previous or subsequent social experience was found to ameliorate these effects. The most marked effect of transection was on animals reared alone. Although some of the transected males in the Dahlof and Larsson study did show intromission and ejaculation, Lodder and Zeilmaker (1976) reported a more profound elimination of intromission with a similar desensitization procedure. The basis of the discrepancy is unclear.

The results from genitally desensitized rats, like those on olfactory restriction, point to a coaction of sensory and social factors in the development of sexual behavior in rats. Male rats make use of several sensory modalities when they copulate. When one is eliminated, others may be sufficient for completed copulation. Social and possibly sexual experience with companions enables the male rat to use the remaining modalities more effectively. However, both olfaction and genital input contribute to the fine structure of copulatory behavior in experienced or naive rats so that their elimination does lead to an altered temporal pattern. This suggests that socially provided stimulation normally carried through these modalities contributes to the development of neural mechanisms that pace sexual behavior.

Female sexual behavior is altered by genital denervation (Diakow, 1970, 1971), but no effects of either social or sensory restriction on the development of female sexual behavior have been determined.

A thoughtful analysis and more complete review of sensory and social factors in the performance and development of mammalian sexual behavior have been provided by Diakow (1974).

Effects of Social Stimulation During Preweaning Periods

Maternal rats interact extensively with their pups during the entire period of litter dependency. All maternal behavior contributes to the stimulative environment of young pups, but maternal licking and handling (see Figure 2.1) are major sources of stimulus change within the nest. Licking and handling provide thermal (Barnett & Walker, 1974), tactile, and vestibular stimulation of pups. Although all pups are licked and handled, males receive substantially more licking, particularly of their anogenital regions (Moore & Morelli, 1979). Anogenital licking stimulates release of urine and feces, thus providing an essential aspect of early maternal care. The response also functions to recycle a large percentage of maternal fluid and salts lost through lactation (Baverstock & Green, 1975; Friedman & Bruno, 1976; Gubernick & Alberts, 1982). Behaviorally, the anogenital licking response typically consists of holding the pup with the forepaws, turning it upside down, and drawing it near the mouth for licking. The response is stimulated by chemical cues, at least some of which are present in urine. Urine from male pups is more effective than that from female pups in stimulating maternal anogenital licking (Moore, 1981). Therefore, male pups normally stimulate their mothers to provide them with relatively high levels of genital stimulation during early developmental stages.

In an effort to determine whether genital stimulation could contribute to the development of male sexual behavior, female pups, which ordinarily are pro-

FIG. 2.1.   Maternal anogenital licking in a laboratory rat.

vided with relatively low levels of anogenital stimulation by their mothers, were stimulated daily with an oiled camel's-hair brush which was vibrated at 60 cycles per second. The stimulus was applied to the perigenital region five times daily, in 15-second bouts distributed over a 20-minute period, during days 2–14 postpartum. Littermate controls were stimulated on the shoulder. These pups were weaned at 25 days of age, reared in groups of similarly treated females, then ovariectomized, treated with testosterone propionate, and tested for male sexual behavior with an estrogen and progesterone primed female during six separate half-hour tests.

No differences were found in the mounting behavior of anogenitally stimulated females and their controls, and none of the females showed the ejaculatory response. However, anogenitally stimulated females performed significantly more intromission patterns, perhaps in part because the inter-intromission intervals were shorter. A mount by an anogenitally stimulated female was also more likely to lead to an intromission pattern: There were fewer mounts without intromission for each intromission pattern shown by anogenitally stimulated females (see Table 2.1).

It is possible that the additional anogenital stimulation lowered the threshold of responsiveness to stimuli encountered by the genitalia of copulating adults, making it more likely that these females would perform motorically defined intromission responses, despite there having been no effects of the early stimulation on genital growth. Alternatively, the early stimulation may have altered the timing of the neural mechanisms that pace intromissions. Either or both possibilities can account for the observed effect on behavior.

Even though the stimuli used in this study had only some of the features of the natural stimuli provided by maternal anogenital licking, it was effective in enhancing some components of male sexual behavior. This suggests that stimulation provided by the mother while caring for her young may also contribute to the development of mechanisms that underlie male sexual behavior. In normally developing males, this maternal contribution would undoubtedly coact with other stimulative and hormonal effects to produce complete copulatory behavior.

TABLE 2.1

Male Sexual Behavior in Female Rats that had Received Daily Vibrotactile Stimulation in Anogenital or Shoulder Regions during Infancy. Values are Means and Standard Deviations of Litter Medians within Treatment.

	Anogenital	Shoulder	p
Number mounts	100.83 ± 106.72	117.38 ± 77.51	NS
Number intromission patterns	14.63 ± 8.54	8.13 ± 3.42	< 0.05
Mounts per intromission pattern	6.67 ± 2.73	14.66 ± 4.14	< 0.02
Median interintromission interval (min)	2.43 ± 0.68	4.47 ± 1.56	< 0.02

($n = 4$ litters and 11 females per condition; p levels are for student's t test for related measures.)

To determine whether naturally occurring maternal stimulation does contribute to the development of male sexual behavior, a controlled-rearing study was done in which male laboratory rats were reared by mothers that licked and stimulated them less (Moore, 1984). Because maternal licking is elicited by pup odors (Moore, 1981), olfactory deficits were imposed by lining the nares with polyethylene tubing (Ruddy, 1980) so that odorous substances from the pups could not reach the olfactory mucosa. This had the expected effect of reducing maternal licking, including licking of the anogenital regions of the developing pups. When later tested for sexual behavior, male offspring of the treated mothers were found to have a more slowly paced copulatory pattern than the offspring of control mothers. In particular, both the ejaculatory latency and the latency from ejaculation to the next intromission pattern were significantly longer. Further, more intromissions were required before an ejaculation in males that had been less stimulated as infants. These data suggest that maternally provided stimulation may not only arouse and direct the development of socially oriented behavior that is required for the later performance of sexual behavior, but that it may also participate in setting the neural mechanisms that underlie the timing of male copulatory performance.

Like other sex differences that have been studied, sex differences in characteristics that stimulate maternal licking originate in the early hormonal differences of males and females. If female rat pups are injected on the day of birth with testosterone, they will subsequently stimulate equivalent levels of licking from dams as do males (Moore, 1982). Testosterone is not unique in this effect; dihydrotestosterone has a similar effect, as does estrogen, at least at high doses. The relationship between pup hormones and maternal behavior raises the possibility that maternal behavior may mediate some of the effects of early hormones on the development of sexual behavior.

Mothers in various mammalian species often devote a great deal of attention to the genitalia of their young. This has been commented on in primates (Fedigan, 1982; Hanby, 1976; Rowell, 1972). Maternal primates also treat males and females differently (reviewed by Fedigan, 1982). Unfortunately, there is no information on the developmental sequelae of this maternal attention in primates or other species.

Hormone-Experience Interactions

Hormones are involved in the development of sexual behavior during two major ontogenetic stages: perinatal and pubertal. Perinatal hormones originate conditions that contribute to the development of sensory, motor, and central neural mechanisms that serve as essential elements of later sexual behavior. Gonadal hormones that are secreted beginning at puberty and continuing through reproductive life are thought to bring previously established but latent mechanisms into play, or to activate perinatally organized mechanisms (e.g., Goy & McEwen, 1980). However, sexual behavior cannot have been fully organized by perinatal hormones, because as described in a previous section, adult hormones only have activational effects on sexual behavior when certain intervening social experiences have been obtained. Perinatal hormones may create some of the conditions for sex-appropriate social experience.

Interactions of hormones with socially provided experience have been more extensively studied for pubertal than for perinatal periods. These studies permit two generalizations. First, pubertal hormones can act to integrate previous social experience and to focus it into specifically sexual behavior, at least in males of some mammalian species. Second, pubertal hormones and the concurrent sexual experience that they help to generate can also terminate behavioral plasticity in some mammals, so that sexual behavioral patterns appropriate to previously secreted hormones are maintained even in the absence of these hormones.

Perinatal Hormones. Hormones present during early ontogenetic stages have extensive effects on the development of male and female sexual behavior. The most widely used developmental paradigm has been to manipulate early neonatal or prenatal hormones and to measure the subsequent probability of occurrence of copulatory behavior. When this is done in rats, it is found that prenatal or neonatal testosterone increases the probability of occurrence of mounting, intromission pattern, and ejaculatory pattern when adult animals are again injected with testosterone. Testosterone present early in life also decreases the probability of occurrence of lordosis when androgenized animals are injected as adults with estrogen or a combination of estrogen and progesterone. These phenomena and the hypothesized mechanisms on which they rest have been reviewed extensively (e.g., Baum, 1979; Beach, 1971; Bermant & Davidson, 1974; Goy & Goldfoot, 1973; Goy & McEwen, 1980).

The potentiation of masculine copulatory behavior by early testosterone has been observed in all species studied, although there are important species differences in the hormone-behavior relationships. For example, mounting behavior normally develops in both male and female rats, but only in male hamsters. Female rats apparently receive prenatally sufficient testosterone from neighboring male fetuses for mounting to develop (Clemens, Gladue, & Coniglio, 1978). Because testosterone potentiates mòunting postnatally in hamsters, developing females of this species do not have access to testosterone and are far less likely to develop mounting than are female rats or male hamsters (Noble, 1977). It is possible that species differences in ontogenetic timing of hormone action account for many species differences in the relationship between early hormones and copulatory behavior (Goy & McEwen, 1981).

One possible way in which early hormones increase the likelihood of mounting is through increasing the sensitivity of relevant neural or other tissues to the testosterone that is essential to the performance of the behavior by adults (Beach, 1971). Since mounting is stimulated by olfactory and other cues from the female partner, it is also possible that the testosterone present in early life somehow contributes to the process by which these stimuli become attractive. The interest that mammals express in intact males or in estrous females depends in part on the hormonal condition at the time of the behavior. However, the effectiveness of hormones on attraction to partners of a particular sex can be modified by early hormone-dependent processes. Early androgenization of female beagles decreases the effect that estradiol in their systems later has on increased attraction to males and further increases the effect that testosterone has on attraction to estrous females (Beach, Johnson, Anisko, & Dunbar, 1977).

The likelihood of intromission and ejaculation is also increased by early testosterone. At least two separate mechanisms have been identified to account for this effect. One involves the morphological development of the penis, which depends on the presence of androgen during prenatal or neonatal periods. Either testosterone or its reduced metabolite, dihydrotestosterone, is effective for normal genital development, but estrogen is not. When male rats are castrated neonatally and treated with dihydrotestosterone, they develop normal penises and show mounting and intromission behavior when treated as adults with testosterone, but they do not perform ejaculatory patterns (Booth, 1977; Hart, 1977). Further, the probability of performing intromission patterns has been found to vary with the completeness of penile development in male rats (Beach, Noble, & Orndoff, 1969). It should be pointed out here that the intromission pattern is distinguished from mounts without intromission by a characteristic dismount; neither by definition nor in fact does the motor pattern require a penis. However, the hormone studies are consistent with the notion that having a penis contributes greatly to the performance of the motor pattern. It is also likely that this hormone-dependent structure contributes to the emergence of the intromission pattern during the frequent mounting behavior of pubertal males. A similar sequence was suggested by Hanby (1976) for the development of intromission by infant monkeys reared with adult female partners. Laboratory-reared monkeys provided only with age-mates as social and sexual partners do not exhibit intromission until 2 or 3 years after they begin to mount with footclasp (Goy & Goldfoot, 1974). Therefore, the possession of a penis is not sufficient for the performance of intromission. The animal must also have an appropriate partner and an interest in mounting.

Despite morphologically normal penises, rats neonatally castrated and treated with dihydrotestosterone do not perform the ejaculatory pattern (Booth, 1977; Hart, 1977), which, like the intromission pattern, is identified by a characteristic dismount, and not by the ejaculation that accompanies it. However, if the castrated male neonates are treated with both dihydrotestosterone and a synthetic estrogen that can escape extracellular estrogen binding proteins and enter cells, they will not only show the intromission pattern but they will also perform the ejaculatory pattern when subsequently treated with testosterone (Booth, 1977). From this and other supporting evidence (Goy & McEwen, 1980), it seems that the complete development of male copulatory behavior requires the aromatization of testosterone to estradiol, presumably in central neural tissue. It is at present unclear how these neuroendocrine events affect subsequent behavior, but some hypotheses may be generated by examining the mechanisms that underlie ejaculation in adult rats.

In rats, multiple intromissions are thought to provide increments to a hypothesized level of excitation so that an ejaculatory threshold is eventually reached (e.g., Sachs & Barfield, 1976). Not all individual rats that show multiple intromissions succeed in ejaculating, possibly because the postulated arousal never reaches sufficiently high levels. Female rats, for example, can show repeated intromissions under appropriate test conditions, but they do not spontaneously ejaculate. If such a female is provided additional arousing stimulation, such as a tail pinch or peripheral electric shock, she will exhibit the ejaculatory pattern (Emery & Sachs, 1975; Krieger & Barfield, 1976). Peripheral shock can also stimulate ejaculatory behavior in developing male rats at an earlier age than it would otherwise be shown (Goldfoot & Baum, 1972). From this and additional evidence (Sachs & Barfield, 1976), it may be hypothesized that the aromatized estrogen present early in development somehow leads to the development of mechanisms in male rats that more efficiently accumulate arousal from repeated intromissions. Whether this developmental effect is achieved during the perinatal periods in which estradiol is present or whether it is achieved in later stages as a result of processes set in motion by perinatal hormones is at present unknown.

The performance of lordosis is highly dependent on concurrent ovarian hormones. Estrogen provides a necessary condition for naturally occurring lordosis in all nonprimate mammals that have been studied, and progesterone has a secondary facilitating effect in some but not all species. When testosterone is present in early developmental stages, as it is in male mammals, the potentiating effect of estrogen or progesterone on lordosis will be reduced in some species (e.g., rats) and not affected in others (e.g., ferrets) (reviewed by Baum, 1979). In those species where early testosterone can interfere with the development of estrogen-activated lordosis, neonatally injected estrogen may have similar effects (Feder, 1967). However, estrogen present in rats during later but still prepubertal stages increases the ease with which lordosis can be stimulated by flank and perineal stimulation after subsequent acute treatment with estrogen (Gerall, Dunlap, & Hendricks, 1973). This effect may be interpreted as due in part to increased sensitivity to estrogen of the estrogen-activated neural mechanisms that underlie lordosis.

The neuromotor elements of lordosis include massive activation of extensor reflexes and concomitant suppression of flexor reflexes (Komisaruk, 1974). Infant rats are capable of performing the motor elements of lordosis when treated with estrogen and tested under the right conditions (Williams, 1982). The interesting developmental questions are how the female comes to integrate these reflexes with precopulatory behavioral patterns and how their performance comes to be linked with such specificity to cyclical hormonal events.

The ''present'' posture of monkeys in some of its contextual manifestations is functionally analogous to lordosis, but the underlying mechanisms and developmental processes do not seem at all similar. Presenting is not tied to any particular hormonal condition at the time of performance (Rowell, 1972), nor is it affected by prenatal hormones (Goy & Resko, 1972). Motorically, it is highly variable in form, not having the reflex quality of lordosis as it is exhibited in various other mammalian species. Little is known of the development of presenting as a sexually receptive pattern.

Early hormones have pervasive effects on the development of sexual behavior, although the nature of the effects will vary with sex and species. Hormones that are present either prenatally or neonatally are likely to contribute to the development of many separate mechanisms that ultimately must be integrated before sexual behavior can be performed. Most studies have conceptualized perinatal hormones as affecting behavioral development through morphological or physiological changes imposed on cells by direct action of the hormones. Debate has centered around the relative importance of central and peripheral structures that are differentiated by early hormone action (Beach, 1971; Goy & McEwen, 1980). Little attention has been paid to the possibility that central and peripheral effects of hormones interact not only in adult behavioral performance, but in the developmental processes through which neural mechanisms underlying sexual behavior are formed. As we know from social isolation studies, these processes must continue in the absence of hormones because the development of sexual behavior is not complete at the end of critical periods of perinatal hormone action.

There has also been little attention to the possibility that hormones may interact with social stimuli during infancy to develop behavioral patterns, although this is generally accepted to occur during juvenile periods. Yet perinatal hormones do alter social stimulation of neonates in ways that are relevant to the development of sexual behavior. As described in the previous section, maternal licking provides stimulation that contributes to the development of male sexual behavior in rats, and this licking is affected by the hormonal status of the young (Moore, 1982, 1984).

Pubertal Hormones.   The onset of copulatory behavior is correlated with the secretion of gonadal hormones at puberty for both males and females. This development stage is a period when the various elements of sexual behavior that have developed during earlier stages become integrated into a fully functional pattern that is maintained for the duration of reproductive life. Two elements are essential for this integration: appropriate hormones and experience with appropriate partners.

Prepubertal castration interferes with the development of male sexual behavior in mammals. The most relevant aspect of puberty is the acquisition of sexual experience, but this experience can be acquired only while gonadal hormones are present in the system. The interactions of hormones and experience in the development of sexual behavior have been extensively studied in cats (Rosenblatt, 1965; Rosenblatt & Aronson, 1958a, 1958b). If male cats are castrated as juveniles, they will not engage in sexual behavior when a sexually receptive female is made available to them. However, if they are treated with testosterone during the time that they are exposed to the female, complete patterns of sexual behavior will be performed. Treatment of castrates with testosterone has no effect unless there is concurrent exposure to a sexual partner. Further, postpubertal castration of sexually inexperienced males is as effective as prepubertal castration in preventing the organization of sexual behavior.

Testosterone seems to play essential roles in integrating the various elements of male copulation into a pattern that is focused on a female partner. Once this process has occurred, testosterone is no longer necessary to the performance of the behavior. Cats that are castrated after they have attained sexual experience and therefore have fully developed the copulatory pattern will continue to copulate even though no testosterone is in the system. The same is true of cats that attain their experience after castration but while treated with exogenous testosterone. Testosterone does not trigger or induce copulation in cats, but does provide a necessary component for its organization during puberty.

The medial preoptic area (MPOA) of the hypothalamus is apparently involved in the pubertal integration of sexual behavior. When adult male rats are lesioned in this region, their copulatory behavior is significantly impaired (Heimer & Larsson, 1967; Twiggs, Popolow, & Gerall, 1978). However, if the lesion is made prepubertally, normal copulatory behavior can still develop, provided that the lesioned rats are reared in heterosexual groups during the recovery period (Leedy, Vela, Popolow, & Gerall, 1980; Twiggs et al. 1978). The lesioned rats show normal levels of playing during the post-lesion period. Leedy et al. (1980) suggest that the ability to perform copulatory behavior develops out of this prepubertal play behavior. When rats are reared in social isolation between the time of the lesion and testing after sexual maturity, they will not copulate (Twiggs et al., 1978). Presumably the MPOA is a brain region that would ordinarily be involved in the prepubertal development of copulatory capacity, but when it is damaged, other regions will assume the same function.

Testosterone may be important for maintaining sexual behavior over long periods as well as for its initial development, although the degree of importance varies with both species and individuals (Bermant & Davidson, 1974). Experienced, castrated cats undergo a slow and individually variable decline in sexual behavior, which can be reversed with testosterone treatment. The decline is correlated to some extent with structural deterioration of the penis (Rosenblatt & Aronson, 1958a). The effects of previous sexual experience survive the castration related decline: Treatment with testosterone reinstates the same level of sexual activity as previously performed (Rosenblatt, 1965). Similar lasting effects of previous sexual experience have been reported for guinea pigs (Valenstein & Young, 1955).

A relationship between hormones and experience similar to that of cats has been found in rats (Larsson, 1978). Sexually experienced males continued to copulate after castration but sexually naive males did not. The experienced castrates gradually declined in sexual performance over several weeks of testing. When testosterone was replaced, copulatory behavior was performed by all groups, but was slower to emerge in previously isolated males than in either sexually or socially experienced males. Thus it appears that experience with copulation is required for sexual behavior to be maintained after hormone withdrawal, but that social experience is sufficient in coaction with testosterone for the initial development of the behavior.

INDIVIDUAL SELECTION AND INTERACTIVE DEVELOPMENT

A goal of developmental studies is to explain behavior in terms of its origins within individuals. However, sexual behavior can occur only if two individuals interact, and the patterns that are comprised by sexual behavior are often best thought of as properties of the interaction and not of individuals. Thus, the cooperation of a mounted partner is essential before footclasp mounting can be performed by rhesus monkeys; although males do the mounting, the mounting cannot be done without active female participation (Goy, 1970). This realization encourages one to look toward premounting interactions for the elements that elicit the cooperation. The interactive nature of sexual behavior means that some factors that alter the likelihood or the nature of the performance of sexual behavioral patterns may do so indirectly, because odors and other communicative properties are changed so that the partner will behave differently toward the affected animal (c.f. Diakow, 1974).

Because no description can be complete, general explanations can be made more powerful by having more than one kind of description (Golani, 1976). Although descriptions in terms of individual motor patterns and acts have led to major advances, it may also be useful for future studies of sexual behavior and its development to create descriptive units for social and sexual dyads rather than to rely solely on behavioral units such as displays described as properties of individuals. Efforts in this direction may yield new insights into the development of sexual behavior that cannot be attained by focusing on individuals. Although individuals are the traditional units of developmental study, nothing precludes the application of developmental methods to supraindividual units. For example, the transitions from mother-pup, to sibling-sibling, to adult male-female dyads might reasonably be a focus of a developmental study of sexual behavior in rats.

The importance of social context is not limited to dyads. Both male and female rats pace their sexual behavior, but the optimal interval between intromissions is not the same for each sex. For females, multiple intromissions stimulate the progestational state required for implantation and successful pregnancy, but when the interval between intromissions is too short, sperm transport through the cervix may be interfered with (Adler, 1978). For males, multiple intromissions are required before ejaculation can occur (Sachs & Barfield, 1976). The optimal inter-intromission interval is shorter for males than for females, and a single male-female pair may be considered to be in conflict so far as the pacing of copulation goes. However, if several males and several females are allowed to copulate in a group session, the males will take turns copulating, and each male will copulate with more than one female within each series of intromissions. When inter-intromission intervals are calculated separately for individual males and females in these groups, it is found that they are not only different but near the optimal value for each sex (McClintock & Anisko, 1982; McClintock, Anisko, & Adler, 1981). The characteristic that is adaptive in this case resides to a large extent in the group process.

In view of the importance of partners and other companions for reproductive behavior, it is perhaps paradoxical that evolutionary theory has come to focus so completely on individuals. The goal of evolutionary studies of behavior is to explain the origins of differences between populations, but individuals have usually been accepted to be the units on which natural selection acts. This understanding has led those who are interested in sexual behavior to describe it in terms of individual adaptive strategies. Since males and females differ in their nonbehavioral investment for perpetuating genes into future generations, there will be selection for them also to differ in behavioral investment so as to maximize the likelihood of efficient use of prior nonbehavioral investments such as gamete size (Williams, 1975; Wilson, 1975).

At a basic level, the argument is that females produce a relatively small number of relatively large and immobile gametes; therefore, they should behave in ways that help to ensure the survival of each gamete. This promotes the evolution of careful selection of mates, protection of fertilized eggs, and care of young. Males, on the other hand, produce relatively large numbers of relatively small and mobile gametes. Like females, they should also behave in ways to promote gametic success, but this will often entail different, even competitive, behavior. Unlike females, males may be selected to fertilize as many mates as possible with their numerous and more expendable gametes, even though some mates may turn out to be bad risks. Ecological conditions may accentuate sex differences in reproductive strategies in some populations, leading to marked dimorphisms in behavior and other characteristics.

A focus on individuals as the unit through which natural selection acts has been enormously useful for generating powerful explanatory principles of evolution. However, the strategy metaphor so often used by sociobiologists to capture the nature of selective pressures on sexual behavior of individuals is inappropriate to describe behavioral organization. As this review reveals, sexual behavioral mechanisms are not unitary. It is also the case that many of the behavioral capacities that underlie successful copulation may also underlie a large number of other social and nonsocial functions. The same skills that are involved in controlling one's movement with respect to the movements of a conspecific may underlie successful copulation, territorial defense, and socially directed food getting. Therefore, a focus on individuals as functional strategists is not likely to assist in developmental studies because proximate analysis has already gone well beyond what can be categorized with the functional-economic vocabulary appropriate to the concerns of current sociobiology. As Lehrman (1970) has argued, functional considerations may identify interesting problems worthy of developmental study, but functional distinctions cannot be used to guide the developmental inquiry.

Gould (1982) has argued that evolutionary theorists must find ways of characterizing the action of natural selection on units larger than individuals, because higher-level units, such as demes, species, and clades, are natural phenomena that can no more be reduced to the individuals within them than individuals can be reduced to genes. With respect to behavior at least, there is very little that proximate analysis currently has to offer to such an endeavor. However, attention to the social nexus may lead to the postulation of supraindividual proximate mechanisms that may provide a vocabulary and a set of concepts of use to evolutionists as they attempt to deal with groups.

COMPARATIVE BEHAVIORAL DEVELOPMENT OF LABORATORY RATS AND RHESUS MONKEYS

There are interesting similarities in the sexual behavior of laboratory rats and rhesus monkeys. In each species hormones affect sexual behavior in both early ontogenetic stages and at puberty, and sex differences in sexual behavior within each species can be traced to origins in early hormone secretion. Male sexual behavior in each species develops during social interactions in prepubertal stages. This is illustrated in each case by the deleterious effects of social restriction. There are perceptual-motor skills in the sexual behavior of both rats and monkeys that also function in nonsexual, social contexts in each case. These include skills underlying mounting, a well-defined motor pattern that is usually considered as diagnostic of masculine sexuality, but that also has nonsexual functions. Despite these compelling similarities, there are equally compelling differences between the two species that caution against facile generalization of mechanisms and developmental processes across mammals.

Although the difficulty that previously isolated male rhesus monkeys have with copulation is superficially similar to that expressed by previously isolated male rats, it is likely that the underlying problems are only partly the same. The improper orientation to the female partner may originate from lack of experience in adjusting body position to a partner in each case, but how does one account for the fact that male rats can benefit from experience with sexually receptive females to overcome this problem but monkeys, with their clearly superior perceptual-motor capacities, cannot? The most likely reason is that sexual behavior for monkeys involves its proper integration into complex social exchanges

(Goy & Goldfoot, 1974; Hanby, 1976; Rowell, 1972). Social restriction in a developing monkey precludes opportunity to practice motor elements of social behavior but, far more importantly, it precludes opportunity to learn the consequences of performing social behavior and the social dynamics of a group and to form appropriate interaction routines. Fear and aggression are typically shown by previously isolated monkeys in a sexual situation (Goy, Wallen, & Goldfoot, 1974). Therefore, when a socially naive monkey is stimulated to mount an estrous female, it is very likely that inadequate or inappropriate social exchanges or interaction routines will interfere with acquiring the correct mounting pattern. Naive rats, with their simpler social context for copulation, would not have this problem.

It may in fact be the case that some of the incorrect orientation exhibited by previously isolated monkeys is a consequence of interference from competing responses rather than a result of failure to know what the correct orientation should be. Previous isolates can orient "correctly" to a crude dummy of a monkey, a stimulus that does not arouse fearful or agressive behavior (Deutsch & Larsson, 1974). Further, rhesus monkeys captured as subadults and housed singly before being treated with a female in captivity initially showed incorrectly oriented mounting. After mounting correctly and achieving their first coital ejaculation, these monkeys thereafter had well-executed mounts (Michael & Wilson, 1973). If it is assumed that these feral monkeys had normal social experiences before capture and that they had therefore previously learned as infants how to orient properly for intromission (Hanby, 1976), it may be that the inadequate initial orientation of the pubertal males in this study was a side effect of the tension resulting from being placed with a strange adult female.

Social restriction leaves lordosis intact in female rats, but eliminates the "present" posture of monkeys. Perhaps this is because lordosis, the diagnostic pattern for female sexuality in rats, is neither a skilled motor pattern nor a skilled social pattern while the present posture, the indicator of female sexuality in monkeys, is both. The present posture and lordosis have some functional equivalence in that both allow copulation to occur, but have very different developmental histories and proximate causes. Lordosis is reflexive and highly dependent on endocrine state; the present posture is variable in form and independent of endocrine state. Lordosis is performed only in sexual contexts, whereas male and female, young and mature monkeys perform the present posture in a variety of contexts, including sexual ones. To perform the present posture, monkeys must become able to orient to a partner from a distance; it may be a more difficult pattern to acquire than mounting (Hanby, 1976). For female monkeys to use the present posture in a sexual context, they must undergo social development analogous to that described for sexual behavior of male monkeys. To perform lordosis in a sexual context, female rats must only be able to adopt a posture in response to tactile stimuli on the flank and perineum; the mechanism for this can be described in terms of estrogenic effects on tactile sensitivity and spinal reflexes (Bermant & Davidson, 1974). Therefore, the differences in behavioral complexity of the patterns most often used as indicators of female sexuality in rats and monkeys are very great. Not only is this difference of importance for restricting the range of explanatory generalization across species, but it has important implications for how sex differences are understood. General conceptions such as masculinity and femininity (e.g., Goy & McEwen, 1980) are commonly used across species to refer to what are in fact very different processes. If lordosis and presenting are indicators of femininity, to be feminine and a monkey requires far more of development than to be feminine and a rat. Using similar criteria, it can be said that it is more difficult to achieve masculinity than femininity in rats while the reverse is true in monkeys. Unfortunately, these kinds of comparisons may say more about premature selection of criteria for hypothesized underlying constructs than about either sex or species differences. To more fully understand sexual development in each sex and species, future studies must depart from attending only to component motor patterns and attend also to the social aspects of sexual behavior.

Overall, the differences between rats and rhesus monkeys constitute a levels difference, as described by Schneirla (1957). The relationship between structure (hormone-dependent physiology and anatomy) and behavior is more complex and remote in the case of monkeys. Further, monkeys must not only acquire necessary perceptual-motor skills during their early social experience; they must also acquire a large social behavior repertoire and the ability to select appropriately from it.

CONCLUDING COMMENTS

Sexual behavior has greater coherence and unity when described in terms of its evolutionary function than when described in terms of its organization or development. First, it is quite possible for common evolutionary function to be achieved by very different proximate mechanisms in different species. The organization of sexual behavior in laboratory rats and rhesus monkeys was compared and found to have important differences as well as similarities. Although some of these differences may reflect responses to different selective pressures, others may reflect different pathways to similar adaptations. Second, when a single species is considered, processes are found to contribute toward sexual behavior that also are essential components of other functional systems. Despite the relevance of functional analyses of behavior in identifying phenomena important to study, the use of functional categories in developmental studies may be a hindrance. This review has demonstrated some ways in which the development of sexual behavior can be better understood by crossing functional boundaries to find common processes. The appropriate identification of and orientation toward a sexual partner in rats, for example, involve skills that are used in many social contexts and that develop gradually, beginning in the early mother-infant interactions surrounding suckling.

Because sexual behavior is necessarily social, many of its qualities reside in the social interaction and cannot entirely be accounted for by proximate mechanisms within an individual. The probability of mounting in a male rhesus monkey, for example, very much depends on the behavior of his partner. Therefore, future research will need to examine ontogenetic changes in dyadic interactions, including the contributions of each developing individual to this process. Both the analysis of development across functional categories and the attention to dyads will lead developmental psychobiologists away from the current concern of sociobiology with individual, functional, reproductive strategies. It is expected, however, that these research directions will ultimately lead to a fuller understanding of the proximate mechanisms and developmental pathways through which members of different species achieve successful reproduction.

ACKNOWLEDGEMENTS

Some of the research reported here was supported by grants BNS 77-24788 and BNS 80-14669 from the National Science Foundation. I am indebted to George F. Michel and to E. S. Gollin and his graduate students at the University of Colorado for useful comments on the manuscript and to Phyllis Doucette for typing it.

REFERENCES

Adler, N. T. (1978). Social and environmental control of reproductive processes in animals. In T. E. McGill, D. A. Dewsbury, & B. D. Sachs (Eds.), *Sex and behavior* (pp. 115–160). New York: Plenum Press.

Adler, N. & Bermant, G. (1966). Sexual behavior of male rats: Effects of reduced sensory feedback. *Journal of Comparative and Physiological Psychology, 61,* 240–243.

Alberts, J. R. (1976). Olfactory contributions to behavioral development in rodents. In R. L. Doty (Ed.), *Mammalian olfaction, reproductive processes, and behavior* (pp. 67–94). New York: Academic Press.

Alberts, J. R. (1978). Huddling by rat pups: Multisensory control of contact behavior. *Journal of Comparative and Physiological Psychology, 92,* 220–230.

Alberts, J. R., & Leimbach, M. P. (1980). The first foray: Maternal influences in nest egression in the weanling rat. *Developmental Psychobiology, 13,* 417–429.

Aronson, L. R., & Cooper, M. L. (1968). Desensitization of the glans penis and sexual behavior in cats. In M. Diamond (Ed.), *Perspectives in reproduction and behavior.* (pp. 51–82). Bloomington: Indiana University Press.

Aronson, L. R., & Cooper, M. L. (1974). Olfactory deprivation and mating behavior in sexually experienced male cats. *Behavioral Biology, 11,* 459–480.

Barnett, S. A., & Walker, K. Z. (1974). Early stimulation, parental behavior, and the temperature of infant mice. *Developmental Psychobiology, 7,* 563–577.

Bastock, M. (1967). *Courtship.* Chicago: Aldine.

Baum, M. J. (1979). Differentiation of coital behavior in mammals: A comparative analysis. *Neuroscience & Biobehavioral Reviews, 3,* 265–284.

Baverstock, P., & Green, P. (1975). Water recycling in lactation. *Science, 187,* 657–658.

Beach, F. A. (1942). Male and female mating behavior in prepuberally castrated female rats treated with androgens. *Endocrinology, 31,* 673–678.

Beach, F. A. (1956). Characteristics of masculine "sex drive." In M. Jones (Ed.), *Nebraska Symposium on Motivation* (pp. 1–31). Lincoln: University of Nebraska Press.

Beach, F. A. (1965). Retrospect and prospect. In F. A. Beach (Ed.), *Sex and behavior* (pp. 535–569). New York: Wiley.

Beach, F. A. (1968). Coital behavior in dogs. III. Effects of early isolation on mating in males. *Behaviour, 30,* 218–238.

Beach, F. A. (1971). Hormonal factors controlling the differentiation, development, and display of copulatory behavior in the ramstergig and related species. In E. Tobach, L. R. Aronson, & E. Shaw (Eds.), *The biopsychology of development* (pp. 249–296). New York: Academic Press.

Beach, F. A. (1976). Sexual attractivity, proceptivity, and receptivity in female mammals. *Hormones and Behavior, 7,* 105–133.

Beach, F. A., Johnson, A. I., Anisko, J. J., & Dunbar, I. A. (1977). Hormonal control of sexual attraction in pseudohermaphroditic female dogs. *Journal of Comparative and Physiological Psychology, 91,* 711–715.

Beach, F. A., Noble, R. G., & Orndoff, R. K. (1969). Effects of perinatal androgen treatment on responses of male rats to gonadal hormones in adulthood. *Journal of Comparative and Physiological Psychology, 68,* 490–497.

Bermant, G., & Davidson, J. M. (1974) *Biological bases of sexual behavior.* New York: Harper & Row.

Booth, J. E. (1977). Sexual behavior of neonatally castrated rats injected during infancy with estrogen and dihydrotestosterone. *The Journal of Endocrinology, 72,* 135–141.

Carlsson, S. G., & Larsson, K. (1964). Mating in male rats after local anesthetization of the glans penis. *Zeitschrift fur Tierpsychologie, 21,* 854–856.

Clemens, G., Gladue, B. A., & Coniglio, L. P. (1978). Prenatal endogenous androgenic influences on masculine sexual behavior and genital morphology in male and female rats. *Hormones and Behavior, 10,* 40–53.

Cooper, M., & Aronson, L. R. (1962). Effects of a sensory deprivation on the sexual behavior of experienced adult male cats. *American Zoologist, 2,* 514–515.

Dahlof, L. G., & Larsson, K. (1976). Interactional effects of pudendal nerve section and social restriction on male rat sexual behavior. *Physiology & Behavior, 6,* 757–762.

Daly, M., & Wilson, M. (1978). *Sex, evolution, and behavior.* North Scituate, MA: Duxbury Press.

Deutsch, J., & Larsson, K. (1974). Model-oriented sexual behavior in surrogate-reared rhesus monkeys. *Brain, Behavior, and Evolution, 9,* 157–164.

Dewsbury, D. A. (1978). The comparative method in studies of reproductive behavior. In T. E. McGill, D. A. Dewsbury, & B. D. Sachs (Eds.), *Sex and behavior: Status and prospectus* (pp. 83–112). New York: Plenum Press.

Diakow, C. (1970). Effects of genital desensitization on the mating pattern of female rats as determined by motion picture analysis. *American Zoologist, 10,* 486.

Diakow, C. (1971). Effects of genital desensitization on mating behavior and ovulation in the female cat. *Physiology and Behavior, 7,* 47–54.

Diakow, C. (1974). Male-female interactions and the organization of mammalian mating patterns. In D. S. Lehrman, J. S. Rosenblatt, R. A. Hinde, & E. Shaw (Eds.), *Advances in the study of behavior* (Vol. 5). (pp. 227–268). New York: Academic Press.

Doty, R. L. (1974). A cry for the liberation of the female rodent: courtship and copulation in *Rodentia. Psychological Bulletin, 81,* 159–172.

Duffy, J. A., & Hendricks, S. E. (1973). Influences of social isolation during development on sexual behavior of the rat. *Animal Learning & Behavior, 1,* 223–227.

Eisenberg, J. F., & Golani, I. (1977). Communication in methatheria. In T. A. Sebeok (Ed.), *How animals communicate* (pp. 575–599). Bloomington: Indiana University Press.

Emery, D. E., & Sachs, B. D. (1975). Ejaculatory pattern in female rats without androgen treatment. *Science, 190,* 484–486.

Feder, H. H. (1967). Specificity of testosterone and estradiol in the differentiating neonatal rat. *Anatomical Record, 157,* 79–86.

Fedigan, L. M. (1982) *Primate paradigms: Sex roles and social bonds.* Montreal: Eden Press.

Folman, Y., & Drori, P. (1965). Normal and aberrant copulatory behaviour in male rats (*R. norvegicus*) reared in isolation. *Animal Behaviour, 13,* 427–429.

Friedman, M. I., & Bruno, J. P. (1976). Exchange of water during lactation. *Science, 191,* 409–410.

Galef, B. G., & Clark, M. M. (1972). Mother's milk and adult presence: Two factors determining initial dietary selection by weanling rats. *Journal of Comparative and Physiological Psychology, 38,* 220–225.

Gerall, A. A. (1963). An exploratory study of the effects of social isolation on the sexual behaviour of guinea pigs. *Animal Behaviour, 11,* 274–282.

Gerall, A. A., Dunlap, J. L., & Hendricks, S. E. (1973). Effect of ovarian secretions on female behavioral potentiality in the rat. *Journal of Comparative and Physiological Psychology, 82,* 449–465.

Gerall, A. A., & Ward, I. L. (1966). Effects of prenatal exogenous androgen on the sexual behavior of the female albino rat. *Journal of Comparative and Physiological Psychology, 62,* 370–375.

Gerall, H. D., Ward, I. L., & Gerall, A. A. (1967). Disruption of the male rat's sexual behavior induced by social isolation. *Animal Behaviour, 15,* 54–58.

Golani, I. (1976). Homeostatic motor processes in mammalian interactions: A choreography of display. In P. P. G. Bateson & R. A. Hinde (Eds.), *Perspectives in ethology* (Vol. 2). (pp. 69–134). New York: Plenum Press.

Goldfoot, D. A., & Baum, M. J. (1972). Initiation of mating behavior in developing male rats following peripheral electric shock. *Physiology and Behavior, 8,* 857–863.

Goldfoot, D. A., & Wallen, L. (1978). Development of gender role behaviors in heterosexual and isosexual groups of infant rhesus monkeys. In D. C. Chivers (Ed.), *Recent Advances in Primatology: Vol. I. Behaviour* (pp. 155–159). London: Academic Press.

Gould, S. J. (1982). Darwinism and the expansion of evolutionary theory. *Science, 216,* 380–387.

Goy, R. W. (1968). Organizing effects of androgen on the behaviour of rhesus monkeys. In R. P. Michael (Ed.), *Endocrinology and human behavior.* (pp. 12–21). New York: Oxford University Press.

Goy, R. W. (1970). Early hormonal influences on the development of sexual and sex-related behavior. In F. O. Schmitt (Ed.), *The neurosciences: Second study program* (pp. 196–207). New York: Rockefeller University Press.

Goy, R. W. (1978). Development of play and mounting behaviour in female rhesus virilized prenatally with esters of testosterone or dihydrotestosterone. In D. C. Chivers (Ed.), *Recent Advances in Primatology: Vol. 1. Behaviour* (pp. 449–462). London: Academic Press.

Goy, R. W., & Goldfoot, D. A. (1973). Hormonal influences on sexually dimorphic behavior. In R. O. Greep (Ed.), *Handbook of physiology: Sec. 7. Endocrinology.* Vol. 2. *Female reproductive system* (pp. 169–186). Baltimore: Williams & Wilkins.

Goy, R. W., & Goldfoot, D. A. (1974). Experiential and hormonal factors influencing development of sexual behavior in the male rhesus monkey. In F. O. Schmitt & F. G. Worden (Eds.), *The neurosciences: Third study program.* (pp. 571–581). Cambridge, MA.: MIT Press.

Goy, R. W., & McEwen, B. S. (1980). *Sexual differentiation of the brain.* Cambridge, MA: MIT Press.

Goy, R. W., & Resko, J. A. (1972). Gonadal hormones and behavior of normal and pseudohermaphroditic nonhuman female primates. *Recent Progress in Hormone Research, 28,* 707–733.

Goy, R. W., Wallen, K., & Goldfoot, D. A. (1974). Social factors affecting the development of mounting behavior in male rhesus monkeys. In W. Montagna, & W. A. Sadler (Eds.), *Reproductive behavior* (pp. 223–247). New York: Plenum Press.

Gregory, E. H., & Pfaff, D. W. (1971). Development of olfactory-guided behavior in infant rats. *Physiology and Behavior, 6,* 573–576.

Gruendel, A. D., & Arnold, W. J. (1969). Effects of early social deprivation on reproductive behavior of male rats. *Journal of Comparative and Physiological Psychology, 67,* 123–128.

Gruendel, A. D., & Arnold, W. J. (1974). Influence of preadolescent experiential factors on the development of sexual behavior in the albino rat. *Journal of Comparative and Physiological Psychology, 86,* 172–178.

Gubernick, D. J., & Alberts, J. R. (1982). *Maternal licking of young: resource exchange and proximate controls.* Paper presented at *International Society for Developmental Psychobiology,* Minneapolis, October.

Hanby, J. (1976). Sociosexual development in primates. In P. P. G. Bateson, & P. H. Klopfer (Eds.), *Perspectives in ethology* (Vol. 2) (pp. 1–67). New York: Plenum Press.

Hård, E., & Larsson, K. (1968). Dependence of adult mating behavior in male rats on the presence of littermates in infancy. *Brain, Behavior, and Evolution, 1,* 405–419.

Hård, E., & Larsson, K. (1971). Climbing behavior patterns in prepubertal rats. *Brain, Behavior, and Evolution, 4,* 151–161.

Harlow, H. F. (1965). Sexual behavior in rhesus monkeys. In F. A. Beach (Ed.), *Sex and Behavior* (pp. 234–265). New York: Wiley.

Harlow, H. F., Joslyn, W. D., Senko, M. G., & Dopp, A. (1966). Behavioral aspects of reproduction in primates. *Journal of Animal Science, 25,* 49–67.

Harris, G. W., & Levine, S. (1962). Sexual differentiation of the brain and its experimental control. *Journal of Physiology* (London), *163,* 42–43.

Harris, G. W., & Levine, S. (1965). Sexual differentiation of the brain and its experimental control. *Journal of Physiology (London), 181,* 379–400.

Hart, B. L. (1977). Neonatal dihydrotestosterone and estrogen stimulation: Effects on sexual behavior of male rats. *Hormones and Behavior. 8,* 193–201.

Heimer, L., & Larsson, K. (1967). Impairment of mating behavior in male rats following lesions in the preoptic-anterior hypothalamic continuum. *Brain Research, 3,* 248–263.

Herbert, J. (1973). The role of the dorsal nerves of the penis in the sexual behaviour of the male rhesus monkey. *Physiology and Behavior, 10,* 293–300.

Hofer, M. A., Shair, H., & Singh, P. (1976). Evidence that maternal ventral skin substances promote suckling in infant rats. *Physiology and Behavior, 17,* 131–137.

Keverne, E. B., & Michael, R. P. (1971). Sex attractant properties of ether extracts of vaginal secretions from rhesus monkeys. *Journal of Endocrinology, 51,* 313–322.

Komisaruk, B. R. (1974). Neural and hormonal interactions in the reproductive behavior of female rats. In W. Montagna and W. A. Sadler (Eds.), *Reproductive behavior* (pp. 97–129). New York: Plenum Press.

Krieger, M. S., & Barfield, R. J. (1976). Masculine sexual behavior: pacing and ejaculatory patterns in female rats induced by electrical shock. *Physiology and Behavior, 16,* 671–675.

Larsson, K. (1971). Impaired mating performances in male rats after anosmia induced peripherally or centrally. *Brain, Behavior and Evolution, 4,* 463–471.

Larsson, K. (1978). Experiential factors in the development of sexual behaviour. In J. B. Hutchinson (Ed.), *Biological determinants of sexual behaviour* (pp. 54–86). New York: Wiley.

Larsson, K., & Södersten, P. (1973). Mating in male rats after section of the dorsal penile nerve. *Physiology and Behavior, 10,* 567–571.

Leedy, M. G., Vela, E. A., Popolow, H. B., & Gerall, A. A. (1980). Effect of prepubertal medial preoptic area lesions on male rat sexual behavior. *Physiology and Behavior, 24,* 341–346.

Lehrman, D. S. (1970). Semantic and conceptual issues in the nature-nurture problem. In L. R. Aronson, E. Tobach, D. S. Lehrman, & J. S. Rosenblatt (Eds.), *Development and evolution of behavior* (pp. 17–52). San Francisco: Freeman.

Leon, M., & Moltz, H. (1972). The development of the pheromonal bond in the albino rat. *Physiology and Behavior, 8*, 683–686.

Lodder, J., & Zeilmaker, G. H. (1976). Effects of pelvic nerve and pudendal nerve transection on mating behavior in the male rat. *Physiology and Behavior, 16*, 745–751.

Mason, W. A. (1960). The effects of social restriction on the behavior of rhesus monkeys. I. Free social behavior. *Journal of Comparative and Physiological Psychology, 53*, 582–589.

Mayr, E. (1963). *Animal species and evolution.* Cambridge, MA.: Harvard University Press.

McClintock, M. K., & Anisko, J. J. (1982). Group mating among Norway rats I. Sex differences in the pattern and neuroendocrine consequences of copulation. *Animal Behaviour, 30*, 398–409.

McClintock, M. K., Anisko, J. J., & Adler, N. T. (1982). Group mating among Norway rats II. The social dynamics of copulation: competition, cooperation, and mate choice. *Animal Behaviour, 30*, 410–425.

Meaney, M. J., & Stewart, J. (1981). A descriptive study of social development in the rat (*Rattus norvegicus*). *Animal Behaviour, 29*, 34–45.

Michael, R. P., & Wilson, M. (1973). Changes in the sexual behaviour of male rhesus monkeys (*M. mulatta*) at puberty. *Folia primatologica, 19*, 384–403.

Michel, G. F., & Moore, C. L. (1978). *Biological perspectives in developmental psychology.* Monterey: Brooks/Cole.

Missakian, E. (1969). Reproductive behavior of socially deprived adult male rhesus monkeys (*Macaca mulatta*). *Journal of Comparative and Physiological Psychology, 69*, 403–407.

Moore, C. L. (1981). An olfactory basis for maternal discrimination of sex of offspring in rats (*Rattus norvegicus*). *Animal Behaviour, 29*, 383–386.

Moore, C. L. (1982). Maternal behavior of rats is affected by hormonal condition of pups. *Journal of Comparative and Physiological Psychology, 96*, 123–129.

Moore, C. L. (1984). Maternal contributions to the development of masculine sexual behavior in laboratory rats. *Developmental Psychobiology, 17*, 347–356.

Moore, C. L., & Morelli, G. A. (1979). Mother rats interact differently with male and female offspring. *Journal of Comparative and Physiological Psychology, 93*, 677–684.

Murphy, M. R., & Schneider, G. E. (1970). Olfactory bulb removal eliminates mating behavior in the male golden hamster. *Science, 167*, 302–304.

Noble, R. G. (1977). Mounting in female hamsters: Effects of different hormone regimes. *Physiology and Behavior, 19*, 519–526.

Olioff, M., & Stewart, J. (1978). Sex differences in the play behavior of prepubescent rats. *Physiology and Behavior, 20*, 113–115.

Pollak, E. I., & Sachs, B. D. (1975). Male copulatory behavior and female maternal behavior in neonatally bulbectomized rats. *Physiology and Behavior, 14*, 337–343.

Powers, J. B., & Winans, S. S. (1975). Vomeronasal organ: Critical role in mediating sexual behavior of the male hamster. *Science, 187*, 961–963.

Rosenblatt, J. S. (1965). Effects of experience on sexual behavior in male cats. In F. A. Beach (Ed.), *Sex and behavior* (pp. 416–439). New York: Wiley.

Rosenblatt, J. S. (1976). Stages in the early behavioral development of altricial young of selected species of non-primate mammals. In P. P. G. Bateson & R. A. Hinde (Eds.), *Growing points in ethology* (pp. 345–383). Cambridge: Cambridge University Press.

Rosenblatt, J. S., & Aronson, L. R. (1958a). The decline of sexual behavior in male cats after castration with special reference to the role of prior sexual experience. *Behaviour, 12*, 285–338.

Rosenblatt, J. S., & Aronson, L. R. (1958b). The influence of experience on the behavioral effects of androgen in prepubertally castrated male cats. *Animal Behaviour, 6*, 171–182.

Rosenblatt, J. S., & Lehrman, D. S. (1963). Maternal behavior of the laboratory rat. In H. L. Rheingold (Ed.), *Maternal behavior in mammals* (pp. 8–57). New York: Wiley.

Rowell, T. (1972). *Social behaviour of monkeys.* Middlesex, England: Penguin Books.

Ruddy, L. L. (1980). Nasal intubation: a minimally obstrusive anosmia technique applied to rats. *Physiology and Behavior, 24,* 881–883.

Sachs, B. D. (1978). Conceptual and neural mechanisms of masculine copulatory behavior. In T. E. McGill, D. A. Dewsbury, & B. D. Sachs (Eds.), *Sex and behavior* (pp. 267–295). New York: Plenum Press.

Sachs, B. D., & Barfield, R. J. (1976). Functional analysis of masculine copulatory behavior in the rat. In J. S. Rosenblatt, R. A. Hinde, E. Shaw, & C. Beer (Eds.), *Advances in the study of behavior,* (Vol. 7) (pp. 91–154). New York: Academic Press.

Sachs, B. D., & Meisel, R. L. (1979). Pubertal development of penile reflexes and copulation in male rats. *Psychoneuroendocrinology, 4,* 287–296.

Schneirla, T. C. (1957). The concept of development in comparative psychology. In D. B. Harris (Ed.), *The concept of development* (pp. 78–108). Minneapolis: University of Minnesota Press.

Simpson, M. J. A. (1978). Tactile experience and sexual behavior: Aspects of development with special reference to primates. In J. B. Hutchinson (Ed.), *Biological determinants of sexual behaviour* (pp. 785–807). New York: Wiley.

Södersten, P., Damassa, D. A., & Smith, E. R. (1977). Sexual behavior in developing male rats. *Hormones and Behavior, 8,* 320–341.

Spaulding, W. D., & Peck, C. K. (1974). Sexual behavior of male rats following removal of the glans penis at weaning. *Developmental Psychobiology, 7,* 43–46.

Teicher, M. H., & Blass, E. M. (1976). Suckling in newborn rats: Eliminated by nipple lavage, reinstated by pup saliva. *Science, 193,* 422–425.

Twiggs, D. G., Popolow, H. B., & Gerall, A. A. (1978). Medial preoptic lesions and male sexual behavior: Age and environmental interactions. *Science, 200,* 1414–1415.

Valenstein, E. S., & Young, W. C. (1955). An experiential factor influencing the effectiveness of testosterone propionate in eliciting sexual behavior in male guinea pigs. *Endocrinology, 56,* 173–177.

Valenstein, E. S., Riss, W., & Young, W. C. (1955). Experiential and genetic factors in the organization of sexual behavior in male guinea pigs. *Journal of Comparative and Physiological Psychology, 48,* 397–403.

Welker, W. I. (1964). Analysis of sniffing in the albino rat. *Behaviour, 22,* 223–244.

Wilhelmsson, M., & Larsson, K. (1973). The development of sexual behavior in anosmic male rats reared under various social conditions. *Physiology and Behavior, 11,* 227–232.

Williams, C. L. (1982, October). *Precocious steroid-facilitated lordosis and ear wiggling in 6-day-old rats.* Paper presented at International Society for Developmental Psychobiology, Minneapolis.

Williams, G. C. (1966). *Adaptation and natural selection.* New Jersey: Princeton University Press.

Williams, G. C. (1975). *Sex and evolution.* New Jersey: Princeton University Press.

Wilson, E. O. (1975). *Sociobiology: The new synthesis.* Cambridge, MA.: Harvard University Press.

Zimbardo, P. G. (1958). The effects of early avoidance training and rearing conditions upon the sexual behavior of the male rat. *Journal of Comparative and Physiological Psychology, 51,* 764–769.

3

Development of Locomotion in Vertebrates: A Comparative Perspective

Anne Bekoff
University of Colorado

INTRODUCTION

The field of behavioral embryology has produced a multitude of studies on the development of motility and/or locomotion in a wide variety of vertebrates. These have been reviewed recently from neuroembryological and behavioral perspectives (e.g., Bekoff, 1981a; Carmichael, 1970; Hamburger, 1963; Oppenheim, 1981).

The purpose of this review is to look at the available studies of the development of locomotion in vertebrates from a comparative and evolutionary perspective. The goal of this analysis is to try to understand better both the evolutionary history and the current adaptive significance of particular stages in the development of locomotion in a variety of vertebrates. In general, development, particularly of the earlier stages, tends to be a conservative process (Romer & Parsons, 1977). Therefore, we should expect to find some features of the development of locomotion that are phylogenetically conservative: some stages, most likely those occurring earlier in ontogeny, should be common to most developing vertebrates, from fishes to mammals. Those features that are found to be similar in a variety of vertebrates are presumably derived from the ancestral condition. Evidence from many other systems suggests that ontogeny in a particular species is most likely to repeat developmental steps that were seen in its ancestors when they are structurally or functionally necessary or when they have adaptive significance for the derived type's own development (Romer & Parsons, 1977). In addition to those features that have been conserved during evolution of the vertebrates, comparative analysis should reveal other features that are found only in particular groups. These are most likely to represent adaptations to unique aspects of the embryonic and/or postnatal conditions that developing animals of different species must face.

In the following discussion the term "locomotion" is used very generally to mean the process in which an animal uses its own musculoskeletal system to move itself from one point to another. There can be no disputing the fact that it is essential for almost all adult vertebrates to be able to locomote in order to survive. In adult vertebrates, locomotion is typically involved in such basic endeavors as obtaining food, avoiding predators, and finding shelter. Furthermore, activities such as courtship and aggressive displays are often derived from locomotor acts (Barlow, 1977).

There is a remarkable diversity of modes of locomotion among adult vertebrates—swimming, walking, flying, to name just a few. We know a great deal about the adaptive changes that have occurred in the musculoskeletal system during the phylogenetic progression from fishes to mammals (Kluge, 1977). We know a great deal less about the evolution of the neural circuitry that generates the pattern of musculoskeletal movements involved in locomotion, primarily because this is not a structure that is preserved in the fossil record. In thinking about the evolution of the neural control mechanisms for locomotion, then, we are more or less limited to comparative studies of living vertebrates. The advantage of working with living vertebrates is that we can study on-going function as well as structure. That is, we can observe animals in the process of locomotion, make electrophysiological recordings from nerves and muscles that are involved in movement, and experimentally manipulate the system in order to gain insight into the underlying mechanisms. However, we must also keep in mind that in trying to derive evolutionary relationships, the living vertebrates that are available for comparative studies may not be representative of the ancestral types. This is particularly obvious in considering locomotion in vertebrates where, in some cases, there is as much diversity in modes of locomotion within a Class as between Classes. For example, compare frog jumping to newt walking, or alligator walking to serpentine locomotion in snakes, or cat walking to whale swimming. Obviously, for each species, we must consider which elements are conservative, i.e., derived from ancestral species, and which represent specific adaptations to particular life-styles or habitats.

EVOLUTION OF LOCOMOTION IN VERTEBRATES

With this information in mind, let us first consider the general plan of evolution of locomotion in adult vertebrates. This section is not meant to provide a comprehensive survey, but rather to point out some of the major trends. More detailed descriptions and additional references can be found in Romer (1959), Alexander (1975), Kluge (1977), Romer and Parsons (1977) and Day (1981). A simplified family tree of the classes of vertebrates is given in Figure 3.1. The ancestral

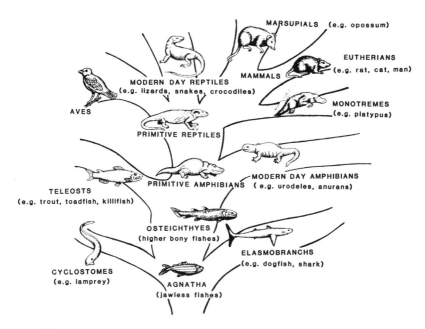

FIG. 3.1. A simplified family tree of the classes of vertebrates (modified after Romer).

vertebrate evolved in an aquatic environment and was certainly a swimmer (Romer & Parsons, 1977). Presumably it swam using its axial (trunk and tail) muscles because paired fins did not evolve until later. The axial muscles were arranged segmentally along the body and may have looked similar to those of the ammocoete larvae of the lamprey, a primitive fish of the Class Agnatha (Fig. 3.2a). While swimming has not, unfortunately, been studied in ammocoete larvae, it has been analyzed in adult lamprey (Cohen & Wallén, 1980; Rovainen, 1979). Despite many degenerative changes that are found in adult lamprey as adaptations to their parasitic or scavenging life-style, their mode of locomotion appears to be primitive rather than degenerate and therefore may provide insight into the ancestral vertebrate condition. Lamprey swim using their segmentally arranged axial muscles that are called myomeres (Fig. 3.2b). Within one segment, myomeres on the right and left sides of the body contract alternately (intrasegmental coordination). At the same time, myomeres along one side contract sequentially with a short phase lag between segments (intersegmental coordination). Contractions normally begin at the anterior end so that what are observed are waves of contraction, which bend the body alternately to the right and to the left and which move in an anterior to posterior direction (Cohen & Wallén, 1980).

a.

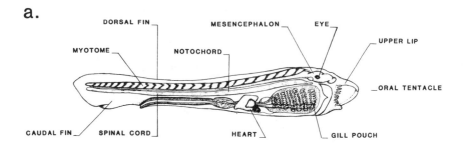

b.

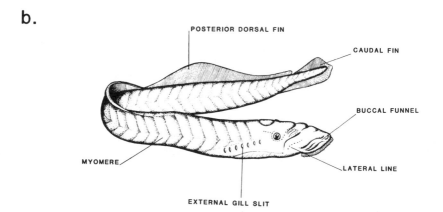

FIG. 3.2.   a. Lateral view of an ammocoete larva of the lamprey. b. Lateral view of an adult sea lamprey.

The next major advance, the development of fins, occurred in the now extinct Placoderms of the Class Elasmobranchiomorphi. These new appendages can be seen today in many living fish of the Class Elasmobranchiomorphi (e.g., sharks) and of the other major Class of fish, the Osteichthyes, which is descended from the Placoderms and includes the most familiar group of fish, teleosts (e.g., goldfish, trout.). In the vast majority of these fish the axial musculature still provides most of the major propulsive force for locomotion (Webb, 1975). Pectoral fins are used primarily in balancing, steering and braking although, in some fish, they can be used in slow swimming (Alexander, 1975; Blake, 1981). In the extinct group of crossopterygian fish (Class Osteichthyes) which gave rise to amphibians, the pectoral fins were evidently used for walking (Alexander, 1975).

Although the crossopterygian fish are believed to have used their limbs only to travel to better aquatic habitats during times of drought, the amphibians were the first Class of vertebrates to emerge onto land for considerable parts of their life cycle. Their limbs evolved further as weight-bearing organs that could be employed for the major terrestrial mode of locomotion—walking. It is important to keep in mind that during embryonic and larval stages of development these primitive amphibians (like most living amphibians) were aquatic. In all amphibians, limbs first appear at metamorphosis, the dramatic transformation that changes an aquatic larva into a terrestrial adult. Thus, swimming using the axial musculature is the mode of locomotion typically employed by young amphibian larvae before the legs emerge. The saltatory (jumping) mode of locomotion, which along with a reduction in axial musculature and development of specialized hindlimb structure characterizes adult anuran amphibians (frogs and toads), is thought to be a recent specialization rather than a primitive feature. It has been suggested that jumping represents an adaptation for quickly returning to water when escape is necessary (Alexander, 1975). In contrast, it is the walking pattern of adult urodele amphibians (newts and salamanders) which is thought to be similar to the ancestral pattern (Kluge, 1977; Romer, 1959). The basic pattern consists of lateral undulations of the trunk, during which the forelimb on the convex side is protracted and the hindlimb on the convex side is retracted (Figure 3.3). The limb movements are largely in a horizontal plane as a result of the sprawling limb posture maintained in urodeles (Rewcastle, 1981).

Primitive reptiles probably showed locomotion patterns quite similar to those of adult urodele amphibians. The major differences include the absence of a free-swimming larval stage, a reduction of lateral bending of the trunk during walking, and a reorientation of the limbs so as to support the trunk further off the ground. This allows freer and more efficient use of the legs. Locomotion of present-day crocodiles is probably close to the ancestral reptilian condition. Other living reptiles show a variety of locomotor specializations, from limbless, serpentine locomotion in snakes to bipedal running in lizards.

Birds are thought to have evolved from bipedal, lizard-like reptilian ancestors. They are an unusually homogeneous group, due to the structural limitations imposed on them by their primary mode of locomotion—flight. Thus, like the earliest birds, most living birds use their modified forelimbs, or wings, for flying. However, most birds also use bipedal locomition, walking or hopping, extensively, and some modern birds are flightless, using bipedal locomotion exclusively (e.g., ostrich).

Mammals also evolved from reptiles, but from a different branch than birds. Like their reptilian ancestors, the earliest mammals were quadrupedal. However, they used even less lateral vertebral movement during walking and had limbs oriented under the body for more efficient locomotion (Alexander, 1975). The opossum probably shows a pattern of locomotion similar to that of the ancestral mammal. Again, modern mammals have radiated widely and numerous modes of locomotion can be found today.

FIG. 3.3.   Series of diagrams showing one step cycle in a urodele amphibian.

TYPES OF EARLY DEVELOPMENT IN VERTEBRATES

Having briefly considered the evolution of locomotion in adult vertebrates, we can now turn to a general consideration of development. Along with the evolutionary trend in which adult vertebrates moved from primarily aquatic to terrestrial habitats, there were correlated changes in egg type and in the stage of locomotor development present at hatching.

The vast majority of fishes are oviparous and lay their eggs in water. Many of these eggs have a limited supply of yolk. This is true of lamprey as well as most teleost fish and presumably represents the ancestral condition. Other fish, including many sharks and some teleosts, lay eggs containing large yolk supplies (Romer & Parsons, 1977). The fertilized egg of an oviparous fish is typically surrounded by two membranes, a thin, usually transparent, vitelline membrane and an outer, chitinous, chorion. In a few cases, eggs are retained in the body of the female where they pass through embryonic development and then are born. If such an embryo is nourished entirely by the yolk of the egg, then development is termed ovoviviparous (e.g., dogfish shark). If it obtains part of its food from maternal tissues, it is viviparous.

In all cases, at the end of embryonic development, the fish embryo hatches out of the egg membranes. Then, if it has only a limited supply of yolk, as in the primitive condition, it immediately becomes free-swimming and capable of feeding itself. Alternatively, in sharks and other fish with large yolk supplies, the hatched fish may continue to develop during a larval stage in which it is nourished by a yolk sac that is often so large that it impedes locomotion. There are also, of course, all gradations between these two extremes.

Like fishes, most amphibians are also oviparous; a few are ovoviviparous. Viviparity is quite rare. The amphibian egg is not much different from the typical fish egg. It has a limited yolk supply and the embryo is surrounded by a thin vitelline membrane. Instead of a chorion, it has a protective jelly coat. Amphibian eggs always develop in a very moist environment, usually in the water. After amphibians hatch out of their eggs, they typically undergo a larval period of development during which they are free-swimming aquatic gill-breathers before metamorphosing into terrestrial adults. The larvae of urodele amphibians often have well-developed legs at hatching; anuran larvae, however, are usually free-swimming tadpoles before the legs begin to appear. A few species of amphibians undergo direct development. That is, they pass through metamorphosis in the egg and hatch out as miniature adults (e.g., the West Indian toad, *Eleutherodactylus martinicensis*).

As in fishes and amphibians, most reptiles are oviparous, although some lizards and snakes are ovoviviparous and a few are viviparous. However, the eggs of oviparous reptiles are dramatically different from those of amphibians and fishes because they are designed to be laid on land. The embryo floats in a fluid-filled membrane called the amnion. Together with its large yolk sac it is enclosed within protective layers of albumen, a chorionic membrane (not homologous with the chorion of fish eggs), shell membranes and a leathery or calcium salt-impregnated shell. When reptiles hatch, they do not go through a larval aquatic stage, but instead emerge as miniature adults, ready to walk and feed themselves on land.

Birds are all oviparous. Their eggs are quite similar in structure to reptilian eggs, having similar membranes and a large yolk supply. The major difference is that bird eggs have an increased percentage of calcium salts in the shell, which makes it harder and more brittle than the typical leathery reptilian egg. Nest building, incubation, and parental care are much more elaborately developed in birds than in most reptiles. In many species the young are precocial and thus, like newly hatched reptiles, can walk and feed themselves immediately after hatching. Flight, however, develops later after down feathers are replaced by the adult plumage. In other species the young are altricial. That is, they may need the care of parents to supply warmth in the nest and food until they develop feathers and the ability to locomote and obtain their own food. Altricial and precocial development, of course, represent two extremes of a continuum. It should be noted that even the most altricial bird must be well enough developed at the end of the embryonic period to be able to hatch from its hard-shelled egg.

With the exception of the monotremes (e.g., platypus) which are oviparous, all mammals are viviparous. The young of viviparous mammals develop and are nourished within the uterus of the mother and are born rather than hatching out of an egg. In contrast to the situation in hatching, the muscular effort necessary for birth is provided by the mother; the young are passive. Mammalian young, like birds, can be precocial (e.g., guinea pig, sheep) or altricial (e.g., rat, cat, human) at birth. Marsupials (e.g., kangaroo, opossum) represent a special case in which the young are extremely immature at birth with the exception of the forelimb locomotor abilities. The forelimbs are used by the newborn marsupial to crawl from the birth canal to the pouch where it then attaches to the nipple and continues development.

Thus the type of embryonic development and the level of maturity at birth place constraints on the type of locomotory system that will be used by the newly hatched or newborn animal.

THE DEVELOPMENT OF LOCOMOTION

To the greatest extent possible, the discussion to follow focuses on studies of spontaneously performed behavior. In this chapter *spontaneous* is used to refer to behavior occurring in the absence of obvious external stimulation (Hamburger, 1963). The reason for concentrating on spontaneous behavior is that this is presumably representative of the behavior normally performed by the undisturbed animal.

Many early studies dealt exclusively with behavior elicited in response to stimulation, usually tactile (for review, see Carmichael 1970). These studies were based on the assumption that locomotion and other coordinated behaviors were produced by chains of reflexes rather than being centrally programmed. Thus, it was thought that the development of locomotion could be studied by observing the development of reflex responses. In contrast, we now know that adult locomotion typically involves both central programming and peripheral feedback (for reviews, see Grillner, 1975, 1981). The role of sensory input is to allow the animal to react to, and compensate for, environmental variables and perturbations. Furthermore, central pattern-generating circuits can modulate the nature of reflex responses so that, for example, the same tactile stimulus may elicit different reflex responses at different points in the step cycle during centrally generated walking (Duysens & Pearson, 1976; Forssberg, Grillner, Rossignol, & Wallén, 1976). Therefore, behavior elicited in response to tactile stimulaton may not be representative of normally occurring behavior. Moreover, as discussed later, embryos developing inside eggs may be well insulated from the kinds of stimuli that can be applied by an experimenter. For these reasons, then, it seems more reasonable to make no assumptions about the central versus reflexogenic nature of embryonic behavior in the absence of experimental data and to place greater reliance on observations of spontaneously performed behavior than on observations of responses to stimulation.

For the sake of convenience, the development of locomotion is divided into stages in the subsequent discussion. However, it should be kept in mind that development is, in fact, continuous. The transitions from one stage to the next are usually quite gradual and the decision about where one ends and where the next one begins is arbitrary.

First Movements: Head Flexure Stage

In all vertebrate embryos that have been studied so far, muscular activity begins with contraction of a few segments of axial musculature in the anterior trunk (or future neck) region. This movement, called a head flexure, appears as a slow bend of the anterior trunk and head to one side, followed by a slow relaxation (*lamprey:* Piavis, 1971; *sharks:* Harris & Whiting, 1954; *teleost fish:* Abu Gideiri, 1966; Armstrong, 1964; Coghill, 1933; Harris & Whiting, 1954; Tracy, 1926; *amphibians:* Abu Gideiri, 1971; Coghill, 1929; Macklin & Wojtkowski, 1973; Muntz, 1975; Wang & Lu, 1941; Youngstrom, 1938; *reptiles;* Decker, 1967; Hughes, Bryant, & Bellairs, 1967; Tuge, 1931; *birds:* Hamburger, 1963; Orr & Windle, 1934; *mammals:* Angulo y Gonzalez, 1932; Barcroft & Barron, 1939; Carmichael, 1934; Windle & Griffin, 1931). No coordination is seen between right and left sides. That is, a contraction to the right may be followed by another to the right, a contraction to the left, or no contraction. In the vast majority of species the early movements occur at irregular intervals (*lamprey:* Whiting, 1954; *teleosts:* Abu Gideiri, 1966, 1968; Armstrong, 1964; Armstrong & Higgins, 1971; Coghill, 1933; Kimmel, Patterson & Kimmel, 1974; Tracy, 1926; Whiting, 1954; *reptiles:* Smith & Daniel, 1946; Hughes et al., 1967; *birds:* Hamburger, 1963; *mammals:* Angulo y Gonzalez, 1932). Only in the dogfish shark have the early movements been described as regular and rhythmic (Harris & Whiting, 1954). In sharks, the early movements are known to be myogenic, that is, due to spontaneously occurring muscle contractions rather than to nerve-induced (neurogenic) muscle activity.

At the stage of development at which these first movements are seen, the axial musculature typically consists of segmentally organized myotomes (Fig. 3.4).

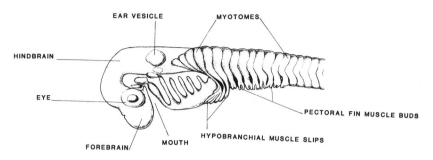

FIG. 3.4. Diagrammatic view of shark embryo, showing the developing myotomes.

These early movements appear to involve slow, simultaneous contractions of a few myotomes, although this has not been tested using recording techniques capable of resolving sequential versus simultaneous contractions.

These movements appear to begin almost as soon as the musculature is capable of contracting. In cases where this has been studied, it has been found that contractions begin very soon after the first time that muscles can be stimulated to contract electrically or mechanically (*rat:* Angulo y Gonzalez, 1932; *amphibians:* Blackshaw & Warner, 1976; Muntz, 1975). The basis for the slowness of the contractions at this stage is not known. It could be due to immature muscle membrane or contractile properties (Muntz, 1975; Whiting, 1954). In the case of neurogenic movements, the slow relaxation could be due to a lack of acetylcholinesterase to break down the neuromuscular transmitter acetylcholine (Sawyer, 1944).

These early head flexures occur spontaneously. That is, they occur in the absence of any obvious external stimulus. In many cases, the first movements appear before responses can be elicited by sensory stimulation and thus are clearly non-reflexogenic (*lamprey:* Whiting, 1954; *shark:* Harris & Whiting, 1954; *teleost fish:* Abu Gideiri, 1968, 1969; Coghill, 1933; Tracy, 1926; *amphibians:* Youngstrom, 1938; *reptiles:* Decker, 1967; Hughes et al., 1967; Tuge, 1931; *birds:* Hamburger, 1963; Preyer, 1885). In a few cases, responses to stimulation appear at the same time as spontaneous movements (*amphibians:* Coghill, 1929; Macklin & Wojtkowski, 1973; Muntz, 1975; *mammals:* Angulo y Gonzalez, 1932; Barcroft & Barron, 1939; Bodian, Melby & Taylor, 1968; Carmichael, 1934; Hooker, 1952; Windle, 1940). In these species, in the absence of experimental manipulation, it is not possible to determine whether or not the movements are centrally generated (see Bekoff, 1981a; Hamburger, 1963 for reviews).

Thus the form and location of the first movements in vertebrates appear to be phylogenetically very conservative. In most species examined, this is presumably a result of the early development of the nervous system in the anterior trunk region, with development proceeding both caudally and rostrally from this point (Jacobson, 1978). It has been suggested that in sharks and in some teleost fish the early embryonic motility is myogenic rather than neurogenic. That is, the movements are due to spontaneously occurring contractions of muscle, independent of nerve activity. Because myogenic activity is found in these lower vertebrates, it might be thought that this was the ancestral condition.

There are, however, two problems with the assumption that myogenic activity is ancestral. The first is that sharks, the only species in which myogenic contractions have been demonstrated with certainty, are not ancestral to either teleost fishes or other higher vertebrates, but rather represent an evolutionary side branch (Fig. 3.1). The second problem is that, except for sharks, the evidence for myogenic activity is relatively weak. In the case of the dogfish shark, the first contractions have unambiguously been shown to be myogenic. These contractions are very regular and rhythmical. They continue after injection of curare (Whiting, 1954) or, even more convincing, after the removal of the entire central nervous system (Harris & Whiting, 1954; Wintrebert, 1920). In this case there appears to be a pacemaker located in the anterior myotomes which initiates a local depolarization. This depolarization is then transmitted to adjacent myotomes, presumably via gap junctions, although the presence of these structures has not yet been demonstrated in this system. It has been suggested that specialized bands of muscle lying at the sides of the notochord may be responsible for the myogenic contractions (Harris & Whiting, 1954; Whiting, 1954).

The evidence for myogenic activity is less convincing in other cases for which it has been proposed. The first line of evidence is based on pharmacological studies. Coghill (1933) injected curare into the yolk sac of killifish (*Fundulus heteroclitus*) embryos and observed that the earliest movements continued unabated. Because curare is known to block acetylcholine receptors in adult muscles and therefore to prevent depolarization by acetylcholine, this evidence has been used to suggest that the observed movements are not neurogenic. Furthermore, Sawyer (1944) found that eserine did not prolong the earliest contractions. In adults eserine inhibits acetylcholinesterase, the enzyme that normally inactivates acetylcholine, thus prolonging the action of acetylcholine at the neuromuscular junction. Thus the absence of an effect when eserine was added was interpreted as indicating that neuromuscular transmission was not yet functional. Nevertheless, these negative results are difficult to interpret for several reasons. First, it is difficult to know whether or not either of these drugs actually reached the motor endplates at sufficient concentrations to have an observable effect. Second, curare can have a direct excitatory effect on embryonic rat muscle (Ziskind & Dennis, 1978). That is, in contrast to its effect on adult muscle fibers, in rat embryos curare was found to depolarize muscle fibers. Furthermore, eserine cannot have an effect until acetylcholinesterase is present. Although an increase in acetylcholinesterase is usually tightly correlated with the onset of motor neuron function (i.e., the time at which terminals begin to liberate acetylcholine), in several cases nerve contacts have been found to precede the appearance of acetylcholinesterase (Diamond & Miledi, 1962; Letinsky, 1974; Letinsky & Morrison-Graham, 1980). It is entirely possible that in such cases acetylcholine release may precede acetylcholinesterase function. In these cases, eserine would have no detectable effect at the stage when functional neurogenic activity is first seen.

On the other hand there is evidence that the earliest movements are neurogenic in at least some fish. Curare abolished early movements in two species of teleost fish, the bullhead, *Ictalurus nebulosus* (Armstrong, 1964) and a tropical cichlid fish, *Aequidens portalegrensis* (Brinley, 1951). Brinley noted that it took a higher concentration of curare to eliminate movements at early stages than in older animals. This again raises the question of whether previous studies had used sufficient doses of curare.

The second line of evidence that has been used to support the suggestion that the early movements are myogenic is based on studies of when nerves first arrive at the muscles. In several studies of fishes, it has been reported that anterior myotome contractions occur before motor neuron axons have been observed to reach the muscles (e.g., *shark:* Harris & Whiting, 1954; *teleost fish:* Abu Gideiri, 1966, 1968; Whiting, 1954). However, the light microscopic observations of methylene blue- or silver-stained sections that were used might not have detected very fine motor neuron terminals at the earliest stages of neuromuscular synapse formation (Blight, 1978). Therefore, the failure to see nerve terminals on the muscle fibers should not be used as conclusive evidence of their absence. Further studies using ultrastructural techniques are clearly needed.

In all other vertebrates studied, amphibians through mammals, motor neuron axons have been observed to reach the axial muscles at the time that movements begin. Furthermore, in all of the species in which it has been tested, curare has been shown to abolish the earliest movements (e.g., *frog:* Blackshaw & Warner, 1976; *chick:* Hamburger, 1963; Kuo, 1039; *rat:* Angulo y Gonzalez, 1932). In *Xenopus,* where the myotomes are electrically coupled to one another via gap junctions, contractions still do not begin until motor neuron terminals reach the anterior myotomes (Blackshaw & Warner, 1976; Hayes, 1975; Muntz, 1975). At stage 24, when the first contractions are seen, spontaneous end plate potentials can be recorded from anterior myotomes (Blackshaw & Warner, 1976). Furthermore, these can be blocked with 2mM Mn^{++} or curare, both of which block normal adult neuromuscular transmission. It therefore appears that contractions are initiated neurogenically in the anterior myotomes, then the depolarization is passively transmitted to more posterior myotomes via electrical coupling.

In any case, in vertebrates above fish, it appears that even the earliest contractions are neurogenic (Hamburger, 1963; Hooker, 1952; Muntz, 1975). The mechanism underlying these spontaneous neurogenic contractions is not understood. Presumably either motor neurons are spontaneously active, or they are activated by other spontaneously active neurons. In the bullhead, a teleost fish in which the early movements appear to be neurogenic, they occur before any axons from the brain reach the spinal cord and continue after the spinal cord is transected just behind the brain (Armstrong & Higgins, 1971). Thus, the early movements appear to be generated by spinal mechanisms and are not dependent on descending activation from the brain.

These first movements typically appear in the first 25% to 30% of the embryonic period, but vary from an early first occurrence at 3.5 days in the chick, less than 20% of the way through the 21-day incubation period, to a late first occurrence at 15.5 days in the rat, about 75% of the way through the 21-day gestation period. There does not appear to be any phylogenetic trend here either in terms of absolute time or percentage of embryonic period elapsed. For example, both zebrafish (Kimmel, Patterson & Kimmel, 1974) and human embryos (Hooker, 1952) begin movements very early in embryonic life. Nor is there a good correlation between time of movement onset and a particular stage of morphological development (Hamburger, 1963). For example, in mammalian embryos movement begins at a much more advanced stage of morphological development than in many submammalian forms. Thus, at the stage when head flexures first appear, human embryos have well-formed limbs with digits and the eyelids and nose are visible. In contrast, chick embryos have only small wing and leg buds and no eyelids or beak have yet formed at the head flexure stage.

Thus, the point in development at which the first movements begin, whether measured in absolute time, or relative to morphological development, appears to vary widely among species. The reason for this variability is not readily apparent. There does not appear to be any obvious correlation with ecological variables or future life-style. The only phylogentic correlation that can be made is that mammals begin activity at a more advanced morphological stage than do lower vertebrates. It is possible that although overall stage of morphological development at the time of first movement may differ in different species, the actual stage of development of the structures in the moving part, in this case the vertebrae, muscles and spinal cord neurons of the anterior trunk (or neck) region, may be comparable. This issue warrants further study.

The C-coil Stage: Coordination of Ipsilateral Muscles

The next stage in the embryonic development of motor behavior is also quite similar in appearance among all vertebrates studied (*shark:* Harris & Whiting, 1954; *teleost fish:* Abu Gideiri, 1966, 1968, 1969; Armstrong, 1964; Armstrong & Higgins, 1971; Coghill, 1933; Pollack & Crain, 1972; Tracy, 1926; *amphibians:* Abu Gideiri, 1971; Coghill, 1929; Macklin & Wojtkowski, 1973; Muntz, 1975; Youngstrom, 1938; *reptiles:* Decker, 1967; Hughes et al., 1967; Smith & Daniel, 1946; *birds:* Hamburger & Balaban, 1963; Orr & Windle, 1934; *mammals:* Angulo y Gonzalez, 1932; Barcroft & Barron, 1939; Narayanan, Fox & Hamburger, 1971; Windle & Griffin, 1931). Soon after the first contractions begin in the anterior myotomes, more posterior myotomes are progressively incorporated into the movements. Once a myotome is capable of contracting, it always appears to contract along with all of the other contracting myotomes on one side of the trunk; independent, localized contractions are not seen. By the end of this stage, a typical movement episode consists of a C-coil. That is, all of the myotomes on one side appear to contract together bending the embryo into a C shape. In some cases the C shape may be held for up to a second or more before the muscles relax. The movements are still myogenic at this stage in dogfish sharks (Harris & Whiting, 1954). It has been suggested that they are myogenic in trout (Abu Gideiri, 1966; Whiting, 1954) and *Tilapia nilotica* (Abu Gideiri, 1968), but the results are again equivocal for the same reasons discussed in the previous section. In all other embryos studied, the C-coil appears to be wholly or in part neurogenic.

Although the behavioral observations suggest that all functional myotomes on a side contract simultaneously, this has not been rigorously shown. Electromyogram (EMG) or nerve recordings would be useful in determining the actual pattern of contraction. In the anuran amphibians, *Xenopus laevis* and *Bombina orientalis,* electrical coupling between adjacent myotomes occurs and may contribute to simultaneity of the contractions (Blackshaw & Warner, 1976; Hayes, 1975). However, it is not known how widely this mechanism is distributed among vertebrates. For example, it is not even universal among amphibians: electrical coupling has not been found in the urodele amphibian, *Ambystoma mexicanum* (Blackshaw & Warner, 1976).

The contractions of the C-coil stage can be initiated at more than one point along the spinal cord. In dogfish sharks, trout, and toadfish, experimental studies have shown that contractions can be anterior or posterior to a mid-trunk spinal cord transection (Tracy, 1926; Whiting, 1954). Although activity in sharks at this stage of development is myogenic, activity is neurogenic in the toadfish and may be neurogenic in the trout. Thus there appear to be multiple potential initiation sites, independent of whether the activity is neurogenic or myogenic.

In all vertebrates studied so far, except in dogfish sharks, the C-coils occur at irregular intervals, but often at a higher frequency than the earlier head flexures. Right and left sides still contract independently.

As in the previous stage, C-coils occur spontaneously in all animals. Furthermore, in those animals that respond to tactile stimulation at this stage, a light touch elicits behavior indistinguishable from that performed spontaneously (e.g., Narayanan et al., 1971; Tracy, 1926).

As the form of the C-coils appears similar in all vertebrates so far, the major difference lies in the frequency with which the C-coils are performed in different species. Tracy (1926) has suggested that the frequency of embryonic movements may be related to future adult life-style. For example, he observed that the toadfish, which is relatively sedentary as an adult, is quite inactive during embryonic stages in comparison to embryos of a more active fish like the killifish.

S-Wave Stage: Bilateral Coordination and Ipsilateral Phase Lag

In the next stage of development, undulatory movements first appear. This S-wave stage, sometimes called the early swimming, or alternating flexure, stage is seen in all vertebrates studied so far (*lamprey:* Piavis, 1971; *shark:* Harris & Whiting, 1954; *teleost fish:* Abu Gideiri, 1966, 1968, 1969; Armstrong, 1964; Armstrong & Higgins, 1971; Coghill, 1933; Pollack & Crain, 1972; Tracy, 1926; *amphibians:* Abu Gideiri, 1971; Coghill, 1929; Macklin & Wojtkowski, 1973; Muntz, 1975; Wang & Lu, 1941; *reptiles:* Decker, 1967; Smith & Daniel, 1946; *birds:* Hamburger & Balaban, 1963; Orr & Windle, 1934; *mammals:* Barcroft & Barron, 1939; Hamburger, 1975; Windle & Griffin, 1931; Windle, O'Donnell & Glasshagle, 1933; Windle, Minear, Austin, & Orr, 1935). The transition from C-coil to S-wave has been described as involving two independent changes (Coghill, 1929). One change is that the axial muscles of one side no longer contract synchronously. Instead, an intersegmental phase lag is introduced so that a rostrocaudal wave of contraction travels down the body. The other change is the development of coordination between left and right sides so that flexions to one side alternate with flexions to the other side. The neural mechanisms for producing the rostrocaudal intersegmental phase lag and the alternation of left and right sides are separable in adult fish and in amphibian embryos (Cohen & Wallén, 1980; Grillner, Perrett & Zangger, 1976; Roberts, Kahn, Soffe, & Clarke, 1981). Functionally, alternation of right and left sides without a rostrocaudal phase lag would produce a standing wave of contraction, whereas addition of a rostrocaudal lag would produce a traveling wave. Nevertheless, the two are difficult to distinguish behaviorally in the absence of detailed analysis of high speed films or EMG recordings.

The assumption that a rostrocaudal phase lag in axial muscle contraction occurs during the S-wave stage has recently been questioned in several studies. Based on EMG recordings, Blight (1976) has suggested that even at an early swimming stage (stage 37), the newt, *Triturus helviticus,* moves by synchronously contracting the anterior trunk muscles on one side at a time. He suggests that this produces a flexion that is passively conducted posteriorly and does not involve active contraction of posterior trunk muscles. When left and right sides alternate, a standing wave is produced to yield the S-type movements. However, it is possible that the time resolution of the EMG recordings used in this study was insufficient to detect a short rostrocaudal phase lag. Absence of a rostrocaudal phase lag has also been suggested for early *Xenopus laevis* embryos, in which only the anterior myotomes are innervated (Muntz, 1975), but are electrically coupled to the more posterior myotomes (Blackshaw & Warner, 1976). Frame-by-frame analysis of films made at 50 frames per second of *Xenopus* support this suggestion because what appear to be S-waves when observed under a microscope at normal speed, are in fact alternate C-coils (Macklin

& Wojtkowski, 1973). Thus, although behavior at the S-wave stage gives the appearance of involving rostrocaudal waves of contraction, there is no unambiguous evidence to show this. Nevertheless some of the behavioral descriptions of rostrocaudal waves of contraction are quite vivid (e.g. Coghill, 1929; Tracy, 1926) and such cases would benefit from reinvestigation with modern recording techniques.

At present, then, the only confirmed change underlying the transition from C-coils to S-wave stage is the development of coordination between left and right sides. This change requires the development of a neural mechanism for coordinating the two sides. This mechanism is clearly located in the spinal cord rather than in the brain because cervical spinal transections do not interfere with attainment of this stage of development (e.g., *shark:* Harris & Whiting, 1954; *teleost fish:* Armstrong & Higgins, 1971; *frog:* Wang & Lu, 1941; *chick:* Oppenheim, 1975).

The movements of the S-wave stage are not yet truly locomotory. Even when prematurely released from the confinement of the egg membranes, fish and amphibian embryos at the S-wave stage do not show progression (Armstrong, 1964; Macklin & Wojtkowski, 1973). Nevertheless, it has been suggested that these movements are direct precursors of swimming, but that they occur at a frequency and amplitude too low for effective locomotion. As mentioned above, the possibility that a rostrocaudal intersegmental phase lag has not yet developed needs to be examined further.

As discussed below, the S-wave movements may play an important role in hatching in anamniotes (fishes and amphibians). However, some anamniotes have already reached the next stage of motor development, the swimming stage, at the time of hatching (Abu Gideiri, 1966, 1971; Armstrong, 1964; Kyushin, 1968; Piavis, 1971; Tooker & Miller, 1980; White, 1915; Whiting, 1954; Youngstrom, 1938). These latter species tend to be relatively inactive immediately after hatching and, unless disturbed, do not begin to swim actively until several hours, or even days, later.

As in embryos still enclosed within the egg membranes, hatched larvae that are at the S-wave stage perform S-waves spontaneously. In addition, most but not all vertebrates at the S-wave stage respond to tactile stimuli. For those species which have hatched, the S-wave may serve an adaptive function in changing the location of the larva (although not in a predictable direction) when local conditions are not favorable. For example, tactile stimuli associated with the approach of a predator might elicit a series of S-waves that would serve to displace the larva although it could not yet swim. On the other hand, it is equally probable that escape may be mediated instead by a behavior called the C-start, which can also be initiated by tactile stimuli in young fish (Eaton, Farley, Kimmel, & Schabtach, 1977). The C-start is discussed further in the section on hatching. The significant point to note here is that visual descriptions of C-starts and vigorous S-waves are very similar. Because most studies of embryonic behaviors were carried out before the C-start had been characterized, there is a need for new studies using techniques that can distinguish between these two behaviors.

Swimming

At the end of the S-stage, the first major divergence occurs between those forms that use axial musculature in swimming as the primary mode of locomotion immediately after hatching (the anamniotes: fishes and amphibians) and those that use limbs for locomotion (most amniotes: reptiles, birds and mammals). In anamniotes the coordination pattern for swimming usually develops either prior to, or soon after, hatching.

However, some fishes, such as the toadfish (Tracy, 1926) and trout (White, 1915) have large yolk sacs that impede movements so that free swimming does not begin for some time after hatching. These forms tend to be fairly inactive until the yolk sac is absorbed. From the available behavioral descriptions, however, it appears that the coordinated swimming pattern can be produced, but simply is not effective in moving the animal due to the bulk of the yolk sac. In addition, swimming mechanisms are not as effective because embryos tend to wag the head, side to side, during swimming (Eaton, Bombardieri & Meyer, 1977).

A number of studies of spinalized animals have shown that the neural circuitry that produces coordinated swimming is located in the spinal cord in adult fish (*lamprey:* Cohen & Wallén, 1980; Poon, 1980; *sharks:* Gray & Sand, 1936a, 1936b; Grillner, Perrett, & Zangger, 1976; LeMare, 1936; Lissman, 1946; Roberts, 1969; *teleost fish:* Gray & Sand, 1936; LeMare, 1936; Lissman, 1946) and in larval teleosts and frogs (Armstrong & Higgins, 1971; Kahn & Roberts, 1978; Roberts, Kahn, Soffe & Clarke, 1981; Stehouwer & Farel, 1980; Wang & Lu, 1941).

The basic swimming pattern consists of a strict alternation between the sides within any given segment and a phase lag between segments on the same side (for review see Grillner & Kashin, 1976). As mentioned in the previous section, alternation between the sides develops in the S-stage. However, it is not clear when the rostrocaudal (intersegmental) phase lag develops relative to the appearance of adult-type swimming. *Xenopus laevis* embryos at stage 37/38, just before hatching, already show an intersegmental phase lag during swimming (Kahn & Roberts, 1978; Roberts, Kahn, Soffe & Clarke, 1981). It was initially reported that if released from the egg membranes at a similar stage of morphological development, *Triturus helviticus* embryos swim using simultaneous contraction of the axial muscles of each side and that a rostrocaudal phase lag did not appear until near metamorphosis, at stage 55c (Blight, 1976, 1977). However, a more recent study, using recording techniques that permit detection of short phase lags show that the rostrocaudal phase lag is present at stages 33 to 35 (Soffe, Clarke, & Roberts, 1983).

One question that remains is whether the transition from S-waves to swimming involves the addition of a rostrocaudal phase lag in intersegmental coordination. Alternatively, the rostrocaudal lag could be established during the S-wave stage, in which case the onset of swimming would simply involve a speeding up of the frequency of alternation of right and left sides. In other words, is there a qualitative difference in the motor output pattern that distinguishes the S-wave stage from swimming or just a quantitative one? Again, this would seem to be a fruitful area for further research, one in which EMG recordings from axial muscles, perhaps combined with high speed frame-by-frame film analysis, would be useful in distinguishing between alternative possibilities.

In any case, at the end of this stage, most anamniotes are capable of adaptive locomotion. Although further studies are needed to confirm this, the picture first presented by Coghill (1929) in which head flexures develop into C-coils, which then develop into S-waves, which then develop into swimming, seems to be a reasonable one for anamniotes. Thus, for these lower vertebrates, swimming develops in an evolutionarily conservative sequence. In contrast, the development of coordinated swimming gets short-circuited at the S-wave stage in amniotes.

Type I Motility

In the reptiles, birds and mammals that have been studied, the three earliest stages of spontaneous embryonic movements (e.g., head flexion, C-coil and S-wave) are telescoped at the very beginning of motility and a transition to swimming is not seen. Instead the S-waves break up into apparently disorganized movements (*reptiles:* Decker, 1967; Hughes, Bryant & Bellairs, 1967; Smith & Daniel, 1946; Tuge, 1931; *birds:* Hamburger, 1963; Hamburger & Balaban, 1963; Orr & Windle, 1934; *mammals:* Hamburger, 1975; Narayanan, Fox & Hamburger, 1971; Windle & Griffin, 1931; Windle, O'Donnell & Glasshagle, 1933; Windle, Minear, Austin & Orr, 1935;) Hamburger (1963) has called this type of embryonic behavior Type I embryonic motility. During Type I motility, all body parts whose neuromuscular connections are functional appear to be active. However, the movements of different body parts are not integrated into a recognizable coordinated behavior. As found for behaviors at earlier stages, Type I motility normally occurs spontaneously. However, it can also be elicited in response to tactile stimulation. The frequency with which Type I motility occurs varies with both stage of development and species. For example, in the chick embryo at 7 days of incubation, Type I motility occurs at a low rate (Hamburger, 1963). By 12–13 days it occurs almost continuously. The frequency drops again toward the time of hatching (21 days). In the lizard, *Lacerta vivipara,* an increase to a peak at mid-incubation followed by a decrease toward the time of hatching is also seen (Hughes, Bryant & Bellairs, 1967). However, the frequency of Type I motility at the peak is much lower than in chick embryos. Here again, one could pose the hypothesis put forward by Tracy (1926) suggesting a correlation between overall frequency of embryonic motility and adult lifestyle.

Very little is known about the neural basis underlying the initiation of Type I motility. In chick embryos, Type I motility appears to result from nearly synchronous activation of neurons throughout the spinal cord (Provine, 1971; Provine & Rogers, 1977). Nevertheless, when multi-unit recordings are made at two locations in the spinal cord, the onset of activity is rarely simultaneous. Lags of 0 to 100 milliseconds are seen (Provine, 1971). No attempt has yet been made to determine whether or not there is a consistent initiation site. It is clear, however, that the necessary circuitry is located in the spinal cord because activity has been shown to continue in chick, rat, and sheep embryos after spinal transections have been made (Barcroft & Barron, 1937; Hamburger, Balaban, Oppenheim, & Wenger, 1965; Hooker & Nicholas, 1930; Oppenheim, 1975; Provine & Rogers, 1977).

As noted above, Type I motility appears to be typical of amniotes, that is, those vertebrate groups that use limbs rather than axial musculature in the first mode of locomotion to develop after hatching or birth. Although Type I motility has been observed in all amniote embryos that have been studied to date, it is not known whether or not Type I motility occurs in the embryos of amniotes, such as snakes or whales, which now exclusively use axial muscles for locomotion. Because snakes evolved from limbed reptilian ancestors and whales from terrestrial, limbed mammalian ancestors, it seems reasonable to suppose that their embryos would retain Type I motility in the behavior repertoire, with coordinated locomotion developing later in ontogeny as it does in other amniotes. However, studies are needed to determine whether or not this is true.

The converse question of whether or not Type I motility ever appears in anamniotes that do not use swimming as the major mode of locomotion immediately after hatching can also be asked. Only one such anamniote has been studied, *Eleutherodactylus martinicensis* (Hughes, 1965, 1966). *Eleutherodactylus* is a toad with a wholly embryonic development. Instead of hatching as a swimming larva, then metamorphosing into an adult, it goes through metamorphosis within the egg and hatches as a small adult that can walk immediately and swims using its legs rather than trunk muscles. Because the emphasis of the published studies of *Eleutherodactylus* was on leg movements, it is difficult to tell whether the trunk movements ever develop into fully coordinated swimming movements during embryonic life, although this is suggested by the description of ''wriggles'' (Hughes, 1965). The trunk movements apparently decrease with age, and no mention is made of their becoming less coordinated. Thus it appears unlikely that Type I movements, which are uncoordinated in appearance, occur in *Eleutherodactylus*. Nevertheless, further studies of this species or of others with direct development would be useful.

It has been suggested that the role of the spontaneous Type I motility in amniote embryos is to ensure adequate activity despite reduced sensory stimulation (see Bekoff, 1981b, for review). Whereas anamniote embryos typically hatch at, or soon after, the time they reach the S-wave stage, amniotes remain in the embryonic environment for an extended period after this stage of development has been reached. During this period, the embryos float in a pool of amniotic fluid that limits or attenuates most incoming stimuli (Bradley & Mistretta, 1975; Reynolds, 1962). Furthermore, they are often less responsive to stimuli than adults (Oppenheim, 1972; Bradley & Mistretta, 1975; Sedlacek, 1971). Thus, the continuation of some kind of spontaneously generated activity may be necessary to maintain adequate levels of activity during this prolonged period of embryonic development. However, because for the typical amniote (and certainly for the ancestral members of each amniote class) the mode of locomotion at hatching or birth will not be swimming, there may be no need to maintain the pattern of coordination typical of swimming through the embryonic period.

It thus appears that Type I motility is an innovation introduced in the amniotes as an adaptation to the new terrestrial life style. In this pattern a larval aquatic stage is eliminated and the embryonic period extended until the developing amniote is prepared to survive on land.

Hatching

At first glance, the inclusion of a section on hatching in a discussion of the development of locomotion might seem unwarranted. Nevertheless, as discussed below, there is some suggestive evidence that the same neural circuitry that is used to produce locomotory behaviors may be used in the production of hatching. Hatching is a problem faced by all non-viviparous vertebrates (see Oppenheim, 1973, for an excellent review of this topic). Among the non-viviparous vertebrates are included the majority of fish, amphibians and reptiles, all birds, and the monotreme mammals. The goal of hatching is to permit the escape of the embryo from the egg at the appropriate time. Because hatching is common to so many vertebrates, including the ancestral groups in each Class, we might expect to find common mechanisms involved.

Descriptions of hatching in anamniotes do suggest strong similarities. For example, studies of a variety of different fish and amphibian species all describe the C-coil and S-wave movements as getting stronger and more vigorous near the time of hatching (Abu Gideiri, 1966; Bragg, 1940; Carrol & Hedrick, 1974; Eaton, Bombardieri, & Meyer, 1977; Petranka, Just, & Crawford, 1982; Piavis,

1971; Tracy, 1926; Volpe, Wilkens, & Dobie, 1961; White, 1915; Youngstrom, 1938). It is usually suggested that these movements eventually result in a tear in the egg membranes and thus allow the escape of the embryo from the egg. In some species, the prior action of a hatching enzyme may also be required to weaken the egg membranes (Armstrong, 1936; Carrol & Hedrick, 1974; Petranka et al., 1982). A few cases have been reported of fish or amphibian embryos that normally hatch without muscular effort (Bragg, 1940; Youngstrom, 1938) or that normally show movements, but can hatch even if anaesthetized (Wintrebert, 1920). Nevertheless, motor activity is used during hatching by most fish and amphibian embryos that have been studied.

Based on the behavioral descriptions that are available, then, it appears that hatching in amniotes may not involve the use of new and different motor patterns, but instead may represent a continuation of on-going behavior. According to this scheme, the major difference between C-coil and S-wave movements on the one hand and hatching on the other would be the increased frequency and/or amplitude of the movements. Assuming, as suggested earlier, that C-coil movements develop into S-wave movements and S-wave movements develop gradually into swimming movements, then hatching would also be closely related to swimming in the sense that both behaviors would presumably use the same neural circuitry. This would seem to be an economical arrangement in that development of a new and separate circuit, which would be used just once in the animal's life, would not be required. Instead the neural circuit that will later be used for locomotion (swimming) is used for hatching.

An alternative suggestion has been made by Eaton and his co-workers (1977). Based on their studies of zebrafish embryos, they suggest that a circuit involving the Mauthner neurons might be involved in hatching. This pair of large cells develops very early during embryonic development, well before the time of hatching, in all fish and amphibians studied so far (Kimmel & Model, 1978). It presists into adulthood in most fish, but regresses at metamorphosis in amphibians. Mauthner neurons have not yet been found in amniotes at any stage of development. These cells thus seem to be associated with an aquatic life-style. However, the Mauthner cells do not participate in swimming (Eaton & Bombardieri, 1978). Instead, studies of adult fish have shown that the behavior produced when one of the Mauthner cells fires is a highly stereotyped startle reflex, called the C-start, which tends to move the animal abruptly away from a tactile or vibrational stimulus (Eaton, Lavender & Wieland, 1981). This behavior appears to involve simultaneous contraction of all of the axial muscles on one side of the body, although detailed EMG recordings have not been done to confirm this. The C-start thus shows a strong resemblance to the vigorous movements described during hatching in anamniote embryos. In addition, the Mauthner neurons of zebrafish embryos show two properties that make them suitable for hatching. First, in contrast to the adult Mauthner neuron, which typically fires only once and is not spontaneously active, the embryonic cell is believed to fire repetitively, and spontaneously (Eaton, Farley, Kimmel & Schabtach, 1977). Second, it fires in response to tactile stimulation anywhere on the body. Eaton and his colleagues have presented evidence that the same kind of tactile stimulus that is thought to cause the Mauthner cell to fire in an embryo will also evoke premature hatching. Thus, the firing of the Mauthner cell may be sufficient to elicit hatching in some circumstances, such as an attack on an egg by a predator.

As mentioned above, the C-start strongly resembles movements used during hatching. It also shows a resemblance to the C-coil of early embryonic stages. There is, however, evidence that the Mauthner cell is not involved in any of the early embryonic behaviors, including the C-coil. Armstrong and Higgins (1971) state that, in bullhead embryos, spinal transection has no effect on motor activity at head flexure and C-coil stages. Also, Wang and Lu (1941) imply that no differences from normal behavior were seen until after swimming developed in spinalized *Rana guntheri* tadpoles. Because spinal transection would cut all axons descending to the spinal cord from the brain, including the axons of the Mauthner neurons, whose cell bodies are located in the medulla and whose axons synapse on motor neurons in the spinal cord, it would eliminate any behaviors, such as the C-start, which are dependent on the Mauthner neuron. It is clear that the Mauthner cells are not necessary either for escape movements (Eaton, 1983; Eaton, Lavender, & Wieland, 1982), or for hatching. Not all fish have them (Zottoli, 1978) and in zebrafish, which do, elimination of the Mauthner cells does not prevent hatching (Kimmel, Eaton, & Powell, 1980).

One possibility is that there may be multiple circuits for various locomotor behaviors developing in the anamniote embryos. Some circuits may be used for swimming, others for escape. It is also possible that more than one circuit can be used for hatching (e.g., C-start and C-coil circuits) depending on the circumstances.

It is clear that what are needed are more detailed studies of the actual movements used in hatching along with careful comparisons among C-coils, S-waves, hatching, and C-starts. This could best be done using a combination of film, EMG and Mauthner neuron recordings during these behaviors to help resolve the issue. An ideal preparation for these studies would be the zebrafish because both normal and Mauthner-deleted animals are available.

In the only amniote in which hatching has been studied in detail, the chick, escape from the egg is effected by a very distinct, stereotyped behavior that bears little resemblance to earlier C-coils, S-waves, or Type I motor activity (for review see Oppenheim, 1973). In recognition of this difference, hatching, and the behaviors used to fold the chick into the hatching position, are called Type III behaviors (Hamburger & Oppenheim, 1967). The chick begins to hatch with its head tucked underneath its right wing and its legs tightly flexed. The behavior consists of synchronous thrusts of right and left legs, coupled with rotatory movements of the upper body and back thrusts of the head during which the beak cracks the shell (Bakhuis, 1974; Hamburger & Oppenheim, 1967). This stereo-typed motor program occurs in episodes of 1–3-seconds duration, at 10–30-second intervals over the period of 45–90 minutes that it takes to complete hatching.

Behavioral observations suggest that hatching behavior develops gradually during the last few days of incubation (Hamburger & Oppenheim, 1967). Nevertheless, EMG recordings suggest that during hatching, chick embryos make use of neural circuitry that developed much earlier and was used for Type I motility, which predominates throughout most of development and is quite different in appearance from the Type III hatching behavior (Bekoff, 1976). Furthermore it has been suggested that some of the same circuitry may be re-used after hatching to produce other behaviors such as walking (Bekoff, 1978, 1981a). Thus, like fish and amphibians, chicks appear to make economical use of circuitry for motor behaviors.

Almost all birds use a very similar behavior pattern for hatching (Oppenheim, 1973). However, almost nothing is known about the movements used in hatching in other amniotes such as reptiles (Hughes, Bryant & Bellairs, 1967; Oppenheim, 1973). It is possible that there is an evolutionary trend from the use of uncoordinated or nonspecific motor behaviors to the use of highly specific, stereotyped behavior during hatching. Alternatively, the type of behavior used may correlate more closely with eggshell thickness or strength. This area of research is wide open.

The other amniotes whose young must hatch out of eggs are the Monotreme mammals. However, little is known about the movements used in this group (Oppenheim, 1973).

Thus, on the basis of the available data, it seems that anamniotes and amniotes have solved the problem of hatching in distinctly different ways. That is, anamniotes use what appears to be simply a more vigorous version of on-going behavior (either C-coils and S-waves or C-starts) to help them escape from their egg membranes. Hatching enzymes are commonly used to weaken the membranes and in some cases hatching is accomplished in the absence of movement.

In contrast, birds, the only amniote for which detailed information is available, use a distinctive behavior involving coordinated leg, wing, and head movements. This hatching behavior is quite different in appearance from on-going Type I behavior nor does it resemble C-coils or S-waves. It seems reasonable to suppose that this type of hatching behavior represents an adaptation for escaping from the hard-shelled amniote egg. Nevertheless, data are needed on hatching in the other amniotes, reptiles and monotreme mammals, to determine whether the situation in birds is, in fact, common to other amniotes.

Although differences are observed in the actual behaviors used for hatching when anamniotes and amniotes (at least birds) are compared, there is one underlying similarity. That is, in both groups the hatching behavior appears to be produced by neural circuitry that will be re-used at later stages to generate other behaviors.

First Limb Movements

In most vertebrates that have been studied, the first limb movements appear to be obligatorily coupled with trunk movements. That is, limbs do not move except during trunk movements (for review see Hamburger, 1963). However, several exceptions have been reported in which discrete fin or limb movements were occasionally observed to occur in the absence of trunk movements (Armstrong & Higgins, 1971; Barcroft & Barron, 1939; Bridgman & Carmichael, 1935; Coghill, cited in Herrick, 1949; Faber, 1956; Narayanan, Fox & Hamburger, 1971; Youngstrom, 1938). The coincidence of limb and trunk movements at early stages followed by the progressive independence of limb movements has often accounted for by the observation that the primary motor neurons, which in adults innervate only the axial muscles, appear to send branches to limb muscles at early developmental stages. Later the secondary (lateral) motor neurons grow out to provide the adult innervation of the limb. If true, this would indeed explain coactivation of limbs and trunk during early limb movements. The data supporting this idea are derived from studies of several fish and amphibian species in which silver-stained sections were examined at the light microscopic level (Abu Gideiri, 1966, 1971; Coghill, 1929; Hughes, 1959; Whiting, 1948; Youngstrom, 1940).

However, this has never been confirmed using modern techniques such as electron microscopy, or HRP histochemistry. In several amphibian species primary motor neurons were not found to send branches to both trunk and limb (Blight, 1978; Forehand & Farel, 1982; Letinsky, 1974; Taylor, 1943). Instead, lateral motor neurons innervate limb muscles from the onset of limb function. Furthermore, it is clear in both birds and mammals that only lateral motor neurons innervate limb muscles even at the earliest stages of development (Hamburger, 1963).

Thus, at least in some amphibians and in birds and mammals, the apparently obligatory coupling of the early limb and trunk movements does not depend on innervation of limb and trunk muscles by branches of the same neurons. It seems more likely that separate groups of limb and trunk motor neurons receive common excitatory input at these stages. This is suggested by recordings from limb and trunk motor neuron axons in bullfrogs at early tadpole stages, which show activity beginning simultaneously in both groups of motor neurons (Stehouwer & Farel, 1980). Multi-unit spinal cord recordings in chick embryos also show concurrent activity at mid-trunk and limb innervating levels (Provine, 1971).

In contrast to the earliest trunk movements, which appear to involve intersegmental coordination (simultaneous contraction of axial muscles on one side), the earliest limb movements are usually described as trembling, jerky, or uncoordinated (e.g., *teleost fish:* Abu Gideiri, 1966, 1968; Coghill, 1933; Tooker & Miller, 1980; *amphibians:* Abu Gideiri, 1971; Coghill, 1929; Hughes, 1965; Hughes & Prestige, 1967; Youngstrom, 1938; *reptiles:* Decker, 1967; Hughes, Bryant & Bellairs, 1967; Smith & Daniel, 1946; Stehouwer & Farel, 1984; *birds:* Hamburger, 1963; Hamburger & Balaban, 1963; Orr & Windle, 1934; *mammals:* Barcroft & Barron, 1939; Carmichael, 1934; Hamburger, 1975; Narayanan, Fox & Hamburger, 1971; Windle & Griffin, 1931; Windle, O'Donnell, & Glasshagle, 1933). Only one report, on trout, states that the pectoral fin movements are rhythmical and coordinated from the onset (Whiting, 1954).

It has been suggested that the earliest limb movements in the killifish are myogenic, based on the fact that they were not eliminated by curare (Coghill, 1933). However, as discussed earlier with regard to trunk movements, these data are equivocal and this issue should be reexamined.

In anamniotes, limb movements typically begin after swimming with axial musculature has been established. In fish and amphibians the anterior limbs (pectoral fin or forelimb) appear first. However, in anuran amphibians the developing forelimbs typically are hidden by the operculum until after the hindlegs have appeared (Youngstrom, 1938).

In amphibians, after the very brief stage of trembling, the limbs are held against the body during swimming (Coghill, 1929; Hughes & Prestige, 1967). Stehouwer & Farel (1980, 1981, 1983) have recorded from limb motor neuron axons in *Rana catesbiana* tadpoles at stages II and XVIII and found that up to stage X the limb motor neurons are tonically activated during patterned trunk motor neuron activity. This tonic activity seems to underlie the hindlimb extension that is maintained during swimming at these stages of development. It is not yet known whether extensor motor neurons are selectively activated or whether all limb motor neurons are indiscriminately activated. In any case, the extensors prevail.

In amniotes, the limb movements begin soon after trunk movements and are usually described as uncoordinated. At first they occur only during trunk movements (Hamburger, 1963). In studies in which recordings have been made during the early, spontaneous limb movements, it has been found that despite the jerky, uncoordinated appearance of the movements, muscle activity is coordinated: antagonist muscles are activated alternately and synergist muscles are coactivated (Bekoff, Stein, & Hamburger, 1975; Landmesser & O'Donovan, 1984).

In summary, the very earliest limb movements may or may not be the result of coordinated patterns of muscle activation. Further studies are needed to determine whether coactivation of antagonists is common at this stage. If so, this may be analogous to the coactivation of adjacent myotomes which is seen during early stages of trunk movement. While in most cases limb muscles appear to be activated synchronously with trunk muscles, this is not always obligatory. Thus the extensive coupling of limb and trunk muscle activity that is seen at early stages is probably due to common imput, which excites both limb and trunk motor neurons. Although additional species should be examined, recent data make unlikely the possibility that medial motor neurons innervate limb muscles at early stages in fish and amphibians.

Development of Coordination within a Limb

In fishes rhythmic adduction and abduction of pectoral fins appear soon after the first movements but no detailed information is available. As discussed in the previous section, Coghill (1929) and others (e.g., Hughes, 1965; Hughes & Prestige, 1967; Sims, 1962; Youngstrom, 1938) describe the first amphibian limb movements as involving tonic extension (retraction, adduction) during swimming. This appears to be due primarily to hip (or shoulder) extension. Later in development the knee (or elbow) begins to flex during limb movements. Then, still later, flexion occurs at the knee (elbow) independent of hip movements. Subsequently, ankle (wrist) and digit movements appear. The same developmental sequence has been reported in reptiles (Decker, 1967; Hughes, Bryant & Bellairs, 1967; and mammals (e.g., Barron, 1941; Narayanan, Fox & Hamburger, 1971; Windle & Griffin, 1931; Windle, Minear, Austin & Orr, 1935). This is probably a simple reflection of the proximal-distal development of limb muscles and their innervation (Youngstrom, 1938).

To analyze the development of coordination of muscles within a limb, either frame-by-frame analysis of high resolution films or videotapes or EMG or nerve recordings are required (Bekoff, 1978). In the three vertebrates in which this has been done so far, frog, chick, and cat, a gradual refinement in motor coordination has been found (Bekoff, 1976; Landmesser & O'Donovan, 1984; Scheibel & Scheibel, 1970; Stehouwer & Farel, 1983). At least in the chick, limb muscle coordination is found prior to the time at which coordinated behavior is recognized behaviorally. For example, alternation of antagonists is present during very early Type I motility.

Coordination between Right and Left Homologous Limbs

Most accounts indicate that individual limbs first move independently and then become coordinated with each other. For example, this is suggested by the few data that are available on the development of interlimb coordination in pectoral fins in fish (Abu Gideiri, 1966; Coghill, 1933; Tooker & Miller, 1980).

In amphibians, after the first tremblings, the right and left leg movements are coordinated in the sense that both legs extend tonically during swimming (Hughes & Prestige, 1967). During the emergence of walking, various patterns have been observed. In some cases, the legs may first move synchronously in attempts at walking, then later alternate (Abu Gideiri, 1971; Coghill, 1929; Faber, 1956). In others, alternating stepping movements can appear before synchronous kicks for swimming or jumping (Faber, 1956; Hughes & Prestige, 1967; Stehouwer & Farel, 1983). Finally, alternating and synchronous coordination patterns can appear at the same stage (Hughes, 1965). There is no consistent pattern.

One area that should be explored further is the relationship of interlimb coordination and trunk movements during early stages in the development of walking. Several studies of amphibians have noted the correlation of limb and trunk movements. Specifically, during walking, the trunk bends alternately to the right and left. Typically the hindlimb is abducted (protracted) on the concave side while the forelimb on that side is adducted (retracted) (Abu Gideiri, 1971; Coghill, 1929). Coghill (1929) interpreted this result as suggesting that the neural mechanism for swimming is responsible for activating limb movements at this stage. On the other hand, results presented by Faber (1956) show that in urodele amphibians other than *Ambystoma,* the legs can be coordinated with trunk movements in the opposite way (e.g., hindlimb abduction on the convex side) or can occur in the absence of trunk bending. Studies of adult vertebrates have shown that there is a separate neural circuit controlling the movements of each limb during locomotion (Grillner, 1975). The extent to which these are influenced by the neural circuitry controlling trunk movements at early stages is unknown. The available data do not allow us to distinguish whether the limb and trunk pattern generators (1) are identical, (2) share common neuronal elements, or (3) are activated by a common source (Stehouwer & Farel, 1983).

Less is known about the development of interlimb coordination in chicks. However, based on EMG recordings from leg muscles, a recent study has found evidence for alternation at early stages (Cooper, 1984). Provine (1980) has reported a gradual increase in simultaneous movements of right and left wings during the incubation period.

In mammals, there is evidence for prenatal development of interlimb coordination. For example, kitten fetuses have been reported to show interlimb coordination patterns typical of postnatal walking (Brown, 1915; Windle & Griffin, 1931). Recently, Bekoff and Lau (1980) have found evidence for interlimb coordination in 20-day-old rat fetuses through the use of frame-by-frame analysis of videotape records. One interesting finding in this study was that coordination was observed between homologous limbs (forelimb-forelimb or hindlimb-hindlimb) in the fetuses, but coordination between homolateral limbs (right or left forelimb-hindlimb pair) was not. This suggests that neural mechanisms for coordinating homologous limb pairs develop before those for coordinating homolateral pairs. On the day after birth, interlimb coordination for all four limbs can be seen during swimming in both rats and mice (Bekoff & Trainer, 1979; Fentress, 1972). This shows that coordinating pathways among the four limb pattern generators are established by this time.

In summary then, the earliest limb movements appear uncoordinated in all vertebrates. In anamniotes, they soon begin to appear coordinated and gradually the coordinated locomotory pattern develops. In most larval and adult fish, the fin movements are typically used for braking, steering and balancing (Alexander, 1975; Batty, 1981), while axial swimming remains the major mode of locomotion, one which is well suited to the aquatic habitat in which they live. In most amphibians on the other hand, the adults are adapted for a terrestrial existence. Therefore, once the limb movements are fully coordinated, the limbs take over as the major locomotory organs. Axial swimming then disappears entirely, as in anurans, or decreases in importance, as in most urodele amphibians.

In most amniotes, the limbs will be the major organs of locomotion. However, the limbs typically develop relatively early in amniotic life, long before the embryo emerges from the egg or uterus. During most of this embryonic period, limb movements occur as part of the Type I motility and appear uncoordinated. Nevertheless, at least in chick embryos, there is an underlying pattern of coordination which undergoes gradual refinement, despite the uncoordinated appearance of the limb movements (Bekoff, 1976). The adaptive function of these Type I limb movements is unknown. As discussed above, spontaneous Type I activity may be important in maintaining normal muscle, joint, and neuron function in an environment in which activity elicited by stimulation would be likely to be minimal (see also Bekoff, 1981b).

Limb movements that are coordinated in appearance begin to be seen near hatching or birth in amniotes. In birds the coordinated leg movements that appear are all related to hatching (Hamburger & Oppenheim, 1967). Whether or not coordinated leg movements are used during hatching in reptiles has not yet been determined (Decker, 1967; Hughes, Bryant & Bellairs, 1967).

Almost nothing is known of the limb movements used in late embryonic and hatching behavior in monotreme mammals. In the rest of the mammals, which do not hatch, but are born, the coordinated leg movements that occur during late fetal life appear similar to walking (Bekoff & Lau, 1980; Brown, 1915; Windle, O'Donnell & Glasshagle, 1933).

CONCLUSIONS: THE EVOLUTIONARY PERSPECTIVE

If we can look at the motor behavior of the embryos and ammocoete larvae of the lamprey as representative of the most primitive ancestral vertebrates then it appears that the early stages of motor development in all vertebrates are phylogenetically conservative. Although there are relatively few descriptions of embryonic lamprey behavior (Harris & Whiting, 1954; Piavis, 1971; Whiting, 1948, 1954), those that are available are remarkably similar to the descriptions of early behavior in more advanced vertebrates. That is, lateral bending of the anterior region of the trunk is the first movement seen. These movements later become more forceful and more frequent but are not rhythmical. Near hatching the movements are described as undulatory, presumably indicating the development of S-waves. Hatching in lamprey appears to be effected by vigorous movements that appear to be a continuation of the previous embryonic movements, as is true in many other fish and amphibians. Thus the use, in hatching, of neural circuitry that will be used after hatching for locomotion appears to be a primitive (phylogenetically old) characteristic of vertebrates. Whether or not a hatching enzyme or the Mauthner neurons are involved in hatching in lamprey is not known.

It is also not known whether these early spontaneous movements in the lamprey are neurogenic or myogenic. In dogfish sharks, the only species in which the movements have been shown clearly to be myogenic, the movements are rhythmical. In all other vertebrates studied, including lamprey, the earliest movements are nonrhythmical and in most of these species the movements are certainly neurogenic (Hamburger, 1963). Thus, as discussed earlier, while the question of whether or not myogenic movements are a primitive ancestral characteristic of vertebrates or a specialization seen only in sharks is still open, the latter possibility seems most likely.

Early movements in lamprey embryos, as in all other vertebrates, are reported to be spontaneous (Whiting, 1954). Thus this characteristic of vertebrate motor development also appears to be evolutionarily ancient. It is possible that motor activity is important for the normal development and/or maintenance of neural circuitry and that spontaneity provides a mechanism for ensuring adequate activity despite the reduced sensory stimulation usually available to embryos (Bradley & Mistretta, 1975; Oppenheim, 1972; Reynolds, 1962). However, this is speculative as motor activity has not yet been shown to be required. In fact, studies of chlorotone- or xylocaine-anaesthetized amphibian embryos have shown that the neural circuitry and muscles used for axial swimming can develop normally in the total absence of motor activity (Carmichael, 1926; Harrison, 1904; Haverkamp & Oppenheim, 1981; Matthews & Detwiler, 1926). The effect of blocking motor activity during the development of limb movements has not been studied in amphibians. In chicks, as little as 48 hours of paralysis produced by drugs that block muscle activation results in permanent malformation of limb joints and limb muscle atrophy (Drachman & Coulombre, 1962; Hall, 1975; Oppenheim, Pittman, Gray, & Maderdrut, 1978). It is not known, however, how the development of neural circuitry is affected (Bekoff 1981b). Thus while spontaneous activity appears to be characteristic of developing motor systems, its function in the development of locomotion remains unknown.

As discussed earlier, Tracy (1926) has suggested that the amount of spontaneous movement seen in developing vertebrates may correlate with their adult life-style. It would be interesting to test this hypothesis by examining a wide range of vertebrate embryos. It would be particularly interesting to compare embryos of two closely related species, one in which the adults are active and one in which the adults are relatively inactive. For example, the frequency of embryonic movements could be compared in two Iguanid lizards, the desert iguana (*Dipsosaurus*), which is an active, agile predator, and the chuckwalla (*Sauromalus*), which is a less active, sit and wait predator.

The basic pattern of early behavior from the first lateral flexions of the anterior trunk to the stage of S-waves appears to have been laid down in ancestral vertebrates and to be conserved throughout the vertebrates. In fish, and in amphibians that pass through a free-swimming larval stage, the S-waves become more vigorous and continuous and appear to develop into axial swimming. In amniotes that rely on limbs for locomotion, gradual development of axial swimming is not seen after the stage of S-waves. Instead the trunk movements become disorganized and appear as part of the Type I motility (Hamburger, 1963).

The development of limb movements appears to be added on top of the development of trunk movements just as the limbs themselves were added to the basic limbless ancestral vertebrate. In all vertebrates the first limb movements appear after trunk movements. In fish, reptiles and birds, limb movements do not begin until trunk movements have progressed at least to the S-wave stage. In amphibians, axial swimming is usually well established before the limbs move. In mammals, limb movements begin soon after the first trunk movements are observed. Thus there is no obvious evolutionary trend toward either earlier or later development of limb movements. In anamniotes the early limb movements rapdily develop into coordinated locomotory movements. In amniotes, limb movements begin very soon after, or even at the same time as, trunk movements. However, they occur as part of the uncoordinated appearing Type I motility, which has no locomotory function, until late in embryonic life.

One of the most intriguing questions is, what is the evolutionary relationship between the neural circuitry controlling axial swimming and that controlling coordinated limb movements? It is clear that in adult vertebrates the motor neurons innervating axial muscles are different from those innervating limb muscles. This is also true for at least some amphibian larvae (Blight, 1978; Forehand & Farel, 1982; Letinsky, 1974; Taylor, 1943) and for bird and mammalian embryos (Hamburger, 1963). It has been claimed however that in at least some developing fish and amphibians motor neurons that innervate axial muscles send branches to limb muscles and provide the only functional innervation of limbs during early motor activity (Coghill, 1929; Youngstrom, 1940). As discussed earlier, these studies have produced equivocal results and should be repeated using currently available techniques that provide higher resolution.

In all vertebrates, even in birds and mammals where the early motor innervation of the limbs is clearly separate from the beginning, there is a close correlation between occurrence of trunk and limb movements at early stages. That is, with few exceptions, the early limb movements occur during trunk movements. This may suggest that the limb motor neurons are being activated by the circuitry that generates axial swimming. Alternatively, there may be two separate trunk- and limb-moving circuits that receive common imput.

In summary, then, it appears that the basic mechanisms underlying locomotion evolved very early in vertebrate phylogeny and have been conserved. For this reason, the basic patterns of development are very similar among vertebrates. All vertebrates appear to go through the early flexure to C-coil to S-wave stages. Furthermore, although early limb movements appear quite different in anamniotes when compared to amniotes, there are underlying similarities. That is, in both anamniotes and amniotes, limb movements appear to be uncoordinated at their onset, then show rapid or gradual development of coordinated movement, depending on the species. For example, in fish the period of uncoordinated fin movements is quite brief and the fin movements are soon integrated with coordinated axial swimming so that they can play their role in balancing, braking, and steering.

In amphibians, again there is a short period of apparently uncoordinated limb movement, "trembling." However, soon after this the limbs are tonically extended during axial swimming, presumably so as not to interfere with swimming. Subsequently they show a period of progressive development of coordinated locomotory patterns, which is completed at the time the amphibian is ready to emerge onto land and use its limbs in its primary mode of terrestrial locomotion, walking. Our understanding of this period of development is only rudimentary. New approaches, however, promise to yield valuable information in the near future (Stehouwer & Farel, 1980, 1981, 1983).

In amniotes, limb movements appear uncoordinated throughout most of embryonic development, until they are actually used in hatching or walking. However, studies using EMG recordings have shown that despite the uncoordinated appearance of the leg movements in chick embyros, there is an underlying pattern of motor coordination that develops gradually into the pattern seen in hatching and that may be used in later locomotion (Bekoff, 1976, 1978, 1981a, 1982; Bekoff et al., 1975).

Thus it appears that there are indeed some aspects of the development of locomotion, especially during the early stages, that are common to all vertebrates. At later stages, there are distinct differences such as the development of axial swimming in anamniotes, the appearance of Type I motility in amniotes and different hatching mechanisms in oviparous anamniotes and amniotes, all of which appear to represent adaptations to differences in the duration and type of embryonic development.

ACKNOWLEDGMENTS

I would like to thank R. C. Eaton, A. H. Cohen and M. Bekoff for valuable comments on an earlier draft of this manuscript. The figures were done by M. Stollmeyer. Ms. G. Metcalf and Ms. J. Cavanagh did an excellent job of typing the manuscript. Support during the preparation of this review was provided by a grant from the National Science Foundation and a fellowship from the Alfred P. Sloan Foundation.

REFERENCES

Abu,Gideiri, Y. B. (1966). The behaviour and neuro-anatomy of some developing teleost fishes. *Journal of Zoology, 149,* 215–241.

Abu Gideiri, Y. B. (1968). Observations on the behaviour of the developing *Zoarces viviparus* (Zoarcidae). *Hydrobiologia, 31,* 60–64.

Abu Gideiri, Y. B. (1969). The development of behaviour in *Tilapia nilotica* L. *Behaviour, 34,* 17–28.

Abu Gideiri, Y. B. (1971). The development of locomotory mechanisms in *Bufo regularis*. *Behaviour, 38,* 121–131.

Alexander, R. McN. (1975). *The Chordates*. London: Cambridge University Press.

Angulo y Gonzalez, A. W. (1932). The prenatal development of behaviour in the albino rat. *Journal of Comparative Neurology, 55,* 395–442.

Armstrong, P. B. (1936). Mechanism of hatching in *Fundulus heteroclitus*. *Biological Bulletin, 71,* 407.

Armstrong, P. B. (1964). Perotic responses in developing bullhead embryos. *Journal of Comparative Neurology, 123,* 147–159.

Armstrong, P. B., & Higgins, D. C. (1971). Behavioral encephalization in the bullhead embryo and its neuroanatomical correlates. *Journal of Comparative Neurology, 143,* 371–384.

Bakhuis, W. J. (1974). Observations on hatching movements in the chick (*Gallus domesticus*). *Journal of Comparative and Physiological Psychology, 87,* 997–1003.

Barcroft, J. & Barron, D. (1937). II. Movements in midfoetal life in the sheep embryo. *Journal of Physiology (London), 91,* 329–351.

Barcroft, J. & Barron, D. (1939). The development of behaviour in foetal sheep. *Journal of Comparative Neurology, 70,* 477–502.

Barlow, G. W. (1977). Modal action patterns. In T. A. Sebeok (Ed.), *How animals communicate*. Bloomington: Indiana University Press.

Barron, D. H. (1941). The functional development of some mammalian neuromuscular mechanisms. *Biological Reviews, 16,* 1–33.

Batty, R. S. (1981). Locomotion in plaice larvae. *Symposia of the Zoological Society of London, 48,* 53–69.

Bekoff, A. (1976). Ontogeny of leg motor output in the chick embryo: A neural analysis. *Brain Research, 196,* 271–291.

Bekoff, A. (1978). A neuroethological approach to the study of the ontogeny of coordinated behavior. In G. M. Burghardt & M. Bekoff (Eds.), *The development of behavior: Comparative and evolutionary aspects*. New York: Garland.

Bekoff, A. (1981a). Embryonic development of the neural circuitry underlying motor coordination. In W. M. Cowan (Ed.), *Topics in developmental neurobiology: Essays in honor of Viktor Hamburger*. New York: Oxford University Press.

Bekoff, A. (1981b). Behavioural embryology of birds and mammals: neuroembryological studies of the development of motor behavior. In K. Immelmann, G. W. Barlow, L. Petrinovich, & M. Main (Eds.), *Behavioral development*. Cambridge: Cambridge University Press.

Bekoff, A., & Lau, B. (1980). Interlimb coordination in 20-day old rat fetuses. *Journal of Experimental Zoology, 214,* 173–175.

Bekoff, A., Stein, P. S. G., & Hamburger, V. (1975). Coordinated motor output in the hindlimb of the 7-day chick embryo. *Proceedings of the National Academy of Sciences of the United States of America, 72,* 1245–1248.

Bekoff, A., & Trainer, W. (1979). Development of interlimb coordination during swimming in postnatal rats. *Journal of Experimental Biology, 83,* 1–11.

Blackshaw, S. E., & Warner, A. E. (1976). Low resistance junctions between mesoderm cells during development of trunk muscles. *Journal of Physiology, 255,* 209–230.

Blake, R. W. (1981. Mechanics of drag-based mechanisms of propulsion in aquatic vertebrates. *Symposia of the Zoological Society of London, 48,* 29–52.

Blight, A. R. (1976). Undulatory swimming with and without waves of contraction. *Nature, 264,* 352–354.

Blight, A. R. (1977). The muscular control of vertebrate swimming movements. *Biological Reviews, 52,* 181–218.

Blight, A. R. (1978). Golgi-staining of "primary" and "secondary" motoneurons in the developing spinal cord of an amphibian. *Journal of Comparative Neurology, 180,* 679–690.

Bodian, D., Melby, E. C., Jr., & Taylor, N. (1968). Development of fine structure of spinal cord in monkey fetuses. II. Pre-reflex period to period of long intersegmental reflexes. *Journal of Comparative Neurology, 133,* 113–166.

Bradley, R. M., & Mistretta, C. M. (1975). Fetal sensory receptors. *Physiological Reviews, 55,* 352–382.

Bragg, A. N. (1940). Observations on the ecology and natural history of Anura. *Proceedings of the Oklahoma Academy of Science, 20,* 71–74.

Bridgman, C. S., & Carmichael, L. (1935). An experimental study of the onset of behavior in the fetal guinea-pig. *Journal of Genetic Psychology, 47,* 247–267.

Brinley, F. J. (1951). Studies on the effect of curare on spontaneous muscular activity in fish embryos. *Physiological Zoology, 24,* 186–195.

Brown, T. G. (1915). On the activities of the central nervous system of the unborn foetus of the cat; with a discussion of the question whether progression (walking, etc.) is a "learnt" complex. *Journal of Physiology, 49,* 208–215.

Carmichael, L. (1926). The development of behavior in vertebrates experimentally removed from the influence of external stimulation. *Psychological Review, 33,* 51–58.

Carmichael, L. (1927). A further study of the development of behavior in vertebrates experimentally removed from the influence of external stimulation. *Psychological Review, 34,* 34–47.

Carmichael, L. (1934). An experimental study in the prenatal guinea pig of the origin and development of reflexes and patterns of behaviour in relation to the stimulation of specific receptor areas during the period of active fetal life. *Genetic Psychology Monographs, 16,* 337–491.

Carmichael, L. (1970). The onset and early development of behavior. In P. H. Mussen (Ed.), *Carmichael's manual of child psychology* (Vol. 1). New York: Wiley.

Carroll, E. J., & Hedrick, J. L. (1974). Hatching in the toad *Xenopus laevis:* Morphological events and evidence for a hatching enzyme. *Developmental Biology, 38,* 1–13.

Coghill, G. E. (1929). *Anatomy and the problem of behaviour.* New York: Hafner.

Coghill, G. E. (1933). Somatic myogenic action in embryos of *Fundulus heteroclitus. Proceedings of the Society for Experimental Biology and Medicine, 31,* 62–64.

Cohen, A. H., & Wallén, P. (1980). The neuronal correlate of locomotion in fish. *Experimental Brain Research, 41,* 11–18.

Cooper, M. W. (1984). *Development of interlimb coordination in the embryonic chick.* Unpublished doctoral dissertation, Yale University.

Day, M. H. (1981). *Vertebrate Locomotion, Symposia of the Zoological Society of London, 48,* 1–471.

Decker, J. D. (1967). Motility of the turtle embryo, *Chelydra serpentina* (Linné). *Science, 157,* 952–954.

Diamond, J., & Miledi, R. (1962). A study of foetal and new-born rat muscle fibres. *Journal of Physiology, 162,* 393–403.

Drachman, D. B., & Coulombre, A. J. (1962). Experimental clubfoot and arthrogryposis multiplex congenita. *The Lancet, II,* 523–526.

Duysens, J., & Pearson, K. G. (1976). The role of cutaneous afferents from the distal hindlimb in the regulation of the step cycle of thalamic cats. *Experimental Brain Research, 24,* 245–255.

Eaton, R. C., Farley, R. D., Kimmel, C. B., & Schabtach, E. (1977). Functional development in the Mauthner cell system of embryos and larvae of the zebra fish. *Journal of Neurobiology, 8,* 151–172.

Eaton, R. C., Bombardieri, R. A., & Meyer, D. L. (1977). The Mauthner initiated startle response in teleost fish. *Journal of Experimental Biology, 66,* 65–81.

Eaton, R. C., & Bombardieri, R. A. (1978). Behavioral functions of the Mauthner neuron. In D. Faber & H. Korn (Eds.), *Neurobiology of the Mauthner cell.* New York: Raven Press.

Eaton, R. C., Lavender, W. A., & Wieland, C. M. (1981). Identification of Mauthner-initiated response patterns in goldfish: Evidence from simultaneous cinematography and electrophysiology. *Journal of Comparative Physiology, 144,* 521–531.

Eaton, R. C., Lavender, W. A., & Wieland, C. M. (1982). Alternative neural pathways initiate fast-start responses following lesions of the Mauthner neuron in goldfish. *Journal of Comparative Physiology, 145,* 485–496.

Eaton, R. C. (1983). Is the Mauthner cell a vertebrate command neuron? A neuroethological perspective on an evolving concept. In J. P. Ewert, R. R. Capranica & D. I. Ingle (Eds.), *Advances in vertebrate neuroethology.* New York: Plenum Press.

Faber, J. (1956). The development and coordination of larval limb movements in *Triturus taeniatus* and *Ambystoma mexicanum. Archives Neerlandaises de zoologie, 11,* 498–517.

Fentress, J. C. (1972). Development and patterning of movement sequences in inbred mice. In J. A. Kiger (Ed.), *The biology of behavior.* Corvallis, Oregon State University Press.

Forehand, C. J., & Farel, P. B. (1982). Spinal cord development in anuran larvae: I. Primary and secondary neurons. *The Journal of Comparative Neurology, 209,* 386–394.

Forssberg, H., Grillner, S., Rossignol, S., & Wallén, P. (1976). Phasic control of reflexes during locomotion in vertebrates. In R. M. Herman, S. Grillner, P. S. G. Stein, & D. G. Stuart (Eds.), *Neural control of locomotion.* New York: Plenum Press.

Gray, J., & Sand, A. (1936a). The locomotory rhythms of the dogfish (*Scyllium canicula*). *Journal of Experimental Biology, 13,* 200–209.

Gray, J., & Sand, A. (1936b). Spinal reflexes of the dogfish (*Scyllium canicula*). *Journal of Experimental Biology, 13,* 210–218.

Grillner, S. (1975). Locomotion in vertebrates: Central mechanisms and reflex interaction. *Physiological Reviews, 55,* 247–304.

Grillner, S. (1981). Control of locomotion in bipeds, tetrapods, and fish. In *The Handbook of Physiology,* section 1: *The Nervous System,* volume II, part 2. Maryland: American Physiological Society.

Grillner, S., & Kashin, S. (1976). On the generation and performance of swimming in fish. In R. M. Herman, S. Grillner, P. S. G. Stein, & D. Stuart (Eds.), *Neural control of locomotion.* New York: Plenum Press.

Grillner, S., Perrett, C., & Zangger, P. (1976). Central generation of locomotion in the spinal dogfish. *Brain Research, 109,* 255–269.

Hall, B. K. (1975). A simple, single-injection method for inducing long-term paralysis in embryonic chicks, and preliminary observations on growth of the tibia. *Anatomical Record, 181,* 767–778.

Hamburger, V. (1963). Some aspects of the embryology of behavior. *Quarterly Reviews of Biology, 38,* 342–365.

Hamburger, V. (1975). Cell death in the development of the lateral motor column of the chick embryo. *Journal of Comparative Neurology, 160,* 535–546.

Hamburger, V., Balaban, M., Oppenheim, R., & Wenger, E. (1965). Periodic motility of normal and spinal chick embryos between 8 and 17 days of incubation. *Journal of Experimental Zoology, 159,* 1–13.

Hamburger, V., & Balaban, M. (1963). Observations and experiments on spontaneous rhythmical behavior in the chick embryo. *Developmental Biology, 7,* 533–545.

Hamburger, V., & Oppenheim, R. (1967). Prehatching motility and hatching behavior in the chick. *Journal of Experimental Zoology, 166,* 171–204.

Harris, J. E., & Whiting, H. P. (1954). Control of rhythmical activity in the skeletal muscle of the embryonic dogfish. *Journal of Physiology, 124,* 501–524.

Harris, J. E., & Whiting, H. P. (1954). Structure and function in the locomotory system of the dogfish embryo. The myogenic stage of movement. *Journal of Experimental Biology, 31,* 501–524.

Harrison, R. G. (1904). An experimental study of the relation of the nervous system to the developing musculature in the embryo of the frog. *American Journal of Anatomy, 3,* 197–220.

Haverkamp, L. J., & Oppenheim, R. W. (1981). Effects of neural blockade on behavioral development in *Xenopus* embryos. *Society for Neuroscience Abstracts,* 181.

Hayes, B. P. (1975). The distribution of intercellular junctions in the developing myotomes of the clawed toad. *Anatomical Embryology, 147,* 345–354.

Herrick, C. J. (1949). *George Ellett Coghill: Naturalist and Philosopher.* Chicago: University of Chicago Press.

Hooker, D. (1952). *The prenatal origin of behaviour.* Lawrence: University of Kansas Press.

Hooker, D., & Nicholas, J. S. (1930). Spinal cord section in rat fetuses. *Journal of Comparative Neurology, 50,* 413–467.

Hughes, A. (1959). Studies in embryonic and larval development in Amphibia. II. The spinal motor root. *Journal of Embryology and Experimental Morphology, 7,* 128–145.

Hughes, A. (1965). The development of behaviour in *Eleutherodactylus martinicensis (Amphibia, Anura). Proceedings of the Zoological Society of London, 144,* 153–161.

Hughes, A. (1966). Spontaneous movements in the embryo of *Eleutherodactylus martinicensis. Nature, 211,* 51–53.

Hughes, A., Bryant, S. V., & Bellairs, D. A. (1967). Embryonic behaviour in the lizard, *Lacerta vivipara. Journal of Zoology, 153,* 139–152.

Hughes, A., & Prestige, M. C. (1967). Development of behaviour in the hindlimb of *Xenopus laevis. Journal of Zoology, 152,* 347–359.

Jacobson, M. (1978). *Developmental neurobiology.* New York: Plenum Press.

Kahn, J. A., & Roberts, A. (1978). The central nervous generation of the swimming rhythm in an amphibian embryo. *Journal of Physiology, 277,* 20–21.

Kimmel, C. B., Model, P. G. (1978). Developmental studies of the Mauthner cell. In D. S. Faber & H. Korn (Eds.), *Neurobiology of the Mauthner cell.* New York: Raven Press.

Kimmel, C. B., Patterson, J., & Kimmel, R. O. (1974). The development and behavioral characteristics of the startle response in the zebra fish. *Developmental Psychobiology, 7,* 47–60.

Kimmel, C. B., Eaton, R. C., & Powell, S. L. (1980). Decreased fast-start performance of zebrafish larvae lacking Mauthner neurons. *Journal of Comparative Physiology. 140,* 343–350.

Kluge, A. G. (1977). *Chordate structure and function.* New York: Macmillan.

Kuo, Z. Y. (1939). Development of acetylcholine in the chick embryo. *Journal of Neurophysiology, 2,* 488–493.

Kyushin, K. (1968). The embryonic development and larval stages of *Hemitripterus villosus (Pallas). Bulletin of the Faculty of Fisheries, Hokkaido University, 18,* 277–289.

Landmesser, L. T., & O'Donovan, M. J. (1984). Activation patterns of embryonic chick hindlimb muscles recorded in ovo and in an isolated spinal cord preparation. *Journal of Physiology, 347,* 189–204.

LeMare, D. W. (1936). Reflex and rhythmical movements in the dogfish. *Journal of Experimental Biology, 13,* 429–442.

Letinsky, M. S. (1974). The development of nerve-muscle junctions in *Rana catesbeiana* tadpoles. *Developmental Biology, 40,* 129–153.

Letinsky, M. S., & Morrison-Graham, K. (1980). Structure of developing frog neuromuscular junctions. *Journal of Neurocytology, 9,* 321–342.

Lissmann, H. W. (1946). The neurological basis of the locomotory rhythm in the spinal dogfish (*Scyllium canicula, Acanthias vulgaris*). I. Reflex behaviour. *Journal of Experimental Biology, 23*, 143–161.

Macklin, M., & Wojtkowski, W. (1973). Correlates of electrical activity in *Xenopus laevis* embryos. Nonmotile and myogenic behavioral phases. *Journal of Comparative Physiology, 84*, 41–58.

Matthews, S. A., & Detwiler, S. R. (1926). The reactions of Amblystoma embryos following prolonged treatment with chloretone. *Journal of Experimental Zoology, 45*, 279–292.

Muntz, L. (1975). Myogenesis in the trunk and leg during development of the tadpole of *Xenopus laevis* (Daudin 1802). *Journal of Embryology and Experimental Morphology, 33*, 757–774.

Narayanan, C. H., Fox, M. W., & Hamburger, V. (1971). Prenatal development of spontaneous and evoked activity in the rat (*Rattus norvegicus albinus*). *Behaviour, 40*, 100–134.

Oppenheim, R. W. (1972). An experimental investigation of the possible role of tactile and proprioceptive stimulation in certain aspects of embryonic behavior in the chick. *Developmental Psychobiology, 5*, 71–91.

Oppenheim, R. W. (1973). Prehatching and hatching behavior: A comparative and physiological consideration. In G. Gottlieb (Ed.), *Behavioral embryology*. New York: Academic Press.

Oppenheim, R. W. (1975). The role of supraspinal input in embryonic motility: A re-examination in the chick. *Journal of Comparative Neurology, 160*, 37–50.

Oppenheim, R. W. (1981). Ontogenetic adaptations and retrogressive processes in the development of the nervous system and behaviour: a neuroembryological perspective. In K. J. Connolly & H. F. R. Prechtl (Eds.), *Maturation and development: Biological and psychological perspectives*. Philadelphia: Lippincott.

Oppenheim, R. W., Pittman, R., Gray, M., & Maderdrut, J. L. (1978). Embryonic behaviour, hatching and neuromuscular development in the chick following a transient reduction of spontaneous motility and sensory input by neuromuscular blocking agents. *Journal of Comparative Neurology, 179*, 619–640.

Orr, D. W., & Windle, W. F. (1934). The development of behaviour in the chick embryo. *Journal of Comparative Neurology, 60*, 271–285.

Petranka, J. W., Just, J. J., & Crawford, E. C. (1982). Hatching of amphibian embryos: The physiological trigger. *Science, 217*, 257–260.

Piavis, G. W. (1971). Embryology. In M. W. Hardisty & I. Potter (Eds.), *The biology of lampreys* (Vol. 1). New York: Academic Press.

Pollack, E. D., & Crain, S. M. (1972). Development of motility in fish embryos in relation to release from early CNS inhibition. *Journal of Neurobiology, 3*, 381–385.

Preyer, W. (1885). *Specielle physiologie des embryo. Unteruschungen uber die lebenserscheinungen vor der geburt*. Leipzig: Grieben.

Provine, R. R. (1971). Embryonic spinal cord: synchrony and spatial distribution of polyneuronal burst discharges. *Brain Research, 29*, 155–158.

Provine, R. R. (1980). Development of between-limb movement synchronization in the chick embryo. *Developmental Psychobiology, 13*, 151–163.

Provine, R. R., & Rogers, L. (1977). Development of spinal cord bioelectric activity in spinal chick embryos and its behavioural implications. *Journal of Neurobiology, 8*, 217–228.

Rewcastle, S. G. (1981). Stance and gait in tetrapods: An evolutionary scenario. *Symposia of the Zoological Society of London, 48*, 239–267.

Reynolds, S. R. M. (1962). Nature of fetal adaptation to the uterine environment: a problem of sensory deprivation. *American Journal of Obstetrics and Gynecology, 83*, 800–808.

Roberts, B. L. (1969). Spontaneous rhythms in the motoneurons of spinal dogfish (*Scyliorhinus canicula*). *Journal of the Marine Biological Association of the United Kingdom, 49*, 33–49.

Roberts, A., Kahn, J. A., Soffe, S. R., Clarke, J. D. W. (1981). Neural control of swimming in a vertebrate. *Science, 213*, 1032–1034.

Romer, A. S. (1959). *The vertebrate story*. Chicago: University of Chicago Press.

Romer, A. S., & Parsons, T. S. (1977). *The vertebrate body*. Philadelphia: Saunders.

Rovainen, C. M. (1979). Neurobiology of lampreys. *Physiological Reviews, 59,* 1007–1077.

Sawyer, C. H. (1944). Nature of the early somatic movements in *Fundulus heteroclitus. Journal of Cellular and Comparative Physiology, 24,* 71–84.

Scheibel, M. E., & Scheibel, A. B. (1970). Developmental relationship between spinal motoneuron dendrite bundles and patterned activity in the hind limb of cats. *Experimental Neurology, 29,* 328–335.

Sedlacek, J. (1971). Cortical responses to visual stimulation in the developing guinea pig during prenatal and perinatal period. *Physiologia Bohemoslovaca, 20,* 213–220.

Sims, R. T. (1962). Transection of the spinal cord in developing *Xenopus laevis. Journal of Embryology and Experimental Morphology, 10,* 115–126.

Smith, K. U., & Daniel, R. S. (1946). Observations of behavioral development in the loggerhead turtle. *Science, 104,* 154–161.

Soffe, S. R., Clarke, J. D. W., & Roberts, A. (1983). Swimming and other centrally generated motor patterns in newt embryos. *Journal of Comparative Physiology, 152,* 535–544.

Stehouwer, D. J., & Farel, P. B. (1980). Central and peripheral controls of swimming in anuran larvae. *Brain Research, 195,* 323–335.

Stehouwer, D. J., & Farel, P. B. (1981). Sensory interactions with a central motor program in anuran larvae. *Brain Research, 218,* 131–140.

Stehouwer, D. J., & Farel, P. B. (1983). Development of hindlimb locomotor activity in the bullfrog (Rana catesbeiana) studied in vitro. *Science, 219,* 516–518.

Stehouwer, D. J., & Farel, P. B. (1984). Development of hindlimb locomotor behavior in the frog. *Developmental Psychobiology, 17,* 217–232.

Taylor, A. C. (1943). Development of the innervation pattern in the limb bud of the frog. *Anatomical Record, 87,* 379–413.

Tooker, C. P., & Miller, R. J. (1980). The ontogeny of agonistic behaviour in the blue gourami, *Trichogaster trichopterus* (Pisces, anabantoidei). *Animal Behaviour, 28,* 943–988.

Tracy, H. C. (1926). The development of motility and behavior reactions in the toadfish (*Opsanus tau*). *Journal of Comparative Neurology, 40,* 253–369.

Tuge, H. (1931). Early behavior of embryos of the turtle, *Terrapene carolina* (L.). *Society for Experimental Biology and Medicine, 29,* 52–53.

Volpe, E. P., Wilkens, M. A., & Dobie, J. L. (1961). Embryonic and larval development of *Hyla avivoca. Copeia, 1961,* 340–349.

Wang, G. H., & Lu, T. W. (1941). Development of swimming and righting reflexes in frog (*Rana guentheri*): effects thereon of transection of central nervous system before hatching. *Journal of Neurophysiology, 4,* 137–146.

Webb, P. W. (1975). Hydrodynamics and energetics of fish propulsion. *Bulletin of the Fisheries Research Board of Canada, 190,* 1–159.

White, G. M. (1915). The behavior of brook trout embryos from the time of hatching to the absorption of the yolk sac. *Animal Behaviour, 5,* 44–60.

Whiting, H. P. (1948). Nervous structure of the spinal cord of the young larval brook lamprey. *Quarterly Journal of Microscopical Science, 89,* 359–383.

Whiting, H. P. (1954). Functional development in the nervous system. In H. Waelsch (Ed.), *Biochemistry of the developing nervous system*. New York: Academic Press.

Windle, W. F. (1940). *Physiology of the fetus: origin and extent of function in prenatal life*. Philadelphia: Saunders.

Windle, W. F., & Griffin, A. M. (1931). Observations on embryonic and fetal movements of the cat. *Journal of comparative Neurology, 52,* 149–188.

Windle, W. F., Minear, W. L., Austin, M. F., & Orr, D. W. (1935). The origin and early development of somatic behaviour in the albino rat. *Physiological Zoology, 8,* 156–175.

Windle, W. F., O'Donnell, J. E., & Glasshagle, E. E. (1933). The early development of spontaneous and reflex behaviour in cat embryos and fetuses. *Physiological Zoology, 6,* 521–541.

Wintrebert, P. (1920). La contraction rythmée aneurale des myotomes chez les embryons de Selaciens. I. Observation de *Scyliorhinus canicula Gill. Archives de zoologie experimentale et generale, 60,* 221–459.

Youngstrom, K. A. (1938). Studies on the developing behaviour of Anura. *Journal of Comparative Neurology, 68,* 351–379.

Youngstrom, K. A. (1940). A primary and a secondary somatic motor innervation in *Amblystoma. Journal of Comparative Neurology, 73,* 139–151.

Ziskind, L., & Dennis, M. J. (1978). Depolarising effect of curare on embryonic rat muscles. *Nature, 276,* 622–623.

Zottoli, S. J. (1978). Comparative morphology of the Mauthner cell in fish and amphibians. In D. S. Faber & H. Korn (Eds.), *Neurobiology of the Mauthner cell.* New York: Raven Press.

4 Ontogeny of Social Recognition: An Essay On Mechanism and Metaphor In Behavioral Development

Jeffrey R. Alberts
Indiana University

INTRODUCTION

Adaptive behavior, in both its immediate (proximate) and ultimate (evolutionary) senses, is predicated on the ability of organisms to emit appropriate, reliable, nonrandom responses to stimuli in their social and physical environments. Recognition is an essential prerequisite for organized behavior, and it is one of the more fundamental and ubiquitous adaptive skills.

My goal for the present chapter is to review, extend, and explore some ideas and data that are pertinent to an appreciation of the development of social recognition. Such a broadly defined goal can be approached from a variety of perspectives. I use a comparative perspective, one that offers the benefits of viewing the varied means by which Nature solves common problems of adaptation. Processes that are hidden in some animals are vividly apparent in others. To focus on just one species often leads to a narrow view of biological issues. The similarities and differences revealed by a comparative view almost always lead to questions and ideas concerning evolutionary origins and interrelations. Such issues arise in this essay and serve to illustrate the delicate interplays of comparative ontogenesis and evolution.

Social recognition is a behavioral topic. Thus, a major theme of this chapter is the ways in which behavior is organized developmentally—and how to study this organization. These concerns represent an important area of overlap between psychology and biology. The contents of the present volume are a testimonial to the timeliness of such integrative analyses. I hope to show that diverse traditions in psychology and biology have led to exciting revelations on the organization of behavioral processes and have illuminated issues that have long been mysterious, while raising new ontogenetic questions about social recognition.

The plan of this chapter is as follows. In the remainder of the Introduction, I review basic issues that will be encountered throughout the essay; the aim is to anticipate and avoid some common interpretive problems.

Section II is a survey of five different "kinds" of social recognition, defined in terms of recognition cues and the functional roles of recognition. The phenomena reviewed in these discussions exemplify different problems in the ontogeny of social recognition, and they are used as the basis of more detailed considerations throughout later portions of the chapter.

Section III is devoted to discussions of developmental aspects of recognition. First I use the issue of developmental *timing* to compare "congenital" and "postnatal" recognition. Understanding the role of ontogenetic timing can help peel away conceptual complexities that cloud other aspects of development. I then turn to *predetermined* aspects of recognition, a delicate topic because it is reminiscent of the onerous terms, instinctive and innate. Nevertheless, it is crucial to understand genetically linked mechanisms of ontogenesis; and predetermined components of recognition have a place in the development of social behavior. I also examine the vital and subtle roles of both *experiential* and *maturational* aspects of behavioral development. These are probably the most important forces in the development of social recognition but they are often elusive to systematic study. There are, however, examples from contemporary empirical research that promise further insights into these central problems in the ontogeny of social recognition.

The "comparative" theme of the present volume reflects a growing awareness of the close relations between issues of development and evolution. Section IV is comprised of discussions of some evolutionary implications of the developmental features of social recognition that were established in sections II and III. In particular, I draw upon the evolutionary ideas of *coevolution* and genetic *coupling* and apply these to social recognition. I speculate on the evolutionary implications of various types of ontogenetic mechanisms of social recognition. Finally, in section IV, I reconsider the uses (and abuses) of metaphor as a tool for analyzing behavior and development. This appraisal is made from both historical and contemporary points of view, and is offered as a reminder that biobehavioral issues such as those addressed in the present chapter require the collective wisdom of multiple disciplines.

A. Meanings of Recognition

When, during behavioral observations, nonrandom and reliable responses are emitted to the same stimulus, we say recognition occurred. Note, however, that recognition is not an observable or directly measurable event. Recognition is not behavior, per se.

Recognition means, literally, "to know again" or "to know or to be aware that something that is perceived has been perceived before." Etymologically, recognition is derived from the Latin roots, *re* (again) + *cognoscere* (to know). In practice, however, recognition is a *descriptive* term. As such, the etymological meaning of recognition accounts for only a small part of the epistemological uses of the term. It has become customary and correct to use the term recognition metaphorically.

1. Metaphors of Recognition.   We can say that certain serum proteins, the immunoglobulins, can "recognize" classes of foreign substances or antigens, and respond to their presence in a complex, adaptive manner by forming antibodies. We also say that the ciliated protozoan, *Stentor,* recognizes food substances, which it ingests, and can similarly recognize nonfoods, which are actively rejected by contracile movements of its peristomal disc. Newly hatched snakes can respond to chemical extracts of species-typical prey items on first encounter; it is as if they can recognize and respond selectively to the cues of the prey that is preferred by their species (Burghardt, 1970, 1978). A duckling recognizes the maternal call of its species, even if it has been incubated in acoustic isolation from other birds and eggs (Gottlieb, 1971a). Baby rats and humans are reported to recognize maternal odors (Leon & Moltz, 1971; McFarlane, 1975). Human infants can recognize the faces (Fagan, 1972) and voices (DeCasper & Fifer, 1980) of their caregivers. It is valid to use the term recognition in these instances, but it is *not* possible to assume that these phenomena involve any kind of knowledge, cognizance, or even necessarily an integrative perceptual mechanism. And it certainly would be futile to look among these examples for a common or shared basis for recognition. Nevertheless, it is valuable to look for and to discover commonalities and patterns in the means by which recognition is accomplished, and to better understand the structure of the behavior that occurs when we identify recognition as occurring.

2. Recognition as a Behavioral Phenotype.   Recognition is best understood as a *phenotypic pattern of behavior*. It is a descriptive term, used to account for *functional* relationships between inputs and outputs (see Fentress, 1976). The existence of mechanisms (intervening variables) that mediate these functional relationships is *inferred*.

3. Description Versus Explanation.   Recognition can be used as a device to describe, but not to explain, behavior. It is critical to remember that description and explanation are separate enterprises.

When making descriptive statements it is proper to remain at the level of observation. In the present chapter, I am concerned with recognition at a level of behavioral phenomena. It would be incorrect to describe recognition in terms of underlying sensory or neural events, based solely on the nature of the behavioral phenotype. Nevertheless, it is possible, and in my opinion desirable, to cross levels of organization in our analyses. When we examine a phenomenon on multiple levels of organization we should proceed cautiously because it is often tempting to assume that functions are arranged similarly on different levels. But they are not. Parallel processes on different levels are not necessarily isomorphic.

B. Proximate and Ultimate Functions of Recognition

Recognition as a biobehavioral phenomenon can be appreciated from at least two "functional" points of view. Recognition of which foods to eat and to avoid, which conspecific(s) to select as a mate, and the myriad perceptions used to coordinate social behavior are *proximate* functions. Proximate functions include those that serve the needs and adjustments within an organism's lifetime (cf. "somatic adaptations" in Pittendrigh, 1958).

So-called ultimate function refers to evolutionary factors that instigate, shape, preserve or eliminate phenotypic characteristics via the changes in the frequency of various alleles in the gene pool. Such effects are usually evaluated in terms of transgenerational influences, as would be seen in the differential reproductive success of individuals possessing a given characteristic in different degrees.

We can consider the biobehavioral functions of recognition according to the dichotomous scheme described above. Recognition can and should be analyzed in terms of both its proximate and its ultimate functions. As you read the survey of "kinds" of recognition below, it will be instructive to evaluate both the proximate and ultimate roles of recognition processes.

KINDS OF RECOGNITION

As I have already indicated, recognition is a protean concept. In its common, metaphorical uses, recognition is applied to so many situations that it becomes helpful to limit its meaning by referring to particular kinds of recognition. To this end, I have formulated a set of five different kinds of recognition. They are listed in Table 4.1 and I illustrate and discuss each in the order shown. This list is not exhaustive and the categories are not mutually exclusive. My purpose is to present a diversity of examples and to consider the relations within and between each kind. With these examples I hope to capture the flavor of some of the analytic problems to be faced.

It is possible that one might view the various kinds of recognition shown in Table 4.1 as a sort of hierarchy, consisting of increasingly finer discriminations and more complex challenges of recognition. But this would be a mistake. It is vital to remember that there is no categorical *scala naturae* of recognition. These categories are our inventions and tools; they exist only to clarify processes, in this case by capitalizing on nominal similarities.

TABLE 4.1
Kinds of Recognition

Feature, or Cue Recognition
Species Recognition
Group Recognition
Kin Recognition
Individual Recognition

I think that it is most profitable to view the kinds of recognition listed in Table 4.1 as derivatives of different analytic approaches, rather than reflections of a hierarchical scheme of Nature. The different kinds of recognition reflect the different kinds of questions that are asked by researchers who approach problems of behavioral organization from different perspectives. For instance, it is largely from ethological traditions that questions are asked about the precise sensory stimuli that control behavior. From such a perspective arose the concepts of sign stimuli, releasers, and associated "fixed action patterns" of behavior. Interest in the coordination of social groups supported questions about the problem of species recognition, the problem of how to recognize conspecifics for purposes of aggregation, cohabitation, resource sharing and competition, and mating. More recently, sociobiological extrapolations have created some new kinds of recognition; kin recognition is one example.

The categories shown in Table 4.1 are not mutually exclusive or even directly comparable because they are defined according to different criteria. For instance, cue recognition is often related to some central or peripheral mechanisms in the recipient or interpreter, or can signify that an isolated portion of a complex stimulus is used for recognition. Group recognition can refer to any one of a number of possible categorical dimensions or assemblages. Kin recognition implies some common characteristic or element among a set of senders and particular kind of adaptive function for both sender and receiver.

A. Feature, or Cue Recognition

Recognition as a behavioral phenotype can be accomplished by responses to isolated cues. There is, in the classical literature on animal behavior, a type of behavior called "taxis," considered to be one of the simplest forms of behavioral organization (Maier & Schneirla, 1935). A taxis is an oriented response that is dependent for its expression upon the immediate presence of a controlling cue. When the cue is present, the response is elicited. If the cue is removed or obscured, the taxic behavior terminates. Taxes are usually named for the controlling stimulus and valence of the elicited responses. Thus, "phototaxis" refers to the attraction of some insects to sources of light and "negative geotaxis" describes a response pattern that orients animals away from the ground (i.e., against gravity).

There are numerous cases in which young organisms are observed to orient and respond to seemingly complex stimuli in a specific and organized fashion. In many cases, however, experimental analysis reveals that the organisms are responding to only a certain aspect of the stimulus complex that is present.

1. Feature Recognition by Herring Gull Chicks.   The early food-elicitation responses of Herring Gull chicks (cf. Tinbergen, 1960) serves to illustrate feature recognition. Until young chicks can forage independently, the parents alternately make excursions from the nest to find food. Upon returning to the nest (which they of course recognize . . . but that's another story) the parent is greeted by probing pecks by the chicks, aimed at the adult's bill. Figure 4.1 depicts this interaction.

Tinbergen and Perdeck (1950) performed a classic ethological analysis of this interaction. The chick's reaction to the parent is a stereotyped feeding adaptation, essential to elicit regurgitation of food for the chick by the adult. The parent's elongated bill, particularly the red spot on its underside (at which the

FIG. 4.1.   Young Herring chicks peck at the red spot on the parent's lower mandible, which evokes regurgitation and presentation of food for the chick. (Drawing based on photograph in Tinbergen, 1960.)

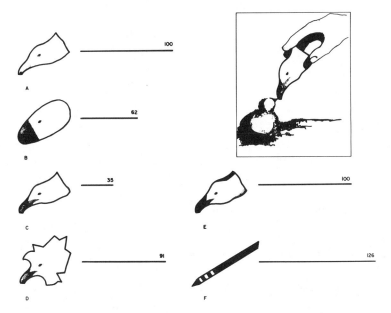

FIG. 4.2.   Field experiments were performed in which Herring gull chicks were presented with various models (insert) and their pecking responses were quantified. The pecking scores were normalized in relation to a score of 100 for the most realistic models. "Recognition" of the parental stimulus is determined by particular features, such as the presence of a red spot, in the context of an elongated form, whereas other features such as the shape of the head or the form of the bill are less important. (Figure based on Tinbergen, 1960, and Tinbergen & Perdeck, 1950.)

chick's pecking is aimed) is the critical *cue* that is recognized. Indeed, it was shown that the entire parent is not essential to the sequence. Tinbergen and Perdeck presented cardboard targets of different shapes and colors to nestling gulls and counted the number of pecks elicited. Figure 4.2 shows that some of the most effective stimuli bear little resemblance to the head of an adult gull, except for the presence of the spot. From such findings has arisen the concept of "sign stimulus" or "releaser," a cue that is recognized and elicits unlearned, stereotyped responses. This kind of cue recognition is often a graded response. Artificial stimuli can be made to be *more* effective than the normal stimulus found in nature. The most extreme, pencil-shaped stimulus shown in Fig. 4.2 elicited more pecking responses from chicks than a faithful representation of the head of an adult gull.

   2. Olfactory Control of Suckling in Rat Pups.   Many young mammals adapt to their early postnatal environments by responding to olfactory information

(Alberts, 1976, 1981; Cheal, 1975). The olfactory atmosphere of a rat nest contains a vast constellation of odorant stimuli, arising from the mother and infants, and from the organic surround itself. The neonatal rat pup, however, seems to be olfactorily "tuned" to recognize specific odorant molecules for nursing. Anosmic pups do not search for nipples and often die of starvation (Alberts, 1976; Hofer, Shair, & Singh, 1976; Tobach, Rouger, & Scheirla, 1967).

Washing the dam's nipples eliminates the pup's ability to locate the teat, and "painting" the nipples with a distillate of the nipple wash (which contains the chemicals that were originally on the nipples) reinstates nipple attachments (Teicher & Blass, 1978).

Pedersen and Blass (1981) tentatively identify dimethyldisulfide (DMDS) as a cue on the nipples of rat dams that is recognized by pups for nursing. The interpretation that DMDS is a normal cue for nipple recognition was buttressed by the finding that DMDS is found in maternal saliva and amniotic fluid, which are the only natural products that have been found to reinstate attraction to washed nipples (Teicher & Blass, 1976). We return to this phenomenon in a later section of the chapter.

B. Species Recognition

This class of recognition is, by definition, based on specialized, species-specific stimuli that identify the targets. Song characteristics that distinguish different species of birds are good examples (see Smith, this volume). Note that not all specialized characteristics of birdsong can be considered as elements for species identification. Regional regularities in song that constitute local "dialects," for instance, do not represent species differences. Moreover, homospecific interactions can be maintained by cues that are not species-specific and thus without species recognition per se. The "pheromone concept" provides an excellent example of the ways in which criteria for species-specificity for olfactory stimuli can be satisfied (Beauchamp, Doty, Moulton, & Mugford, 1976).

In the natal nest of many mammals, heat cues direct infants into contact with conspecifics—such as warm siblings in a huddle, or toward the warm body of the mother (Alberts, 1978; Leonard, 1974). Under such restricted conditions, a simple thermotaxic response is sufficient to bring neonates into aggregations with siblings. Note that there is nothing "species-specific" about the heat cues, even though the result can be the aggregation of conspecifics.

1. Species Recognition by Ducklings. Mother ducks use species-typical "recruitment calls" to lure their offspring from the nest and to elicit approach and following responses. Wood ducks, for example, nest in hidden recesses such as hollows in tree trunks near the shore, elevated above the easy reach of terrestrial predators. When the mother leaves the nest and makes her solicitous call to the young, she usually is well out of sight and in such cases it is clearly her call to which the young respond. The maternal call of the duck is a powerful attractant. In response to the mother's notes, the young approach the small nest hole, position themselves in the entry, and are motivated to fling themselves into space, whereupon they flap their featherless wings until they splash down in the water near the mother. Gottlieb and others have demonstrated clear species specificity in the maternal call of the wood duck, which is distinct from that of other ducks and gallanaceous birds. Moreover, the behavioral specificity of the responses of the young hatchlings of each species matches the specificity of the calls. In numerous laboratory studies, it has been found that the young ducklings recognize the maternal call of their species upon its initial presentation.

2. Species Recognition by Crickets. Crickets also use acoustic signals for species recognition. Males produce species-specific calls by closing their wings together (a behavior termed stridulation). Hoy and his associates have analyzed the acoustic mediation of social behavior of crickets (Hoy & Casaday, 1979; Hoy, Hahn, & Paul, 1977). The temporal regularities of cricket songs are sufficient to be used by humans for taxonomy and by female crickets for mate selection. Real or synthetic calls can be played through loudspeakers and the orientation of females during tethered flight can be used as a measure of recognition and approach. Hoy used this behavioral test, along with electrophysiological methods, to study behavioral, genetic, and neural aspects of species recognition. Figure 4.3 depicts the sound energy spectra in male calling songs in comparison to the frequency sensitivity of the female cricket ear. Note the match in acoustic tuning. We draw additionally on some of this work in a subsequent section of the chapter.

3. Filial Preferences in Rats. Many altricial animals do not manifest species recognition until some time after birth. In the Norway rat, for instance, the infants do not show selectivity in their behavioral associations during early postnatal life. They are highly social creatures, as evidenced by their propensity to huddle, but as I mentioned earlier, their attraction is simply toward sources of heat and cues of "contact comfort" (Alberts, 1978). At about 2 weeks of age, however, the picture changes considerably. Huddling behavior by rat pups can still be elicited by warm targets, but pups now will display strong preferences for huddling with members of their own species. This form of social recognition and preference is olfactorily mediated (Alberts & Brunjes, 1978). There is abundant evidence for olfactory recognition of species identity (Alberts, 1981; Cheal, 1975; Doty, 1976).

C. Group Recognition

Identities can be established and recognized for numerous groupings other than species per se, e.g., groups defined by dimensions of social status, gender, reproductive state, and residential area can each be recognized. Evidence of

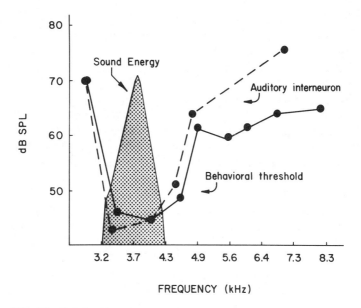

FIG. 4.3.   Relationships among sound energy in the song of *Telegryllus commodus* and responsity of an auditory neuron in a female conspecific and her behavioral threshold. (Figure redrawn from a composite presented by Hoy & Casaday, 1978.)

recognition is usually indirect. Recognition of group membership, for instance, is implied by the observation that territorial residents will often behave aggressively toward nongroup members that cross territorial boundaries. Normally, the ability to discriminate group members from nongroup members presupposes the ability to recognize conspecifics, since group membership is considered to be based on cues that are subsumed under those that identify the larger set, or species. Rarely, however, has such an assumption been tested.

Eibl-Eibesfeldt (1970) has described colonies of wild Norway rats (*Rattus norvegicus*) as "closed anonymous groups." He used this label to suggest that adult group members are recognized according to their colony affiliation, but individuals or other units are not recognized within the group division. Social recognition is based on olfactory identity in rats (Alberts & Galef, 1973; Telle, 1966) and in many other species (Cheal, 1975; Doty, 1976). The ability of animals to discern social affiliation (Alberts & Galef, 1973), dominance (Krames, Carr, & Bergman, 1969), gender (Carr, Loeb, & Dissinger, 1965), individuality (Bowers & Alexander, 1967), and minute genetic differences (Yamazaki, Beauchamp, Bard, Thomas, & Boyse, 1982)—all on the basis of olfaction—is a useful reminder that the cues are often multidimensional and can change or be simultaneously present under different circumstances. Moreover, as is the case with olfaction, one modality can convey numerous different messages.

The existence of regional "dialects" of birdsong is a well-established dimension of recognition and identification (Baker, 1974; Marler & Tamura, 1964). Vocal dialects among passerines represent geographical variations on species-specific themes. It has been suggested that regional dialects function as "reproductive barriers" for white-crowned sparrows.

D. Kin Recognition

Recent evolutionary analyses place special emphasis on the ability of animals to recognize their kin. "Kin recognition," as a capability of animals, is a prediction derived from the concept of "inclusive fitness" (Hamilton, 1964). According to this powerful perspective of modern population genetics, inclusive fitness represents the individual's reproductive success *plus* the reproductive success of the relatives whose fitness is affected by the individual (cf. Grafen, 1982). Genetically, and evolutionarily, relatives are individuals that share alleles in proportion to their degree of relatedness. Evolutionary success, the differential representation of specific alleles in the gene pool, is therefore accomplished by both individual reproduction *and* the reproduction of close relatives that share the same alleles.

From this view has arisen the theory of kin selection (Maynard Smith, 1964), which predicts that behavior among conspecifics will vary as a function of their degrees of relatedness. An "altruistic act" is one for which the immediate benefit to the actor appears to be nil or negligible, whereas the benefit to the recipient is relatively great. However, viewed from the perspective of inclusive fitness, the "altruist" in this situation may be enjoying the sociobiological (genetic) benefit of enhanced reproductive success of an individual with whom it shares alleles. By helping relatives, the altruist increases its genetic representation in the gene pool, and hence its own inclusive fitness.

Recent field and laboratory studies of insects (e.g., Greenberg, 1979), amphibia (Blaustein & O'Hara, 1981; Waldman, 1980; Waldman & Adler, 1979), birds (Bateson, 1976), carnivores (Bertram, 1976; Moehlman, 1979), rodents (Holmes & Sherman, 1982; Porter, Wyrick, & Pankey, 1978), and primates (Wu, Holmes, Medina, & Sackett, 1980) have been interpreted as demonstrations of kin recognition. Sociobiologists continue to pursue kin recognition and differential favoritism of relatives as evolutionarily selected social strategies. It is useful to keep in mind that much of the available data on kin recognition, or on the ability of animals to recognize degrees of genetic relatedness among conspecifics, is derived from studies motivated by sociobiological considerations, as opposed to interest in perceptual processes, or the genetics of phenotypic identities. Thus, in most cases, our knowledge of recognition capabilities is deduced from the overall patterns of behavior, rather than by rigorous tests designed to reveal the perceptual basis of recognition. As an illustration, it will be helpful to review some of the data base.

1. A Possible Genetic Component of Odor Identification.   Greenberg has reported that the eusocial sweat bee, *Lasioglossum zephyrum*, can recognize kin, probably by odor, and uses this information to determine whether a conspecific will be permitted to enter a nest. *L. zephyrum* live in kin groups and inhabit underground burrows that are guarded by one or more colony members. They are derived from a common queen. The guards exclude natural enemies and conspecifics that live in other nests.

Two lines of sweat bees were reared under identical laboratory conditions and subsequently tested for recognition, using the species' natural response to exclude foreigners (non-kin) as a bioassay for recognition. The intruders in these tests had been reared separately and were thus unfamiliar to the guards (the subject bees). The controlled breeding routine permitted calculation of r, the "coefficient or relatedness" (the fraction of genes shared by two individuals due to common recent ancestry), which is purported to be the evolutionary determinant of kin selection. Figure 4.4 illustrates the results of this elegant study. There was a positive linear relationship between coefficient of relatedness and the probability that an unfamiliar bee would be permitted by the guards to pass into the nest. These data, together with previous observations of odor identities in this

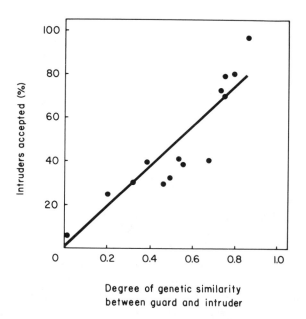

Degree of genetic similarity
between guard and intruder

FIG. 4.4   The probability that female sweat bees (*L. zephyrum*) will accept a conspecific (by permitting it to enter the nest) is a function of their genetic similarity, independent of prior exposure and familiarization. (Redrawn from Greenberg, 1979.)

insect, were interpreted to suggest that there is a genetic component to odor identity that is used by sweat bees for recognition (see Buckle & Greenberg, 1981, for an incisive extension of this analysis).

2. *Kin Recognition in Ground Squirrels.*   Belding's ground squirrels (*Spermophilus beldingi*) are group-living rodents with an ethogram favorable to direct, above-ground observations and extended longitudinal study. Adult female ground squirrels actively defend a territory around their burrow; they also emit alarm calls at the approach of aerial and terrestrial predators. At Tioga Pass, California, the exact age and matrilineal relationship are known for virtually every resident ground squirrel. (Sherman, 1977, 1980a, 1981; Holmes & Sherman, 1982). In *S. beldingi,* male offspring usually disperse before their first winter hibernation. Females do not. On the average, males settle 5–12 times farther than females from the natal burrow and from kin. Although nest burrow proximity among females does not indicate exact genetic relationship, it is coupled to common ancestry (Sherman, 1981).

Careful analyses of hundreds of agonistic and amicable interactions suggest that "nepotism" exists among females but not males in *S. beldingi.* Nepotism in this context is defined as "phenotypically unreciprocated assistance to conspecifics . . . when variations in such favoritism are based on kinship" (Sherman, 1980a, p. 506), or behaviors that favor kin (Sherman, 1980b). Several lines of evidence for nepotism among females were found.

Sherman has suggested that alarm calling in these ground squirrels is nepotistic because callers are typically older, reproductive, resident females with living kin in their vicinity, rather than males, nonresident females, or females without kin. Nest burrow defense also has nepotistic qualities. Intraspecific predation on suckling young is the largest source of mortality for juvenile ground squirrels, so nest defense is a salient aspect of maternal behavior (the polygamous males do not participate in rearing the litter). Unrelated trespassers of both sexes were chased farthest and most vigorously by defending females. Females never killed young of close relatives. These are admittedly circumstantial bits of evidence, but the case becomes more convincing as the data accumulate.

Additional lines of evidence suggesting nepotism, and hence the ability to recognize the kin, consist of the following: (a) close relatives (mother-daughter and sister-sister pairs) fight significantly less than unrelated females when establishing nest burrows, (b) close relatives but not unrelated trespassers are permitted temporary access to burrows in the face of predatory threat, (c) close relatives sometimes co-defend territories, and (d) close relatives warn each other when predatory mammals approach.

I have dwelt on Sherman's observations because they present an instructive analytic problem. Female Belding's ground squirrels interact in ways that favor kin. But there is a paucity of evidence from these observations that the animals use cues of kinship to accomplish their alleged nepotistic acts. The demographic characteristics of their social structure could conceivably provide some alternative routes to behavioral interactions that might favor kin, without kin recognition, per se, playing an active role (Holmes & Sherman, 1982; Sherman, 1980a). *Any* cue that correlates reliably with genetic relatedness could be the organizational basis of the animal's interactions, and this could produce the phenotypic result we call "nepotism." Thus, *S. beldingi* might favor neighbors, whether kin or not, or they may favor familiar conspecifics, kin or not (Sherman, 1980, p. 524). Demographic features of social organization, including some of these displayed by *S. beldingi* could thus work to favor kin, without the direct use of cues of kinship.

Sherman (1980a, 1981), in fact, offers several points of observational data that are inconsistent with the explanation that nepotism in ground squirrels is accomplished solely by indirect means such as mere neighborliness or familiarity. He points out, for example, that although close and distant female relatives live in equal proximity, close kin are still favored. Similarly, analysis of related and nonrelated females whose territories were adjacent for several years, providing a basis for familiarity, nonetheless revealed favoritism of kin.

The congeneric Arctic ground squirrel, *S. parryii,* shares many demographic features with *S. beldingi*. Holmes and Sherman (1982) have complemented their field observations with controlled and manipulative studies: Pups reared together in the laboratory, related or not, treat each other amicably in standardized social tests. In contrast, pups reared apart, even siblings, tend to treat each other agonistically in these tests. *Females* of both species, however, even when raised apart display some behavioral indications that they recognize kin in the social behavior tests. Recently, Davis (1982) repeated Holmes and Sherman's procedures with Richardson's ground squirrels and he, too, found that related pups that were reared apart behaved differently than unrelated, unfamiliar pups.

E. Individual Recognition

Although it is probably assumed that organisms that are capable of recognizing individuals are also capable of recognizing kin, group, and species identities (all "larger" and more "inclusive" categories). This is, however, an untested and unnecessary assumption. Different kinds of recognition are arranged for our conceptual convenience, *not* as a reflection of an ontological scheme.

Individual recognition implies, however, abilities of perceptual registration keen enough to discern features unique to individuals, even closely related individuals. We should remember that such an ability could evolve as a distinct phenotypic specialization, rather than as a generalized ability of perceptual or cognitive processing.

Extraordinary capacity of the central nervous system is not required for individual recognition. Some bees are believed capable of individual recognition

(Barrows, 1975; Breed, 1981). Beecher's (1982) recent work on bank swallows is also consistent with the view that individual recognition is a naturally occurring phenomenon in complex social groups. Field data are accumulating that are being used to establish visual and auditory bases for individual recognition by primates (Cheney & Seyfarth, 1982).

1. Individual Labels in Maternal-Filial Attachments of Goats. Mother goats discriminate between their own and alien kids and can thereby allocate their parental investments in a manner that maximizes the reproductive benefit of their investment (Trivers, 1974). Recognition of offspring also mediates important outcomes on more proximate levels, such as the development of early filial attachments and the development of social behavior (Bowlby, 1969; Harlow & Harlow, 1969). In the parent-offspring system of goats, maternal acceptance is evidenced by a mother's willingness to lick and nurse a kid, whereas rejection is indicated by threats and butting (Gubernick, Jones, & Klopfer, 1979). Recognition works in the service of maternal attachment in goats, and the adults' dichotomous responses (acceptance—rejection) serve as a dependent measure of recognition).

Normally, recognition and attachment are established rapidly, during a brief period shortly after birth. Like other ungulates, goats produce precocious offspring that walk just hours after birth. Prompt and rapid bonding can maintain mother-infant proximity in such mobile, non-nesting species.

If kids are removed from their own mother immediately after birth, they can be accepted by other mothers that might otherwise reject them (Gubernick, 1980). It was found that goat mothers "label" kids with cues transmitted during postpartum licking and nursing bouts, and they learn to recognize these labels. Labeled kids are accepted by mothers that labeled them and thereafter rejected by other mothers. Gubernick (1981) tested recognition of kids following early interactions during which their own mother wore an "udder apron" that prevented the transfer of milk, and/or a muzzle that could be closed to prevent licking interactions (Fig. 4.5). These two avenues functioned additively to provide cues that enabled other mothers to recognize individuals that had been labeled.

Deposition of a cue that serves as an identifier is an elegant and flexible mechanism for recognition. For mother goats with one kid, this form of labeling can mediate individual recognition. However, since it is the label not the individual that is recognized, adjustments in the pattern of cue deposition can transform the same mechanism into one that serves group or kin recognition.

2. Models of Individual Signatures. Currently, some researchers are attempting to create mathematical models of strategies for individual recognition. Beecher (1982), for example, has begun to develop a model to estimate the number of individual phenotypic identities that can be created by variations in a relatively small number of characters. He notes some data on royal terns, a

FIG. 4.5.   A post-parturient goat, fitted with both an udder apron and a muzzle, designed to block two routes by which she can "label" a kid. (Photograph courtesy of D. Gubernick.)

colonial waterbird with a creche system. It has been suggested that parents use the coloration of their chicks for recognition. The coloration of each chick's bill, bill tip, legs, leg blotching, down color and the degree of down spotting vary in an uncorrelated manner. Beecher shows that with these six independent dimensions and five "levels" of each there could exist over 15,000 unique chick color patterns, or individual "signatures." That which is possible and that which is real are not always identical. The potential of the various approaches to some common problems is nonetheless exciting.

The kinds of recognition that I have discussed are categories of convenience and utility, much in the way that recognition is a metaphor that helps unify different kinds of processes. I reiterate that these categories are not an exhaustive set, nor are they based on common criteria. In some cases they are defined largely in terms of their presumed function (e.g., species and kin recognition), while in others the definition is based on the nature of the stimulus (e.g., feature recognition). Some functions were not included (e.g., mate recognition) and many stimulus categories (e.g., auditory and visual recognition) were not used. Instead, my purpose was to provide a survey of diverse phenomena, to convey the breadth and subtlety of the processes that coordinate social interaction. The remainder of this essay is mostly devoted to examining the developmental roots of these patterns of behavior, and some of the evolutionary implications of these powerful and pervasive constructs.

ONTOGENETIC ASPECTS OF RECOGNITION

In the forthcoming section I present some ontogenetic aspects of recognition for purposes of discussing: (1) the roles of *timing* and developmental *rate* in ontogenesis, (2) application of the concept of *innate* to recognition systems, and (3) the ways in which *experience* operates as a developmental mechanism. For each of these interrelated topics I offer some general discussion, followed by one or two empirical examples to make the ideas concrete.

A. Congenital and Postnatal Recognition

Recognition is either *congenital* or *postnatal,* depending on whether the recognition phenotype is manifest at birth (or hatching) or emerges later. The distinction between congenital and postnatal recognition is purely temporal: There can be no inferences made about the underlying formative processes. Congenital simply means "present at birth." Congenital is not innate, and postnatal development is not synonomous with learned or experience-dependent. Innate recognition refers to a form of predetermined phenotype. To cite an example of Arnold's: Congenital birth defects are not innate, even though they can be a regular feature of whole populations of newborns, such as those exposed prenatally to toxins or to malnutrition. The criterional standards associated with innate and predetermined processes are discussed in more detail below and by Arnold (1980).

If the timing of development does not provide an indication about innateness, what does it signify? Developmental timing can be understood as rate regulation along a vector on which lie sequences of ontogenetic changes that serve the adaptive needs of organisms as they move from one developmental niche into another. Although birth is a landmark event in the course of development, it is only one of many markers that describe ontogenetic stages in a life history. The transition from prenatal to postnatal life requires major feats of adaptive reorganization, as do further transitions through subsequent worlds of infancy and adulthood (see Galef, 1981; Oppenheim, 1981, for fuller discussions of such views).

The temporal dimensions of development are therefore significant because they pertain to sequences of ontogenesis. To paraphrase Bonner (1974) on biological reproduction: That which reproduces is not an organism, but a life cycle. Recognition, like any other adaptive skill, is influenced by natural selection to appear in the life cycle at or before the point when the capability is a stage-appropriate adaptation.

Embedded in the temporal vector are other aspects of development that will help us to appreciate the formative forces that lend adaptive organization to behavior as the organism moves through the various niches of its life-cycle. Congenital recognition, then, can be viewed as adaptation to the neonatal niche, expressed through temporal control of phenotypic onset. The two empirical cases described below were selected to illustrate two types of formative inputs that can affect congenital recognition and serve the newborn's adaptation to the early postnatal world.

1. Congenital Recognition of Nipple Cues in Rats. Recall the account of nipple location by rat pups that was introduced in section II.A.2., above. This was discussed as a case of "feature recognition" in which newborn rat pups recognized and responded specifically to maternal saliva and amniotic fluids as stimuli for nursing. Dimethyldisulfide (DMDS) was suggested as a crucial chemical cue for nursing by the neonatal rat.

Blass and his students reasoned that the neonate's congenital attraction to nipples might be produced by prenatal exposure to DMDS in the uterine environment. If DMDS is not a strictly predetermined identification cue established by some heritable mechanism to attract pups to the teat, it might be that if other substances were present in the amniotic fluid, they would also be sufficient to guide early behavior in the immediate postnatal world. The development of an adequate and effective recognition system for the newborn could be achieved by some general, nonspecific mechanism that assigns early postnatal behavior to a cue that is derived from prenatal experience.

To test this hypothesis, a novel chemical odorant was added to the uterine environment. The uteri of pregnant rats were surgically exposed about 4 days before the dams were due to give birth. A catheter was inserted into the space between each fetus and the odorant citral (a lemon-like scent) was added to the amniotic environment. Four days later these pups were delivered by Caesarean section.

Pups exposed to citral *in utero* and briefly after delivery attached to the washed nipples that had been painted with citral, whereas control pups did not (Pedersen & Blass, 1981). These results were interpreted to show that chemical cues present in the uterine environment can act in an inductive manner on the developing olfactory system to establish a congenital phenotype. The mode or the mechanisms by which the influence of the prenatal environment acts upon the fetus is open to speculation (cf. Leonard, 1981). Several of the phenomena discussed earlier in this chapter, such as kin recognition by bees and tadpoles, may well be mediated by similar gestational mechanisms that endow a perceptual memory that can be used by a newborn for recognition.

2. Prenatal Self-Stimulation Can Establish Congenital Phenotype. Mallard and Peking ducklings each show congenital recognition of the maternal call of their species. When placed in a test arena, incubator-hatched birds recognize and preferentially approach a loudspeaker emitting their species' maternal call, in preference to another loudspeaker emitting a different maternal call, such as that of a heterospecific duck or a chicken.

Knowledge of the duckling's prenatal environment suggested that the newly hatched bird is not auditorily naive. Sounds from the outside can penetrate the egg. Moreover, toward the end of the incubation period, the embryo resides with its bill protruding into the airspace at the small end of the egg, as illustrated in Fig. 4.6. In this space the bird can emit audible peeps. At this stage the auditory system of the duckling is responsive to acoustic stimuli. Gottlieb was not concerned that acoustic cues from the mother or from unhatched eggs had influenced his results because his subjects were incubated in acoustic isolation from the mother and other eggs. Nevertheless, an individually incubated bird could still receive prehatching auditory stimulation from its *own* vocalizations.

A method was devised to temporarily *devocalize* unhatched ducklings. Surgery was performed through a small window cut in the egg. A drop of liquid collodion was placed on the surgically exposed vocal syrinx of the embryo, producing a mechanical blockade of the vibrations of the vocal apparatus. The embryos were then replaced and allowed to incubate to term. With this preparation the auditory system is left intact, but is deprived of acoustic self-stimulation normally generated by the embryo.

The results of this ingenious study indicated that high frequency sounds heard prenatally augment perceptual development in the auditory system, particularly the perception of the frequencies that distinguish the maternal call of the species

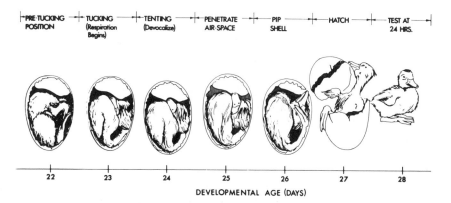

FIG. 4.6.   Late embryonic and hatchling stages of development in Peking duckling (*Anas platyrhynchos*). Gottlieb (1975) devocalized embryonic ducklings in the Tenting stage, prior to the stage when their bill penetrates the air space of the egg. Muted birds, thus deprived of auditory self-stimulation, do not show species-typical auditory recognition upon hatching. (Figure used with permission of G. Gottlieb.)

(Gottlieb, 1975). Devocalized birds could not make the discrimination necessary for species recognition. Self-stimulation by prenatal vocalizations is apparently the key to the elaboration of the appropriate perceptual development for congenital recognition.

More recently, there has been a report of early auditory recognition of maternal speech sounds by human neonates. One-day-old infants oriented preferentially toward a loudspeaker playing their own mother's voice, relative to a loudspeaker that played the voice of another mother with both voices reading the same passages (DeCasper & Fifer, 1980). It has been reported that the uterine environment of the human infant is probably sound permeable—particularly for acoustic stimuli in the range of the fundamental frequencies of human voice.

B. Predetermined Recognition

I use the term *predetermined recognition* to refer to the kinds of recognition for which the identification stimulus (e.g., odor, taste, color, acoustic frequency, a pattern, or some combined gestalt) is developmentally predetermined. The defining characteristics of developmentally predetermined recognition are chronotypy of phenotype, coupling between the sender's identification stimulus and the response bias of the receiver's perceptual system, and heritability of phenotype, as discussed below. Although this criterional profile is not easy to satisfy, it is attainable.

My thinking about the nature of "predetermined" phenotypes has been strongly influenced by Arnold's discussion of *innate* (1980, pp. 411–415), which I found to be an unusually lucid and rigorous treatment of a timeworn source of confusion. Arnold has reserved the term *innate* for features that are present at birth and that meet additional operational standards. But Arnold's perspective was derived as a basis for his analysis of feeding phenotypes in newborn snakes, taxa which are superbly precocious. Newborn snakes receive no parental care and therefore must independently adapt to a postnatal environment that is substantially equivalent to that faced by their adult counterparts. Altricially born infants, particularly those of mammals, emerge into a neonatal world that is substantially different from that of their adult counterparts. It is correspondingly less likely that altricial young will manifest lasting phenotypic attributes at the time of birth. Nevertheless, in the course of its ontogenesis, the altricially born organism can manifest attributes that are entirely predetermined and which, if they were present congenitally, would be termed innate. Thus, I use the term *predetermined* to label phenotypes that meet the criteria described below and that would, if present at birth, be defined as innate, according to relatively rigorous standards of evaluation.

1. Chronotypy.   This is a dimension of ontogenesis that concerns timing or rate. Chronotypic features are those that appear according to a fixed sequence and at a particular age or point of maturation. Congenital recognition is, by definition, chronotypic; postnatal recognition can also display chronotypy.

Revelations of molecular genetics have raised our awareness of the existence and importance of "regulator genes," whose function is to control when during development particular processes are initiated and the rates at which they are expressed. Theorists such as deBeer (1958), Gould (1977), and others have explored in thoughtful detail the implications of such regulation of development (often referred to as heterochrony), which they see as a central mechanism for the expression of evolutionary change and phylogenesis.

2. Coupling. In predetermined recognition systems, coupling must exist between sender and receiver. This means that the identifier cue presented by the sender is stable, heritable, and species-typical. The characteristics of the receiver are coupled to the sender in the sense that the receiver is equipped with a sensory-perceptual system that is predetermined to recognize the cue emitted by a coupled sender. Pheromonal systems, in their strictest sense, represent a form of coupling. Such pheromonal communication involves the emission of a species-specific chemical signal that is usually produced by a specialized effector mechanism. This signal is recognized by a receiver equipped with a sensory-perceptual apparatus that is specifically tuned or biased or otherwise coupled to the precise identification signal (Beauchamp et al., 1976).

3. Heritability. By definition, heritability represents the proportion of phenotypic variance due to additive genetic variance. Heritability is a parameter of populations, not individuals. Heritability is *not* a property of traits and it is misleading to view a phenotype as "consisting" of a heritable component. It is necessary to apply standard techniques of empirical population genetics in order to measure heritability. It is both possible and essential to include this dimension in thorough considerations of innate and predetermined processes. Arnold (1981) has done this in his analyses of prey recognition in snakes. He points out that heritability as a parameter changes with differences in gene frequency and can vary with environmental changes, maturation, and experience. The interested reader should examine his work for insights. I review some of the highlights pertinent to the present discussion.

4. An Analysis of Predetermined Recognition of Prey Species. Increased rates of tongue flicking toward a target is an excellent indicator of food recognition in snakes (Burghardt, 1967). The flicking of the forked, serpentine tongue collects molecules and deposits them through two openings in the roof of the mouth into a specialized portion of the olfactory system, called the vomeronasal organ. Arnold (1981) studied geographically isolated populations of the garter snake species, *Thamnophilus elegans*. Adult *T. elegans* captured on the California coast recognize and respond to terrestrial prey such as slugs. In contrast, congeners from inland populations forage for aquatic prey; inland *T. elegans* recognize leech extracts but not slugs. Prey recognition by *T. elegans* is congenital. Newly hatched, naive snakes showed the same specificity as their parent populations, even when they were incubated in isolation and hatched under constant conditions in the laboratory (Arnold, 1980). Neonatal recognition of prey items is not influenced by maternal diet (Burghardt, 1978). "Chemoreception scores" to different food cues were generated with laboratory tests. Such measures are crucial for estimating the degree to which congenital characteristics are heritable (Arnold, 1980). Arnold compared the variability in the feeding phenotypes both within and among known relatives, and thus established heritability values (see above) for the feeding preferences. These are reputed to be the first estimates of behavioral variability for any natural population of vertebrates.

The chemoreception scores, presumed to have a threshold relationship to underlying genetic variation, were used by Arnold to model the temporal parameters for the evolutionary divergence of the snakes' perceptual recognition of chemical cues. Assuming different, but seemingly reasonable parameters for the intensity of selection and a heritability of .17 (found in both populations), the phenotypic divergence found in nature could evolve in as little as 780 years! This startling analysis represents, to me, an impressive synthesis of sensory, behavioral, and evolutionary research, and reflects the important interdependence of methods and concepts of different disciplines. I realize that prey recognition by snakes may appear to be a digression from the topic of social recognition, but these analyses represent analytic and methodological approaches that are germane to this essay.

C. Experiential and Maturational Determinants

In the vocabulary of behavioral embryology, there exist different types of precursors that influence the course of development and the expression of phenotype. Earlier (section III.B.) I alluded to the ability of extrinsic and intrinsic events to alter *rate* of development. The term *facilitative precursor* is applied here to stimuli that accelerate maturation. Such precursors have no effect on *whether* a particular feature develops, nor on *which* features develop. They influence only *when* they are manifested.

In contrast, the term *determinative precursor* refers to stimulation that functions to channel development in a particular direction, or to specify a particular phenotype from a larger set of possibilities (they affect "whether" and "which"). Gottlieb (1973) has provided helpful exposition on the roles of determinative precursors in the development of behavior (see also Bateson, 1976; Gottlieb, 1976; Kuo, 1967). For purposes of the present discussion, I would like to consider some ways in which *experience* and *maturation* can act as determinative precursors.

Experience is primarily a form of stimulation to the organism. Like any form of stimulation, it varies in quality and in quantity.

Maturational determinants of recognition are ontogenetic factors that play direct, "permissive" roles—allowing the expression of a determined feature of recognition. One broad class of maturational determinants that we have discussed is sensory-perceptual development. Onset of function or the achievement of a level of perceptual function is maturational determinant of recognition. I will describe "emergent discrimination" as an example of a maturational determinant that adds specificity to early recognition.

Recent research has enabled us to conceptualize different ways in which experience and maturation can operate on an organism and its development. These factors, though separable for analytical purposes, are not mutually exclusive. Moreover, multiple forces can act upon the development of a singular phenotype. One task for students of development is to unravel the formative processes that determine developmental expression of phenotype.

At least three types of processes that involve experience or maturation can be found to enter into the expression of social recognition. They are separable and can operate simultaneously to establish, refine, and maintain well-articulated, specific phenotypes. The three processes are familiarization, associative learning, and emergent discrimination. I will use the development of olfactory attractions in rats to illustrate some principles that I consider useful in appreciating how experiences and maturation can establish recognition.

1. Familiarization. This term refers to a general, nonassociative form of learning that is accomplished without the existence of contingencies that produce "reinforcement" or associative learning. Familiarization is a form of learning in the sense that it exerts a relatively long-lasting effect on responsivity to particular cues on the basis of prior experience. Some researchers, such as Sluckin (1965), use the more specific term *exposure learning* to refer to this type of process, and use it as a parsimonious explanation of numerous forms of acquired behavior. It is believed that familiarization, or exposure learning, can occur simply on the basis of "perceptual registration" in the absence of any contiguous events or associative forces.

Familiarization has been invoked as a powerful general explanation of some phenomena that appeared to be highly specific. For example, Leon and Moltz (1971) described the existence of a "maternal pheromone" in Norway rats. They observed that 2-week-old rat pups reliably approached an airstream that had passed through a compartment in which a lactating rat was confined. The developmental onset of the approach response was perfectly correlated with the onset of the emission of the olfactant by the dams, since pups did not approach the airstream odors of nonlactating rats or the odors of rats that had been lactating for less than 2 weeks. (The effective olfactant in these tests was contained in the anal excreta of the adults.) In addition, the pups' response waned at the same developmental point that the attractiveness of the dam ceased (Leon & Moltz, 1972). The interindividual regulation underlying the endocrine control of the emission of the olfactory cue has been extensively studied (Leon, 1974).

Nevertheless, it has been shown that the pups' attraction to the maternal scent is not what one might expect for a "pheromone," at least in the strict sense of the term. Further experimentation revealed that the attractiveness of a lactating female was based on the food that she had been eating (Leon, 1975). Moreover, it was shown that the same tendency of pups to approach the maternal pheromone could be established for the arbitrary odor of peppermint, simply by exposing the pups to the odor of peppermint for a few hours each day until they were two weeks old (Leon, Galef, & Behse, 1977). This is an important result, not just because it leads to a possible reinterpretation of data on the maternal pheromone in rats, but because it demonstrates how behavior that is highly specific in appearance can be mediated by the most general of underlying mechanisms.

It is therefore possible to understand that familiarity can give specificity to behavior in either of two ways. Behavior can be directed toward stimuli that are "recognized" and for which there are particular associations for the organism. Alternatively, the same *behavioral phenotype of recognition* can result if the organism simply avoids stimuli that it "recognizes" as novel, in favor of stimuli that are relatively familiar. This is a fundamental distinction in the organization of behavior. Developmentally, the picture is further elaborated by the possibility that the underlying mechanisms can change while the phenotypic continuity (i.e., the same behavior) is maintained. The lack of necessary correlation between phenotype and mechanism emphasizes the importance of careful analyses.

How can we dissociate the control of behavior by familiarization from the control of behavior by other, more specific forms of learned recognition? If both types of process operate simultaneously, can we identify the action of the more specific mechanisms?

2. Induction of Perceptual Preference by Associative Processes. To examine a route to recognition in which it is possible to dissociate an associative process from familiarization, I will briefly describe some results of my research on the development of huddling behavior in the Norway rat.

Rats are a "contact species" (Barnett, 1963), meaning that their social behavior is dominated by interactions that involve bodily contact, especially huddling. The huddling phenotype is present from birth. The newborns live in a world of constant social contact that occurs within a pile of huddling littermates as well as with the mother. Huddling with other rats remains a prominent, lifelong feature of their social life.

We found that the phenotypic continuity of huddling masks major ontogenetic discontinuity in the sensory control of the behavior. The results of one series of experiments indicated that infant rats (5 and 10 days of age) recognize targets for huddling by thermal cues. Pups at this early stage of development huddle as readily and as much with a member of a different species as with a conspecific rat (Alberts & Brunjes, 1978). In fact, these pups huddle readily with an inanimate cylinder heated to the surface temperature of the live target. By 15 days of age, however, there is a dramatic shift in the sensory control of contact behavior. Huddling is now dominated by olfactory stimuli and the behavior is preferentially expressed at targets that bear the odors of the species. Figure 4.7 illustrates this developmental phenomenon. The results in the graph show the amount of time spent huddling by rat pups with either an anesthetized rat or an anesthetized gerbil. There is no evidence of species recognition before Day 15, and clear filial attraction thereafter. The results of additional experiments indicated that the pups' emergent attraction to the rat stimulus in these huddling preference tests was based on their perception of the *odors* of the conspecific (Alberts, 1978; Alberts & Brunjes, 1978).

We have argued that the recognition of rat odors as an affiliative signal is acquired through an experience-sensitive process. Rat pups reared by perfumed

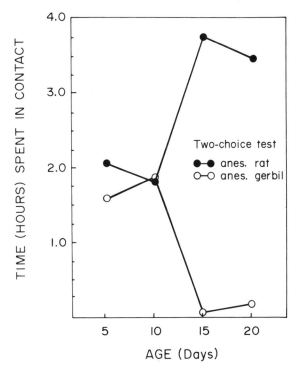

FIG. 4.7.   The development of huddling preferences of rat pups (*Rattus norvegicus*). Younger rats huddle equally with an anesthetized rat and gerbil. By Day 15, there is a pronounced preference for the conspecific target. (From Alberts & Brunjes, 1978.)

foster mothers developed stronger filial attractions to animals with the perfume scent than to the normal, species-typical stimulus (Brunjes & Alberts, 1979).

Note, however, that this behavioral preference could be based on a form of nonassociative exposure learning. Indeed, we have evidence consistent with the possibility that familiarization can produce a filial attraction in a test of huddling preferences. Figure 4.8 summarizes a recently completed series of experiments (Alberts, 1981; Alberts & May, in press). The first two rows of the figure show that daily exposure (4 hr/day) to a scented, lactating foster mother (top row) or daily familiarization (2nd row) leads to similarly dramatic olfactorily guided huddling preferences when the test odor is compared to a novel odor. When pups were given *both* types of experience (i.e., dam and mere exposure), however, each with a distinctive olfactory "tag," we were able to evaluate separately the effects of familiarization and the effects of pairing an odor with maternal care.

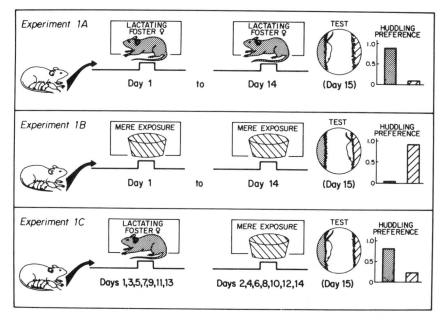

FIG. 4.8.   Paradigms and results of experiments designed to evaluate the contributions of maternal stimuli and "mere exposure" in the establishment of olfactory preferences for huddling by rat pups. Daily sessions with foster dams or odor exposures were associated with different scents. Subsequent preferences were measured in two-choice huddling tests with scented pelts. Experience with a scented foster dam and mere exposure were both sufficient to produce robust behavioral preferences for specific odors. The maternal effect proved to be stronger than mere exposure in pups given both types of experiences, each with a different odor. (From Alberts & May, 1984.)

The results shown in the bottom row of Fig. 4.8 indicate that stronger preferences are formed to the odor paired with the dam. That is, familiarization is *sufficient* to produce a behavioral preference for an odor, relative to a novel scent, but the preference established by the same amount of stimulation in association with maternal care is stronger than that from mere familiarization.

These experiments have been extended to inquire into the precise experiences that establish filial recognition. We found, somewhat surprisingly, that the nursing relationship between mother and infant is *not* part of the induction of the odor preference. Nonlactating foster dams induce preferences as strong as those induced by lactating foster mothers. Instead, it appears that thermotactile stimulation contiguous with an odor leads to the development of filial associations to the odor (Alberts & May, 1984).

It appears that maturational processes mediate the transition from thermally controlled huddling to olfactorily controlled huddling, but experiential mechanisms are the determinative precursors (see above). In the development of filial huddling, thermotactile stimulation specifies the odor toward which the recognition phenotype (huddling preference) is canalized. The roles of familiarization and specific experiences can be studied separately and can act simultaneously in the service of a stable phenotype. Moreover, the phenotype can remain constant while the underlying mechanisms change with maturation.

3. Emergent Discrimination. This is a term derived from Jaynes' (1958) work on imprinting in precocious birds. Imprinting has long been viewed as one type of mechanism for the establishment of filial recognition and attachment. A stimulus to which a duckling has been imprinted elicits filial responses such as approach and following, and suppresses the emission of distress reactions to separation. *Initially,* a wide range of stimuli can elicit filial responses from ducklings. After imprinting, however, the subject's filial responsiveness to other stimuli is reduced; alternate cues are no longer recognized in the same manner.

We are accustomed to think of developmental change as an additive or expansive process, rather than one of restriction. It is important to realize that through development there can be a sharpening and increased articulation of phenotype that has as its basis the attrition, inhibition, or "pruning" of more general response characteristics, rather than a simple building or strenthening of features.

Emergent discrimination has been postulated as a maturational factor to explain post-imprinting suppression of filial reactions to previously effective stimuli. Hoffman and his colleagues have conducted a series of laboratory studies of the postnatal imprinting process, particularly the behavioral changes that characterize emergent discrimination (Hoffman, 1978; Hoffman, Ratner, & Eiserer, 1972; Hoffman, Stratton, Newby, & Barrett, 1970). Figure 4.9 shows representative results. The two histograms in the left of each panel show that the two test stimuli, a rotating light and a moving block, were both effective in suppressing distress vocalizations in ducklings before imprinting. After imprinting, however,

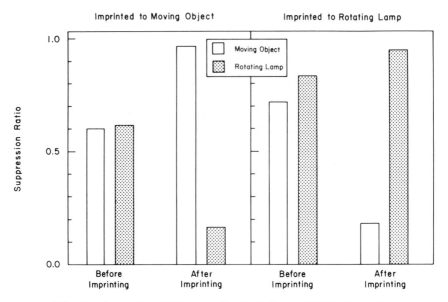

FIG. 4.9.   Suppression of distress vocalization during the initial (preimprinting) and final (postimprinting) tests of ducklings. Before imprinting, distress calls were equivalent in the presence of each test object. Either object could become a calming stimulus after the imprinting procedures. (Redrawn from Hoffman, Ratner, & Eiserer, 1972.)

the same stimuli were *not* effective. If ducklings were imprinted to the moving object, the lamp lost its potency to suppress distress calls. If the lamp was the imprinted object, the moving block became ineffective.

Hoffman's subsequent analyses demonstrated that this form of emergent discrimination has two coordinate bases. After imprinting, the control afforded by the imprinted stimulus either increases slightly or remains about the same. In addition, the control exerted by the nonimprinted stimulus declines significantly. Loss of control by nonimprinted stimuli is an age-related (maturational) phenomenon based, according to Hoffman's analysis, on the development of fear responses to sufficiently unfamiliar stimuli. The effects of forced exposure to nonimprinted stimuli supported this interpretation.

Once again we see that the behavioral phenotype is maintained by the sculpting effects of two or more processes that act simultaneously. Recognition of familiar stimuli can maintain the expression of filial responses, and the specificity of these responses can be further enhanced by the recognition and avoidance of novelty. In addition, there can be formed associative bonds that have an additional specifying role in recognition.

Familiarization, association, and emergent discrimination are three aspects of control that exist separately and operate in unison to produce the developing phenotype. There are other ontogenetic aspects of recognition; these are just a sample of some that we are now able to conceptualize due to empirical paradigms for the analysis of the organization of behavioral control during development.

MECHANISMS AND METAPHORS OF RECOGNITION

In this chapter, I have used "social recognition" to refer to a broad, behavioral phenotype: nonrandom responses to stimuli of social origins, usually arising from conspecifics. By "mechanisms" of recognition I mean the formative events, proximal forces, and anatomical-physiological substrates by which the behavioral phenotype(s) of recognition are realized. By "metaphors" of recognition I mean the use of concepts, vocabulary, or analogies derived from other processes or entities as a means of explaining or analyzing recognition. My goal here is to draw attention to some contemporary metaphors that are applied to the study of recognition, and to make explicit their existence, usefulness, and potential dangers. These metaphors, and the mechanisms that they signify, pertain to both ontogenetic and evolutionary aspects of analysis.

At the outset of this chapter, I indicated that we cannot study recognition directly because it is not an entity or an event. The term is used as a metaphor, to lend some meaning, coherence, and continuity to events in a world of behaving things. It is beyond the scope of the present effort to discuss the structure of metaphorical thought in science. There are numerous works of this type, and they are important to the conduct of science with wisdom and self-awareness.[1] The interested reader could initially consult authors such as Black (1962), Hinde (1960), Kuhn (1962), Lakoff and Johnson (1980), and Popper (1959). My concern here is that we use our metaphors for what they are—*tools*—and that we use these tools skillfully.

Metaphors are invaluable tools and deserve to be treated with the utmost respect. But, at the same time, they should not be taken too seriously.

---

[1]In scientific thought and exposition we most often encounter *ontological metaphors* which are, according to some systematists (e.g., Lakoff & Johnson, 1980), "entity and substance metaphors." Ontological metaphors are those that provide description and clarification by reference to physical objects and processes which are bounded by surfaces and are amenable to categorization, grouping and quantification. Such ontological metaphors enhance our ability to reason better about the processes that gave rise to them. As with any metaphor, we must be cautious with our reasoning, since our understanding is derived from the metaphor, not the actual subject of inquiry.

A. Coevolution and Coupling of Recognition Mechanisms

I use "recognition mechanism" as a functional concept, that is, to denote a process that connects inputs and outputs and, in doing so, integrates the parts of a larger system, namely, the adapted, behaving organism. It is necessary for us to expand and refine our analytical skills to identify and articulate more precisely the ways in which behavioral mechanisms such as recognition act as functional components in life systems.

Thus far, we have been dealing with recognition mechanisms as they pertain to input-output functions within a single organism. The focus of this essay, however, is on *social* recognition, and this connotes interindividual processes. Social recognition is a coordinate exercise in which one organism presents a signal that is recognized by a recipient. Although this is a simple idea, the implications are profound. We must consider not only the interindividual systems, but also the influences of such systems beyond the individuals' lifetimes, i.e., the *evolutionary* implications.

1. Coevolution. The concept of coevolution is a tenet of ecology and evolutionary biology. When two or more taxa have close ecological relationships, they can exert reciprocal selective pressures that make the evolution of either taxon partially dependent upon the evolution of the other, even though no genes are exchanged (Ehrlich & Raven, 1964). The concept of coevolution is commonly used to characterize the interdependent evolutionary relations between plants and herbivorous animals (Pianka, 1974). The concept of coevolution is sometimes also extended to include other forms of interactions including competition, predation, and mutualism (Pianka, 1974).

It is possible to use coevolution as a metaphor and to apply it as a heuristic for appreciating a novel aspect of systems of social recognition. Most instances of social recognition that we have considered in this essay involve single taxa—conspecific groups in which genes are shared and exchanged, so that here the concept of coevolution is metaphorical.

Consider sender-receiver recognition systems as functional units that are subject to pressures analogous to those of coevolution. In such a coevolving unit at least two different participants depend on appropriate recognition by the other. It is crucial that senders present stimuli that can be recognized by receivers. Acoustic signals must be within the perceptible range of the receiver, color patterns contain light of appropriate wavelengths, and so forth. In fact, it tends to be the case that most important identification cues are not merely perceptible to the receiver. Such signals are usually tailored to the ranges of maximum sensitivity or behavioral biases of potential receivers (e.g., Fig. 4.3).

The existence of coordinated interdependence in a recognition system has implications for evolutionary changes in organisms that, at any point in their lives, engage in reproductively relevant interactions that involve identification cues. Phenotypic changes are constrained, not only by factors intrinsic to the organism, but also by characteristics of recipients. If a phenotypic change results in identification cues that lie outside the perceptual ranges of appropriate receivers, or if the change renders the receiver less responsive to some cues for social recognition, the result could be deleterious to the phenotype—and it would tend not to be repeated.

In recognition systems for which identification cues and reception mechanisms are narrowly and *rigidly* specified, this type of system might operate as a powerfully conservative influence on phenotypic change. In general, we might expect predetermined recognition systems (Section III.B.) to have the most inertia for phenotypic change. Competitively viable, alternate phenotypes would be limited by incremental tolerance of the recognition mechanisms for alternate signals, or the ability of identification cues to activate recognition mechanisms with new parameters. Rate of intergenerational phenotypic change would be limited by the extent that survival and reproduction involve such recognition mechanisms.

The concept of coevolution, originally applied by ecologists to plant-animal relations, thus has heuristic value in appreciating possible implications of predetermined recognition mechanisms. When the receiver "expects" a predetermined identification signal, or when the sender "expects" the operating characteristics of the receiver to be rigid and tuned with narrow specificity, there will be a higher degree of intolerance (i.e., fixity) in the system.

Within the same general framework, however, we can consider the possible consequences of a "probabilitistically determined" recognition system (cf. Gottlieb, 1973; section III.C., above) on possible rates of evolutionary change. Probabilistic systems should have less inertia for change than predetermined systems. In probabilistic systems the operating characteristics of the receiver's perceptual apparatus will tend to be broadly tuned, since the nature of the important identification cues from the environment are relatively unspecified. The receiver must be capable of transducing a broader range of stimuli, even if only a narrow set is established for use. The sender in this situation enjoys freedom from the fetters of a specified, selective receptor that must be satisfied if the system is going to "work." It would seem, therefore, that evolutionary changes can be actuated more rapidly, because there are fewer constraints on the operating characteristics of the system as a whole. In evaluating the implications of these arrangements, it is important to remember that we are examining possible consequences of different mechanisms on the evolution of phenotype. Whether the mechanism is predetermined or probabilistic, the resultant phenotypes can be species-specific. This point reemphasizes the importance of dissociating between proximate mechanisms and outcomes in evolution (Lehrman, 1970). The nature of one is not necessarily reflected in the form of the other.

Only careful experimental dissection can fully reveal the mechanism-outcome relationship. This has been one of the major concerns of the present essay.

2. *Genetic Coupling.* Earlier in this chapter I used the concept of "coupling" between sender and receiver as a descriptive characteristic of recognition systems. It was noted that the signals in predetermined systems of recognition probably involve closer or tighter coupling than in more unspecified, experience-dependent systems.

Armchair intuition was brought to bear upon speculations about the evolutionary plasticity of different kinds of recognition systems. In particular, I suggested that intergenerational variations in tightly coupled sender-receiver systems would be constrained by the deleterious effects of decoupling: Phenotype of the sender and receiver could not deviate too much without rendering the system inoperable or less effective.

The recognition system of crickets, however, provides a striking solution to the problems of evolutionary inertia and the threat of uncoupling, as I have discussed them. In virtually all respects, species recognition by crickets is tightly tuned, rigidly controlled and predetermined. According to the logic of the scheme developed above, such a recognition system would be destined to phenotypic conservatism because phenotypic variations that altered the male's call, or changed receptivity of the female's auditory system, would suffer a reproductive disadvantage due to the specificity and fixity of the interindividual recognition system. Despite these logically derived caveats, the species recognition mechanism of crickets can withstand drastic transgenerational perturbation and, in doing so, provides an important instance of *genetic coupling* in a recognition system.

The male's stridulation/song pattern (identification) and the responsivity of the female cricket's auditory operating characteristics (recognition) are apparently controlled by the same gene loci. Thus, a novel acoustic male phenotype, created by an evolutionary genetic change, could easily be reproductively successful, because females with the corresponding genetic variation (i.e., at the same gene loci) will automatically be responsive to the male's novel phenotype.

Figure 4.10 shows the patterned sound pulses of the calling songs of two cricket species, *Teleogryllus oceanicus* and *T. commodus* and their interspecific hybrids. Hybrid males produce calling songs different from either parent species (tracings B and C in the figure). Patterns of hybrid calls are statistically intermediate between parental types. Genetic analyses suggest polygenic control of song pattern. The rhythm of song as reflected in the intertrill interval is, however, sex-linked. The call of each hybrid type resembles that of the maternal line more than the paternal. Hybrid females are more responsive to the calls of their matched hybrid male than to either of the parental stocks or the alternate hybrid variety. This phenomenon has been explored genetically, behaviorally, and neurally by Bentley, Hoy and their colleagues (Bentley & Hoy, 1972; Hoy & Paul,

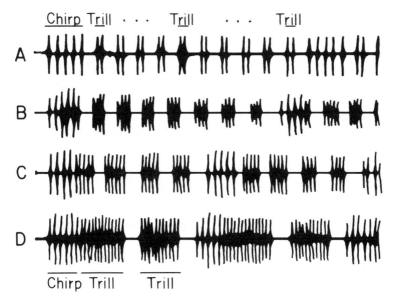

FIG. 4.10. Temporal pattern of acoustic pulses in the calling songs of male crickets from two species and their interspecific hybrids (genus *Teleogryllus*). Songs can be characterized by their phrase structure, which is based on the chirp and subsequent series of trills. Songs and song responsivity are species-specific and linked to genetic lineage. Tracing A: Song of *T. oceanicus*. B: Song of hybrid *T. oceanicus* male × *T. commodus* female. C: Song of hybrid *T. commodus* male and *T. oceanicus* female. D: Song of *T. commodus*. (Redrawn from oscillograms of Bentley & Hoy, 1972.)

1973; Hoy, Hahn, & Paul, 1977). Frequency of cross-species matings in nature and the rates of genetic variation in such crickets are not known. The valuable lesson here is that the operating characteristics of two seemingly different phenotypic characteristics (stridulation in male crickets and auditory nerve sensitivity in females) are based, developmentally, on the same loci of genetic determination. With such complete and simple coupling, coevolution could proceed in the absence of the problem of coordinating disparate events. The phenomenon of coupling between heteromorphic components in a social recognition system reminds us to assume as little as possible in the interpretation of behavior. Nature can regulate apparent complexity with the simplest of underlying mechanisms and sometimes relies on intricacy of mechanism to maintain a seemingly simple result.

B. The Metaphors of Recognition

In recent years there have proliferated a substantial variety of concepts, hypotheses, constructs, and putative mechanisms, each designed to clarify some aspect of the problem of recognition and behavior. These offerings consist mostly of metaphors, although it is rare that they are explicitly or consistently treated as such.

The concepts of *innate releasing mechanism* (e.g., Lorenz, 1950; Tinbergen, 1951) and *sensory templates* (Marler, 1976) have been extraordinarily influential metaphors in the area of recognition. An innate releasing mechanism (IRM), according to the tenets of classical ethology, was hypothesized to reside in the central nervous system and to hold in restraint the nervous energy of a particular fixed action pattern. IRMs were viewed as the mechanisms that were acted upon by "sign stimuli" to "release" the "action-specific energy", which, in turn, energized the observable "fixed action pattern", which is usually some form of a species-specific behavior. Thus conceived, IRM is a kind of lock-and-key arrangement in which a stimulus acts as a "key" that fits perfectly into a lock (the IRM) to release a predictable response. The IRM and its other attendant metaphors have had terrific appeal. Indeed, the hydraulic energy model in which IRMs usually appear is a common paradigm in the behavioral sciences (see Hinde, 1960).

Although IRM is a metaphor derived from the operations of a classical hydraulic energy model (another metaphor), scientists have long searched for physical mechanisms in peripheral receptors and in the central nervous system that are selectively responsive to species-typical signals. One problem with this approach is that no finding can falsify the existence of the IRM. Some findings, interpreted broadly enough would be consistent with an IRM explanation, but they can neither prove nor reject it. Thus, the metaphor of the IRM was "good" to the extent that it stimulated creative, novel and productive investigations. To the extent that scientists attempted to study the metaphor itself, the work was misguided.

The use of *sensory template* metaphor is similar to the IRM (Marler, 1976). The *metaphor* of the sensory template has been a useful heuristic for many workers, particularly those in the area of avian song learning.

Birdsong can be regarded as a stereotyped, species-typical motor pattern that generates crucial social stimuli. Unlike cricket song calls, however, birdsong does not develop normally in individuals separated from conspecifics, suggesting that avian song is learned. One of the striking findings about the nature of song learning comes from experiments in which isolated birds were tutored by tape recordings. This procedure can be implemented successfully, and isolated birds will learn their species normal song. The template concept became relevant when it was found that there was selectivity in song learning. Isolated birds did not simply learn to sing the patterns to which they were exposed. They learned their species song if they were exposed to it, but they showed little evidence of learning in their songs if they were tutored by an inappropriate stimulus tape. Isolated males that were played several songs, including the song of their species, showed clear selectivity in their learning and acquired the normal song type. It is *as if* the bird has in its head a song template to which acoustic input is matched. In Marler's words, the auditory template is a "notion" that arose from the observed results of different forms of auditory deprivation on the development of song. Auditory templates "are visualized as lying in the neural pathways for auditory processing, sensitizing the organism to certain patterns of stimulation" (1976, p. 320). Such characterizations are not precise, but they are not intended to be. The metaphor is successful in communicating a concept in terms of other, better-understood operations.

There is nothing wrong with the use of metaphor here or elsewhere in science. Indeed, the metaphor of a sensory template has been a stimulating heuristic for a good deal of exciting work and thought (Eimas & Miller, 1981; Green & Marler, 1979; Konishi, 1978). The problems arise when we forget that such metaphors mean *as if*. When the *as ifs* begin to fade, or our awareness of them fades, we become prone to misinterpretation and misapplication of the metaphors. The metaphor of sensory templates is sometimes treated as an hypothesis, which it is not. Hypotheses are constructed for purposes of falsification. In this sense they have a different purpose and reality status than metaphors. It is crucial to keep separate these two tools. The sensory template metaphor has had widespread influence on the study of acoustic recognition in animals and in humans (see Marler, 1980). With its success and popularity, however, comes the likelihood that the metaphor will assume the status of mechanism. The evolution of the concept of "feature detectors" is a similar tale. Drift from metaphor to mechanism is a historical pattern, but one that can be avoided with careful application and explicit use of our metaphorical tools.

C. Return of the Nominal Fallacy?

Metaphors not only *reflect* the ways in which we think about things, they *affect* them as well. In addition to the danger of transforming metaphors into unfalsifiable hypotheses, indiscriminant use of metaphor makes us prone to the so-called nominal fallacy, a classic in the history of science. The nominal fallacy is committed when one confuses naming with explaining. In his important essay on "The Descent of Instinct," the comparative psychologist Frank Beach (1955) began with the following quotation that is ironically pertinent in the present context: "The delusion is extraordinary by which we thus exalt language above nature . . . making language the expositor of nature instead of making nature the expositor of language" (Alexander Brian Johnson: *A Treatise on Language*).

The appearance in the recent literature of terms such as "recognition allele" is a timely reminder that we should remain circumspect. Recognition alleles (or at least the metaphor) were postulated by Hamilton (1964) and have been discussed in the context of genetically based kin recognition (see Dawkins, 1976; Holmes & Sherman, 1982). The ability of some organisms to recognize genetic kin, as evidenced by differential responsiveness to genetically related individuals, can be discussed *as if* there exist "recognition alleles," genetic loci that express themselves through recognition of the same alleles in another organism. Taken literally (and therefore not metaphorically), this is a biological fantasy. Alleles do not recognize. Beyond this, however, is the implication that when organisms manifest recognition of kin, that they are responding to cues of kinship. We know now that this is not necessarily the case. The means by which the kin recognition phenotype is expressed may be related to a response to a cue that happens to covary with kinship. In many forms of social organization this may be accomplished by a mechanism as simple as familiarization (Section III.C.). Bekoff (1981), in fact, charges that some researchers confuse relatedness with familiarity. Awareness and self-regulation can prevent such errors. Empirical ingenuity and finesse give us the ability to dissect experimentally the processes that establish and maintain the organization of behavior, providing the means to move beyond metaphor.

SUMMARY AND CONCLUDING REMARKS

It is appropriate to consider recognition as an adaptive skill but it is necessary to specify the meanings of this designation. In its most literal meaning, recognition is a mentalistic term, viz. the inferred experience, "to know again." In practice, however, the meanings of recognition are metaphorical—devices used as functional principles to describe *behavior*. Recognition is an *adaptive skill* in the sense that it operates both in the service of proximal adjustments to the environment and as a mechanism that directly affects reproductive success.

I dealt with social recognition as an adaptive skill. Treatment of recognition as a behavioral phenotype led to consideration of the way(s) in which the phenotype emerges through *developmental* processes. Three developmental themes (timing, predeterminism, and experiential-maturational mechanisms) were explored. Each proved to have noteworthy *evolutionary* implications.

Congenital and postnatally emergent recognition phenotypes were compared. They differ in *timing,* but not necessarily in underlying mechanisms. Such temporal regulations of development are crucial aspects of adaptation to niches of prenatal and postnatal life. Moreover, differential rates of development (heterochrony) are believed to be an evolutionary mechanism for modifications on the phylogenetic level.

A second developmental theme was the notion of "predetermined" phenotype. I suggested that it is possible to consider some recognition phenotypes as predetermined, but they may be either congenital or postnatal in appearance; typical concepts of innate recognition require modification to encompass postnatal predeterminism. Predetermined recognition was characterized by chronotypy, coupling, and heritability (Section III.B.). Each of these characteristics has evolutionary import, both on mechanistic and theoretical levels. "Genetic coupling'' was examined as one specialized mechanism to coordinate senders and receivers.

Experience was the third developmental theme. Experience can act as a *facilitative precursor* affecting temporal aspects of development, or it can be a *determinative precursor* that canalizes phenotypic expression. I used familiarization and associative learning as examples of experiential mechanisms that can act solely, jointly, or in combination with maturational processes such as emergent discrimination to sharpen recognition. Awareness of recognition mechanisms can enhance appreciation of evolutionary and ecological patterns. Such awareness also raised the reminder about relationships between mechanisms and outcomes. Simple and similar mechanisms can produce elaborate and varied results. Seemingly simple and similar outcomes can be created by different and complicated mechanisms.

Recognition is used most often as a metaphor. A common error, however, is to exaggerate the reality of the metaphor, confuse metaphor and mechanism, explain by describing, and thus commit the ''nominal fallacy.''

The comparative approach to social recognition yields phenomena that are important as adaptive adjustments to the environment. Observational and empirical methods can be used to analyze the underlying ontogenetic architecture. The development of social recognition is an ideal problem for convergent efforts by psychologists, geneticists, physiologists and ecologists.

ACKNOWLEDGMENTS

I thank Professor Gene Gollin, his students and colleagues for the stimulating seminar that gave rise to the present chapter and helped shape it. Other friends and colleagues, such as D. Chiszar, B. Galef, D. Gubernick, W. Holmes, M. Petersen, and P. Sherman contributed comments, critiques and bibliographic resources. I appreciate their assistance. Artwork and graphics were done by Sara Delgado.

Research from the author's laboratory was supported by Grant #MH-28355 and by Research Scientist Development Award #MH-00222, both from the National Institute of Mental Health to J. R. Alberts. This support is gratefully acknowledged.

REFERENCES

Alberts, J. R. (1976). Olfactory contributions to behavioral development in rodents. In R. L. Doty (Ed.), *Mammalian olfaction, reproductive processes and behavior* (pp. 67–94). New York: Academic Press.

Alberts, J. R. (1978). Huddling by rat pups: Multisensory control of contact behavior. *Journal of Comparative and Physiological Psychology, 92,* 220–230.

Alberts, J. R. (1981). Ontogeny of olfaction: Reciprocal roles of sensation and behavior in the development of perception. In R. N. Aslin, J. R. Alberts & M. R. Petersen (Eds.), *Development of perception: psychobiological perspectives* (Vol. 1). New York: Academic Press.

Alberts, J. R., & Brunjes, P. C. (1978). Ontogeny of thermal and olfactory determinants of huddling in the rat. *Journal of Comparative and Physiological Psychology, 92,* 897–906.

Alberts, J. R., & Galef, B. G., Jr. (1973). Olfaction and movement: Stimuli intraspecific aggression in the wild Norway rat. *Journal of Comparative and Physiological Psychology, 85,* 233–242.

Alberts, J. R., & May, B. (1984). Non-nutritive, thermotactile induction of filial huddling in rat pups. *Developmental Psychobiology, 17,* 161–181.

Arnold, S. J. (1980). The microevolution of feeding behavior. In A. Kamil & T. Sargent (Eds.), *Foraging behavior: Ecological, ethological and psychological approaches* (pp. 409–453). New York: Garland Press.

Baker, M. C. (1974). Genetic structure of two populations of white-crowned sparrows with different song dialects. *Condor, 76,* 351–356.

Barnett, S. A. (1963). *The rat: A study in behavior.* London: Methuen.

Barrows, E. M. (1975). Individually distinctive odors in an invertebrate. *Behavioral Biology, 15,* 57–64.

Bateson, P. P. G. (1976). Specificity and the origin of behavior. In J. S. Rosenblatt, R. A. Hinde, E. Shaw, & C. Beer (Eds.), *Advances in the study of behavior* (Vol. 6). (pp. 1–20). New York: Academic Press.

Beach, F. A. (1955). The descent of instinct. *Psychological Reviews, 62,* 401–410.

Beauchamp, G., Doty, R. L., Moulton, D. G., & Mugford, R. A. (1976). The pheromone concept in mammalian chemical communication: A critique. In R. L. Doty (Ed.), *Mammalian olfaction, reproductive processes and behavior.* New York: Academic Press.

Beecher, M. D. (1982). Signature systems and kin recognition. *American Zoologist, 22,* 477–490.

Bekoff, M. (1981). Mammalian sibling interactions: Genes, facilitative environments, and the co-efficient of familiarity. In D. J. Gubernick & P. H. Klopfer (Eds.), *Parental care in mammals* (pp. 307–346). New York: Plenum.

Bentley, D. R., & Hoy, R. R. (1972). Genetic control of neuronal network generating cricket song patterns. *Animal Behaviour, 20,* 478–492.

Bertram, B. C. R. (1976). Kin selection in lions and evolution. In P. P. G. Bateson & R. A. Hinde (Eds.), *Growing points in ethology* (pp. 281–302). Cambridge: Cambridge University Press.

Black, M. (1962). *Models and metaphors.* Ithaca, NY: Cornell University Press.

Blaustein, A. R., & O'Hara, R. K. (1981). Genetic control for sibling recognition? *Nature, 290,* 246–248.

Bonner, J. T. (1974). *On development.* Cambridge, MA: Harvard University Press.

Bowers, J. M., & Alexander, B. L. (1967). Mice: Individual recognition by olfactory cues. *Science, 158,* 1208–1210.

Bowlby, J. (1969). *Attachment, attachment and loss* (Vol. 1). New York: Basic Books.

Breed, M. D. (1981). Individual recognition and learning of queen odors by worker honey bees. *Proceedings of the National Academy of Sciences, 78,* 2635–2637.

Brunjes, P. C., & Alberts, J. R. (1979). Olfactory stimulation induces filial huddling preferences in rat pups. *Journal of Comparative and Physiological Psychology, 93,* 547–555.

Buckle, G. R., & Greenberg, L. (1981). Nestmate recognition in sweat bees (*Lasioglossum zephyrum*): Does an individual recognize its own odour or only odours of its nestmates? *Animal Behaviour, 29,* 802–809.

Burghardt, G. M. (1967). Chemical-cue preferences of inexperienced snakes: Comparative aspects. *Science, 157,* 718–721.

Burghardt, G. M (1970). Chemical perception in reptiles. In J. W. Johnston, Jr., D. G. Moulton, & A. Turk (Eds.), *Communication by chemical signals* (pp. 241–308). New York: Appleton-Century Crofts.

Burghardt, G. M. (1978). Behavioral ontogeny in reptiles: Whence, whither, and why. In G. M. Burghardt & M. Bekoff (Eds.), *The development of behavior: Comparative and evolutionary aspects* (pp. 149–174). New York: Garland STPM Press.

Carr, W. J., Loeb, L. S., & Dissinger, M. L. (1965). Responses of rats to sex odors. *Journal of Comparative and Physiological Psychology, 59*, 370–377.

Cheal, M. (1975). Social olfaction: A review of the ontogeny of olfactory influences on vertebrate behavior. *Behavioral Biology, 15*, 1–25.

Cheney, D., & Seyfarth, R. (1982). Discrimination of individuals within and between groups of free-ranging old world monkeys. *American Zoologist.*

Davis, L. S. (1982). Sibling recognition in Richardson's ground squirrels (*Spermophilus richardsonii*). *Behavioral Ecology and Sociobiology, 11*, 65–70.

Dawkins, R. (1976). *The selfish gene.* New York: Oxford University Press.

deBeer, G. R. (1958). *Embryos and ancestors.* Oxford: Claredon Press.

DeCasper, A. J., & Fifer, W. P. (1980). Of human bonding: Newborns prefer their mothers' voices. *Science, 208*, 1174–1176.

Doty, R. L. (1974). A cry for the liberation of the female rodent: Courtship and copulation in Rodentia. *Psychological Bulletin, 81*, 159–172.

Doty, R. L. (Ed.). (1976). *Mammalian olfaction, reproductive processes and behavior.* New York: Academic Press.

Eibl-Eibesfeldt, I. (1970). *Ethology.* New York: Holt, Rinehart & Winston.

Eimas, P. D., & Miller, J. L. (Eds.).(1981). *Perspectives on the study of speech.* Hillsdale, NJ: Lawrence Erlbaum Associates.

Ehrlich, P. R., & Raven, P. H. (1964). Butterflies and plants: A study in coevolution. *Evolution, 18*, 586–608.

Fagan, J. F. (1972). Infants' recognition memory for faces. *Journal of Experimental Child Psychology, 14*, 453–476.

Fentress, J. C. (1976). System and mechanism in behavioral biology. In J. C. Fentress (Ed.), *Simpler networks and behavior* (pp. 330–340). Sunderland, MA: Sinauer Associates.

Galef, B. G., Jr. (1981). The ecology of weaning. In D. J. Gubernick & P. H. Klopfer (Eds.), *Parental care in mammals* (pp. 211–241). New York: Plenum Press.

Galef, B. G., Jr. (1982). Acquisition and waning of exposure-induced attraction to a non-natural odor in rat pups. *Developmental Psychobiology, 15*, 479–490.

Gottlieb, G. (1971a). *Development of species identification in birds.* Chicago: University of Chicago Press.

Gottlieb, G. (1971b). Ontogenesis of sensory function in birds and mammals. In E. Tobach, L. R. Aronson, & E. Shaw (Eds.), *The biopsychology of development.* New York: Academic Press.

Gottlieb, G. (1973). Introduction to behavioral embryology. In G. Gottlieb (Ed.), *Studies in the development of behavior and the nervous system* I. New York: Academic Press.

Gottlieb, G. (1975). Development of species identification in ducklings: I. Nature of perceptual deficit caused by embryonic auditory deprivation. *Journal of Comparative and Physiological Psychology, 89*, 387–399.

Gottlieb, G. (1976). The roles of experience in the development of behavior and the nervous system. In G. Gottlieb (Ed.), *Studies in the development of behavior and the nervous system* (Vol. 4). New York: Academic Press.

Gould, S. J. (1977). *Ontogeny and phylogeny.* Cambridge, MA: Belknap Press.

Grafen, R. (1982). How not to measure inclusive fitness. *Nature, 298*, 425–426.

Green, S., & Marler, P. (1979). The analysis of animal communication. In P. Marler and J. G. Vandenbergh (Eds.), *Handbook of behavioral neurobiology: Vol. 3, Social behavior and communication* (pp. 73–158). New York: Plenum Press.

Greenberg, L. (1979). Genetic component of bee odor in kin recognition. *Science, 206*, 1095–1097.

Gubernick, D. J., Jones, K. C., & Klopfer, P. H. (1979). Maternal "imprinting" in goats? *Animal Behaviour, 27*, 314–315.

Gubernick, D. J. (1980). Maternal "imprinting" or maternal "labelling" in goats? *Animal Behaviour, 28*, 124–129.

Gubernick, D. J. (1981). Mechanisms of maternal "labelling" in goats. *Animal Behaviour, 29,* 1.

Hamilton, W. D. (1964). The genetical evolution of social behaviour, I. and II. *Journal of Theoretical Biology, 7,* 1–52.

Harlow, H. F., & Harlow, M. K. (1969). Effects of various mother-infant relationships on rhesus monkey behavior. In B. M. Foss (Ed.), *Determinants of infant behavior* (Vol. 4). (pp. 219–256). New York: Wiley.

Hinde, R. A. (1960). Energy models of motivation. *Symposia of the Society for Experimental Biology, 14,* 199–213.

Hofer, M. A., Shair, H., & Singh, P. (1976). Evidence that maternal ventral skin substances promote suckling in infant rats. *Physiology and Behavior, 17,* 131–136.

Hoffman, H. S. (1978). Laboratory investigations of imprinting. In G. M. Burghardt & M. Bekoff (Eds.), *The development of behavior* (pp. 203–212). New York: Garland Press.

Hoffman, H. S., Ratner, A. M., & Eiserer, L. (1972). The role of imprinting in the emergence of specific filial attachments. *Journal of Comparative and Physiological Psychology, 81,* 399–409.

Hoffman, H. S., Stratton, J. W., Newby, V., Barrett, J. E. (1970). Development of behavioral control by an imprinting stimulus. *Journal of Comparative and Physiological Psychology, 71,* 229–236.

Holmes, W. G., & Sherman, P. W. (1982). The ontogeny of kin recognition in two species of ground squirrels. *American Zoologist, 22,* 491–517.

Hoy, R. R., & Casaday, G. B. (1979). Acoustic communication in crickets: Physiological analysis of auditory pathways. In G. M. Burghardt & M. Bekoff (Eds.), *The development of behavior: Comparative and evolutionary aspects* (pp. 43–62). New York: Garland STPM Press.

Hoy, R. R., Hahn, J., & Paul, R. C. (1977). Hybrid cricket auditory behavior: Evidence for genetic coupling in animal communication. *Science, 195,* 82–84.

Hoy, R. R., & Paul, R. R. (1973). Genetic control of song specificity in crickets. *Science, 180,* 82–83.

Jaynes, J. (1958). Imprinting: The interaction of learned and innate behavior: IV. Generalization and emergent discrimination. *Journal of Comparative and Physiological Psychology, 51,* 238–242.

Johnson, A. B. (1947). A treatise on language (D. Rynin, Ed.), Berkeley: University of California Press, p. 58.

Konishi, M. (1978). Auditory environment and vocal development in birds. In R. D. Walk & H. L. Pick (Eds.), *Perception and experience.* New York: Plenum Press.

Krames, L., Carr, W. J., Bergman, B. (1969). A pheromone associated with social dominance among male rats. *Psychonomic Science, 16,* 11–12.

Kuhn, T. S. (1962). *The structure of scientific revolutions.* Illinois: University of Chicago Press.

Kuo, Z.-Y. (1967). The dynamics of behavior development. New York: Random House.

Lakoff, G., & Johnson, M. (1980). *Metaphors we live by.* Illinois: University of Chicago Press.

Lehrman, D. S. (1970). Semantic and conceptual issues in the nature-nuture controversy. In L. R. Aronson, E. Tobach, D. S. Lehrman, & J. S. Rosenblatt (Eds.), *Development and evolution of behavior.* San Francisco: Freeman.

Leon, M. (1974). Maternal pheromone. *Physiology and Behavior, 13,* 441–443.

Leon, M. (1975). Dietary control of maternal pheromone in the lactating rat. *Physiology and Behavior, 14,* 311–319.

Leon, M., Galef, B. G., & Behse, J. H. (1977). Establishment of pheromonal bonds and diet choice in young rats by odor pre-exposure. *Physiology and Behavior, 18,* 387–391.

Leon, M., & Moltz, H. (1971). Maternal pheromone: Discrimination by preweanling albino rats. *Physiology and Behavior, 7,* 265–267.

Leon, M., & Moltz, H. (1972). The development of the pheromonal bond in the albino rat. *Physiology and Behavior, 8,* 683–686.

Leonard, C. M. (1974). Thermotaxis in golden hamster pups. *Journal of Comparative and Physiological Psychology, 86*, 458–469.

Leonard, C. M. (1981). Some speculations concerning neurological mechanisms for early odor recognition. In R. N. Aslin, J. R. Alberts, & M. R. Petersen (Eds.), *The development of perception: Vol. 1. Psychobiological perspectives.* New York: Academic Press.

Lorenz, K. (1950). The comparative method in studying innate behavior patterns. *Symposium of the Society of Experimental Biology, 4*, 221–268.

Maier, N. R. F., & Schneirla, T. C. (1935). *Principles of animal psychology.* New York: Dover.

Marler, P. (1976). Sensory templates in species-specific behaviors. In J. C. Fentress (Ed.), *Simpler networks and behavior* (pp. 314–329). Sunderland, MA: Sinauer Associates.

Marler, P., & Tamura, M. (1964). Culturally transmitted patterns of vocal behavior in sparrows. *Science, 146*, 1483–1486.

Maynard Smith, J. (1964). Group selection and kin selection. *Nature, 201*, 1145–1147.

McFarlane, J. A. (1975). Olfaction in the development of social preferences in the human neonate. In M. A. Hofer (Ed.), *Parent-infant interaction.* Amsterdam: Elsevier.

Moehlman, P. D. (1979). Jackal helpers and pup survival. *Nature, 277*, 382–383.

Moore, C. L. (1981). An olfactory basis for maternal discrimination of sex of offspring in rats (*Rattus norvegicus*). *Animal Behaviour, 29*, 383–386.

Oppenheim, R. W. (1981). Ontogenetic adaptations and retrogressive processes in the development of the nervous system and behavior. In K. Connolly & H. Prechtl (Eds.), *Maturation and behavior development.* London: Spastics Society Publications.

Pedersen, P. E., & Blass, E. M. (1981). Olfactory control over suckling in Albino Rats. In R. N. Aslin, J. R. Alberts, & M. R. Petersen (Eds.), *Development of perception: Vol. 1. Psychobiological perspectives* (pp. 359–382). New York: Academic Press.

Pianka, E. R. (1974). *Evolutionary ecology,* New York: Harper & Row.

Pittendrigh, C. S. (1958). Adaptation, natural selection, and behavior. In A. Roe & G. G. Simpson (Eds.), *Behavior and evolution* (pp. 390–416). New Haven: Yale University Press.

Popper, K. R. (1959). *The logic of scientific discovery,* London: Hutchinson.

Porter, R. H., Wyrick, M., & Pankey, J. (1978). Sibling recognition in spiny mice (*Acomys cahirinus*). *Behavioral Ecology and Sociobiology, 3*, 61–68.

Sherman, P. W. (1977). Nepotism and the evolution of alarm calls. *Science, 197*, 1246–1253.

Sherman, P. W. (1980a). The limits of ground squirrel nepotism. In G. W. Barlow & J. Silverberg (Eds.), *Sociobiology: Beyond Nature/Nurture.* Boulder: Westview Press.

Sherman, P. W. (1980b). The meaning of nepotism. *American Naturalist, 116*, 604–606.

Sherman, P. W. (1981). Kinship, demography, and Belding's ground squirrel nepotism. *Behavioral Ecology and Sociobiology, 8*, 251–259.

Sluckin, W. (1964). *Imprinting and early learning.* Chicago: Aldine.

Teicher, M. H., & Blass, E. M. (1976). Suckling in newborn rats: Eliminated by nipple lavage, reinstated by pup saliva. *Science, 193*, 422–425.

Teicher, M. H., & Blass, E. M. (1978). The role of olfaction and amniotic fluid in the first suckling response of newborn albino rats. *Science, 198*, 635–636.

Telle, H. J. (1966). Bietrag zur kenntnis der verhaltensweise von ratten, vergleichend dargetellt bein, *Rattus norvegicus* and *Rattus rattus. Zeitschrift fur Angewandte Zoologie, 53*, 129–196.

Tinbergen, N. (1951). *The study of instinct.* Oxford: Claredon Press.

Tinbergen, N. (1960). *The herring gull's world.* New York: Harper & Row.

Tingergen, N., & Perdeck, A. C. (1950). On the stimulus situation releasing the begging responses in the newly hatched Herring Gull chick (*Larus a. argentatus* Pont.). *Behaviour, 3*, 1–38.

Tobach, E., Rouger, Y., & Schneirla, T. C. (1967). Development of olfactory function in the rat pup. *American Zoologist, 7*, 792.

Trivers, R. L. (1974). Parent-offspring conflict. *American Zoologist, 14*, 249–264.

Waldman, B. (1980). Sibling recognition in toad tadpoles: The role of experience. *American Zoologist, 20,* 854.

Waldman, B., & Adler, K. (1979). Toad tadpoles associate preferentially with siblings. *Nature, 282,* 611–613.

Wu, H. M. H., Holmes, W. G., Medina, S. R., & Sackett, G. P. (1980). Kin preference in infant *Macca nemestrina. Nature, 285,* 225–227.

Yamazaki, K., Beauchamp, G. K., Bard, J., Thomas, L., & Boyse, E. A. (1982). Chemosensory recognition of phenotypes determined by the *Tla* and *H-2K* regions of chromosome 17 of the mouse. *Proceedings of the National Academy of Sciences, U.S.A., 79,* 7828–7831.

5

The Evolution of Helping Behavior— An Ontogenetic and Comparative Perspective

Jerram L. Brown
State University of New York
Albany

INTRODUCTION

The biological study of social behavior has a long history, dating at least from Charles Darwin (1859). During the 1930s, 1940s and 1950s the approach of evolutionary biologists to social behavior was dominated by the comparative methods employed by Lorenz (1941) and Tinbergen (1959), which emphasized phylogeny and the roles played by drives, displays, and vocalizations in communication. In the 1960s two relatively new approaches brought social behavior into better ecological perspective. *Comparative ecological studies of social systems,* such as those by Orians (1961) on New World blackbirds (Icteridae) and Crook (1962, 1964) on Old World weaverbirds (Ploceidae), emphasized the correlations of ecological factors with social systems. At the same time, *selection models,* such as the polygyny threshold model (Orians, 1969a; Verner, 1964) and the economic defendability model (Brown, 1964), suggested hypotheses with which to study the postulated environmental influences on behavior that are mediated by natural selection.

The study of cooperative social behavior benefited in the 1960s and 1970s from both approaches. The selection model known as Hamilton's (1964) rule focused attention on aid giving in the social insects. The comparative ecological approach revealed some of the ecological correlates of cooperative social systems in primates (Crook & Gartlan, 1966), ungulates (Estes, 1974; Jarman, 1974) and birds (Brown, 1969, 1974; Crook, 1965; Lack, 1968).

Helping behavior is a type of aid giving that has been traditionally defined as parentlike behavior toward young that are not offspring of the helper (Brown, 1978; Skutch, 1935, 1961). Note that considerations involving the effects of helping upon the fitness of the parties involved are not part of the definition. Helping behavior, like parental behavior, need not always have a net benefit to the recipient's direct (individual) fitness.

The act of becoming a helper may be viewed as a decision that is made in response to a complex social environment. The ways in which this choice might be adaptive are not clear. This review of helping attempts to place it in developmental and comparative perspective. Particular attention is given to current controversies and to ways in which they can be scientifically resolved. We concentrate on birds because the issues are most clearly drawn here.

ONTOGENY OF AVIAN HELPING

Patterns of Development of Helping

Helping is not a unitary phenomenon. It varies among species in ecological causation, in the types of behavior involved, and in developmental patterns. With respect to the ontogeny of helping behavior, it is useful to distinguish two modes of origin.

Mating and Mate Sharing

Long recognized as a contributing cause of helping is the difficulty of acquiring a mate. Among birds with male parental care, surplus males—those that fail to acquire a female—rather than wander nomadically may in some species join another male on his territory, sharing in its defense and sometimes sharing copulations with the female as well. A similar phenomenon occurs in African lions (*Panthera leo*) (Bygott, Bertram, & Hanby, 1979; Packer & Pusey, 1982).

The development of helping in these species is relatively simple and straightforward. These are typically males in full breeding condition who have been forced to make a compromise to improve their chances of having offspring; in some species two or more males are needed to defend particularly rich and highly contested resources. In southern hemisphere skuas (*Catharacta lonnbergi*) of lower latitudes, territories in food-rich areas with many individuals of nesting prey species may be defended by two males who both nest and forage there, although the species is usually monogamous (Young, 1978). In the Galapagos hawk (*Buteo galapagoensis*) there is a large surplus of breeding-age adults that compete for a relatively small number of territories. It appears that two or more males are usually needed to successfully maintain a territory with one female (Faaborg, DeVries, Patterson, & Griffin, 1980). Little is known about the relatedness of the males in these cases, though Faaborg et al. speculate that in many trios the males are unrelated. Growing up together may facilitate the development of cooperation in some of these cases.

Another tactic used by unmated males of some species late in the season is to associate with a female after her eggs are laid, sometimes even feeding her young. The prior loss of the female's mate may facilitate such mate replacement. Several such cases have been reported for temperate-zone, migratory species (barn swallow, *Hirundo rustica,* Myers & Waller, 1977; savanna sparrow, *Passerculus sandwichensis,* Weatherhead & Robertson, 1980). Since most pairs in these species are probably formed anew at the onset of the breeding season, these cases of helping by the new mate to feed young of the old male are of doubtful importance for the species as a whole or even for the individuals concerned. They do indicate the existence of greater flexibility in mating and helping than is generally appreciated.

In the above cases the potential helpers are typically males without mates of their own, and their behavior is clearly aimed at acquiring a mate. Adaptations that improve the effectiveness of the male as a helper are virtually absent. An important role for kinship has been claimed for lions (Bertram, 1976; Vehrencamp, 1979) but has not been substantiated for the other cases and may have been overemphasized for lions (Packer & Pusey, 1982).

Prolonging the Nuclear Family

A distinctly different mode of origin of helpers is the persistence of nuclear families by prolonging the period of association of young with each other and with one or both of their parents, usually on their natal territory. In this mode the developmental age of onset of helping is a variable, rather than being confined to the adult stage. It is this mode of origin that has led—mainly in the tropics—to the most extreme adaptations in communal birds and the lives of helpers. In temperate and polar zones with harsh nonbreeding seasons many species migrate long distances, thereby losing one of the factors that tends to keep the family together, the territory. The hazards of migration also promote mixing in the population, create territorial vacancies, and consequently make dispersal relatively more profitable than in the tropics.

Three distinct modes of helping may be recognized in persistent family groups: helping by juveniles, helping by older immatures or subadults, and recipirocal sharing of reproductive tasks among breeders.

Juveniles as Helpers.   The feeding of sibling young by juveniles is conspicuous among tropical species with relatively low survival rates. In the splendid wren (*Malurus splendens*) three or more broods per season may be raised. By 60 days the juveniles "are sufficiently adept to be useful helpers at the nest following the one in which they were hatched" (Rowley 1981, p. 244). The mean interval between broods was 62–70 days. Annual survival in the study area was .71 for males and .43 for females. The situation is similar in these respects for the superb blue wren, *M. cyaneus* (Rowley, 1965). In anis (*Crotophaga* spp.)

juvenile helping is also conspicuous and the juveniles are surprisingly precocious in this respect (Davis, 1940, 1942). Annual survival on the study area in the groove-billed ani (*Crotophaga sulcirostris*) have been estimated at .57–.69 for males and .60–.77 for females (Vehrencamp, 1978). The value of juvenile aid to the recipients and to the juveniles themselves has been largely ignored by field workers. Review and study of juvenile helping are needed.

Subadults as Helpers.   The two most conspicuous examples of adaptations that are concerned with helper status occur at this developmental stage. These are the prolonged immaturity that may accompany delayed breeding in helpers and the distinctive visible markings that identify the young members of the family in many species. The grey-crowned babbler (*Pomatostomus temporalis*) exemplifies these traits (Fig. 5.1). In this species breeding is delayed 1–3 years during which time the birds function as nonbreeding helpers and are usually distinguishable from the breeders by the color of their iris, which varies from dark brown in young helpers to light yellow in mature breeders (Counsilman & King, 1977). Similar delays in breeding accompanied by distinctive markings for

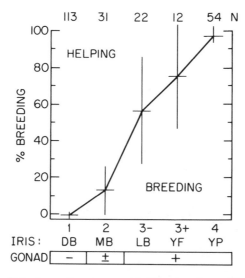

FIG. 5.1.   Percentages of grey-crowned babblers breeding and helping at progressively older ages. Data are for the 1976 breeding season, Meandara, Australia. Mean and 95% confidence intervals are shown for the sample sizes (N) above. Iris colors are DB (dark brown), MB (medium brown), light brown (LB), yellow with dark flecks (YF), and pure yellow without flecks (YP, the adult condition). Approximate ages for each iris-age class are shown in years. Gonads are small and nonfunctional (−) for DBs; functional and adult size (+) for LB, YF, and YP; and intermediate (±) for MB.

the younger helpers are found in several other groups (notably *Aphelocoma ultramarina,* personal observation and *Cyanocorax* spp. (Hardy, 1973).

Delayed breeding is facilitated by high survival rates. The equilibrium fraction of nonbreeders—hence helpers—in the population is determined jointly by their rates of production and survival in relation to the survival of breeders (Brown, 1969). The typical group size in such species is probably determined ontogenetically largely by the number of years spent in the group as a nonbreeding helper.

Task Sharing by Breeders and Potential Breeders. In a few communal species more than one pair or female may breed in a social unit or territory (plural breeding), in some cases laying their eggs in the same nest (joint nesting; references in Brown, 1978). Territory defense, anti-predator vigilance, feeding of young, and in the joint-nesters even incubation may be shared by two or more unit members. Some destruction of each other's eggs may occur in these species (Bertram, 1979; Brown, 1963; Trail, Strahl, & Brown, 1981; Vehrencamp, 1977) and sharing is usually not equal; nevertheless, it is conspicuous. This category differs from the mate sharing origin by originating from the nuclear family and by the possibility of extended families with genealogical lines occupying the same territory over several generations, as in the Mexican jay (*Aph. ultramarina;* Brown & Brown, 1981a).

This simple dichotomy by no means covers all factors in the origin of helping or mentions all systems. It does, however, single out two extremes.

Why Delay Breeding?

Presumably when the age at first breeding, α, is delayed in birds it is because the cost of attempting to breed earlier than α exceeds the strong benefits of breeding early that were emphasized by Cole (1954). The nature of these costs remains poorly known and might vary from species to species. Probably because delayed breeding in communal birds is often discussed in the context of inclusive-fitness theory, some theorists have been tempted to explain the delays as being due to parentally induced altruism (Emlen, 1982b; Vehrencamp, 1979, 1980). As I have argued before (Brown, 1978, p. 135), however, the delays are easily explained by factors such as those discussed below.

Learning To Forage Efficiently

There is some evidence that the length of time preceding α corresponds to the time needed to perfect foraging skills. Immatures are known to find food less effectively than adults in several noncommunal water birds (Buckley & Buckley, 1974; Orians, 1969b; Searcy, 1978). More importantly, MacLean (1982) showed that in three species of *Larus* gulls the length of the period of improvement in foraging efficiency continues at least to α when α is a variable among species. In other words, in a comparative perspective α is a function of age-specific foraging ability.

Information of this kind is not available for any communal bird, but some evidence tentatively suggests a similar pattern. Year-old immature Mexican jays weigh less (personal observation) and deliver food to nestlings at a slower rate than adults (Brown, 1970, 1972). In grey-crowned babblers average body weight increases each year until α, when the full adult iris coloration has been attained (Brown et al., 1982a; Counsilman & King, 1977).

Very little is known about the energy budgets of communal birds. The possibility remains that the energy balance of many helpers, particularly the younger ones would be too easily threatened by the energetic stresses of the reproductive cycle to justify the attempt. Female *Malurus splendens,* which may rear several broods a year, seem to have a markedly lower survival rate than males, suggesting that the costs of reproduction, which are heavier on the females in this species, are exacted in post-breeding mortality (Rowley, 1981).

The rate of foraging success is probably important for reproductive success because the more efficient foragers have more time and energy available for behaviors associated with reproduction and parental care. There may be a threshold rate of energy profit that physiologically permits or stimulates an animal to initiate a breeding attempt (see model in Fig. 5 of Brown, 1982). An individual can be below this threshold for a variety of reasons. Probably an important one, though still poorly documented, is the energy environment. It is well known that among seabirds which delay breeding while young, resource failures in a bad year can cause many older individuals to forego or abandon breeding that year (e.g., Andersson, 1976). Orians et al. (1977) have suggested that low levels of food availability might be responsible for the high frequency of nonbreeding helpers in Argentine marshes and they suggested food shortage as a general cause of helping behavior in birds, a thesis echoed by Emlen (1982a). Orians' hypothesis is especially attractive for colonial species with helpers, since in most of them breeding sites are not limiting and feeding areas are undefended. In most colonial species the saturation hypothesis, which invokes defense of all-purpose territories, is not applicable—at least not in its simplest form.

Emlen (1982a) has proposed that "fluctuating, erratic environments" promote helping in some individuals; however, it is not variability per se but the fact that an individual is below threshold for breeding that is the more important and general factor (Orians' hypothesis). An individual can be below threshold in a constant or variable climate, depending on its foraging skill relative to food availability at the time.

Learning to Build Nests

Building a nest requires still other skills that may require much time for practice. In Mexican jays two-year old males sometimes attempt nest building but usually the nest is not completed and more twigs end up on the ground than in the nest. It is noteworthy that this skill, which appears to require considerable practice, is not usually attempted by yearling helpers, who do little more than break off twigs and immediately drop them.

Dominance

Another requirement for successful breeding in many species, at least for males, is dominance in the territory. Inability to acquire dominance in a territory suitable for breeding has long been considered to be a major cause of delayed breeding by helpers (Brown, 1969). This saturation hypothesis was intended for and applies to stable and unstable environments—Emlen's (1982a) misunderstanding of this notwithstanding. In the Florida scrub jay (*A. c. coerulescens*) helpers are subordinate to breeders of the same sex (Woolfenden & Fitzpatrick, 1977). This suggests that dominance may be crucial in this species, but in Mexican jays and piñon jays it is not uncommon for birds in their first year of life to dominante established male and female breeders (Barkan, Craig, Brown, Stewart, & Strahl, 1981; Balda & Balda, 1978), at least at food.

Age of Role Shift

Variation among Species

In the comparative perspective, the age of role shift from nonbreeding to breeding, α, is a critical variable. Because nonbreeders in communal birds tend to become helpers the number of helpers is determined primarily by the number of nonbreeders. The latter is determined, at least in a comparative perspective, by the age of transition to breeding age, α. For example, in the genus *Aphelocoma* α ranges from 1 year in California populations of *A. coerulescens* to 3 or 4 in Arizona populations of *A. ultramarina* with intermediate values in other populations (Table 5.1). Unit sizes vary accordingly. Similar variation in α presumably occurs in other jays (Fig. 5.2).

A second ontogenetic factor with important social consequences in *Aphelocoma* is the manner of dispersal and acquisition of breeding status. In most temperate zone passerine birds, like California *A. coerulescens*, juveniles leave their parents after the breeding season and may wander long distances from their hatching site before settling on a breeding territory. In Florida *A. coerulescens*, this wandering is reduced to exploratory forays from the natal territory, and males may acquire a territory by a process of "budding" off the natal territory (Woolfenden & Fitzpatrick, 1978). This trend is carried further by Arizona *A. ultramarina*, in which both sexes may "inherit" the entire natal territory (Brown & Brown, 1981a); however, they must share it since more than one pair may breed in a territory. The result is a still larger social unit since the progeny of more than one pair inhabit the same territory together.

This method of acquiring a breeding territory is highly unusual in birds though common in female primates and requires a special tolerance between parent and

TABLE 5.1
Comparison of Four Populations of *Aphelocoma* Jays in
Two Species, the Mexican Jay (*A. ultramarina*)
and the Scrub Jay (*A. coerulescens*).
α = Age at First Breeding.

Population	Approximate α	Typical Unit Sizes	% Breeding	Pairs per Territory	Youth Signals	Dispersal Mechanism
A.c. Cal.[a]	1–2 yr	2	90	1	–	Long and short movements
A.c. Fla.[b]	2–3	2–5	70	1	–	Budding; short movements
A.u. Tex.[c]	2–?	2–4+	50	1	–	?
A.u. Az.[a]	3–4	5–20	18–59	2–4	+	Inheritance; short movements

[a]Brown, 1963, and personal observation.
[b]Woolfenden 1975.
[c]Ligon and Husar 1974.

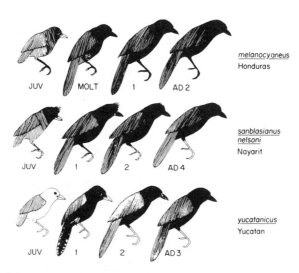

melanocyaneus
Honduras

JUV   MOLT   1   AD 2

sanblasianus
nelsoni
Nayarit

JUV   1   2   AD 4

yucatanicus
Yucatan

JUV   1   2   AD 3

FIG. 5.2. Signals of immaturity in jays of the subgenus *Cissilopha* (genus *Cyanocorax*). Each row shows the ontogenetic sequence of appearances (plumage and soft parts) in one species, beginning with the juvenile plumage (JUV) at left and ending with the full adult condition (AD) at right. The numbers show representative ages for the intermediate appearances and, for the adult, the age at which the full adult appearance is normally first acquired. A light bill and, in some species, a dark iris characterize the pre-adult appearance. After Hardy (1973).

offspring, as well as among unrelated breeders. The ability of some birds in their first year of life to take priority at food sources ("dominance") over established breeders has so far been found only in Mexican and piñon jays (Balda & Balda, 1978; Barkan et al., 1981) and might be related to the inheritance of territory—a point currently under study.

Individual Variation in α Within a Species

In addition to variation among species in α and in consequent behavior of individuals, there is conspicuous variation within species, as already suggested for babblers in Fig. 5.1. Table 5.2 reveals some of the variation among individual Mexican jays. A few rare individuals have bred successfully at age 2 (with an older mate), but the fraction of birds breeding at a given age does not asymptote until age 4, at about 66% (A). Breeding success (at least one young has reached banding age) does not asymptote until age 5 (B). Even for the best breeders, breeding success varies greatly from year to year. The fraction of older birds for whom we have no evidence of nesting (perennial helpers) is quite large in Mexican jays. It decreases with age (C) but does not asymptote at zero. Instead, even by age 3, over half have never tried to breed; and at older ages, around 10% seem to be perennial helpers. In terms of successful nesting, even at

TABLE 5.2

Developmental Changes in Breeding Status in an Arizona Population of the Mexican Jay. Data are for all Birds of Precisely Known Age (Banded as Nestlings or Yearlings) 1969–81. As the Differences Between the Sexes are Small, the Sexes are Combined Here.

	Age in Years								
	1	*2*	*3*	*4*	*5*	*6*	*7*	*8*	*9–12*
A	0	23	42	66	60	62	70	71	100
B	0	.07	.23	.55	1.18	.72	.65	1.07	1.43
N_1	141	102	79	64	40	29	20	14	7
C	100	79	51	22	10	12	13	11	
D	100	97	88	72	54	44	43	39	
N_2	145	108	82	64	41	32	23	18	

A. Percentage of the number of birds alive at the stated age (N_1) for whom a nesting attempt was observed at that age. Data are for successful and unsuccessful nests. A small fraction of nest attempts went undetected; the actual percentage should, therefore, be slightly larger.

B. Age-specific reproductive success. Nestlings of banding age (c. 14 days) produced per bird.

N_1 Sample sizes for A and B.

C. Percentage of the birds that lived at least to the stated age who had no nesting record by that age, i.e., before alpha.

D. Percentage of the birds that lived at least to the stated age who had never fledged young.

N_2 Sample sizes for C and D.

age 5 over 50% of the individual jays have never fledged young. Only by age 6 or 7 is a bird likely to have fledged at least one young.

Reliance on dominance as an exclusive key to future breeding by an individual appears tentatively to be unreliable in Mexican jays. One individual that bred at age 2 was a male who was not the dominant male in his unit. The potential causes of such variation in α, including dominance, are currently being studied.

Signals of Immaturity

In several species of communal birds young individuals retain a distinctive color pattern at least through their first year and sometimes longer, as shown in Figs 5.1 and 5.2. The duration and conspicuousness of these youth signals vary among species of a genus, as shown for the *Cissilopha* subgenus of *Cyanocorax* jays in Fig. 5.2. The signals vary within species, being present in Arizona *A. ultramarina* but absent in the Texas population (Table 5.1). In Arizona *A. ultramarina* these markings can easily be used by a human observer to distinguish individual young from each other, but their adaptive value, if any, is unknown.

Trends

Population Consequences

The two extremes in the spectrum of animal sociality are the ants among the eusocial insects, on the one hand, and the many birds and mammals that breed normally with no more aid than the mother and sometimes the father provide. As previously described, further help may come from additional individuals who, for a variety of reasons, find themselves in a nonbreeding condition. Between these extremes in the trend toward greater sociality, the disposition of the nonbreeders is important. The nonbreeeders may be divided for simplicity into two categories, those that leave and lack territories, termed floaters, and those that stay in their natal unit, here termed helpers. The fraction of the population existing in each of these categories, breeders, floaters, and helpers, is shown for a range of species in Fig. 5.3.

In colonizing species (selected for high birth rate and much dispersal) a surplus of nonbreeders is rare (Fig. 5.3A). In noncolonizers (low birth rate; less dispersal) a surplus is more likely to accumulate. In most species surplus individuals exist as nonterritorial birds often termed floaters. Estimates of their proportion in a population are difficult and speculative, but Smith (1978, p. 579) estimated that 50% of her marked population of rufous-collared sparrows (*Zonotrichia capensis*) were floaters; and removal experiments suggest that the proportion of floaters may be substantial in many species (Brown, 1969; Klomp, 1972; see also Rappole, Warner, & Ramos, 1977), as in Fig. 5.3B. Such condi-

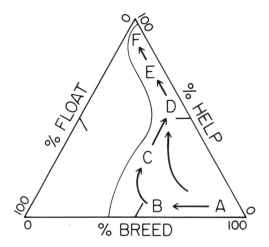

FIG. 5.3. Population fractions in various social systems involving helpers, floaters and breeders. Axes are percentages. At each point in the triangle the percentages sum to 100. A. High-dispersal species with high fecundity and no floaters or helpers. B. Territorial species with floaters but no helpers. C. Communal-colonial birds and other social systems with mixtures of breeders, helpers and floaters. D. and E. Territorial communal birds with variable numbers of helpers but few if any floaters. F. Eusocial species: many helpers, few breeders or floaters. Arrows suggest trends.

tions in a sedentary population create a situation in which it may be more favorable for the parents of a young bird to let it remain with them rather than to cause it to leave ''before its time.''

In most colonial birds there is no feeding territory, and the young may or may not associate with their parents. These are not necessarily colonizing species in the sense used above. Here the word colony refers to the dispersion pattern (not dispersal), which is characterized by clumping of nests. In the piñon jay (*Cyanocephalus gymnorhinus*) most young remain in the colony home range but do not aid their parents (Balda & Bateman, 1971), a situation not far from B in Fig. 5.3. In the pied kingfisher (*Ceryle rudis*) 12% of one population and 31% of another was composed of helpers, and probably even more nonbreeding birds existed in the population (Reyer, 1980). A larger percentage of the population may occur as helpers in territorial species (Fig. 5.3D). For the African yellow-billed shrike (*Corvinella corvina*) Grimes' (1980) data indicate that about 80% of the population is composed of nonbreeding helpers. In the Mexican jay the percentage of helpers in the population over a 9-year period varied from 41 to 82 with a mean of 67% (unpublished data). The extreme shown in E of Fig. 5.3 is not found in birds, but it corresponds roughly to the naked mole-rat (*Heterocephalus glaber*; Jarvis, 1981) and to many eusocial insects.

Prolonged Immaturity

The retention of traits that are characteristic of a brief and early developmental stage into older ages has received many names and much discussion (Gould, 1977; Pierce & Smith, 1978). Both neoteny (Brown, 1963) and paedogenesis (Geist, 1977) have been used to describe this phenomenon in communal birds, but since the use of such terms seems to cause more confusion than clarity, I will not assign them here. This trend can be identified by comparison among species. It is exemplified in the genus *Aphelocoma,* which retains the nestling bill coloration into the second year of life in the most social population (Arizona) while losing it at the time of fledging in less social forms (Table 5.1). Prolonged immaturity is strikingly illustrated in the *Cissilopha* jays (Fig. 5.2) and babblers (Fig. 5.1).

This prolongation of the juvenile period probably involves also a prolonged dependence of the young on their natal social unit. Mexican jays can sometimes be seen begging for food and being fed up to 12 months after hatching, although this is unusual. They are probably dependent in other ways too for a much longer period. Communal species profit from the vigilance of the unit, from the resources of the territory that is defended by the unit, from the nests and body heat of the group if they roost together, and in other ways. This association may be interpreted as extended parental care, which presumably benefits both parents and offspring.

A conspicuous aspect of this prolonged dependency is an extended period of immaturity. Among communal species that defer breeding we can distinguish both obligate and facultative immaturity. For example, in the grey-crowned babbler (Fig. 5.1) the gonads are tiny and nonfunctional in the first year in both sexes, intermediate in size in the second year, and reach full size and function by the third year. Obligate immaturity corresponds to the period of nonfunctional gonads. Facultative immaturity corresponds to the later period during which it is thought that failure to breed is caused by the social or energetic environment, rather than by a physiological limitation of gonadal function.

Earlier Determination of Helper Status

The age of caste determination is a focus of interest, especially in the social insects. In the least social species, such as the solitary wasp *Sphex ichneumoneus* (Brockmann & Dawkins, 1979), determination is late; there are no workers, but breeders may share a burrow (this condition has some similarities to the sharing of a territory). Among birds, male Galapagos hawks and southern hemisphere skuas may share a territory and a female. Thus, each male may care for young of his own and of the other male, being in effect both a breeder and a helper. In these cases determination occurs after or at the stage of initiation of reproduction. In the beta, or subordinate, foundresses in paper wasps (*Polistes*) role determination is settled by dominance interactions resulting in little or no direct reproduction by the beta female (Metcalf & Whitt, 1977; Noonan, 1981). A partial parallel among birds might be in the Australian fairy wrens (*Malurus* spp.), where the helper status of the beta male is determined also by dominance at breeding age.

Role determination at an earlier age, in an immature condition, is characteristic of the honeybee (*Apis mellifera*) and of the birds that depend conspicuously on helpers, such as the grey-crowned babbler (Fig. 5.1) and the Mexican jay. The trend is toward determination of helper status at earlier ontogenetic stages in those species that are more toward the eusocial extreme. Although it is true that birds differ from insects in lacking sterile castes, they may be compared in terms of a more general parameter, namely, the age-specific probability of reaching reproductive status at age x,F_x, if they choose to make the attempt (Brown, 1978; Emlen's ψ, 1982a). This is presumably low for a young helper in species with delayed reproduction. In the grey-crowned babbler the probability that a one-year old will survive to reproductive status is about .5 or less. In Mexican jays it seems that for certain individuals F_x is much lower still, since some never do reproduce even though they may live several years beyond the usual α (Table 5.2). The trend is for earlier determination of role as F at earlier ages becomes smaller.

Relative Permanence of Helper Status: Variability in F_x

The existence of an ontogenetic process of role or caste determination implies some variation among species in degree of reversibility. For example, in the extremely eusocial insects, queens and workers rarely change roles, although some workers may lay male eggs. More generally, in the social insects, however, the probability of switching roles, particularly from worker to queen, is a variable that is often greater than zero. The probability of a switch from nonbreeder to queen may be low in honeybees but high among *Polistes* wasp foundresses.

In birds, the probability that an individual will be able to attain breeding status at a given age, x, is a variable, F_x. In a population of communal birds the proportion of birds breeding increases with age, as shown in Fig. 5.1 for the grey-crowned babbler. For individuals, however, there seems to be considerable variation in F_x at a given age. For some individual Mexican jays, for example, α comes early in life (2 years); for most individuals, at about 4 years; and for others, later or never (Table 5.2). In other words, for some individuals in some species F_x is relatively low compared to other individuals of the same age, while in other species F_x is relatively high and less variable for any age. In the more social species the mean of F_x tends to be lower at early ages than in the less social ones. Probably the variance tends to be greater, with the result that a smaller fraction of individuals at an early age will actually reach reproductive status.

The extreme of this trend has yet to be discovered in a bird, but it seems to have been found in a vertebrate. In the naked mole-rat (*Heterocephalus glaber*), Jarvis (1981) has suggested that there might be a critical period early in life during which determination of those individuals destined to become queen mother occurs. If an existing queen disappears, she is replaced not by the oldest female worker but by a younger female who has not passed the critical age.

Recapitulation

In a survey of ontogenetic patterns in communal birds we have seen variation involving the stage of onset of helping, its duration, termination and permanence, and the retention of juvenile traits, both behavioral and morphological. This variability probably relates to the ecological importance of mutalistic social relationships, which we consider next.

THE SELECTION PRESSURES

Three Theories

Controversy exists about the selection pressures that have been important in the origin, maintenance, and further evolution of helping behavior in birds and mammals. Three theories will be considered.

1. Helping has evolved purely by the mechanisms of classical or direct selection as it was understood in the 1950s (involving kin selection in the form of aid to descendent but not nondescendent relatives). Altruism does not occur.
2. Helping has evolved purely by the mechanism of indirect selection, requiring aid to nondescendent relatives and altruism.
3. Helping has evolved by complex combinations of direct and indirect selection with origins from direct selection and, in some cases, further evolution by a combination of direct and indirect selection. Altruism may or may not occur and is not required.

Theory 1 seems to be favored by Zahavi (1974, 1976, 1981), Woolfenden (1976; Woolfenden & Fitzpatrick, 1978), Ligon and Ligon (1978a; Ligon, 1981a), Verbeek and Butler (1981), Birkhead (1981), and Koenig and Pitelka (1981), although it is often difficult to judge just where a given author stands on this matter. The principal onus and point of attack of these authors seems to be theory 2.

Theory 2, sometimes incorrectly assigned to me (Ligon & Ligon, 1978a; Woolfenden, 1981, p. 257; Woolfenden & Fitzpatrick, 1978), is a straw man (Brown, 1978). There has been no serious scientific publication to my knowledge that advocates theory 2 as an explanation for the evolution of helping in birds or mammals. On the other hand, kin selection has received much speculative and theoretical attention in the natural process of evaluating a new theory; and, in retrospect, its importance seems to have been exaggerated by popularizers.

Theory 3 was an attempt to combine the best from theories 1 and 2, that is, from the classical and the modern (Brown, 1969, 1974; Emlen, 1982a, 1982b; Ricklefs, 1975; Vehrencamp, 1979, 1980). My own version postulated an origin of helping based on any ecological conditions that promoted a surplus of nonbreeding birds, in other words based on direct selection. Later evolutionary phases of helping involved indirect selection also.

Helper status involves a combination of behaviors. It results from a series of decisions. The above way of viewing the controversy obscures these factors, lends itself to the method of advocacy, and tends to polarize and oversimplify a complex problem.

Three Decisions

We may approach problems concerning the evolutionary adaptiveness of behavior by treating the performance of a particular behavior as the outcome of a decision that is made, consciously or unconsciously, by the animal's nervous system making use of the information available to it about the internal and external environments. Individuals that make decisions allowing them to survive and reproduce tend thereby to increase the frequency of their genes in the next generation relative to the genes of individuals whose decisions result in death or nonreproduction. If the predisposition to make a particular correct decision is influenced by genetic differences between successful and unsuccessful individuals, then natural selection can be said to act to favor decisions that are correct under the circumstances. In withdrawal from pain, for example, the nervous system evaluates the noxious stimulus and usually decides to withdraw the appropriate part of the body. In this case the animal is strongly predisposed to make the correct decision.

The physiological mechanisms by which such adaptive decisions are made do not concern us here. It is the consequences of such decisions to the reproductive success of individuals with which we are concerned, for these determine the course of natural selection in a population by acting upon the predispositions of many individuals to make correct decisions. In brief, a "correct" decision is the one that maximizes the individual's inclusive fitness. In the following discussion, therefore, we assume that the behaviors specified, namely those involved in reproduction, dispersal, and "parental" care, have been influenced by natural selection. Justification for such assumptions can be found in textbooks of animal behavior and behavior genetics (e.g., Brown, 1975; Ehrman & Parsons, 1981). Individuals do not, of source, calculate the consequences of each decision in terms of inclusive fitness. They do, however, commonly react to cues and contexts in a way that is correlated with more tangible perceived rewards, involving food, sex, and security. These rewards are typically closely correlated with components of inclusive fitness. In the following discussion this logical linkage is implicit.

Three decisions made by a helper can be considered separately: (1) to attempt breeding or delay it, (2) to remain in the natal territory, usually with the parents, or not, (3) to provide alloparental care (Wilson, 1975) or not. Most authors have neglected these distinctions and have discussed helping as one decision (e.g., Rowley, 1981; Vehrencamp, 1979; Woolfenden & Fitzpatrick, 1978).

1. To Breed or Not

Breeding is delayed in many noncommunal species. Clearly these individuals do not delay breeding altruistically in order to benefit from indirect fitness by becoming helpers because in noncommunal species helping does not occur. This decision is likely to be made on the basis of anticipated effects on future fecundity and risks of survival both to parents and their potential offspring (Stearns & Crandall, 1981; Wiley, 1974) and may involve energy-budget considerations stemming from the acquisition of skills at foraging and dealing with companions (as discussed above).

2. To Stay or Leave—Mutualistic Sharing

Given that a bird has opted for nonbreeding, it must then decide whether to stay home (with the consent of its parents) or to leave. Those who leave may either join another territorial unit or exist as floaters, either in a flock of nonterritorial individuals or in the "underworld" (Smith, 1978), lurking inconspicuously among the interstices of established territories.

In any case and regardless of kinship, the bird must maintain a favorable energy balance if it is to survive to breed at a later time. Many noncommunal birds and mammals choose to live in a nonbreeding group as the best way to survive. Consequently, it has always been clear that such decisions are often more influenced by energy and risk than by kinship and that kinship is probably rarely important in many mutualistic relationships, such as occur in flocking sparrows, herding mammals, and schooling fish.

Therefore, it has been proposed that staying with the parents in a territorial group originated in an environment in which group living was more economical for individuals than living alone or in pairs (Brown, 1969). For nonbreeders during the breeding season their participation in the shared costs of the group provides them a better place to survive than they might otherwise have. For breeders, their additional costs may also be cut in a variety of ways by the nonbreeders.

These concepts have been developed in a simple mathematical model (Brown, 1982), but a graphical portrayal conveys the essence of the model (Fig. 5.4).

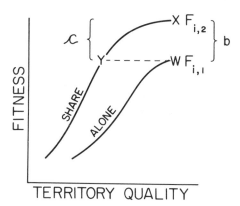

FIG. 5.4.   The threshold of sociality for a lone territory owner occurs when the net fitness in a potentially shared territory, Y, equals the net fitness alone on the same territory, W. b = benefit due to cost-sharing of defense and other tasks ($X - W$). c = cost of loss in resources ($X - Y$).

The fitness of an individual alone on a territory may be conceived to vary with the quality of the territory, as shown for the curve $F_{i,1}$, in Fig. 5.4. The first subscript, i, designates the territory quality by rank, and the second subscript gives the size of the social unit on it. Territories are presumed to fill up in order from best to worst, that is, from right to left. The addition of an individual is conceived to confer a benefit, b, in terms of aid in sharing costs such as defense and vigilance, and a cost, c, in terms of reduction in territory quality through consumption of food and other effects. In Fig. 5.4 the benefit of adding an individual to a given territory is the vertical distance between the curves $F_{i,1}$ and $F_{i,2}$. The benefit in the best territory is the vertical distance, WX. The cost of adding an individual is the vertical distance between X and Y. The result in this case is that the fitness of a lone bird on the best territory is equal to that of sharing with a second bird on the same territory. This can be considered the *threshold of sociality* for the original owner of the best territory. An increase in b or a decrease in c will cause the threshold to be crossed toward sociality.

A subordinate individual seeking a territory will have a choice between taking a lower ranking territory alone, such as at Z in Fig. 5.5, or sharing the best territory. If the result of sharing is a fitness between X and Y for both parties, it should be desirable for both to share, since the fitness of the dominant would be above W and the subordinate above Z. A zone of conflict exists where sharing would raise the subordinate's fitness above Z but would lower the dominant's fitness below W and Y. Under these conditions we should expect the subordinate to continually attempt sharing with the dominant and the latter to refuse. If sharing lowers fitness for both parties below V, then each would be below its respective sociality threshold for the best territory; each would be better off alone.

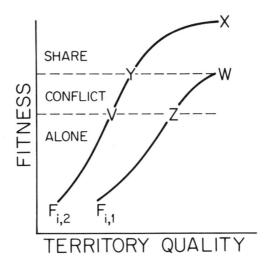

FIG. 5.5. Conditions for ecological conflict of interest between a dominant and subordinate. W = dominant alone on best territory. Z = subordinate alone on best available territory. Y = lowest tolerable fitness for sharing by dominant. V = lowest tolerable fitness for sharing by subordinate. The zone of conflict is defined above by the threshold of sociality of the dominant (dashed line through Y and W) and below by the threshold of sociality of the subordinate (dashed line through V and Z).

In this model both dominant and subordinate may alter their behavior to affect each other's sociality. A subordinate might bring the dominant in the zone of conflict above its sociality threshold (Y) either by lowering costs or raising benefits to the dominant, thereby benefiting the subordinate too by enabling it to share the best territory. A dominant could take advantage of this possibility to raise its own fitness by depressing that of the subordinate. So long as this social suppression maintained the subordinate's fitness above Z, the subordinate should tolerate it. Otherwise, it can leave.

This simple ecological model reveals how competition may persist within a cooperative social relationship. In these cases the fitness axis can be in energy or fitness. The latter can be in direct fitness or inclusive fitness. The addition of indirect fitness would change the costs and benefits to each participant, depending on relatedness, but it would not alter the basic nature of the conflict, which is fundamentally ecological.

Figs. 5.4 and 5.5 show the situation for adding an individual so as to increase unit size from 1 to 2. Similar logic applies at any unit size (i.e., from n to $n+1$). So long as all members and potential members of a unit are above their own threshold for the new group size, addition of a member should be favored.

Situations of this sort are likely to impart unequal costs and benefits to various group members depending on seniority, dominance, and other factors. Sharing tempts cheating, yet sharing persists even without close relatedness probably for two reasons. In a Prisoner's Dilemma situation Tit-for-tat is a stable strategy in most natural contexts (Axelrod & Hamilton, 1981; J. S. Brown, Sanderson, & Michod, 1982). Also many mutualisms are not Prisoner's Dilemmas; cooperation may pay more than cheating regardless of the "opponent's" behavior, even in single games (Brown, 1983b).

The energy costs and benefits of mutualistic relationships have received little attention. Recent work suggests that energetics are important in flocking sparrows (reviewed in Pulliam and Millikan, 1982) and in nonbreeding territorial wagtails (*Motacilla alba,* Davies & Houston, 1981), but these are not communal species. Though no panacea, this approach may provide some fresh insights into the individual decisions concerning group membership.

It has long been clear from field studies on color-banded populations that dispersal is much reduced in communal birds (Greenwood, 1980; Rowley, 1965). It has usually been presumed that this reduction is caused ultimately by the reduced chances of finding a suitable breeding territory with mate by the method of leaving home (low F_x) and by reduced chances of survival (Brown, 1969, and many later authors). Data are rare on this point; but Rowley (1981) has estimated that for a one-year-old male potential helper in the splendid wren (*Malurus splendens*) the chances of acquiring a breeding territory with mate are four times better by staying home than by leaving in its first year.

3. To be an Alloparent or Not?

Given that an individual has chosen not to attempt breeding and that it has chosen to remain in its natal territory, should it then act as an alloparent? For some individuals the answer seems to be no, since they persist in their natal territories or home range even without significant feeding of the nestlings of the breeders (Australian magpie, *Gymnorhina,* Carrick, 1972; crow, *Corvus,* Verbeek and Butler, 1981; piñon jay, Balda & Bateman, 1971; prairie dog, *Cynomys,* Hoogland, 1982). If such nonhelpers were to do significant damage, on average, to parental inclusive fitness, their parents would be selected to drive them away (Brown, 1969, 1982; Gaston, 1978b). Nonhelpers may still benefit breeders through their vigilance toward predators and toward rival territory owners. In typical communal species, however, non-breeders do contribute alloparental care to the breeders. Why? Some potential answers are discussed below.

4. Combining the Three Questions

To consider ways of approaching this question, it is useful first to consider several possible effects of a helper on its own inclusive fitness in the context of our three questions combined. An individual should choose to stay home, forego breeding, and be a helper when its expected inclusive fitness from helping, E_H, exceeds its expected, inclusive fitness from breeding, E_B,

$$E_H > E_B. \qquad (1)$$

Both E_H and E_B can each be broken down into direct and indirect components, corresponding to the classical and modern components of inclusive fitness (effects on descendent and nondescendent kin or co-gene-carriers). Each of these can be further subdivided into present and future components, resulting in four components for each, namely, present direct fitness, D; future direct fitness, d; present indirect fitness, I; and future indirect fitness, i (Brown, 1980). Table 5.3

TABLE 5.3

Components of Inclusive Fitness for the Breeding and Nonbreeding (Helping) Options of a Potential Helper at age x. Assume (1) a Steady-State Population; (2) if Breeding Chosen, Bird does not Help Again; (3) if Helping Chosen, Bird Chooses Breeding the Following Years; (4) One Breeding Pair per Unit

| | Breeding | |
	Present	Future
Direct	$D_{B,x} = m_x r_B$	$d_{B,x} = r_B \sum\limits_{y}^{\infty} l_y m_y$
Indirect	$I_{B,x} \sim 0$	$i_{B,x} \sim 0$

| | Helping | |
	Present	Future
Direct	$D_{H,x} \sim 0$	$d_{H,x} = r_B \sum\limits_{y}^{\infty} l'_y m'_y$
Indirect	$I_{H,x} = \sum\limits_{R} h_{x,R} r_{HR}$	$i_{H,x}$: See Text

B = breeder. H = helper. R = recipient of help. y = future ages. m_x = age specific fecundity of breeder. m_y = future fecundities if breeding chosen. m'_y = future fecundities if helping chosen. r_B = relatedness of breeder to its own offspring, usually 0.5. l_y = survivorship at future ages if breeding chosen, when $l_y = 1.0$. l'_x = survivorship at future ages if helping chosen; $l_x = 1.0$. r_{HR} = relatedness of helper to recipient. h_x = age-specific increment to recipient's m_x. In this paper the symbols D, d, I and i are used for the components of inclusive fitness, rather than for effects on the components of inclusive fitness, as in my previous papers.

shows the components of D, d, I and i for the breeding option, E_B, and the nonbreeding helping option E_H, for a steady state population. The complexity of the question may now be apparent.

The criterion for deciding to be a helper may now be written as

$$D_H + d_H + I_H + i_H > D_B + d_B + I_B + i_B. \tag{2}$$

Omitting terms that approximate zero this becomes

$$d_H + I_H + i_H > D_B + d_B. \tag{3}$$

This formulation reveals the futility of the preoccupation of some authors (e.g., Emlen, 1978; Ligon, 1981a; Ligon & Ligon, 1978a) with the question, "Is helping altruism?" If helping were altruistic $(D_B + d_B) > d_H$ and $(d_H - D_B - d_B)$ would be negative, an interesting though unlikely event (Brown, 1978; Brown & Brown, 1981b). The important question, however, is whether $(I_H + i_H)$ is large or small relative to $(d_H - d_B - D_B)$ when $E_H > E_B$, or in other words, the relative magnitude of the indirect and direct effects of helping on inclusive fitness, when choosing the helping option. Note that the magnitude of $(I_H + i_H)$ is independent of the sign of $(d_H - d_B - D_B)$. In other words, the importance of indirect selection is revealed not by the sign of the direct effects but by the contribution of $I_H + i_H$ in tipping the balance of E_H over E_B.

Expression 3 also reveals the inadvisability of the term "kin altruism" (Vehrencamp, 1979). Some authors (e.g., Koenig & Pitelka, 1981; Ligon, 1981a) have used kin altruism as a synonym for kin selection, which it is not. "Kin altruism" implies that kin selection requires altruism; but, as revealed in expression 3, in kin selection or indirect selection $(d_H - D_B - d_B)$ need not be negative (the condition required for altruism, using the definition of Hamilton, 1964). It is quite possible in theory to have kin selection or indirect selection without altruism and altruism without kin or indirect selection.

Where do we stand in evaluating the components of E_H? Let's look at the main ones briefly.

I_H and i_H

Since Rowley's (1965) study of *Malurus cyaneus* there has been positive support for I_H being measurably large; however, there were several uncontrolled variables (Brown & Balda, 1977; Gaston, 1978a; Lack, 1968; Zahavi, 1974). These were finally controlled in an experimental study that showed reduction of reproductive success when helpers were removed under controlled conditions (Brown et al., 1982).

The existence of i_H was overlooked until recently and its magnitude has not yet been estimated. It would be positive if, by helping, a one-year-old helper learned to become a better helper the following year, which might happen in Mexican jays since they do improve with age. It would also be positive if the additional young attributable to a helper in one year became helpers to the parents of the helper in a subsequent year (the usual case). Probably the overall effect will prove to be small, but it should be at least considered.

d_H

Future reproductive success is most importantly affected by the individual's decision whether to stay or leave and whether to attempt breeding or not. These effects, which have already been discussed, are distinct from the decision to be an alloparent or not.

Three mechanisms have been suggested by which alloparental behavior per se (given that the decision to stay home and not breed has already been made) might increase a helper's reproductive success in future years.

The Augmentation Hypothesis.   Woolfenden (1976; Woolfenden & Fitzpatrick, 1978) suggested that the augmentation of group size (G) caused by the additional reproductive success of the breeders due to the helper, a, would increase the conditional probability that a male helper would be able to get a territory and mate if an attempt were made (F_x).

Woolfenden and Fitzpatrick described a plausible mechanism for this effect, but they have not yet demonstrated the effect itself. According to their hypothesis the probability that a male helper will acquire a territory and mate in the following year is a function of its group size, $F_x = f(G)$. Group size in the Florida scrub jay would normally increase through the parents' efforts, even without the aid of a male helper, by about 0.6 independent young for an experienced pair. With a helper the increase averages about 1.0. Thus the group would go from 3 to 3.6 without the nonbreeder's alloparental care and from 3 to 4.0 with it. The augmentation attributed to the helper, a, is $4.0 - 3.6 = 0.4$ independent young. Although the hypothesis was enthusiastically received by some field workers, none of them has attempted to test it. First it is necessary to test that $F_x = f(G)$. This conditional probability, F_x, would be difficult to estimate, but the fraction of individuals breeding in a given cohort of males, B_x, can be observed. Consequently, we can test the hypothesis $B_x = f(G)$. Second, it is necessary to test the hypothesis that the small augmentation attributable to a helper, a, causes a measurable increase in B_x, i.e., that $B'_x = f(G + a) > f(G) = B_x$.

The mechanism of the proposed effect involves enlarging the group territory and budding off a piece of it for a male helper. The hypothesis does not explain female alloparental care since females do not acquire territories this way. Also, most males do not acquire their territory this way. Though the enthusiasm for this hypothesis has been premature, it does have possibilities.

A slightly different mechanism has been suggested by Ligon (1981b) for the green woodhoopoe (*Phoeniculus purpureus*). It too invokes the idea that the young raised by the helper increase the helper's chance to acquire breeding status. "First, older helpers clearly gain by helping to produce younger flock mates in that the younger birds can be 'used' to obtain breeding status for the older (former) helper and to feed and otherwise care for the older bird's own nestlings'' (p. 242).

This hypothesis suffers from the same difficulties as the Woolfenden version; namely, it has not actually been shown with data that $B_x = f(G)$ or that the augmentation attributable to the helper causes a measurable increase in B'_x for the helper, i.e., that $B'_x > B_x$. Ironically, there is an additional objection to the Ligon hypothesis that stems from their own data. The Ligons (1978b) claim that no augmentation is attributable to the helper. ''Our data over three years do not convincingly demonstrate that more helpers per flock yield more surviving young woodhoopoes'' (Ligon, 1981b, p. 242). If anything, they say, there is an inverse relationship. In other words, Ligon is saying that parents produce just as many young without as with helpers, i.e., a = 0. If this is true—a point worth reexamining—then there is no augmentation at all and the augmentation hypothesis, consequently, must be rejected for woodhoopoes.

More generally I have argued elsewhere that each member of a social unit may have its own optimal group size (Brown 1982), and that it is to the individual's advantage when below its optimum to behave so as to increase or at least maintain the size of the group.

Learning.   It has often been suggested that a young bird learns to be a better breeder by an apprenticeship as a helper (Brown, 1969, 1974; Ricklefs, 1975, and nearly every later writer). Consistent with this idea is the observation that yearling helpers are less effective at feeding nestlings than older helpers in Mexican jays (Brown, 1970, 1972) and probably babblers (Brown, Dow, Brown, & Brown, 1978). Moreover, naive brown jay (*Psilorhinus morio*) helpers showed improvement as the nestlings grew (Lawton & Guindon, 1981), though this may have been caused partly by the increasing age, size, and stimulus strength of the nestlings. Improvement in foraging probably occurs too, but it is to be expected whether a young bird helps or not. Thus the mere observation of improvement with age does not by itself argue that alloparenting per se is responsible. What is needed to test the learning hypothesis is to demonstrate that birds who have alloparented as nonbreeders average more reproductive success in subsequent years (as a result of helping) than birds who did not alloparent or breed for an equivalent time period.

Socialization With or Without Augmentation.   Brown and Brown (1980) have suggested tentatively that helpers enlist social affiliation from the young they feed by the very act of feeding them. They observed unrelated Mexican jays regularly feeding each other's young. By becoming known as individuals to the fed young, the feeders might increase the chances that the young might become socially bonded with the feeder and benefit the feeder in a future year. The helper, in this hypothesis, ''buys'' the loyalty of the young by feeding it repeatedly.

In an earlier paper I referred to this relationship between the totally naive young and its feeders as "unconscious reciprocity" (Brown, 1978, p. 136). I suggest that *generational mutualism* is a preferable term, since "reciprocity" tends to imply conscious score keeping of a tit-for-tat nature.

Aside from anecdotal observations, such as the above, and the reasonable assumption that the young learn the identity of their fellow unit members around the age of fledging, there is virtually no systematic evidence for this hypothesis. It is worth testing.

D_B

The chances of breeding success, should it be attempted in the present season, are likely to be very low for a young bird, for reasons involving foraging ability, food availability, territorial behavior, age of mate, and energy budgets, as discussed above. The small value of D_B for a one-year-old male is one of the main reasons for $E_H > E_B$ in the splendid wren (Rowley, 1981).

d_B

The cost of reproduction (Williams, 1966) could be reflected in $d_{B,x}$. This cost represents the effects of the present reproductive effort on future fitness. Reproduction is probably very expensive when attempted prematurely (Stearns & Crandall, 1981), especially in communal animals in which F_x is low, resulting in low $d_{B,x}$. Even at maturity there is a suggestion in the splendid wren, pied kingfisher, and groove-billed ani of a severe cost to the survival of the incubating bird (Reyer, 1980; Rowley, 1981; Vehrencamp, 1978). This factor also seems to be important in causing $E_H > E_B$ at young ages. On the other hand, in older, successful breeders the young produced become an asset and may convert this cost into a net benefit (Brown & Brown, 1981b). By minimizing the negative effect of premature efforts at reproduction in the first few years on E_B, the life history of the grey-crowned babbler and many other communally breeding birds resembles the bet-hedging strategy of Stearns (1976; Brown, 1978).

5. The Third Question Reconsidered

The relative importance of the direct components in tipping the balance toward helping can be expressed as a simple fraction,

$$Q_I = (I_H + i_H)/(E_H - E_B). \tag{4}$$

Although not identical, Q_I resembles Vehrencamp's (1979) index of kin selection, I_K. Estimates of I_K made by Vehrencamp and Rowley (1981) are 0.51 for lions, 0.55 for Florida scrub jays, 1.89 for *Polistes* wasps, and 0.43 for the splendid wren.

As explained by Vehrencamp, values greater than 1.0 indicate altruism; values between 0 and 1 may be taken as fractions of the combined difference in inclusive fitness due to indirect effects in a mutualistic relationship.

Such estimates reveal that indirect fitness is not insigificant. Though a step in the right direction, they fail to answer the third and most vexatious question. The main factors contributing to the direct component in I_K or Q_I are those that affect the first two questions, namely dispersal, survival, costs of reproduction, and chances of success when attempting breeding under conditions of a surplus of potential breeders. On these points there has long been general agreement (Brown, 1969). These indices, therefore, do not reveal the relative importance of the more controversial, speculative components of d_H discussed above.

Mutualism

To qualify as mutualism a relationship between two individuals must result in a net gain to direct fitness for both, compared to individuals that do not choose the relationship. Therefore, in choosing helping it must be true for the helper that $d_H > d_B + D_B$ and for the recipient that $D_B^* + d_B^* > D_B + d_B$, where the left side is for help present and the right side is for help absent.

In mutualism the indirect fitness of the helper $(I_H + i_H)$ is not specified. Therefore, the hypothesis of mutualism is not necessarily mutually exclusive with an important role for indirect fitness, contrary to the implication of some authors (e.g., Ligon & Ligon, 1978a, 1982; Packer & Pusey, 1982). Indeed, in many cases of probable mutualism indirect fitness appears to be significant, even if some helpers and recipients are unrelated.

Of particular interest is the fact that in both mutualism and indirect selection an identical requirement exists. If breeder benefit from the helper is not present, then the hypotheses of mutualism and indirect selection must both be rejected. Since the Ligons have argued that there is no breeder benefit from helpers in the green woodhoopoe (see quote above), the hypothesis of mutualism, or "reciprocity" as they call it, must be rejected for their species along with hypotheses involving indirect selection. Since the case of the green woodhoopoe has been widely publicized as an example of "reciprocity" it is important that the lack of statistically significant, empirical evidence for such an interpretation not be overlooked.

That some aspects of a helper's life could be interpreted as "unconscious reciprocation" was noted by Brown (1978, p. 136) and Ligon and Ligon (1978a), who pointed out that the young reared by a helper might in a few years aid the former helper. To qualify as reciprocity in the more useful sense of the word however, "anticipation that the recipient will return the favor" must be demonstrated (Waltz, 1981). Therefore, it is safer to refer to such situations as long-term or generational mutualism (Brown, 1983), to avoid the issues of anticipation or conscious expectation of return of benefits.

The best evidence available for reciprocal aid giving in communal birds with short-term return of benefits was provided by Brown and Brown (1980), who showed that breeding Mexican jays fed each other's young indiscriminately.

Even in this case, however, indirect selection and anticipation remain complications. A mathematical theory for the evolution of helping and other cooperative behaviors based on mutualistic, short-term benefits was described by Brown (1982). This model illustrates the theoretical possibility of the evolution of several kinds of aid giving without the necessity of indirect selection or generational mutualism.

In a series of papers the Ligons have adapted the original augmentation hypothesis into a scenario referred to as "reciprocity." This interpretation is in need of critical appraisal. The stimulating but speculative nature of the augmentation hypothesis has already been discussed.

Ligon and Ligon (1978a) advocated "reciprocity" as an alternative to "kin-selected altruism," but this claim was based mainly on an incorrect rejection of indirect selection (see Brown, 1979, 1983) and on the use of "kin-selected altruism" as a straw man (see above). The Ligons' (1983) interpretation of "reciprocity" in the green woodhoopoe is suspect (see above). Ligon's (1983) survey of "reciprocity" repeats the same arguments and attempts to acquire support from Axelrod and Hamilton (1981); however, Ligon failed to consider that major assumptions made by Axelrod and Hamilton are not met in communal birds (see below).

Helping as a Prisoner's Dilemma

Recent game theoretic models of cooperation in animal groups (Axelrod & Hamilton, 1981; J. S. Brown et al., 1982) have stimulated a second look at the use of the Prisoner's Dilemma as a paradigm of cooperative social systems (Brown, 1983; Pulliam & Caraco, 1984). These models are useful for showing that cooperation can in theory evolve without indirect selection, even under assumptions that were formerly thought to favor noncooperation. There is a danger, however, that the current popularity of game-theory models may blind us to certain limitations of the Prisoner's Dilemma as a model for helping behavior.

Game theory and inclusive fitness are, of course, not theoretical alternatives but nicely complement each other (Axelrod & Hamilton, 1981)—despite such titles as "Cooperation . . . kin selection or game theory?" (Packer & Pusey, 1982). In the end this argument still boils down to the relative importance of direct and indirect components of inclusive fitness.

The most important failure is the assumption of symmetry or equality of participants. In many avian communal breeding systems dominance appears to determine which individuals breed (reviewed in Brown, 1978, p. 137). The introduction of asymmetry into the Prisoner's Dilemma makes cooperating easier if subordinates cannot gain by leaving (Fig. 5.5; see also Pulliam & Caraco, 1984). In most communally breeding species, male helpers have less access to breeding females than do male breeders. In a few species, females might be shared equally by two or more male breeders, but this remains to be confirmed genetically. The requirement of symmetry is probably rarely met. This is important because asymmetry may be a strong factor favoring indirect selection for helping.

Another violation of assumptions in the Prisoner's Dilemma is that helping is not a two-party game. It is a game involving at least three parties, the helper and the recipient as a potentially cooperative unit against other such units (Brown, 1982, 1983).

Still another failure is the requirement that cheating or defecting against a cooperator pays more than cooperation in single contests. This requirement forces us to ask just what a single contest is and over what period of time it is played. If the time period is trivially short, it may indeed pay to cheat, rob, or kill one's cooperator for that period, but over any realistic longer time period such a view appears highly contrived. It may, therefore, be more illuminating to use models based on realistic and specified time periods for the return of the benefits.

Ockham's Razor

Reviewing the evidence, it is clear that a helper can often increase the reproductive success of nondescendent relatives, contributing to the indirect fitness of the helper significantly. This effect has been demonstrated frequently under uncontrolled conditions (references in Brown, 1978; Emlen, 1978) and once under controlled conditions (Brown et al., 1982b). The magnitude of the effect has been measured and shown to be small relative to what an unaided pair can do (Brown, 1978; Brown & Brown, 1981b; Emlen, 1978). Though previously questioned (Brown & Balda, 1977; Lack, 1968; Zahavi, 1974; and others) and though not always demonstrable (Gaston, 1973, 1978a; Ligon & Ligon, 1978b), it is a generally accepted phenomenon (Oring, 1982) and constitutes good evidence for a real contribution of I_H to E_H. Furthermore, in such cases there should usually be an additional contribution to i_H.

In contrast, an effect of alloparenting per se on d_H has never been demonstrated or measured. Its existence is usually inferred when I_H appears to be negligible, such as when the author thinks that nonbreeding helpers are unrelated to the recipients (Faaborg, DeVries, Patterson, & Griffin, 1981; Kepler, 1977; Ligon & Ligon, 1978a; Reyer, 1980), or when $h_{x,R}$, the beneficial effect to the breeder (Table 5.3), is not significantly different from zero (Gaston, 1973, 1978a; Ligon & Ligon, 1978b; Zahavi, 1974). That alloparenting has positive effects on d_H is a plausible hypothesis, but until hypothesized effects are convincingly demonstrated by strong-inference tests (Platt, 1964), they can hardly be considered parsimonious explanations for the evolution of alloparenting per se.

It has been suggested that "kin selection" (presumably meaning exclusively indirect selection) is never a parsimonious hypothesis and that, in contrast, direct selection must always be more parsimonious (Zahavi, 1974). This is a misapplication of Ockham's razor. William of Ockham intended that the argument with the stronger evidence and the lesser reliance on speculation should be preferred over the argument with the weaker evidence and greater reliance on unsubstantiated ideas ("it is vain to do by more what can be done by fewer" in Hutchinson, 1978, p. 33). Were we to follow his advice, we would accept I_H (theory 2) and reject d_H (theory 1) as the main cause of alloparenting per se in most species. This conclusion, I believe, would be unfortunate. Surely we are not engaged in politics here; we desire not to "win" but instead to find the truth. Attempts to settle the issue by Ockham's razor are only postponing the day when we can settle the issue by strong-inference testing.

Dual Origins

Part of the difficulty in assessing the components of E_H is that the indirect effects must derive from preexisting behaviors that have evolved entirely via direct selection. For example, a nonbreeder stays on its natal territory because it is the best base on which to survive and seek a territory vacancy nearby (direct benefits), but in so doing it is set up to benefit its indirect fitness too, by providing care to its parents' offspring, behavior that might also benefit the helper's future, direct fitness. Thus, phase 1 "sets the stage" for phase 2 (Brown, 1974, p. 77; Emlen, 1982a, p. 40).

Similarly two sibling lions may cooperate in establishing themselves in a pride of females, benefiting their inclusive fitness both directly and indirectly (Bygott, Bertram, & Hanby, 1979). It is sometimes said that if a direct benefit occurs, that is enough to explain the evolution of the behavior. The error in such statements may be realized by reconsidering the criterion for choosing helping over breeding, $E_H > E_B$. It is the *sum* of components of E_H that must exceed the sum for E_B. The direct benefit to E_H alone, even though positive may not be sufficient to exceed E_B. The contribution from $I + i$ may be needed for E_H to exceed E_B.

Retrospective

In 1972 I delivered a paper about the evolution of "altruism" and cooperative breeding in jays (Brown, 1974) that was an elaboration of a theory outlined earlier (Brown, 1969) in the light of new data on Mexican jays. No claims were made that the theory applied to other birds; indeed, other mechanisms were suggested for some other groups, such as an excess of males over females. The theory had three parts: (1) an origin based purely on classical direct selection in a specified demographic context involving a surplus of potential breeders with its effects on dispersal and alpha, (2) a role for indirect selection in small family units, and (3) the inheritance of territories, especially in large social units and for high-quality territories. What has been the fate of these three concepts?

Phase 1 received widespread acceptance. The concept of habitat saturation has been embraced by many subsequent field workers (e.g., Emlen, 1982a; Koenig & Pietelka, 1981; Stacey, 1979; Woolfenden, 1975; Woolfenden & Fitzpatrick, 1978; to name a few). Some authors (Emlen, 1982a) seem to have been misled by the label that I attached to this phase, "K-selection phase." The text, however, revealed that the essential features of the model did not include K-selection or stable environments. These features can result from K-selection (hence the label) but also from bet-hedging in a variable environment (Brown, 1978, pp. 145–147; Stearns, 1976). Contrary to Emlen, my theory has never been limited to "stable environments" (see retraction by Emlen, 1983).

Phase 2, or indirect selection combined with direct selection, has been controversial. That an increment to the helper's indirect fitness results from helping in some species has finally been confirmed after much dispute (e.g., Brown et al., 1982b). The evidence for indirect selection is widespread and difficult now to refute.

Phase 3 relied heavily on the inheritance of territories and on differences in quality among territories. Quality differences have been documented for communal birds, for babblers (Brown & Balda, 1977; Brown & Brown, 1981b; Gaston, 1978a), acorn woodpeckers (Trail, 1980), and white-browed sparrow weavers (*Plocepasser mahali,* Lewis, 1981). Variations on the theme of territorial inheritance have been documented for Australian wrens (Rowley, 1965, 1981), jays (Brown & Brown, 1981a; Woolfenden & Fitzpatrick, 1978) and several other species of communal birds. This phase had something in common with trait-group selection (D. S. Wilson, 1975) in that "Individual genotypes are selected mainly as they function harmoniously in a flock." Although we cannot yet provide a strong inference test of this statement, it should be noted that the genetic structure of one population of babblers is suitable for trait-group selection (Johnson & Brown, 1980), and that social relationships within such groups do seem more harmonious than in similar sized flocks of noncommunal species.

In 1974 I proposed 14 "testable predictions" of the 3-phase theory. Most of these, especially the more important ones, have been confirmed; a few are testable only with difficulty. Some of the predictions have notable exceptions in non-corvid species, and there have been some semantic problems; but by and large, the agreement between these predictions and the results from subsequent field studies has been good.

Much has been learned about communal birds since 1974. Many species fit the jay model, but there are several interesting species that depart considerably from it, particularly in respect to mate sharing. The biggest development since 1974 has been an increased sensitivity to possibilities for mutualisms that are not dependent on kinship (although this is inherent in phase 1 of my 1969 and 1974 models). We now have theoretical models of mutualism (Axelrod & Hamilton, 1981; J. S. Brown et al., 1982; J. L. Brown, 1982), and scattered anecdotal data that are at least consistent with the theory; however, theorists and empiricists are still far apart in this realm, and much theoretical and empirical work will be required before the pieces of the puzzle reveal their picture.

CONCLUSION

Helping behavior in many animals characterizes a stage in development. This period may occur early, as in juveniles, late, as in breeders sharing a task, or at any time between, depending on species and circumstance. Consequently, to gain insight into the evolution of helping we must view it in the broader context of the individual's entire ontogeny. To do this it is convenient to treat ontogeny as a Markovian sequence of behavioral states. During its development the individual must frequently decide whether to stay in its present state or to move to another one. Even in relatively fixed sequences, such as nestling-fledgling-juvenile-helper-breeder, variability arises in the length of time in a state and in the ability to revert from a later state, such as breeder, to an earlier one, such as helping. Since many alternative states are available and since these may be assembled in many different orders, an indefinitely large number of sequences may occur.

In asocial species the sequence, or "ontogenetic trajectory" (Wiley, 1980), is relatively invariant. Sociality introduces additional contingencies. Species with prominent helping behavior are more flexible. Indeed, ontogenetic flexibility may be a hallmark of communaly breeding birds (Brown, 1978, p. 148).

In this review we first surveyed various ontogenetic sequences characteristic of helping species in the second section. Then in the third section we viewed the transitions between states of these sequences as decision processes and considered the costs and benefits of particular choices. This section introduces a new ecological model of social conflict that is relevant to parent-offspring conflict (Fig 5.5). The discussion of costs and benefits is presented in a newly expanded version of inclusive fitness theory. The particular constellations of costs and benefits responsible for "shaping" by natural selection the characteristic state sequences for various species are controversial. By analyzing costs and benefits as components of inclusive fitness an attempt is made to clarify some of the issues.

ACKNOWLEDGMENTS

I thank E. S. Gollin and his students as well as E. R. Brown and C. P. L. Barkan for comments. Research by the author was supported by the National Institute of Mental Health and by the National Science Foundation. Figures by R. Loos; typing by R. Lee.

REFERENCES

Andersson, M. (1976). Population ecology of the longtailed skua (*Stercorarius longicaudus* Vieill.). *Journal of Animal Ecology, 45*, 537–559.
Axelrod, R., & Hamilton, W. D. (1981). The evolution of cooperation. *Science, 211*, 1390–1396.

Balda, R. P., & Balda, J. H. (1978). The care of young pinon jays (*Gymnorhinus cyanocephalus*) and their integration into the flock. *Journal fur Ornithologie, 119,* 146–171.

Balda, R. P., & Bateman, G. C. (1971). Flocking and annual cycle of the pinon jay, *Gymnorhinus cyanocephalus. Condor, 73,* 287–302.

Barkan, C. P. L., Craig, J. L., Brown, J. L., Stewart, A. M., & Strahl, S. D. (1981). Dominance in social units of communal Mexican jays. *American Zoologist, 21,* 948.

Bertram, B. C. R. (1976). Kin selection in lions and in evolution. In P. P. G. Bateson & R. A. Hinde (Eds.), *Growing points of ethology.* Cambridge: Cambridge University Press.

Bertram, B. C. R. (1979). Ostriches recognize their own eggs and discard others. *Nature, 279,* 233–234.

Birkhead, M. E. (1981). The social behaviour of the Dunnock *Prunella modularis. Ibis, 123,* 75–84.

Brockmann, H. J., & Dawkins, R. (1979). Joint nesting in a digger wasp as an evolutionary stable preadaptation to social life. *Behaviour, 71,* 203–245.

Brown, J. L. (1963). Social organization and behavior of the Mexican jay. *Condor, 65,* 126–153.

Brown, J. L. (1964). The evolution of diversity in avian territorial systems. *Wilson Bulletin, 76,* 160–169.

Brown, J. L. (1969). Territorial behavior and population regulation in birds. *Wilson Bulletin, 81,* 293–329.

Brown, J. L. (1970). Cooperative breeding and altruistic behaviour in the Mexican jay, *Aphelocoma ultramarina. Animal Behaviour, 18,* 366–378.

Brown, J. L. (1972). Communal feeding of nestlings in the Mexican jay (*Aphelocoma ultramarina*): interflock comparisons. *Animal Behaviour, 20,* 395–403.

Brown, J. L. (1974). Alternate routes to sociality in jays with a theory for the evolution of altruism and communal breeding. *American Zoologist, 14,* 63–80.

Brown, J. L. (1975). *The evolution of behavior.* New York: Norton.

Brown, J. L. (1978). Avian communal breeding systems. *Annual Review of Ecology & Systematics, 9,* 123–155.

Brown, J. L. (1979). Another interpretation of communal breeding in green woodhoopoes. *Nature, 280,* 174.

Brown, J. L. (1980). Fitness in complex avian social systems. In H. Markl (Ed.), *Evolution of social behavior: Hypotheses and empirical tests.* Dahlem Konferenzen. Weinheim: Verlag Chemie.

Brown, J. L. (1982). Optimal group size in territorial animals. *Journal of Theoretical Biology, 95,* 793–810.

Brown, J. L. (1983). Cooperation—a biologists dilemma. In J. S. Rosenblatt (Ed.), *Advances in behavior,* New York: Academic Press.

Brown, J. L., & Balda, R. P. (1977). The relationship of habitat quality to group size in Hall's babbler (*Pomatostomus halli*). *Condor, 79,* 312–320.

Brown, J. L., & Brown, E. R. (1980). Reciprocal aid-giving in a communal bird. *Zeitschrift fur Tierpsychologie, 53,* 313–324.

Brown, J. L., & Brown, E. R. (1981a). Extended family system in a communal bird. *Science, 211,* 959–960.

Brown, J. L., & Brown, E. R. (1981b). Kin selection and individual selection in babblers. In R. D. Alexander & D. Tinkle (Eds.), *Natural selection and social behavior: Recent results and new theory.* New York: Chiron Press.

Brown, J. L., Brown, E. R., & Brown, S. D. (1982a). Morphological variation in a population of grey-crowned babblers: correlations with variables affecting social behavior. *Behavioral Ecology & Sociobiology, 10,* 281–287.

Brown, J. L., Brown, E. R., Brown, S. D., & Dow, D. D. (1982b). Helpers: Effects of experimental removal on reproductive success. *Science, 215,* 421–422.

Brown, J. L., Dow, D. D., Brown, E. R., & Brown, S. D. (1978). Effects of nestlings in the grey-crowned babbler (*Pomatostomus temporalis*). *Behavioral Ecology & Sociobiology, 4,* 43–59.

Brown, J. S., Sanderson, M. J., & Michod, R. E. (1982). The evolution of social behavior by reciprocation. *Journal of Theoretical Biology, 99,* 319–339.

Buckley, F. G., & Buckley, P. A. (1974). Comparative feeding ecology of wintering adult and juvenile royal terns (Aves: Laridae, Sterninae). *Ecology, 55,* 1053–1063.

Bygott, J. D., Bertram, B. C. R., & Hanby, J. P. (1979). Male lions in large coalitions gain reproductive advantages. *Nature, 282,* 839–841.

Carrick, R. (1972). Population ecology of the Australian black-backed magpie, royal penguin, and silver gull. In *Population ecology of migratory birds: A symposium.* United States Department Interior Wildlife Research Report 2.

Cole, L. C. (1954). The population consequences of life history phenomena. *Quarterly Review of Biology, 29,* 103–137.

Counsilman, J. L., & King, B. (1977). Ageing and sexing the grey-crowned babbler (*Pomatostomus temporalis*). *Babbler, 1,* 23–41.

Crook, J. H. (1962). The adaptive significance of pair formation types in weaverbirds. *Symposium of the Zoological Society, London, 8,* 57–70.

Crook, J. H. (1964). The evolution of social organization and visual communication in the weaver-birds (Ploceidae). *Behaviour Supplement, 10,* 1–178.

Crook, J. H. C. (1965). The adaptive significance of avian social organizations. *Symposium of the Zoological Society, London, 14,* 181–218.

Crook, J. H., & Gartlan, J. S. (1966). Evolution of primate societies. *Nature, 210,* 1200–1203.

Darwin, C. (1928). *The origin of species.* New York: Dutton. (First published in 1859.)

Davies, N. B., & Houston, A. I. (1981). Owners and satellites: The economics of territory defense in the pied wagtail, *Motacila alba. Journal of Animal Ecology, 50,* 157–180.

Davis, D. E. (1940). Social nesting habits of the smooth-billed ani. *Auk, 57,* 179–218.

Davis, D. E. (1942). The phylogeny of social nesting in the Crotophaginae. *Quarterly Review of Biology, 17,* 115–134.

Ehrman, L., & P. Parsons. (1981). *Behavior genetics.* New York: McGraw-Hill.

Emlen, S. T. (1978). Cooperative breeding. In J. R. Krebs & N. B. Davies (Eds.), *Behavioural ecology: An evolutionary approach.* Oxford: Blackwell.

Emlen, S. T. (1982a). The evolution of helping. I. An ecological constraints model. *American Naturalist, 119,* 29–39.

Emlen, S. T. (1982b). The evolution of helping. II. The role of behavioral conflict. *American Naturalist, 119,* 40–53.

Emlen, S. T. (1983). Erratum. *American Naturalist, 121,* 755.

Estes, R. D. (1974). Social organization of the African Bovidae. In V. Geist & F. Walther (Eds.), *The behavior of ungulates and its relation to management.* Morges: International Union for Conservation of Nature and Natural Resources.

Faaborg, J., De Vries, T., Patterson, C. B., & Griffin, C. R. (1980). Preliminary observations on the occurrence and evolution of polyandry in the Galapagos hawl (*Buteo galapagoensis*). *Auk, 97,* 581–590.

Gaston, A. J. (1973). The ecology and behaviour of the long-tailed tit. *Ibis, 115,* 330–351.

Gaston, A. J. (1978a). Demography of the jungle babbler *Turdoides striatus. Journal of Animal Ecology, 47,* 845–870.

Gaston, A. J. (1978b). The evolution of group territorial behavior and cooperative breeding. *American Naturalist, 112,* 1091–1100.

Geist, V. (1977). A comparison of social adaptations in relation to ecology in gallinaceous bird and ungulate societies. *Annual Review of Ecology and Systematics, 8,* 193–207.

Gould, S. J. (1977). *Ontogeny and phylogeny.* Cambridge, MA: Belknap Press.

Greenwood, P. J. (1980). Mating systems, philopatry and dispersal in birds and mammals. *Animal Behaviour 28,* 1140–1162.

Grimes, L. G. (1980). Observations of group behaviour and breeding biology of the yellow-billed shrike *Corvinella corvina. Ibis, 122,* 166–192.

Hamilton, W. D. (1964). The genetical evolution of social behavior. I & II. *Journal of Theoretical Biology, 7,* 1–51.

Hardy, J. W. (1973). Age and sex differences in the black-and-blue jays of Middle America. *Bird-Banding, 44,* 81–90.

Hoogland, J. L. (1982). Prairie dogs avoid extreme inbreeding. *Science, 215,* 1639–1641.

Hutchinson, G. E. (1978). *An introduction to population ecology.* New Haven: Yale University Press.

Jarman, P. J. (1974). The social organization of antelope in relation to their ecology. *Behaviour, 48,* 215–267.

Jarvis, J. U. M. (1981). Eusociality in a mammal: Cooperative breeding in naked mole-rat colonies. *Science, 212,* 571–573.

Johnson, M. S., & Brown, J. L. (1980). Genetic variation among trait groups and apparent absence of close inbreeding in grey-crowned babblers. *Behavioral Ecology and Sociobiology, 7,* 93–98.

Kepler, A. K. (1977). Comparative study of todies (Todidae) with emphasis on the Puerto Rican tody, *Todus mexicanus. Publication of the Nuttall Ornitholical Club, 16,* 1–190.

Klomp, H. (1972). Regulation of the size of bird populations by means of territorial behaviour. *Netherlands Journal of Zoology, 22,* 456–488.

Koenig, W. D., & Pitelka, E. H. (1981). Ecological factors and kin selection in the evolution of cooperative breeding in birds. In R. D. Alexander & D. W. Tinkle (Eds.), *Natural selection and social behavior: Recent research and new theory.* New York: Chiron Press.

Lack, D. (1968). *Ecological adaptations for breeding in birds.* London: Methuen.

Lawton, M. F., & Guindon, C. F. (1981). Flock composition, breeding success, and learning in the brown jay. *Condor, 82,* 27–33.

Lewis, D. M. (1981). Determinants of reproductive success of the white-browed sparrow weaver, *Plocepasser mahali. Behavioral Ecology and Sociobiology, 9,* 83–93.

Ligon, J. D. (1981a). Sociobiology is for the birds. *Auk, 98,* 409–412.

Ligon, J. D. (1981b). Demographic patterns and communal breeding in the green woodhoopoe, *Phoeniculus purpureus.* In R. D. Alexander & D. W. Tinkle (Eds.), *Natural selection and social behavior.* New York: Chiron Press.

Ligon, J. D. (1983). Cooperation and reciprocity in avian social systems. *American Naturalist, 121,* 366–384.

Ligon, J. D., & Husar, S. L. (1974). Notes on the behavioral ecology of Couch's Mexican jay. *Auk, 91,* 841–843.

Ligon, J. D., & Ligon, S. H. (1978a). Communal breeding in green woodhoopoes as a case for reciprocity. *Nature, 280,* 174.

Ligon, J. D., & Ligon, S. H. (1978b). The communal social system of the green woodhoopoe in Kenya. *Living Bird, 17,* 159–197.

Ligon, J. D., & Ligon, S. H. (1982). The cooperative breeding behavior of the green woodhoopoe. *Scientific American, 247,* 126–134.

Ligon, J. D., & Ligon, S. H. (1983). Reciprocity in the green woodhoopoe (*Phoeniculus purpureus*). *Animal Behaviour 31,* 480–489.

Lorenz, K. (1941). Vergleichende Bewegungsstudien bei Anatiden. *Journal für Ornithologie, 89,* 194–294.

MacLean, A. A. E. (1982). *A comparative study of the improvement of foraging success with age in three species of gulls on the Niagara River: Relationships to deferred breeding.* Ph.D. Thesis, University of Rochester, Rochester, N.Y.

Metcalf, R. A., & Whitt, G. S. (1977). Relative inclusive fitness in the social wasp *Polistes metricus. Behavioral Ecology and Sociobiology, 2,* 353–360.

Myers, G. R., & Waller, D. W. (1977). Helpers at the nest in barn swallows. *Auk, 94,* 596.

Noonan, K. M. (1981). Individual strategies of inclusive-fitness-maximizing in *Polistes fuscatus* foundresses. In R. D. Alexander & D. W. Tinkle (Eds.), *Natural selection and social behavior.* New York: Chiron Press.

Orians, G. H. (1961). The ecology of blackbrid (*Agelaius*) social systems. *Ecological Monographs, 31,* 285–312.

Orians, G. H. (1969a). On the evolution of mating systems in birds and mammals. *American Naturalist, 103,* 589–603.

Orians, G. H. (1969b). Age and hunting success in the brown pelican (*Pelecanus occidentalis*). *Animal Behavior, 17,* 316–319.

Orians, G. H., Orians, C. E., & Orians, K. J. (1977). Helpers at the nest in some Argentine blackbirds. In B. Stonehouse & C. Perrins (Eds.), *Evolutionary ecology.* London & New York, University Park Press.

Oring, L. (1982). Avian mating systems. In D. Farner, J. King, & K. Parkes (Eds.), *Avian biology, VI.* New York: Academic Press.

Packer, C., & Pusey, A. E. (1982). Cooperation and competition within coalitions of male lions: Kin selection or game theory. *Nature, 296,* 740–742.

Pierce, B. A., & Smith, H. M. (1978). Neoteny or paedogenesis. *Journal of Herpetology, 13,* 119–121.

Platt, J. R. (1964). Strong inference. *Science, 146,* 347–353.

Pulliam, H. R., & Caraco, T. (1984). Living in groups: Is there an optimal group size? In N. B. Davies & J. R. Krebs (Eds.), *Behavioural ecology* (2nd ed.). Sunderland, MA: Sinauer.

Pulliam, H. R., & Millikan, G. C. (1982). Social behavior in the non-reproductive season. In D. Farner, J. King, & K. Parkes (Eds.), *Avian biology, VI,* New York: Academic Press.

Rappole, J. H., Warner, D. W., & Ramos, M. (1977). Territoriality and population structure in a small passerine community. *American Midland Naturalist, 97,* 110–119.

Reyer, H. U. (1980). Flexible helper structure as an ecological adaptation in the pied kingfisher (*Ceryle rudis rudis* L.). *Behavioral Ecology and Sociobiology, 6,* 219–227.

Ricklefs, R. E. (1975). The evolution of co-operative breeding in birds. *Ibis, 117,* 531–534.

Rowley, I. (1965). The life history of the superb blue wren, *Malurus cyaneus. Emu, 64,* 251–297.

Rowley, I. (1981). The communal way of life in the splendid wren, *Malurus splendens. Zeitschrift für Tierpsychologie, 55,* 228–267.

Searcy, W. A. (1978). Foraging success in three age classes of glaucous-winged gulls. *Auk, 95,* 586–588.

Skutch, A. F. (1935). Helpers at the nest. *Auk, 52,* 257–273.

Skutch, A. F. (1961). Helpers among birds. *Condor, 63,* 198–226.

Smith, S. M. (1978). The underworld in a territorial sparrow: Adaptive strategy for floaters. *American Naturalist, 112,* 571–582.

Stacey, P. B. (1979). Habitat saturation and communal breeding in the acorn woodpecker. *Animal Behavior, 27,* 1153–1166.

Stearns, S. C. (1976). Life-history tactics: A review of the ideas. *Quarterly Review of Biology, 51,* 3–47.

Stearns, S. C., & Crandall, R. E. (1981). Quantitative predictions of delayed maturity. *Evolution, 35,* 455–463.

Tinbergen, N. (1959). Comparative studies of the behavior of gulls (Laridae): A progress report. *Behaviour, 15,* 1–70.

Trail, P. S., Strahl, S. D., & Brown, J. L. (1981). Infanticide and selfish behavior in a communaly breeding bird, the Mexican jay (*Aphelocoma ultramarina*). *American Naturalist, 118,* 72–82.

Trail, P. W. (1980). Ecological correlates of social organization in a communaly breeding bird, the acorn woodpecker, *Melanerpes formicivorus. Behavioral Ecology and Sociobiology, 7,* 83–92.

Vehrencamp, S. L. (1977). Relative fecundity and parental effort in communaly nesting anis, *Crotophaga sulcirostris. Science, 197,* 403–405.

Vehrencamp, S. L. (1978). The adapative significance of communal nesting in groove-billed anis (*Crotophaga sulcirostris*). *Behavioral Ecology and Sociobiology, 4,* 1–33.

Vehrencamp, S. L. (1979). The roles of individual, kin, and group selection in the evolution of sociality. In P. Marler & J. G. Vandenbergh (Eds.), *Handbook of behavioral neurobiology 3*, New York: Plenum Press.

Vehrencamp, S. L. (1980). To skew or not to skew. *Symposium International Ornithological Congress, 17*, 869–874.

Verbeek, N. A. M., & Butler, R. W. (1981). Cooperative breeding of the northwestern crow *Corvus caurinus* in British Columbia. *Ibis, 123*, 183–189.

Verner, J. (1964). Evolution of polygyny in the long-billed marsh wren. *Evolution, 18*, 252–261.

Waltz, E. C. (1981). Reciprocal altruism and spite in gulls: a comment. *American Naturalist, 118*, 588–592.

Weatherhead, P. J., & Robertson, R. J. (1980). Altruism in the savannah sparrow. *Behavioral Ecology and Sociobiology, 6*, 185–186.

Wiley, R. H. (1974). Effects of delayed reproduction on survival, fecundity, and the rate of population increase. *American Naturalist, 108*, 705–709.

Wiley, R. H. (1980). Social structure and individual ontogenesis: problems of description, mechanism, and evolution. In P. P. G. Bateson & P. H. Klopfer (Eds.), *Perspectives in ethology* (Vol. 4). New York: Plenum Press.

Williams, G. D. (1966). Natural selection, the costs of reproduction, and a refinement of Lack's principle. *American Naturalist, 100*, 687–690.

Wilson, D. S. (1975). A theory of group selection. *Proceedings of the National Academy of Science, 72*, 143–146.

Wilson, E. O. (1975). *Sociobiology*. Cambridge, MA: Harvard University Press.

Woolfenden, G. E. (1976). Co-operative breeding in American birds. *Proceedings of the International Ornithological Congress, 16*, 674–684.

Woolfenden, G. E. (1981). Selfish behavior by Florida scrub jay helpers. In R. D. Alexander & D. W. Tinkle (Eds.), *Natural selection and social behavior*. New York: Chiron Press.

Woolfenden, G. E., & Fitzpatrick, J. W. (1977). Dominance in the Florida scrub jay. *Condor, 79*, 1–12.

Woolfenden, G. E., & Fitzpatrick, J. W. (1978). The inheritance of territory in group-breeding birds. *Bioscience, 28*, 104–108.

Young, E. C. (1978). Behavioural ecology of *Lonnbergi* skuas in relation to environment of the Chatham islands, New Zealand. *New Zealand Journal of Zoology, 5*, 401–416.

Zahavi, A. (1974). Communal nesting by the Arabian babbler. *Ibis, 116*, 84–87.

Zahavi, A. (1976). Co-operative nesting in Eurasian birds. *Proceedings of the International Ornithological Congress, 16*, 685–693.

Zahavi, A. (1981). Some comments on sociobiology. *Auk, 98*, 412–415.

6

Comparative Study of the Ontogeny of Communication

W. John Smith
University of Pennsylvania

INTRODUCTION

Ethologists who study animal communication have not paid sufficient attention to the broad range of problems and opportunities presented to different animals in the course of ontogeny. What knowledge we have consists largely of descriptive catalogues of immature repertoires and accounts of the appearance of adults' signals during the development of members of various species. There has been no concerted attempt to ask such general questions as what kinds of information can be made available by signaling at different stages in the development of social behavior? how are skills of signaling and responding to signals developed? how is information from various sources sought and used at different stages? or how do different aspects of relationships and the organization of social groups affect the evolution and character of ontogenetic procedures basic to skilled communicating? Despite considerable research on the development of some kinds of skills, in particular the learning of ''dialects'' by birds, the scope of the field remains to be mapped.

Communication does not appear *de novo* in the evolution of each species, and it is reasonable to expect some features of the process to occur widely among animals. Even very different species have some social needs and environmental problems in common, and are similarly constrained by genetics and developmental options. Indeed, available evidence suggests that the kinds of information provided by the ''displays'' (behavioral units specialized as signals, see below) of most vertebrate species are remarkably similar in spite of differences in the life-styles of the species, as are the numbers of such signals in each species' repertoire (see Smith, 1977a). Yet similarities such as these are less obvious on first impression than are differences among species in such matters as the forms of their signals, the amount of signaling members of each species do, the situations in which they signal, and the kinds of functions their signaling appears to generate.

Such diversity demands explanation. If there is a best way to communicate, why does this way differ among species? Species differ in physical and behavioral capabilities, of course. Further, different species are not all faced with the same problems, and need to obtain different advantages from signaling. Even to the extent that their problems are similar, identical procedures cannot evolve and be kept identical over large numbers of generations in different lineages—there is too much genetic and other diversification over time. Yet if diversity is inevitable, it is also limited. Many differences among species should accord with general patterns, generated by such issues as the comparable needs of individuals developing with different amounts of parental care, or in social groups of different size or complexity.

We can only learn what general principles govern the behavior of communicating by comparing how numerous different species have met their evolutionary challenges. Only through such comparisons can we separate adaptations to basic requirements from those to less widespread demands, separate divergences peculiar to opportunism in the evolutionary histories of different lineages from those imposed by adapting to different social or ecological environments, separate similarities due to common ancestry from those due to convergence upon common solutions demanded by underlying functional problems, and discern trends that would go unnoticed in studies of one or a very few species. The evolution of large numbers of species in diverse lineages provides us with results of a large set of natural experiments in which procedures for communicating have been molded successfully to environmental requirements. Comparisons enable us to work out and test hypotheses about the key historical conditions of those experiments.

A comparative, evolutionary approach enables us to ask why animals have the particular mechanisms that underlie behavior. For example, north temperate birds of some species respond to the shortening day length of summer and autumn by migrating south, others by setting up local territories, and others by joining wandering nomadic flocks. The "proximate" causes of these behavioral changes (i.e., the mechanisms effecting them) begin with shifts in hormonal balance induced by perception of shortening days. The "ultimate" cause, the reason why the hormonally mediated behavioral predispositions exist, is the need to secure access to a supply of food (for discussion of "proximate" vs. "ultimate" causes see Mayr, 1961). In the winter some species organize socially to exploit local resources, but others may obtain resources in other regions. The key environmental differences are in the kinds and distributions of foods used by species with different histories. Most purely insectivorous species cannot winter in the far north, whereas granivores can, although some have to wander seeking locally abundant patches of food.

Darwin (1872) offered such comparisons in asking why the forms of some signaling movements show widespread trends among phylogenetically diverse species. He noted, for example, that carnivores, horses, kangaroos, and some other mammals "draw their ears back when feeling savage" (p. 111), and that to do so gives the ears some protection in fighting. He further noted that cattle, sheep, and goats do not lay back their ears "when enraged" (p. 112), and also do not fight with their teeth. Flattened-back ears have evolved as a signal position only in the former species. Many further examples exist in which comparisons among species have revealed evolutionary origins and phylogenetic limits of signaling movements.

Less extensive comparative study of the ontogeny of signaling has been done. Perhaps the best example involves differences among those species of birds in which social learning is required in order to develop song or, in some cases, other vocalizations. There are interspecific similarities and differences in when during ontogeny the learning occurs, and in what individuals and vocal characteristics can serve as models. The patterns being found begin to suggest possible functions of such learning, and are discussed later (see p. 196).

The aim of this chapter is to show that a comparative approach can suggest many kinds of questions that will help us to define central issues and themes in the ontogeny of the behavior of communicating. The chapter begins with short accounts of characteristics of communication and its study by ethologists, the social milieu in which communication functions, and the kinds of ontogenetic changes in individuals and their social behavior that are of basic importance to developmental trends in communicating. It then examines the kinds of things we know about the ontogeny of formalized signaling, including developmental changes in the stimuli eliciting signaling behavior. Finally, it reviews development of appropriate responding to signaling in changing circumstances.

CHARACTERISTICS OF COMMUNICATION

A. Communication and its Ethological Study

Communication occurs when information is shared. The usual concern of ethologists is with social communication: the sharing of information between or among individual animals. When individuals who lack information receive it from another, they obtain increased ability to predict the course of events, and to choose their responses accordingly. This is how we recognize and define "information": an abstract property of all things and events that makes something about them predictable to any entity capable of perceiving it.

Interacting individuals obtain information from many sources, including each other. Every perceivable feature of an individual is informative: its height, shape, whether it moves surely or falters, whether it is sleeping, eating, or departing, and so forth. Some of this information is useful to other participants in an interaction, yet much additional information that could be useful is not readily accessible. Some of the latter is private, as, for example, much of the information about each individual's internal states. Other is potentially public, but may be difficult to obtain, such as information about the whereabouts of individual members of a group trying to travel together at night or in dense vegetation. Because individuals can profit from sharing some of this information with each other, behavior specialized to make it more available has evolved—both biologically and culturally. These special signaling actions can be referred to as "formalized" behavior (Smith, 1977a, pp. 2, 9–10, 326–330, 389–425). Comparable specializations have evolved in markings of hair, feathers, and the like that characterize species and age or sex classes, scents that attract mates, and other structural features or products.

Ethologists customarily focus their studies of communication on behavior and other features that have been specialized as sources of information. These should be among the most relevant or continuously pertinent of the various sources of information that contribute to interactional decisions.

Some ethological research concentrates on the form of these specializations, for instance, asking how they are made distinctive or how they are adapted to particular environments. Other research seeks to learn their "referents" (Smith, 1977a, 1981): what becomes knowable or predictable through signaling performances as a contribution just of the signaling itself, as distinct from the contributions of other sources of information. Referents can be studied either by determining what correlates with signaling performances, or by observing how recipients of signaling respond. Each procedure leaves ambiguities. The former because it does not demonstrate which of the correlates are significant to recipients of the signaling. The latter because recipients always base their responses to a considerable extent on information from sources other than the signaling. In practice, the effects of contextual sources of information are so diverse and pervasive as to render the latter procedure by far the more problematic in studies of referents. The need to determine the relevant sources of different kinds of information and their contributions also makes study of the responses to and functions of signaling difficult. Often ethologists simply infer these from observations of behavior in uncontrolled natural situations. Some control is achieved by studying responses to presentations of artificial signals, such as recorded or simulated vocalizations, although this requires great care to minimize the number and significance of relevant contextual sources of information. In spite of the complexity, ethologists characteristically prefer to observe or experiment with communication in natural or near-natural circumstances, however. They try to avoid problems that arise when animals face the confusingly impoverished situations inherent in highly controlled laboratory settings.

The ethological emphasis on naturally occurring behavior reflects the perspective of evolutionary biology. The behavior of communicating, and characteristics of its ontogeny, are seen as adaptive—as enabling individuals to operate in the natural world and thus to contribute to future gene pools.

B. Repertoires of Formalized Signaling Behavior

Each species has a repertoire of formalized signals. The signal units correspond to the "displays" of traditional ethology—or most do; some traditionally recognized displays are compounds of such units. Familiar examples of signal units are (roughly speaking) the chirps, twitters, songs and crest raisings of birds; the barks, growls, snarls, howls, tail-wags and urine marking of dogs; and the laughs, groans, smiles and eyebrow raising of humans. These are the basic formalized vehicles for carrying information, and each unit provides not one but several kinds of information (see below, section D).

In most species there also appears to be a repertoire of procedures for varying the form of these basic units. For example, both visible and vocal display units can be performed at a range of amplitudes, and each unit can be completed within a range of durations. Vocalizations can also be harshened, altered in their frequency spread or fundamental frequency, inflected, quavered or complexly modulated, and so on—the ways a basic form can be noticeably altered and yet remain recognizable are quite numerous. Exactly what is produced in any particular instance of signaling thus depends on both what signal unit is selected and what set of procedures is employed in performing it.

Each consistent procedure for varying unit form seems to be specialized to provide information, either modifying the information of the basic unit or adding further information to it (examples below, section D). Because each way of varying form is typically continuously graded, it can be difficult for a recipient to discern just where on the gradients a particular instance of signaling lies. The problem is avoided, however, if the recipient needs to make only relative judgments during events in which signaling shifts about, comparing any particular performance with those just before or after it (Smith, 1977a, p. 400). The opportunities for such use are probably greatest for animals that spend much time together and signal copiously (Moynihan, 1966), but are significant for any kind of signaling behavior that tends to be repeated during an event, even by relatively asocial species.

In addition, some, perhaps most, species also have repertoires of ways of making simultaneous or sequential combinations of display units. Gulls, e.g., may simultaneously combine one of various bill angles and degrees of lifting of the carpals with an extended neck in the "upright" position, or with a withdrawn neck in the "hunched" (names of the combinations are from Tinbergen, 1959, who treated the combinations as fundamental units rather than the recombinable bill angles, carpal positions, and neck positions). Birds of various species combine different song forms into grammatical sequences (avoiding ungrammatical ones) that may continue unbroken for tens of minutes at a time and inform about a singer's shifting patterns of behavior (reviewed by Smith, 1977a, 1977b).

Still another repertoire is built of cooperative performances that each require two or more participants. The signaling units of this repertoire are not displays but "formalized interactions" (Smith, 1977a, pp. 426–457), and they add to the kinds of information that can be made available by signaling behavior. A human handshake is a simple example. No one of us can perform it alone, yet we all recognize it as a signaling unit and can participate in its performance. Greetings are more complexly patterned examples, sometimes involving long sequences of mutually coordinated moves. Some formalized interactions are relatively fixed, except for iterative and restart flexibility, as in the courtship of certain butterflies (see Bastock, 1967). Others are very fluid and often have many steps, as in the T-sequences of golden jackals (Golani & Mendelssohn, 1971)—which are also termed "courtship" in ethological jargon. The ontogenetic strategies for acquiring skill at the last of these may involve much flexibility. Play interactions (e.g., M. Bekoff, 1974; Fagen, 1981) are obvious examples of formalized interactions that become elaborated as individuals become practiced in performing with each other as partners.

Like display units, units of formalized interaction are variable in form—which in their case includes internal sequencing and other combinations, as well as the forms of component acts. Also like displays, formalized interactions can be variously combined with one another. That is, there are repertoires of form variation and of combinatorial procedures at this level of cooperative performance, too.

All of these repertoires are based on rules for performing formalized behavior (Smith, 1977a, p. 464), rules that generate units or vary the forms and combinations of these. Each set of "performance rules" gives rise to a repertoire of signaling specializations.

C. Signaling and Responding in Different Events

Considerable range and subtlety is given to communication by the several repertoires just discussed. Taken together, they permit signaling to be fit much more closely to characteristics of different events than would be possible with, say, simply a limited repertoire of invariable display units. Additional capacity to make distinctions and adjustments in signaling and also in responding to signals is achieved by several means (Smith, in press a), all much affected by ontogeny.

As individuals develop, signaling can be adjusted to their changing needs and capabilities through changes in its form and in the information it makes available. Some changes in form are inevitable products of growth, e.g., changes in the sounds of vocalizations as vocal tracts change in size and shape. Others are perhaps specializations incorporated into signaling ontogeny to mark other maturational changes. Whatever their origins, these changes in the form of signaling coincide with shifts in the information being made available. This can be compared with effects of the repertoire of ways of varying the form of signal units, mentioned above. But the ontogenetic changes differ in being largely unidirectional and irreversible.

Further adjustments arise in development as signalers mature and gain experience. They learn to signal in response to different stimuli as their needs change, or to be more discriminating in the stimuli they accept as sufficient to elicit signaling. For instance, the sorts of stimuli that will elicit escape responses and "alarm" signals are much broader for young mammals than for old (e.g., in beavers, Hodgdon & Larson, 1973; ponies, Tyler, 1972; and vervet monkeys, Seyfarth, Cheney, & Marler, 1980). Progressive narrowing of stimuli to those that are most appropriate has been shown in the vervet case. The information made available by such signals does not necessarily change, for example, if it is that there is an escape-eliciting stimulus and that the signaler may flee. Nonetheless, recipient individuals who are aware of the extent of the signaler's experience (or of some approximate correlate, such as its age) can adjust their responses accordingly. Their expectations are determined partly by the information provided by the signal, and partly by information about how readily signalers of different degrees of experience are frightened into escape behavior.

In this example, recipients of a signal bias their selection of responses on the basis not just of the information it provides but also in terms of information from other sources (from sources indicating the experience of the signaler, and probably from memories of learned relations between experience or age and the breadth of stimuli eliciting "alarm" signaling; memories are stored sources of information). Their responses to the signal are context-dependent, and can differ from event to event. Such predispositions to respond are modifiable by learning, at least in most vertebrate species.

Context-dependency is both a general characteristic of response behavior and a fundamentally important procedure for making distinctions appropriate to particular events. There are numerous sources of information that can be relevant in addition to signaling (see Table 6.1).

Finally, it is sometimes suggested that the referents of signals should shift from moment to moment, i.e., that signals should make different information available in different events. Perhaps some do. We humans sometimes use signals this way, both when informing creatively and when misinforming. But the procedure endangers intelligibility. It makes it less likely that recipients will know what information is being provided. (This, of course, is its advantage when misinforming.)

Probably the context-dependent nature of responding is what usually gives the appearance of such short-term "semantic flexibility," not changes in the referents of signals themselves. Recipient individuals do respond to information that differs among events in which the same form of signaling behavior occurs. However, much of their information comes from sources contextual to the signal, and those sources do differ. Reversible, short-term semantic flexibility may contribute little to reliable communicating, at least in the social interactions of nonhuman animals.

D. Kinds of Information Made Available

The kinds of information made available by formalized signaling other than speech are not what might be expected if we assumed that deliberate linguistic

TABLE 6.1
Sources of Information in Communicating

Formalized
Behavioral
    1. Repertoires of signaling units ("displays")
    2. Repertoires of ways to vary unit form
    3. Repertoires of ways to combine units ("grammars")
      a) simultaneously
      b) sequentially
    4. Formalized interactions (Cooperative performances)
Nonbehavioral
    1. Badges (formalized features of individual appearance)
    2. Constructions (signaling devices built by animals)
    3. Some pheromones (excreted chemicals specialized to be informative)
    4. Some tokens (things from the environment, modified and incorporated into signaling)
Not Formalized
    Any perceivable event or thing, including all nonformalized behavior, all chemicals excreted simply as metabolic products (still termed "pheromones"), all unmodified environmental objects involved in signaling or peripheral to it but relevant to recipients of the signals, all memories and genetic stores of information—including the "codes" that make formal signaling intelligible. Together, these are by far the most numerous sources of information, but in any event usually only a few are as relevant to interacting individuals as is formalized signaling. (They can, of course, be more relevant, and even render formalized signaling unnecessary, but when it is performed it tends to rank among the more important sources.)

communication were the standard. Human speech, with noun phrases, verb phrases, their subcategories and relations, is an inappropriate guide to most nonspeech communication. Clear-cut noun-verb distinctions have not been found in the latter, for instance. Speech and nonspeech signaling differ greatly in organization and content, and in the capacity to formulate propositional statements, questions, and commands—even though functional analogues of commands can be generated without speech. The signaling actions of most nonspeech communication do not package information in the same ways that most words do.

Various kinds of information are made available by each display (i.e., by each basic signal unit, see section B above). They include information about the signaler's behavior: what it is doing or may do in addition to the act of signaling. A signal usually indicates different kinds of behavior among which the signaler is selecting, and also provides information about the relative probabilities of each selection, the "intensity" with which it would be performed, and sometimes the direction the action could take. The predictions engendered are conditional, and changes in its situation can dispose the signaler to behave otherwise.

For example, a typical display performed in, say, courting, could provide the information that the signaler might select among three categories within its whole repertoire of behavior. It might either interact or flee, but is more likely to behave indecisively and do neither immediately. The information about interactional behavior is broadly predictive, subsuming diverse options. There are fewer ways to flee or to behave indecisively—the information about these categories is more narrowly predictive. In a courting event, different responses by the recipient of this display might lead the signaler to approach and associate with it, groom it, lead it to a nest, or try to mount it, or to withdraw or continue to vacillate at a safe distance. Departure of that other participant could lead to following or to a sufficiently changed event that the signaler would do none of the predicted behavior and turn instead to self-maintenance activities such as foraging.

Current evidence suggests that most displays of most species of at least mammals and birds may provide information about only a dozen or so categories of behavior (Smith, 1977a; see Table 6.2). Thus members of species very different in social behavior, ecology, and phylogenetic histories appear to communicate with largely the same basic set of categories. If this generalization holds as more comparative research is completed, it may find explanation in the rather small size of display repertoires. Few species have more than 45 or so display units, counting those adapted for reception by all sensory modalities. With so

TABLE 6.2
Categories of Behavior About Which the Display Units of Diverse
Species Provide Information

Interactional behavior: attempting to interact in any way, or to avoid interacting. This category is broad, and does not specify the kind of interacting.

Associating behavior: interacting just by remaining in the company of another individual.

Copulation behavior: attempting to inseminate or be inseminated, or to carry out whatever procedure for fertilization is characteristic of the species.

Attack behavior: attempting to injure, by any means.

Escape behavior: any procedures for withdrawing or avoiding (in many species includes immobile "freezing" as one option).

Locomotory behavior: moving from place to place by walking, flying, swimming, etc.

Behavior of remaining with site: restricting movements to a particular neighborhood or point.

Attentive behavior: paying attention to a stimulus; monitoring.

Seeking behavior: attempting to gain the opportunity to perform some other behavior, such as associating or escaping.

Receptive behavior: preparing to accept interactional behavior (or some specified subset of it) from another individual.

Indecisive behavior: vacillating or hesitating between other patterns of behavior.

General set of behavior patterns: diverse options from the part of the behavioral repertoire that is incompatible with some other category of behavior about which a display provides information.

The above are categories of behavior ("selections" from the behavioral repertoire) about which information appears to be made available by the display units of a large number of very diverse species of birds, mammals, and other animals. Although some display units do make information available about additional categories, few if any of those appear to be widespread among species, and most species may have few or no displays that deal with them.

few available, each display must have to be useful either in the broadest possible range of events, or in events that must be resolved quickly or without misunderstanding. Information about broadly delimited categories, such as interactional behavior, must increase the range of usefulness of a display, whereas that about narrower categories must serve where less ambiguity can be tolerated. Few categories of behavior may be as useful in communication as the dozen that are now known from the displays of diverse species.

Communication about behavior is not as limited as this quick outline of the information made available by display units might suggest, however. These units represent only one kind of repertoire of formalized signaling behavior. In the performance of a display, the repertoire of ways of varying its form can be employed either to modify its information (e.g., altering the relative probabilities of the different behavioral selections) or to add further information that may specify additional categories of behavior. The range of categories is just beginning to be explored. Information is also provided by using grammatical repertoires to combine performances of display units. Apart from the grammars of speech, however, it is not yet clear that most such recombining adds novel information. The main function of the grammars may be to place display units in patterned juxtaposition when their combined informative contributions are appropriate and, for sequences, to make obvious the relative frequencies with which each unit is repeated (see Smith, 1977a, p. 421, and Smith, Pawlukiewicz, & Smith, 1978). Finally, information is markedly augmented when an individual signals in a formalized cooperative performance with one or more other participants. Some, perhaps much of the information made available appears to be about behavior, but these "formalized interactions" have yet to be analyzed for the kinds of information they contribute.

Because signaling makes information available about behavior, it can be interpreted as informing about the internal states that underlie the behavior. With our current understanding of motivational states and emotions, such interpretation is difficult. It is clear, however, that displays are not simply "expressions of emotions," as is sometimes claimed. The extent to which they provide information about emotions has yet to be adequately tested.

Formalized signaling also provides information about more than behavior and underlying internal states. It identifies the individuals who perform, usually to species and often to infraspecific classes, extending even to identification as a particular individual. Sometimes information is provided about physiological classes (e.g., sex, maturity) and even social membership (e.g., in a family or pair). The physical characteristics of audible displaying also provide binaural listeners with some information about the location of a signaler, i.e., about its direction and distance relative to a recipient of the sound.

Finally, some displays or variants provide information about things other than the signaler (e.g., about predators and possibly food, feeding sites, nests or nest sites, territories, or kinds of circumstances in which the signaler finds itself). For example, it was recently shown that some variants of a ground squirrel vocal display are performed only in response to predators, and that different of these variants distinguish among predators of different classes (Owings & Leger, 1980). Each variant of this vocalization also provides distinctive information about the signaler's behavior, ranging from alert monitoring to particular forms of escape. Honey bee dances (von Frisch, 1967) provide information about flights to be made to some resource, although the dance formalization does not itself specify the kind of resource more precisely. Well-documented examples of displays with such referents remain rare, although it is not clear to what extent this is because most putative cases are inadequately tested or because such displays are relatively uncommon. Research on this issue is increasing at present.

E. Responding

Responses by recipients of signals are crucial to the evolution of formalized signaling. They alone generate the functions of communicating. An individual profits from making information available only if that information affects the behavior of another individual. Although not all of the consequences of the latter's responses will be beneficial to the signaler, evolutionary pressures can develop and maintain formalized signaling behavior if there is an overall excess of benefits to costs. Similarly, predispositions to respond are shaped by evolution to provide benefits for the responder. Signaling that misinforms and misleads responding individuals to the advantage only of a signaler is evolutionarily unstable (Smith, 1977a, p. 10), as natural selection reduces or eliminates costly response predispositions. For the most part, the information provided by a signal must be such that both signaler and recipient profit (although not necessarily equally) from the latter's responses.

A fundamentally important characteristic of responding has already been mentioned as a means by which the effects of signaling are adjusted to particular events. Responses are made on the basis of information not just from formalized signals, but also from sources contextual to those signals. Some of the latter sources provide more or less immediate context, e.g., the signaler's actions other than signaling, perceivable characteristics of the signaler and of the setting. Others provide historical context: information stored in memory or in genetic predispositions, e.g., predispositions to respond appropriately to different formalizations, amounting to a knowledge of a species-specific "code." Context-dependency is a pervasive feature of communication.

THE SOCIAL ARENA FOR COMMUNICATION

Communication must be understood within the arena where it functions. It is one of the principal tools with which participants give order and direction to their social encounters and, through them, to their enduring relationships and coherent groups. Its arena is thus all social behavior.

Social behavior is more complex and difficult to manage than are most other kinds of behavior. Its orderliness can rarely be imposed by the actions of a single individual. Order must be constructed in interactions, the participants both affecting and being affected by one another as each makes its moves.

Interactions are events in which individuals influence each other's choices of action. Communication facilitates orderly interactional behavior by enabling each participant to anticipate the other's in some ways. With every increment in predictability, each can better adopt appropriate tactics for integrating its behavior with that of the other. Each can better decide how far to go in attempts to control the event, in what ways to accommodate, and what information to share. In even moderately social species, individuals must be able to interact in many ways (e.g., to greet, to threaten and respond to threats, to associate with other individuals, or to aid), with many classes of other individuals (e.g., strangers, neighbors, peer-level members of troops, mates, or parents and offspring), and over many issues (e.g., joining another individual peaceably, controlling resources or achieving a stand-off, or mutually maintaining the coherence of a traveling group). The greater the diversity, the more is required of communicative behavior.

Interactions are the moment by moment, local building blocks of other social integration that extends further through time or space: enduring relationships and groups. Such integration has, in turn, characteristics that shape and limit the kinds of interactions that can be appropriate. Thus communication both affects and is affected by every way in which social behavior is integrated.

Relationships that endure beyond an interaction, linking the successive interactions of two individuals in patterned ways, become variously specialized. They must be integrated over long periods, including time in which the parties to the relationship are not interacting with one another. They become characterized by mutually tailored, in some ways unique, patterns of interacting. The patterns develop as the expectancies of the participants become adapted to each other's idiosyncracies and are shaped by familiarity, function, and efficiency. Such enduring relationships may be stable, or may change in quality or into other kinds of relationships. A bond can persist between the parties even as relationships change, giving the individuals continued access to one another.

Interacting individuals comprise a group, a social network of mutually accessible members. A cohesive group has an organization beyond that of the organized flow of the interactions of its members, and of their patterned relationships. Some of its characteristics are species specific, while others are peculiar to the group's environment, which determines possibilities for interacting, the safety of group members, the ways in which they can forage, and so forth. The characteristics of a cohesive group include the workable spatial arrangements and numbers of its members, the network of their relationships, and particular assortments of age, sex, and other classes. A special set of interactional procedures is needed to sustain the group as a persistently organized social unit and enable its members, as a group, to establish and maintain relationships with other groups.

This arena for communicating, the whole complexly interwoven social structure whose order depends on effective communicating, is not fixed. Changes are imposed during the life of an individual, for instance as demographic parameters change. More predictably, it alters during ontogeny as an individual changes through maturation, learning, and in social behavior and position. The species-specific and individually variable course of ontogeny must considerably influence the acquisition of communicative skills.

ONTOGENETIC CHANGES IN INDIVIDUALS
AND THEIR SOCIAL BEHAVIOR

Consider the course of social development of a savanna baboon. The following selected highlights are abstracted from accounts of Altmann (1980), Packer (1980), Hausfater, Altmann, and Altmann (1982), Busse and Hamilton (1981), Owens (1975a, 1975b), and Ransom and Ransom (1971).

The initial interactions of an infant baboon are with its mother, and are simple. She feeds it, carries it, and protects it. It seeks food from her and rests in her arms. It has an inelaborate, dependent-to-caregiver relationship, and she is the other member of its only group. Soon it is able to cling to her, to climb about on her body and play in simple ways with her and, with further physical development and motor competence, to move short distances from her and return. These new ways to interact add relationships to the continuing dependent:caregiver one between mother and infant. The two individuals become play partners, and with the infant's increasing exploration a tester:controller relationship becomes more evident and more elaborate. It is not a static relationship, and control shifts gradually to the infant (Hinde, 1974; Hinde & Atkinson, 1970; Hinde & Herrmann, 1977; Nash, 1978; Simpson & Howe, 1980).

The infant also broaches membership in an expanding group. Other baboons begin to take it from the mother, some to groom or play with, others to carry in dangerous social events. At this stage relationships are being begun with individuals of diverse ages and both sexes, and these too will be elaborated as many new kinds of interactions are incorporated. The youngster's group now includes various subgroups: its family (mother and older siblings), adult females with various relationships with its mother, perhaps some juvenile females, and usually at least one or two adult males.

Gradually the dependent:caregiver relationship with the mother wanes. The youngster begins to play more and more with its peers, becoming more proficient in agonistic and protosexual interactions. Eventually, with widening familiarity with troop members of other ages its working awareness of groups extends to its troop, a closer subtroop within it, the other subgroups of its ontogenetic history, and to the neighboring troops that are encountered. If it is a female, she settles within her natal troop. She contests for a dominance position with individuals familiar to her through their relationships with her family, and achieves a rank below that of her mother and above her older sisters. She becomes sexually active, preferring to copulate with novel males—even enticing them to immigrate into her troop from neighboring troops. Eventually she begins to raise young herself. With the birth of her second offspring or later she may establish a special relationship with one adult male.

A maturing male savanna baboon passes from life in a peer group to emigration from his natal troop, severing his bonds and relationships with its members. He establishes a dominance rank among the adult males of his new troop, and forms supportive alliances. He may gradually develop close bonds with particular individual females and their growing young. As an immigrant he must adjust his expectations to fit his new social environment, learning the temperaments and idiosyncracies of new individuals, the properties of a new mixture of group members, and on what issues, when, how, and how forcefully to test his new companions. His sensitivity to idiosyncratic signaling and other behavior must be renewed. In turn, his intrusion into the new group changes its fabric, and may act as a selective agent for communicative flexibility in the natal animals.

The point of this sketchy history is to emphasize the number and magnitude of the changes, and the extent of the elaboration that can occur within the social life of an individual. The case is complex, but basically representative. Vertebrate animals, especially birds and mammals of many kinds, experience many of the same steps. For example, as increasingly competent infants they pass through series of relationships with caregivers. They enter wider social spheres as juveniles. By emigrating or meeting immigrants, they must establish relationships with new individuals at sexual maturity. Like savanna baboons, they must manage the necessary interactions of each phase, and this places a succession of demands on their ability to communicate that must affect it greatly.

There are various ontogenetic sources of social change, and various kinds of changes that affect communication. How communication is affected, the changes wrought in it, is the topic of later sections.

A. Sources of Social Change

During ontogeny, in particular its early phases, an individual's physical characteristics change relatively rapidly. It grows larger and develops increased motor ability and skill, changes that affect both the ways it can interact socially and the ways it needs to. Its cognitive capacities also enlarge, permitting more detailed assessments of events and more differentiated and flexible responding. Its overall behavioral repertoire, initially both different from and much narrower than that of adults, broadens and becomes more "adult"—although in many species there are special adaptations to the needs of particular stages, and behavior that appears is characteristic neither of early infants nor mature adults (various forms of play are obvious examples).

The physical and cognitive growth and increasing experience are sources of social change. They allow an individual to be more and more independent of other individuals for its simple maintenance (i.e., for obtaining nutrition, shelter, etc.). But they also lead it to become dependent, often elaborately, in other ways. Its social needs do not cease, but change.

As the individual changes, its social opportunities also change and different demands are made upon it by other individuals. Thus the sources and pressures underlying its changes in social behavior come from both developments in itself and changes in its social environment.

B. Kinds of Social Change

During ontogeny an individual masters more intricate, subtle, differentiated and flexible forms of social behavior, and a wider range of social moves. It also becomes increasingly adept at interpreting the social behavior of others, and integrating information from multiple kinds of sources as it selects its responses. With increased competence it enters into and invites a different, usually much expanded, set of social situations. As in the baboon example, these changes can be seen in an individual's interactional behavior, its relationships with other individuals, and the groups it joins. As this ontogenetic course progresses, demands on its communicative behavior change radically.

DEVELOPMENT OF FORMALIZED SIGNALING BEHAVIOR

As individuals develop in capability they enter social regimes in which their communication must deal with different issues and serve new or altered functions. New signaling forms appear and previously existing forms may change, and all must be intelligible to the individuals with whom they interact. The information that is made available changes as signal form does, and there are changes in the stimuli that elicit signaling.

A. Normalization

As formalized signaling appears and develops, its forms and referents must be recognizable and intelligible within the community in which it functions. It must conform to the norms. There are two routes for its normalization: genetic evolution and socially learned shaping. Both can operate on the same signaling.

Zivin (1982) categorized human nonverbal signaling on the basis of these routes. Her concern was with ontogenetic shifts that yield increasingly voluntary control of signaling that is modifiable on a scale far exceeding that found in most nonhuman species. The following adaptation employs three major categories in an attempt to adapt her scheme to serve a broadly comparative approach.

Signaling that is Normalized Through Evolution. This category includes the "displays" of traditional ethology, as well as results of genetically programmed rules that generate the other repertoires discussed on pp. 177–178 of this chapter. Ethologists refer to this class of behavior as "ritualized." The term is used here to mean that features of form are governed by genetic programming, physical constraints, and maturational processes other than social learning. There are four possible ontogenetic courses of this sort, two of which involve significant changes in form during ontogeny.

(a) Signaling behavior may develop as soon as it is physically feasible for performers, and then be (with at most only brief practice) in adult form. An example may be the canid "play bow." When it first appears in the fourth week of life in coyotes, wolves, and dogs, its form does not differ from that of older animals, even in individuals reared apart from others of their species (M. Bekoff, 1977a).

(b) Signaling patterns may appear as soon as feasible, but their forms may then undergo noticeable changes arising from anatomical changes of the growing performers. For example, vocalizations are likely to become lower in frequency as the dimensions of the vocal tract are altered by physical growth. Although we might loosely classify signals (e.g., cries, laughs) that appear in this way as being "the same signals" throughout ontogeny, they are better viewed as serial members of classes of signals ("laughs" would thus be a class of signals, represented by different forms during ontogeny). Recipient individuals could distinguish among members of the series by the progressive changes of form. They should base different expectations on different forms to the extent that these represent signalers with the capacities typical of different ontogenetic stages.

(c) Signaling behavior may also develop through specialized modification of displays from earlier ontogenetic stages. A relatively small number of signaling units, each varying in form, may progressively change and diverge.

Young Franklin's and ring-billed gulls, for instance, hatch out already uttering a set of intergrading vocalizations that range from a loud, hoarse, quavered call to a soft, whistle-like "cheep." After a few days an abbreviated, repetitively uttered version of the former differentiates. A few days later the softer call changes to resemble the begging call of adults. The hoarse call breaks into at least three calls that diverge, yielding a vocabulary of approximately five distinctive vocal displays that are elaborations of the initial variable set. As the calls segregate out, several visible display movements and postures develop. These at first vary, but each gradually becomes more stereotyped and some then begin to be exaggerated. After the young gulls fledge, their displays change little until the birds begin to become reproductively active. Then the adult display repertoire appears suddenly, apparently through modifications of form of the juvenile displays (Moynihan, 1959). When such transformations appear fully in individuals raised under conditions of social deprivation, they are presumably results of maturational processes rather than of social learning.

(d) Finally, particular signals may also appear only when needed by the developing individual, often at maturational stages long after they would be physically feasible. A signal may appear full-blown in adult form, or may require practice—as does the song of birds, even in species that do not learn from social models.

Evolved Signaling that is Further Normalized Socially.   The forms of some signaling patterns are set to a considerable extent by genetic evolution, and yet open to modification through learning, from social models, of what we might call "conventions." The signals come to have both conventionalized and ritualized features. ("Conventionalization" and "ritualization," subsumed under "formalization," are discussed by Smith, 1977a, pp. 326–330.)

Examples include songs of birds. There are species in which some features are learned from a parent, neighbor, neighborhood group, or member of a larger geographical region. Infant and in most species juvenile birds do not sing. Nonetheless, they may learn to recognize by ear the locally sung variants of their species' songs. In such cases they are genetically constrained to recognize songs of their own species and to avoid learning, in natural circumstances at least, to sing like members of other species (unless songs of the latter are incorporated into their species-specific performances, as they are in species known as "mimics"). For instance, experiments in which Marler and Peters (1980) presented artificially constructed song stimuli to infant swamp sparrows have shown that males select the models from which they learn to sing on the basis of appropriate structural components (termed "syllables") within the songs, largely disattending the temporal patterns in which these components are organized. Months later, when they finally produce their own songs, both syllable structure and temporal organizations are species specific, but the details of syllable form show the influence of the models each infant had available to copy.

As the time to breed approaches, male birds begin a "subsong" phase, singing with great variability and with few obvious characteristics of adult song. Numerous features gradually develop, and options are winnowed down through successive "subplastic" and "plastic" stages, finally "crystallizing" into the form of adult song (see Marler & Peters, 1981). An individual may pass through the subsong to full song developmental sequence each year, having ceased singing in the nonbreeding season. In at least the canary, a region of his brain actually increases and decreases in volume seasonally (Nottebohm, 1981).

In nonhuman primates, also, immatures may have highly variable, intergrading signals that they make less variable as they grow older (Newman & Symmes, 1983). Snowdon (1982) reports that infants of both pygmy marmosets and cotton-top tamarins "go through an extensive period of 'babbling'" in which they utter a stream of highly variable vocalizations in inappropriate juxtapositions. This may be analogous to the babbling of human infants practicing speech sounds, although without the cooperative (and presumably instructive) signaling exchanges with adults that we offer in response to some of our infants' vocalizing. Yet the form of primate displays can also be modified during ontogeny without any stage of high variability, as it is in the "isolation peep" vocalization of squirrel monkeys (Lieblich, Symmes, Newman, & Shapiro, 1980). And in all of these cases there are indications of some socially learned features of the eventual form.

That human nonverbal signaling can depend both on genetic programming and on socially learned rules is strongly suggested by comparisons of different populations (e.g., by Ekman & Friesen, 1969; reviewed by Ekman & Oster, 1979). These show that people in the United States, Brazil, Japan and New Guinea are alike in matching photographs of certain posed facial appearances with a list of "primary affects" (emotional states, in particular "happiness," "anger" and "fear"). Ekman and Friesen also showed that members of different cultures (e.g., natives of Japan and the United States) do not perform these facial "expressions" in fully overlapping ranges of circumstances. By applying what Ekman calls "display rules" ("display" here means visible appearance, not the display units discussed above), members of one culture modify facial signaling and increase or decrease the amount performed in comparison with members of another culture (Ekman, 1977).

Signaling Normalized Entirely Through Convention.   The forms of purely conventionalized signaling patterns are entirely learned from social sources, whether through conditioning or imitation. (They are, of course, constrained by the evolved physical capabilities of the signaling organism.) The most obvious nonspeech class includes many of those human signals that Ekman and Friesen (1969, elaborated by Ekman in 1972) term "emblems": nonverbal acts that have "a direct verbal translation." Among examples are a chopping motion with the edge of the hand to the throat (kill, or turn off noisy equipment), thumb held vertically upward (things are all right), and the sign alphabet of deaf language. Some behavior that Ekman and Friesen classify as emblems, however, may not be purely conventionalized. For example, shaking a fist could be a genetically evolved threat display of our species, modifiable by local custom. We may not always be able to tell readily whether acts belong to this or the previous category.

Some purely conventionalized acts accord with cultural norms and are in widespread use. Others are conventionalized just within the repertoires of particular dyads of individuals, and presumably some are even performed only by single individuals. The last function if one or more other individuals grasp their consistency and can interpret them—can decode them. Dyadic and idiosyncratic conventions must arise primarily when individuals have close, enduring relationships. With considerable familiarity, they can begin learning one another's behavior from subtle clues. The increasingly smooth and efficient flow of their interacting becomes a reward for producing those clues with increasing consistency or even slight exaggeration.

There should be comparable phenomena in the interactions of nonhuman species, although research is lacking. Involvement of at least chimpanzees in communicating with limited and highly conventionalized signaling has been fostered in recent years in experimental research on cognition (e.g., Premack, 1971), but shows us only what members of that species can do, not necessarily how they do communicate in nature. We have long seen basically comparable use of artificial and often limited conventions in our interactions with household pets.

B. Ontogenetic Changes in Information Made Available

As the form of signaling changes, so does the information that is made available. This can be information that identifies the signaler, information that renders it locatable, or information about its behavior.

Information that Identifies.   As the course of song learning is studied in more and more species of birds, several patterns are emerging. All suggest that the learned features of song provide information identifying the singer. Significantly, the learned distinguishing characteristics appear to serve no single function. Predispositions to learn aspects of the form of loud, species-specific "song" vocalizations have apparently arisen in response to different evolutionary pressures in different species.

In several species, song learning appears to underlie procedures for controlling gene flow. As suggested by Nottebohm (1969) for the sparrow *Zonotrichia capensis,* learned "dialects" could help males to settle in the general region of their birth, where their natal type of habitat may occur, if they establish territories near males singing the appropriate song forms. Then females, also having learned local song forms as infants (see, e.g., experiments by Kern & King, 1972; Milligan & Verner, 1971) can settle in the same region and select mates from their natal population.

Nottebohm (1969, 1975) found that *Z. capensis* males are differentiable on two features of their songs. One, the "terminal trill," is characteristic of whole local populations and differs between adjacent populations that live in different habitats. Trills mark the dialects he recognized. The other feature, "introductory whistles," gives rise to different "themes." Nottebohm defined a theme as a "series of notes always rendered in the same order and with set pitch relationships" (1969, p. 302). Within a local population, neighbors within mutual hearing tend to sing the same theme. Where neighbors are more dispersed, in populations of low density, they are less likely to share themes. Although the juvenile emigration patterns and models for learning are not known in this species, the distribution of song forms suggests that young males learn the trill of their natal neighborhood, then may move within the population sharing that trill and learn a neighbor's song on settling or, lacking a close neighbor, select from a sampling of available themes sharing the appropriate trill. But why should there be these two different features that differentiate among the songs of males?

In principle, there is an optimum level of inbreeding. A mate should be selected from the population adapted to the natal habitat, but not from such close relatives that excessive homozygosity is conferred on the offspring. Members of one species, the Japanese quail, have actually shown in laboratory tests a preference for mating with first cousins rather than closer or more distant relatives (Bateson, 1982). We have no idea how many species tune their preferences this finely in the wild, but many could if the right information can be made available.

Avoidance of close inbreeding on the basis of learned song forms may be easiest for species in which sons learn from fathers (Nottebohm, 1972), as in bullfinches (Nicolai, 1959) and zebra finches (Immelman, 1969). It has also been suggested in the case of a New Zealand passerine bird in which sons disperse and learn from territorial neighbors where they settle (Jenkins, 1978). Jenkins did not suggest how females choose mates in such a case, although the implication is that to avoid mating with a brother a female should mate only with a bird singing like her father. She should thus disperse only within the local group that sings that song, and recognize her father himself by other means, or be recognized and avoided by him.

Further species are known in which males disperse and then learn to sing the song forms of their neighbors. In the marsh wren, males born late in a season do this (Kroodsma & Pickert, 1980). By learning the songs of a neighbor, a marsh wren can vie for "leader" roles in counter-singing with that bird as they progress through a sequence of different song forms. The functional significance is not fully clear, but the procedure somehow helps territorial neighbors to establish and advertise an aspect of their relationships. In the indigo bunting, in which a dispersed young male learns to sing a song like that of one of his established neighbors, Payne (1981, 1982) suggests he is "deceiving" other males into misidentifying him as the older individual. Payne found that newly dispersed males who mimic an established neighbor breed more successfully than those who do not. Nonetheless, their songs are imperfect copies, are sung from different sites than those used by the model, and must often be uttered more or less simultaneously with his songs. That they should be successful in misinforming seems unlikely. To be misled, responding males would have to be very undiscriminating, and to forego both checking them, by probing into the territories of the mimic and his model, and challenging them in direct encounters. Why a young immigrant should learn an established neighbor's song or songs thus remains to be discovered, and may differ among species.

In parasitic African viduine indigo birds, in which young are reared by hosts of other species, two categories of songs are learned, but from two different classes of models. One set is species specific to the parasites, and also specific to a local group of about 100 adults. The remaining song is learned from the host species that rears each young indigo bird (Payne, 1973).

Social learning may also influence the development of forms of vocalizations less elaborate than song, adding to their identifying information. Pine grosbeaks, for instance, have a "location call" (Adkisson, 1981) that is uttered when flocks are traveling or individuals are seeking to rejoin flocks. Its form varies among populations across North America, and sufficiently that birds are unresponsive to those calls least like their own. Adkisson showed that young pine grosbeaks between 8 and 15 weeks of age learn the form of call uttered by adults who are rearing them. By cross-fostering, i.e., having members of one population hatch out and raise young from another, he showed that the form learned need not be that of their true parents.

Learned forms of calls may also identify members of other infraspecific groups. In the American goldfinch and related species, features of what has been termed the "flight call" are alterable by social learning, perhaps on a cyclical schedule. Nestlings learn the form of their parents. Later, form is altered in pair formation so that mates come to share the same form (either sex may imitate, or both may converge). When winter flocks form, their members may also adopt a common form (Mundinger, 1970, based partly on studies of captive birds). In many species of birds that "duet," i.e., sing or call together in formalized patterns, mates or family members learn and can utter each other's forms (reviewed by Smith, 1977b).

There are often limits to how far the normalization of form is carried. As vocalizations are learned, they may not be copied in exact detail. The resultant forms can be used to identify individuals. Further, Marler and Peters (1981) have shown that as developing male swamp sparrows practice singing, each incorporates unique inventions into its song. Neighboring male birds of many species can recognize each other as individuals by characteristics of their songs (see, e.g., Baker, Thompson, & Sherman, 1981; Falls, 1969).

Finally, to the extent that changes in the form of signaling are typical of developmental stages, part of the identifying information they make available is about the level of "maturity" of the signaler. Effectively, this is information about membership in a class defined by physiology. And as these classes coincide with changes in behavioral repertoires, the signaling also informs about behavior. Not necessarily about particular behavioral selections, but about stage-specific subrepertoires with their baseline probabilities for different behavior.

Information About Location.   Developmental changes in signaling have also been reported that alter the information vocalizing provides about a signaler's location. Nestling birds, for instance, beg food with calls that are less readily locatable (according to Marler, 1955) than are their begging calls after they fledge and scatter. Similar phenomena may be widespread.

Information About Behavior.   Developmental influences on the form of bird-song can affect information that is made available about behavior; as well. For instance, young male brown-headed cowbirds differ markedly in their song forms if raised in captivity as isolates or in all-male groups. The songs of isolate raised males have been shown to be by far the most "attractive" to females, using response with precopulatory posture as a bioassay. Further, these attractive song forms correlate with male dominance: in a group of males, only the dominant individual utters the most attractive form (King & West, 1977; West & King, 1980; West, King, & Eastzer, 1981). Different song forms in this species thus predict at least readiness to fight or to defer. Each male learns to utter forms appropriate to his capacities within a particular group, adjusting form to his current skills and consequently to his social rank.

What information is made available about agonistic behavior by an individual cowbird's song is thus influenced by the social conditions prevailing during maturation. Because there has been little effort in ethology to study the ontogeny of communicating about behavior, we do not know whether this sort of ontogenetic shaping is widespread. For example, do coyote pups who do not form close bonds and then emigrate from their natal groups (M. Bekoff, 1977b) differ in their signaling from their more companionable littermates who remain behind? Do young macaques or savanna baboons of low-ranking mothers develop different repertoires of signaling variations from those of peers whose higher status mothers protect them more during their ontogeny? Do young male Florida scrub jays growing up in the presence of several dominating older male siblings (see Woolfenden & Fitzpatrick, 1977) have repertoires that differ in any characteristics from those siblings? To what extent are repertoires modifiable later in life if an individual's social options change? Is such an individual condemned to work with an incompletely applicable vocabulary, or can it acquire signaling forms it has not performed before, in correlation with its altered nonsignal behavior? (The effects of rearing on cowbirds are reversible.) And if such signaling differences among individuals arise, are they largely confined to providing information only about some kinds of behavior, for example, of competitive sorts of interactional behavior and escape, or do they extend to information about indecisive or locomotory behavior, or the behavior of "associating" with other animals or being receptive to their advances (all examples of behavioral information known to be provided by the displays of diverse species, see Table 6.2)?

It is unfortunate that there has been so little research on the ontogenetic development of signaling about behavior. Although identifying information is universally important, there is much more to communicating than simply identifying one's self.

C. Ontogenetic Changes in Stimuli Eliciting Signaling

Whether signal form changes or not during ontogeny, many of the stimuli to which individuals respond by signaling do change (Barlow, 1977; Burghardt, 1977). As an individual develops, the competence with which it interprets many kinds of events increases and the kinds of interpretations it makes change. It seeks different kinds of information from different sources and becomes more resourceful in the quest. It learns what stimuli are important and what to expect in different circumstances, how to discriminate among similar stimuli, only some of which are significant, and what kinds of information are needed from sources contextual to them. With increased and sharpened cognitive capacity, "there are shifts in environmental saliences, in causal attributions, in the ability to integrate events over time, as well as in the ability to shift behavior in the face of changing demands . . . the organism determines what will and will not serve as a stimulus, and what the stimulus will signify" (Gollin, 1981, p. 245).

The change and diversification of stimuli that can be relevant in eliciting formalized signaling behavior are seen in Green's account of a vocalization of Japanese macaques (1981). This "uh" sound varies in form, although Green does not indicate if any variations are limited to ontogenetic phases. Struggling infants utter "uh" when they succeed in reaching a mother's nipple. Juveniles do not nurse, but utter some form of "uh" when finally managing to struggle into a huddled group of relatives (males gradually utter it less in this circumstance, but females retain this use throughout their lives). Adult and subadult females utter an "uh" when they eventually become calm after running screaming from a fight. Adult males sometimes utter it just prior to dismounting after copulating. While all these and apparently other cases have in common the transition of the vocalizing animal to relaxed behavior after vigorous social activity, there is a great elaboration with maturation of the range of events in which the vocalization is uttered and in the stimuli eliciting it.

If the shift from vigorous to relaxed social behavior, common to all cases, is the information that is made available about behavior by the "uh," then it does not change during ontogeny even though the circumstances eliciting vocalizing do. (Just how the relaxing signaler will behave in different events is evident from contextual clues.) Changes in eliciting stimuli do not need to entail changes in this information.

An example in which human nonverbal signaling becomes elicited by a wider range of stimuli involves a chin-up posture of the head. Zivin (1977, 1982) reports that very young children hold their chins at an upward angle when staring directly with medially raised brows at an opponent in a competitive encounter. She terms this combination of three units the "plus face." Older children use the chin-up unit in response to quite different stimuli in diverse circumstances in which they appear to be giving the impression of assured behavior or competence—often in events in which they pit themselves against a task and have no social opponent.

The stimuli eliciting signaling that provides information about "things" and "situations," to the extent that such referents occur, may be especially modifiable as developing mammals and birds gain experience. Infant and juvenile vervet monkeys, for instance, are much more likely than adults to utter their "eagle alarm" at the sight of birds such as storks, herons, and pigeons that are not dangerous to them, and even occasionally on seeing a falling leaf (Seyfarth & Cheney, 1980). Adult vervets, on the other hand, make few such errors and narrow performances of this signal primarily to sightings of martial eagles, their most dangerous predators, and to two similar species. When Seyfarth and Cheney played back recordings of the call, they found that infants spent increased time looking at their mothers, individuals from whom they could learn to associate that vocalization with the most appropriate stimuli.

DEVELOPMENT OF RESPONSES TO FORMALIZED SIGNALING

As individuals develop and their needs change, they must adjust the ways they respond to many things, including signaling behavior. The adjustments may depend in some ways on maturing response biases, and in others on learning what consequences to expect of their responses. Much of it has to do with obtaining the necessary information to permit functional responding.

A. Learning to Rely Upon Multiple Sources of Information

Infants are usually biased innately to respond in preordained ways to simply defined stimuli. This led early ethologists to describe "releasers" of behavior. For example, a newly hatched gull chick will seek food by pecking at a bill of optimal width traversing a horizontal arc at a certain speed. Parent gulls provide these stimuli when presenting food (Hailman, 1967). With the experience of its first few days with its parents, however, a gull chick comes to require more complex stimuli. It no longer gives its pecking response to simple models, and may respond to them with avoidance. It now needs to see a good, three-dimensional approximation of an adult gull's head, with a body behind it. It has developed expectations of relations between the cues it perceives, each cue providing a necessary part of the context of the others. Thus its innate bias toward simple stimuli is replaced in development by a bias to learn simultaneously available sources of information, and to become reliant on information integrated from multiple sources for its responding.

Formal signaling is not the only nor, in many events, necessarily even the major source of information during communication. It does provide focal points: sources of information that are usually especially significant if only because formal signaling has evolved to be informative. But *all* formalized signaling is interpreted by recipients in accordance with sources contextual to it (Smith, 1963, 1977a). For some species it may require considerable experience to do this effectively, but all animals should evolve to do it. They cannot evolve the expectation of being fully informed by signaling, both because signaling repertoires are small, and because information is always withheld by signalers.

Responding individuals must be prepared for, or prepared to learn, the limits of what information is made available, and the most effective ways to employ contextual sources of information in responding to signaling. This requires developing the ability to evaluate the relevance in different circumstances of numerous sources of information, and even propensities to seek particular sources at times. Individuals also need to accumulate stores of information, e.g., on the idiosyncracies, temperaments, and social status of individuals they encounter, or the significance of particular places, to be brought to bear in responding to signaling in future events.

Developing the ability to respond to formalized signaling contextually is not a unique problem, however. It is a fundamental feature of perception that available stimuli need to be sorted into figures and ground, and the ways in which figures are interpreted depends upon characteristics of the ground, and upon experience. Social communication of the sorts usually studied by ethologists is special in part because evolutionary or cultural processes have specialized some stimuli to be salient "figures."

Some contextual sources are made readily available as a part of signaling; e.g., displays are presented in the context of badges, or of other displays. Visible signals have the rest of the signaling animal as sources of contextual information: its size, shape, visible sexual characteristics, orientation, location with respect to recipients or features such as territories, and its intention movements and other nonformal behavior. Other sources can be readily available to an animal but difficult for an observer to evaluate because they lie in information that the animal has stored. For example, individuals of some species spend much time together and get to know each other as individuals. They can develop experience with each other's temperaments: the long-term behavioral predispositions of each. They can become skilled at reading changes in each other's moods: states that set individuals to respond in particular ways, e.g., irritably, aggressively, calmly. Opportunities for such development differ among species.

B. Calibrating Individuals

In developing capacities to respond to unique yet predictable social partners, an animal must learn to compensate for individualistic signaling. Just as no two individuals are identical in other characteristics of their structure and behavior, they differ in the form and referents of their signaling. These differences are not usually extreme, or communicating would be inefficient. Nonetheless, they are inevitable.

Where sufficient opportunities exist during the development of relationships, individuals can learn and adjust to one another's signaling idiosyncracies. This requires a degree of "openness" in the way animals are prepared to recognize the referents of each other's signaling behavior. Any responding individual must a priori expect a certain range of information from each formalization; this is based on the "shared code" of its species. Its expectations must be adjusted as it learns what can be predicted from a given kind of signaling in the context of information that identifies individual signalers. To whatever extent it can, it should calibrate the signaling peculiarities of each individual with whom it must deal.

Just how far animals can carry such calibration is largely unknown. Opportunities to calibrate must vary with the extent of social interacting and time available for developing detailed relationships. There is some anecdotal evidence. Tinbergen (1939, 1953), for instance, reports that within colonies of herring gulls, individuals who "alarm call" unusually readily are apparently known by their neighbors and their alarms are largely disattended. And there is experimental evidence, for at least two species, on recognition by neighbors of conspecific individuals with extremely individualistic songs. Richards (1979) reports that occasional red-eyed towhees sing imitations of the very different songs of Carolina wrens, and yet can defend territories and attract mates. By playing back tape recordings he showed that neighbors of such individuals recognize them and respond strongly, whereas non-neighbors do not. Similarly, Rice (1981) found a mated, territorial red-eyed vireo with a grossly aberrant song and showed that its neighbors responded to playback of the song but strangers did not. Neighbors somehow learned to accept these aberrant singers, whether through peculiarities of their songs, clues from their locations, utterances as the singers challenged them, or a diversity of means. The ontogenetic processes by which those neighbors developed responsiveness to territorial singing must have prepared them for their own species' songs, but also left them open to use non-song sources of information to calibrate individuals with highly aberrant songs.

C. Calibration and Reliability

That responding individuals calibrate signaling through their knowledge of individual signalers has fundamental implications. It permits more distinctions to be made in communicating as, indeed, all context-dependent responding does (Smith, in press a). Calibration also implies limits on the extent to which signaling can evolve through advantages it brings signalers who misinform other individuals. Unreliable signaling is known in interspecific communicating (e.g., in Batesian mimicry) where the stakes are life and death, but it creates such evolutionary instability that in most intraspecific communicating it may be short-lived.

By actively seeking sources of information contextual to signaling, animals can check the information being signaled. Checking must defeat some potential kinds of misinforming. For instance, it has been suggested that a bird might gain advantages in territorial competition by singing songs of more than one form. According to the "Beau Geste" postulate (Krebs, 1977) this might mislead others into believing the singer to be more than one individual, and dissuade them from settling locally in the apparently dense population. However, territorial songbirds trespass on one another's territories. In some species, such as the great tit for which Krebs formulated his postulate, such trespass is frequent both before and during the breeding season (Gibb, 1956; Hinde, 1952; Krebs, 1971). Trespassers see the individuals who inhabit each area, and must also learn what each sings. They should be no more readily misled than is a competent bird-watcher, who is not fooled. Their intrusive probings are probably adaptive largely because of the information they uncover.

Testing is an even more active way to obtain information with which to evaluate signaling. Males of Rocky Mountain sheep (Geist, 1971) or red deer (Clutton-Brock & Albon, 1979), for instance, use testing to work out their closest dominance relationships. More distant ranks are settled at a glance: larger horned (or antlered) individuals are deferred to by smaller horned ones. Animals similar in appearance confront each other and head-butt or antler-wrestle, testing each other's strength and endurance. The signaling of these characteristics by horn or antler size (evolved badges) is kept reliable not only by these direct tests, but also by a checking procedure. Less well-endowed individuals gather and watch jousting bouts. Afterward, one usually challenges the loser. Even though larger than such a challenger, a loser is momentarily fatigued and rendered less dangerous. Any individual with deceptively large horns or antlers will be discovered and reduced in such tests to its appropriate rank, having risked fights with more powerful individuals to no gain.

Testing and checking keep the evolution of displays and badges reliable by keeping their wearers calibrated. During individual life spans they keep individuals from misinforming as they develop relationships with one another.

Individuals who do not signal reliably are devalued on being calibrated (Smith, in press b). A parallel to their devaluation is seen during ontogenetic development, in cases in which young, inexperienced animals have not yet learned appropriate stimuli for signaling well enough to be useful sources of information, and are largely ignored by adults, as mentioned on pp. 178–179. But it is not just inexperienced individuals who devalue the signaling of naive ones. Calibrating other individuals must be a recurrent or continuous developmental process that enables each individual, at all stages, to fine-tune adjustment of its responses to signaling to the particular social relationships and groups with which it makes its life.

D. Development of Formalized Interactions

As an individual gains experience, and ability to evaluate and integrate information from multiple sources in any event, its responses to signaling should permit increasing elaboration of its interactional behavior. As a result, the forms of one signaling repertoire could become richer: formalized interactions, signaling patterns that incorporate interactions in their structure.

Each formalized interactional unit requires the integrated participation of two or more contributors. Especially in the case of formalized interactions acquired and normalized largely as conventions, appropriate performance must develop only with experience. Among other abilities, participants in formalized interactions must develop sensitivity to the predictive clues offered in the orientation, timing, and specific acts of other participants. They must become competent in recognizing sequential patterns and choice points for different subroutines. They must stabilize their own contributions within the normative limits of each kind of formalized interaction.

It is the complexity of this kind of signaling behavior that led A. Bekoff (1978) to question whether detailed ontogenetic analyses of all kinds of signaling were feasible. Her specific example was a formalized interaction of geese known as the "Triumph Ceremony." Probably the development of formalized interactions can be analyzed, but it will require breaking down each into component motor patterns of the participants plus a set of formalized rules that regulate (often flexibly) the performance of these acts according to the parts being played by different participants (see pp. 177–178, and Smith, 1977a, chapter 14).

COMPARATIVE RESEARCH ON THE ONTOGENY OF COMMUNICATION

We have only fragmentary descriptions from a scattering of species of the many ways in which developing individuals change their communicative behavior. These reveal both similarities and divergences among species, as expected: different species have needs in common as well as different needs and histories.

An example of divergence among species can be seen in the most detailed comparisons ethology has yet produced in studying the development of signaling, the learning of characteristics of form of their vocalizations by young birds. First, the functions of learning differ markedly among species and among kinds of signals. Second, as the functions differ, so do some parameters of the ontogeny: the "sensitive period" for learning from a social model differs in timing, and renewed sensitive periods may occur if there are appropriate times; the models an individual is biased to select and the parts of the signal repertoire modifiable by learning differ. Third, all this specialization is based on important general features. For instance, each species must have an appropriate means of choosing a model, and an appropriately timed period or periods in which to learn.

The potential advantages of comparative research are considerable. By learning what social problems the young of different species must face in common as they develop, and what causes divergence and specialization, we can establish a framework for posing and relating questions about the ontogeny of communication, and thus for guiding research. To be suitable, a conceptual framework must relate features and stages of individual and social development to changes in communicating for diverse species. That is, it must take into account needs and capacities at different ontogenetic phases, as developing individuals engage in progressively different kinds of interactions and relationships, and become functioning members of different groups. It must relate these changing needs and capacities to changes in the form of signaling, stimuli eliciting signaling, and the kinds of information made available by several different classes of formalized signaling repertoires: display units, rules for varying the forms of these units, grammatical rules, and formalized interactions—as well as changes in nonbehavioral formalizations such as badges and scents, and provision of information by nonformalized sources. It must further relate changing needs and capacities to changes in the ways developing individuals respond to signaling.

A suitable conceptual framework must recognize that developing individuals contend simultaneously with two tasks: becoming adult and having appropriate behavior for each ontogenetic phase. Each individual, in common with its development of other social behavior, must form expectations of different situations and the kinds of resolution it should seek of them. It must develop means to seek and deal with information from many sources as it selects among its options in each situation, and among these sources are formalized signals. It must develop propensities to respond to some stimuli by providing information, when this can bias the responding of other individuals in ways favorable to it, and in doing so must develop its performance of signaling.

Surely the ways in which it develops its communicative behavior depend on the complexity and uncertainty of the issues it must face. In some species, development can perhaps be largely governed by preprogrammed maturational shifts. These, however, cannot provide an individual with the finely tuned responses it could use in dealing with the idiosyncracies of the individuals with which it must interact. In other species, development must equip each individual to deal with many others and form many kinds of relationships with them, in social environments that cannot be predicted in important details. In these latter species, the conditions prevailing during an individual's ontogeny must determine many features of its signaling and responding—but what features, how flexibly is their development governed, and to what extent are the developmental adjustments alterable later in ontogeny?

Ethology is only beginning to recognize and explore the range of social behavior shown by vertebrate animals. We have few concepts with which to understand how social groups are integrated, and fewer for understanding the characteristics of relationships and interactions. Yet it is in interactional events that communication does most of its work. Thus we know rather little about the communicative needs of organisms, or how these change during ontogeny. But it is not too early to begin seeking central themes for the comparative study of the ontogeny of communication. Only if we adopt a framework, however gross and provisional, for guiding research can we hope to ask the kinds of questions that will eventually lead us to general principles.

ACKNOWLEDGMENTS

I am indebted to Gene Gollin, Liz Rozin, Paul Rozin, and Jon Schul for advice on matters of development and for criticizing drafts of this paper.

REFERENCES

Adkisson, C. S. (1981). Geographic variation in vocalizations and evolution of North American pine grosbeaks. *Condor, 83,* 277–288.

Altmann, J. (1980). *Baboon mothers and infants.* Cambridge: Harvard University Press.

Baker, M. C., Thompson, D. B., & Sherman, G. L. (1981). Neighbor/stranger discrimination in white-crowned sparrows. *Condor, 83,* 265–267.

Barlow, G. W. (1977). Modal action patterns. In T. A. Sebeok (Ed.), *How animals communicate.* Bloomington: Indiana University Press.

Bastock, M. (1967). *Courtship: an ethological study.* Chicago: Aldine.

Bateson, P. (1982). Preferences for cousins in Japanese quail. *Nature, 295,* 236–237.

Bekoff, A. (1978). A neuroethological approach to the study of the ontogeny of coordinated behavior. In G. M. Burghardt & M. Bekoff (Eds.), *The development of behavior. Comparative and evolutionary aspects.* New York: Garland.

Bekoff, M. (1972). The development of social interaction, play, and metacommunication in mammals: an ethological perspective. *Quarterly Review of Biology, 47,* 412–434.

Bekoff, M. (1974). Social play and play-soliciting by infant canids. *American Zoologist, 14,* 323–340.

Bekoff, M. (1977a). Social communication in canids: Evidence for the evolution of a stereotyped mammalian display. *Science, 197,* 1097–1099.

Bekoff, M. (1977b). Mammalian dispersal and the ontogeny of individual behavioral phenotypes. *American Naturalist, 111,* 715–732.

Burghardt, G. M. (1977). Ontogeny of communication. In T. A. Sebeok (Ed.), *How animals communicate.* Bloomington: Indiana University Press.

Busse, C., & Hamilton, W. J., III. (1981). Infant carrying by male chacma baboons. *Science, 212,* 1281–1283.

Clutton-Brock, T. H., & Albon, S. D. (1979). The roaring of red deer and the evolution of honest advertisement. *Behaviour, 69,* 145–169.

Darwin, C. (1872). *The expression of the emotions in man and animals.* London: Appleton.

Ekman, P. (1972). Universals and cultural differences in facial expression of emotion. In J. Cole (Ed.), *Nebraska Symposium on motivation, 1971.* Lincoln: University of Nebraska Press.

Ekman, P. (1977). Biological and cultural contributions to body and facial movement. In J. Blacking (Ed.), *The anthropology of the body, A.S.A. Monograph, 15.* London: Academic Press.

Ekman, P., & Friesen, W. V. (1969). The repertoire of nonverbal behavior: Categories, origins, usage, and coding. *Semiotica, 1,* 49–98.

Ekman, P., & Oster, H. (1979). Facial expressions of emotion. *Annual Review of Psychology, 30,* 527–554.

Fagen, R. (1981). *Animal play behaviour.* New York: Oxford University Press.

Falls, J. B. (1969). Functions of territorial song in the white-throated sparrow. In R. A. Hinde (Ed.), *Bird vocalizations.* New York: Cambridge University Press.

Geist, V. (1971). *Mountain sheep.* Chicago: University of Chicago Press.

Gibb, J. (1956). Territory in the genus *Parus. Ibis, 98,* 420–429.

Golani, I., & Mendelssohn, H. (1971). Sequences of precopulatory behavior of the jackal (*Canis aureus* L.). *Behaviour, 38,* 169–192.

Gollin, E. S. (1981). Development and plasticity. In E. S. Gollin (Ed.), *Developmental plasticity.* New York: Academic Press.

Green, S. M. (1981). Sex differences and age gradations in vocalizations of Japanese and lion-tailed monkeys (*Macaca fuscata* and *Macaca silenus*). *American Zoologist, 21,* 165–183.

Hailman, J. P. (1967). The ontogeny of an instinct. *Behaviour Supplement, 15.*

Hausfater, G., Altmann, J., & Altmann, S. (1982). Long-term consistency of dominance relations among female baboons (*Papio cynocephalus*). *Science, 217,* 752–755.

Hinde, R. A. (1952). The behaviour of the great tit (*Parus major*) and some other related species. *Behaviour,* Suppl. II.

Hinde, R. A. (1974). *Biological bases of human social behaviour.* New York: McGraw-Hill.

Hinde, R. A., & Atkinson, S. (1970). Assessing the roles of social partners in maintaining mutual proximity, as exemplified by mother-infant relations in rhesus monkeys. *Animal Behaviour, 18,* 169–176.

Hinde, R. A., & Herrmann, J. (1977). Frequencies, durations, derived measures and their correlations in studying dyadic and triadic relationships. In H. R. Schaffer (Ed.), *Studies in mother-infant interactions.* London: Academic Press.

Hodgdon, H. E., & Larson, J. S. (1973). Some sexual differences in behaviour within a colony of marked beavers (*Castor canadensis*). *Animal Behaviour, 21,* 147–152.

Immelmann, K. (1969). Song development in the zebra finch and other estrildid finches. In R. A. Hinde (Ed.), *Bird vocalizations.* New York: Cambridge University Press.

Jenkins, P. F. (1978). Cultural transmission of song patterns and dialect development in a free-living bird population. *Animal Behaviour, 26,* 50–78.

Kern, M. D., & King, J. R. (1972). Testosterone-induced singing in female white-crowned sparrows. *Condor, 74,* 204–209.

King, A. P., & West, M. J. (1977). Species identification in the North American cowbird: appropriate responses to abnormal song. *Science, 195,* 1002–1004.

Krebs, J. R. (1971). Territory and breeding density in the great tit, *Parus major* L. *Ecology, 52,* 2–22.

Krebs, J. R. (1977). The significance of song repertoires: the Beau Geste hypothesis. *Animal Behaviour, 25,* 475–478.

Kroodsma, D. E., & Pickert, R. (1980). Environmentally dependent sensitive periods for avian vocal learning. *Nature, 288,* 477–479.

Lieblich, A. K., Symmes, D., Newman, J. D., & Shapiro, M. (1980). Development of the isolation peep in laboratory-bred squirrel monkeys. *Animal Behaviour, 28,* 1–9.

Marler, P. (1955). Characteristics of some animal calls. *Nature, 176,* 6–8.

Marler, P., & Peters, S. (1980). Birdsong and speech: evidence for special processing. In P. Eimas & J. Miller (Eds.), *Perspectives on the study of speech.* Hillsdale, NJ: Lawrence Erlbaum Associates.

Marler, P., & Peters, S. (1981). Sparrows learn adult song and more from memory. *Science, 213*, 780–782.

Mayr, E. (1961). Cause and effect in biology. *Science, 134*, 1501–1506.

Milligan, M. M., & Verner, J. (1971). Inter-populational song dialect discrimination in the white-crowned sparrow. *Condor, 73*, 208–213.

Moynihan, M. (1959). Notes on the behavior of some North American gulls. IV. The ontogeny of hostile behavior and display patterns. *Behaviour, 14*, 214–239.

Moynihan, M. (1966). Display patterns of tropical American "nine-primaried" songbirds. IV. The yellow-rumped tanager. *Smithsonian Miscellaneous Collection, 149*(5), 1–34.

Mundinger, P. C. (1970). Vocal imitation and individual recognition of finch calls. *Science, 168*, 480–482.

Nash, L. T. (1978). The development of the mother-infant relationship in wild baboons (*Papio anubis*). *Animal Behaviour, 26*, 746–759.

Newman, J. D., & Symmes, D. (1983). Inheritance and experience in the acquisition of primate acoustic behavior. In C. T. Snowdon, C. H. Brown, & M. R. Petersen (Eds.), *Primate communication*. New York: Cambridge University Press.

Nicolai, J. (1959). Familientradition in der Gesangsentwicklung des Gimpels (*Pyrrhula pyrrhula* L.). *Journal für Ornithologie, 100*, 39–46.

Nottebohm, F. (1969). The song of the chingolo, *Zonotrichia capensis* in Argentina: Description and evaluation of a system of dialects. *Condor, 71*, 299–315.

Nottebohm, F. (1974). The origins of vocal learning. *American Naturalist, 106*, 116–140.

Nottebohm, F. (1975). Continental patterns of song variability in *Zonotrichia capensis:* some possible ecological correlates. *American Naturalist, 109*, 605–624.

Nottebohm, F. (1981). A brain for all seasons: Cyclic anatomical changes in song control nuclei of the canary brain. *Science, 214*, 1368–1370.

Owens, N. W. (1975a). Social play behaviour in free-living baboons, *Papio anubis*. *Animal Behaviour, 23*, 387–408.

Owens, N. W. (1975b). A comparison of aggressive play and aggression in free-living baboons, *Papio anubis*. *Animal Behaviour, 23*, 757–765.

Owings, D. H., & Leger, D. W. (1980). Chatter vocalizations of California ground squirrels: predator- and social-role specificity. *Zeitschrift für Tierpsychologie, 54*, 163–184.

Packer, C. (1980). Male care and exploitation of infants in *Papio anubis*. *Animal Behaviour, 28*, 512–520.

Payne, R. B. (1973). Vocal mimicry of the paradise whydahs (*Vidua*) and response of female whydahs to the songs of their hosts (*Pytilia*) and their mimics. *Animal Behaviour, 21*, 762–771.

Payne, R. B. (1981). Song learning and social interaction in indigo buntings. *Animal Behaviour, 29*, 688–697.

Payne, R. B. (1982). Ecological consequences of song matching: Breeding success and intraspecific song mimicry in indigo buntings. *Ecology, 63*, 401–411.

Premack, D. (1971). Language in chimpanzee? *Science, 172*, 808–822.

Ransom, T. W., & Ransom, B. S. (1971). Adult male-infant relations among baboons (*Papio anubis*). *Folia Primatologica, 16*, 179–195.

Richards, D. G. (1979). Recognition of neighbors by associative learning in rufous-sided towhees. *Auk, 96*, 688–693.

Rice, J. C. (1981). Behavioral implications of aberrant song of a red-eyed vireo. *Wilson Bulletin, 93*, 383–390.

Seyfarth, R. M., & Cheney, D. L. (1980). The ontogeny of vervet monkey alarm calling behavior: A preliminary report. *Zeitschrift für Tierpsychologie, 54*, 37–56.

Seyfarth, R. M., Cheney, D. L., & Marler, P. (1980). Vervet monkey alarm calls: semantic communication in a free-ranging primate. *Animal Behaviour, 28*, 1070–1094.

Simpson, M. J. A., & Howe, S. (1980). The interpretation of individual differences in rhesus monkey infants. *Behaviour, 72,* 127–155.

Smith, W. J. (1963). Vocal communication of information in birds. *American Naturalist, 97,* 117–125.

Smith, W. J. (1977a). *The behavior of communicating. An ethological approach.* Cambridge: Harvard University Press.

Smith, W. J. (1977b). Communication in birds. In T. A. Sebeok (Ed.), *How animals communicate.* Bloomington: University of Indiana Press.

Smith, W. J. (1981). Referents of animal communication. *Animal Behaviour, 29,* 1273–1275.

Smith, W. J. (in press a). Consistency and change in communication. In G. Zivon (Ed.), *The development of expressive behavior: Biology–environment interactions.* New York: Academic Press.

Smith, W. J. (in press b). An "informational" perspective on manipulation. In R. W. Mitchell & N. S. Thompson (Eds.), *Deception: perspectives on human and non-human deceit.* State University of New York Press.

Smith, W. J., Pawlukiewicz, J., & Smith, S. T. (1978). Kinds of activities correlated with singing patterns in the yellow-throated vireo. *Animal Behaviour, 26,* 862–884.

Snowdon, C. T. (1983). Linguistic and psycholinguistic approaches to primate communication. In C. T. Snowdon, C. H. Brown, & M. R. Petersen (Eds.), *Primate communication.* New York: Cambridge University Press.

Tinbergen, N. (1939). On the analysis of social organization among vertebrates, with special reference to birds. *American Midland Naturalist, 21,* 210–234.

Tinbergen, N. (1953). *The herring gull's world.* London: Collins.

Tinbergen, N. (1959). Comparative studies of the behaviour of gulls. *Behaviour, 15,* 1–70.

Tyler, S. J. (1972). The behaviour and social organization of the New Forest ponies. *Animal Behaviour Monograph, 5*(2), 87–196.

von Frisch, K. (1967). *The dance language and orientation of bees.* Cambridge: Harvard University Press.

West, M. J., & King, P. (1980). Enriching cowbird song by social deprivation. *Journal of Comparative and Physiological Psychology, 94,* 263–270.

West, M. J., King, A. P., & Eastzer, D. H. (1981). Validating the female bioassay of cowbird song: Relating differences in song potency to mating success. *Animal Behaviour, 29,* 490–501.

Woolfenden, G. E., & Fitzpatrick, J. W. (1977). Dominance in the Florida scrub jay. *Condor, 79,* 1–12.

Zivin, G. (1977). On becoming subtle: age and social rank changes in the use of a facial gesture. *Child Development, 48,* 1314–1321.

Zivin, G. (1982). Watching the sands shift: Conceptualizing development of nonverbal mastery with the assistance of instabilities and discontinuities. In R. S. Feldman (Ed.), *The development of nonverbal communication in children.* New York: Springer.

7 Ontogeny of Communicative Behaviors

David Chiszar
University of Colorado and National Science Foundation

INTRODUCTION

This chapter has two missions. The first is to review data and theory dealing with the development of communicative skills in animals. The second is to discuss methodological and conceptual issues that are particularly important in the developmental analysis of communication. Since these two missions are clearly interdependent, both sets of considerations are treated in parallel rather than in sequence.

The chapter reaches three main conclusions that can be stated briefly to provide the reader with an orientation toward the arguments to be presented. First, the term *communication* denotes a very important psychobiological domain that contains a heterogeneous set of partially understood processes, and the single label—communication—has come to impart to these processes a false sense of unity. Communication is not a single process. Understanding communication requires that we come to terms with the diversity of mechanisms that produce events with semantic value. This brings up the second conclusion, namely, that communicative skills have evolved because of contributions they make to fitness. Understanding a communicative process requires that we understand the environment in which it has evolved and the functions it serves. Finally, all psychobiological processes have an ontogenetic dimension. Hence, another requirement for understanding communication is that we take a developmental perspective, and this point demands greater elaboration.

TAKING A DEVELOPMENTAL PERSPECTIVE

At first glance it may seem as though a developmental perspective simply implies that we should be sensitive to the conditions under which signals emerge during ontogeny and to the processes that establish their semantic value. That is, we should be attentive to ontogenetic events occurring in the sender that have the effects of generating, shaping, and/or delivering the signal, and we should also study ontogenetic events in the receiver that facilitate reception, interpretation, and appropriate response.

There is no doubt about the value of developmental analyses of the sort described in the previous paragraph. However, there is a major omission in this statement, and this omission derives from the adult-centered orientation of much research on animal (and human) communication.

It is as if many researchers believe that adults are the proper models of any particular species, and that pre-adults are incompletely formed versions that must undergo a variety of finishing processes. Such a view clearly emphasizes the valuable task of studying the finishing processes and of understanding how individuals make the transition from imperfect juveniles to perfect adults. But, this view attaches no special importance to communication arising from and/or directed at immature animals. As an example, many researchers have studied development of primate affectional systems, and the focus of this valuable work has usually been upon the early socioenvironmental determinants of behavioral patterns seen in adulthood (see Mason, Davenport, & Menzel, 1968, for a review). The same can be said about much of the research on early determinants of social and/or emotional behavior in dogs, cats, and rodents (for reviews see Newton & Levine, 1968; Stevenson, Hess, & Rheingold, 1967). Experimental manipulations were typically introduced at some point during the period of maternal care, and terminal measures were taken at some point after puberty. In many of the rodent studies no data were gathered during the intervening time, emphasizing the fact that this research usually has an orientation toward the final form of adult social skills rather than an orientation toward the early functions of the behavioral systems under consideration. Neonatal treatments that had no effects on behavior in adulthood were often regarded as theoretically uninteresting, even though the treatments might have had strong effects for short periods after their administration.[1] This research generated the important concept of "developmental homeostasis"—the idea that many developmental systems can compensate for significant exteroceptive or interoceptive perturbations and pro-

---

[1] I recognize that the case has been slightly overstated here, and that some workers have long taken the sort of developmental perspective advocated in this section. The references given earlier in this paragraph are excellent summaries of the literature, and the interested reader can consult them for a more detailed presentation of research on early experience. I believe the reader will then agree with my main theme, particularly for the rodent literature through the 1960s.

duce essentially normal adaptive traits even in suboptimal environments (Alcock, 1979; Mayr, 1963). Yet, because early aspects of ontogeny were often not recorded, we have little understanding of the plasticity (i.e., compensatory) mechanisms implied by developmental homeostasis (Gollin, 1981; Gollin, 1984). Also, we have little understanding of the functions of early manifestations of behaviors known to be adaptive later in adulthood. Accordingly, we are frequently placed in the curious situation of seeing (at least in outline) the trajectories leading to adult expressiveness without a simultaneous view of the adaptedness of any of the early stages along those trajectories. This has sometimes led to assertions denying any significant function for early behaviors other than their proactive (i.e., practice and/or exercise) effects. The following quotation from Scott (1958) will illustrate this point.

> *Development of behavior.*—The young lambs did not behave exactly like the adults, and in order to get the complete picture of behavior we had to follow their activity from birth until they reached maturity. One of the first activities was their special type of ingestive behavior, nursing. After a while it became obvious that the mothers always allowed the lambs to nurse just after they came when called. This appeared to train them to follow their mothers.
>
> Within a few days the lambs began to eat grass but spent much less time grazing then did their elders. Instead they spent a good deal of time in play activities. As we watched, we saw that most of the play consisted of immature forms of adult types of adaptation, directed to no particular end. The young lambs would run and leap together in a playful form of allelomimetic behavior. Occasional mounting was obviously a playful form of sexual behavior. As they grew older their behavior became more and more like that of the adult sheep. (pp. 23–24)

This conceptual situation is reminiscent of the Cuvier-St. Hilaire controversy (circa 1930) regarding the manner in which invertebrates and embryos should be viewed within phylogenetic and embryological theory, respectively (Gould, 1977). The "Natur Philosophen" imagined that all animals developed according to a single plan or ontogenetic trajectory, and that development was propelled by an energy called formative force. The distance along the trajectory achieved by an organism was determined by the amount of formative force it contained. The end point of the trajectory was, of course, *Homo sapiens,* and all other species were more or less imperfect humans since they had insufficient formative force to proceed to the full extent possible along the common ontogenetic path. This view did not see invertebrates as forms adapted for functions, and it inspired no ecologically sound understanding of these multitudinous species. They were simply imperfect embryos or monstrosities relative to perfect adult humans (particularly German and French males). It took a scientific revolution to replace this conceptualization of ontogeny and phylogeny with an ecologically informed one. No longer are other species seen as embryonic humans, yet there is still a tendency to think of immature animals as imperfect adults. Just as "lower species'' must be understood as forms adapted to functions within particular ecosystems, young animals must be seen as having adaptations fitting them to environments that are usually quite different from the environments inhabited by adults. Although a young animal may be incompetent at executing adult actions, it is self-evident that young animals must be rather competent at being themselves.

Although it may in some cases be true that early behaviors have only proactive (if any) consequences, it is hazardous to extend this conclusion to early behavior in general. Indeed, the accumulating evidence strongly advises against this. The safest strategy is to take a developmental perspective that combines an interest in the early determinants of adult motor patterns with an interest in the topography and function of the neonatal and juvenile patterns that eventually give rise to the adult forms. This is particularly important for the analysis of communication because the functions of certain motor patterns in adulthood can often be understood from the use to which the precursor patterns are put by neonates. Research focusing only on the final emergence and/or form of adult expressiveness may therefore overlook an important source of hypotheses and explanations regarding the semantic value of motor patterns.

THE ADAPTEDNESS OF EARLY COMMUNICATION

It will be necessary in this section and elsewhere to take a broad view of communication (see Sebeok, 1968, and Sebeok & Ramsay, 1969, for attempts to define communication and for encyclopedic treatments of the topic). Specifically, I want to include luring behavior in this discussion even though such predatory tactics (as well as most other interspecific interactions) are traditionally excluded from the domain of communication.[2]

A number of snakes are born with brightly colored tails and with an ability to wiggle their tails in a manner simulating a worm or a larval insect (Heatwole & Dawson, 1976; Henderson, 1970; Neill, 1960; Radcliffe, Chiszar, & Smith, 1980). Caudal luring thus attracts lizards and possibly other potential prey to the snake. Although several species of snake are known to retain these adaptations into adulthood, many species seem to exploit caudal luring only during infancy (i.e., roughly the first year of life) when lizards are primary prey and when the frequency of successful predatory episodes is of particular significance. Indeed,

---

[2]The advantage of including luring behavior in this section derives from the fact that the contemporaneous adaptive significance of these juvenile actions is beyond doubt. I do not care to argue that luring represents a kind of deceptive communication, although I believe this to be the case (Mitchell, 1982; Weldon, 1982). Instead, it is my goal to use juvenile luring behavior only as a metaphor in arguing that other forms of juvenile behavior (especially intraspecific communication) are also of adaptive significance at the time they occur.

the first season of life is a critical one for many reptiles and amphibians because (1) the frequency of feeding determines the probability of surviving the first hibernation, and (2) the frequency of feeding determines the rate of growth and, hence, the rapidity with which individuals pass out of the size range of maximum vulnerability to predation. The fact of greatest interest here is that neonates are well equipped not only to recognize potential prey (Burghardt, 1970) but also to emit signals that attract them into striking range. There is no doubt about either the effectiveness of the luring signals or the contribution they make to fitness. Hence, no one would judge these behaviors to be without immediate consequence or to be executed mainly to provide practice for use later in adulthood.

The case is obviously similar for neonatal behaviors that subserve mother-offspring bonding or that elicit care from parents. Infants of many avian and mammalian species must be regarded as competent in controlling maternal resources, and numerous aspects of infant morphology and behavior must be understood as semantic adaptations serving to elicit care, comfort, feeding, or protection. Again, no one would question the contemporaneous instrumental significance of these behaviors or propose that they are emitted mainly to serve some proactive or "perfecting" consequences.

It is not difficult to find other examples of neonatal or juvenile behaviors that produce immediate advantages for the organisms executing them. The well-known studies of Japanese monkeys (*Macaca fuscata*) are especially instructive because here we see the rapid spread of juvenile-invented adaptive behaviors (sweet-potato washing, "placer-mining" of wheat) throughout a population (Itani, 1958; Tsumori, 1967). Such findings led Harper (1970) to suggest that neonate-adolescent inventiveness may be a generally important source of behavioral adaptations in primates.

Nonetheless, when we arrive at the phenomenon of play we come to a domain of behaviors that is sometimes defined with explicit reference to the not-immediately-functional character of the activities involved (see the above quotation from Scott, 1958). Play may, therefore, be an exception to the assertion developed above that each stage in the behavioral trajectory leading to adulthood is probably adaptive in its own right (i.e., contemporaneously as well as proactively). Certainly it is possible that the enormous proactive and/or exercise effects usually attributed to play can justify a relatively long period of investment in practice and shaping without contemporaneous adaptive benefit, especially if the developing animals are protected and nourished by adults during this period (see Bekoff, 1976a; Fagen, 1976; and West, 1974, for additional discussions of this point). On the other hand, it is worth looking more closely at the matter to discern whether or not some more or less immediate consequences of play have been overlooked.

Three potential effects of play seem especially worthy of consideration (see also Bekoff, Byers, & Bekoff, 1980). First, playful activities undoubtedly have communicative properties not only to playmates but also to adults. Indeed, the socially integrative consequences of play may be quite important for family and/or group cohesion (Peters, 1980). Moreover, it may be that play, like many other characteristics of young animals, has care-eliciting or instruction-eliciting significance (Lorenz, 1965, 1981). Second, inasmuch as play is a demonstrative activity, adults may be able to make judgments about offspring competence based on observations of play. Such judgments may lead to differential invest- ment of resources by parents or other adults (Trivers, 1972, 1974). Third, it seems possible that playful activities can generate a sense of ''self-confidence'' (Maier & Seligman, 1976) in addition to providing an opportunity for the topo- graphical development of social or hunting skills. Recognizing that repeated experience of failure generates learned helplessness and that early success can immunize animals against learned helplessness (Moye, Grau, Coon, & Maier, 1981; Seligman, Maier, & Geer, 1968), it might be possible to conceptualize early play as a relatively harmless opportunity for animals to experience the instrumental significance of their own actions in the context of social-commu- nicative relationships with peers. If young animals were forced to deal com- petitively with larger, stronger adults, then it might very well happen that the former would suffer a steady sequence of failures precisely when this would be exceedingly destructive not only to the acquisition of particular skills but also to the motivation needed to sustain the young animal's interaction with its environ- ment. Accordingly, play might represent immunization against learned help- lessness or at least shelter from the contingencies that would produce learned helplessness. No data currently exist to confirm or disconfirm this idea (S. Maier, personal communication).

Although these ideas about play are highly speculative, they point to the likelihood that play may indeed have some relatively immediate adaptive conse- quences as well as long-term, proactive benefits. Moreover, all three hypotheses emphasize potential communicative functions of play that would probably be overlooked by investigators taking only a prospective view of the contribution of play to the motor performance of adult animals. Research aimed at the three hypotheses described above is much needed, and such work may revolutionize our conceptualization of play and the creatures that engage in it.

SIGNALS AND THEIR EVOLUTIONARY ORIGINS: RITUALIZATION

It is axiomatic in modern ethology that many behaviors with signal value have arisen through ritualization. Threat, assertion, and certain advertising displays are often highly ritualized aggressive responses. The initial components of the original (source) sequence are often elaborated temporally and supplemented with features that augment the conspicuousness of the action. Warning, alarm, and tension-indicating displays often evolve from the initial components of escape sequences. Displacement responses spawned by simultaneous arousal of two conflicting motivational systems can be emancipated from their original motivational context and used for entirely different purposes (Tinbergen, 1952).

Clearly, ethologists have generated a rich conceptual framework around the evolution of responses having signal value. Most attention has been given to signals involved in threat, courtship, and care eliciting; and, these signals have been traced to sources including aggression, copulation, conflict, feeding, grooming, and infantile actions and appearances.

These ethological ideas deal mainly with the phylogeny of display topography, and they also generate expectations regarding ontogeny of displays in the same way that knowledge of morphological evolution can lead to ontogenetic predictions (Gould, 1977). There is, however, the important issue of stimulus control that is left unanalyzed in such discussion. Note that the issue of stimulus control contains two parts: (1) What are the stimulus elements that are responsible for releasing displays? and (2) What behavior(s) of recipient conspecifics are controlled by displays? When we restrict our attention to social interaction in which displays by one animal result in the same displays by another, then the two questions are identical. But, in virtually all other situations (e.g., facilitation of predator avoidance by alarm calls), the two questions are likely to have quite different answers.

It is well known that some stimuli are able to trigger appropriate responses in naive animals (Burghardt, 1970), indicating the existence of an innate releasing mechanism that requires little or no experiential sharpening. Nevertheless, there is ample evidence that stimulus control is often sharpened by experience (Hailman, 1967), and in some cases stimulus control is established entirely by experience. Accordingly, it should always be remembered that knowledge about the phylogenetic derivation of the topography of a communicative act represents only a part (albeit an important part) of what we eventually must know in order to piece together a complete understanding of communication. It is equally important to understand the stimuli that release the act as well as the semantic value of the act itself. The relationship between stimulus control and experience is considered in the final section of this chapter.

There is a relatively new addition to the list of sources from which displays are derived. This insight came from a reconceptualization of bonding, especially between parents and offspring (Eibl-Eibesfeldt, 1981). It goes without saying that the evolution of birds and mammals has involved the appearance of intimate and nurturant attachment formation between parents and neonates. Traditionally the emphasis has always been on the role that bonding plays vis-à-vis the delivery of resources to offspring by parents. Recently, the reciprocities inherent in the parent-young relationship have come more sharply into focus (Alberts & Gubernick, in press; Harper, 1970). But, the full ethological meaning of parent-offspring bonding (as well as other bonding phenomena) has only just begun to be recognized. Whereas bonding almost certainly came into existence as a post-adaptation to the long ontogenetic dependency of relatively altricial young, bonding immediately became a preadaptation for social control. That is, behaviors that cement and/or affirm bonds can be withheld, and withholding of affection or of intimate contact can be an effective means of controlling the behavior of others. Additionally, the availability of bond-affirming behaviors from individual A can be made contingent upon the behavior of individual B, providing yet another device for social control (see the first paragraph of the earlier quotation from Scott, 1958). A new kind of threat thus becomes possible between bonded individuals, not a threat of aggression but a threat of rejection (i.e., a threat to sever the bond). Clearly, these considerations have far-reaching implications, most of which cannot be explored here. The one point of special interest in a chapter on the ontogeny of communication is that we must consider neonates not only to be invested with effective care-eliciting features and behaviors but also with the capacity to control their caregivers by withholding affection and/or by threatening rejection. Indeed, the ontogeny of communication must involve the emergence of signals that express these intentions and it probably also involves the emergence of some perceptual-cognitive process that registers the instrumental power of those signals. Of course, the latter point refers to reinforcement, and it can be phrased in the mechanistic S-R language of traditional learning theory, or it can be articulated in more modern cognitive terminology. However we choose to verbalize it, the fact remains that many young birds and mammals sooner or later acquire control over each other and over caregivers in part by emitting signals that negate or threaten to negate the bonds that link them to each other. In addition to increasing our understanding of the ontogeny of communication, these new ideas have great importance for theoretical speculation about the biological bases of human social behavior (Hinde, 1974).

MECHANISMS REGULATING THE TIME OF SIGNAL DEVELOPMENT

"Signal development" is here used to refer to initial *emission* of signals, and it must be kept in mind that development of *reception, interpretation, and response* to the signal may follow a different temporal pattern and may be based upon entirely different processes. This distinction is fundamental, particularly because the literature on the ontogeny of communication has been concerned mainly with the first process (emission) and we know relatively little about the second. It would be the greatest error to assume that the psychology of impression can straightforwardly be deduced from the psychology of expression.

Furthermore, it is worth noting that the literature on signal emergence is largely a literature about song development in birds. Since males are usually singers while females are listeners, the psychology of expression has been mainly a study of male behavior. The creation of a complementary psychology of impression will involve much study of females, especially from a developmental perspective (Kroodsma, 1976).

Research on song development has been summarized by Hinde (1969), Konishi & Nottebohm (1969), Kroodsma (1978), Marler (1967), and West, King, & Eastzer (1981) and there is no need to reiterate this material. It is important only to mention the major generalizations: (1) song is largely innate in some species (Mulligan, 1966; but see Kroodsma, 1977); (2) experience of an external model plays an important role in many species (Marler, 1970; Thorpe, 1958); (3) the latter species usually possess sensitive periods within the first 3 months of life during which hearing adult song is of special importance (Marler, 1970; Nottebohm, 1969); (4) young males are selective with respect to which songs they will learn (Kroodsma, 1978); and (5) the duration of the sensitive period can be altered by environmental variables such as photoperiod and quali-ty-quantity of available adult song (Kroodsma & Pickert, 1980; see also Not-tebohm, 1969; Verner, 1975). The last point is particularly important since the sensitive period can literally be extended until the next year for neonates who have heard insufficient adult song, indicating a surprising degree of adaptive plasticity in the ontogeny of a complex communicative system.

Behavioral varability deriving from adaptive plasticity is receiving consider-able theoretical attention these days not only in the field of animal communica-tion but in ethology in general. Differential timing of skill emergence in different individuals of the same population or in closely related species is always a captivating observation. It seems reasonable to infer that some environments are permissive or encouraging with respect to song variability whereas other en-vironments are restrictive. In the latter case, song development is likely to be guided either by direct genetic underwriting and/or by parental provision of unambiguous post-hatch model stimulation during a well-defined sensitive peri-od. In more permissive environments there would be less need for investment in such precise mechanisms, and song development might occur over prolonged periods according to ordinary principles of associative learning. The evolution-ary point implicit here is that "leisurely" song acquisition by associative learn-ing may have been the primitive condition whereas canalized song acquisition is the derived state. If this is so, then research on canalized song learning ought not to be taken as representative of the ancestral song learning process; at least it should be recognized that canalized systems may represent specializations brought about by variability-restricting selective pressures. The environmental relativity of song acquisition mechanisms requires that theoretical attention be given to ultimate as well as proximate causal factors, especially if part of our goal is to understand the environmental conditions that give rise to particular song acquisition systems. Consider that some oscine species (e.g., Henslow's sparrow, *Passerherbulus henslowii*) have but a single, simple species-specific song whereas other species have extraordinarily complex repertoires containing more than 100 song types that can be organized into elaborate and variable sequences (e.g., Marsh wren, *Cistothorus palustris;* Verner, 1975). A complex song sequence minimizes the probability that listeners habituate. This, in turn, maximizes the stimulatory consequences of song (Petrinovich, Patterson, & Peeke, 1976). Discovery of environmental correlates of song complexity (Hartshorne, 1973; Kroodsma, 1977) will illuminate the ultimate causation of this dramatic aspect of avian behavior, and analysis of the ontogeny of complex songs may reveal variability-enhancing (entropy-increasing) processes analogous to human creativity. Hence, we can envision a continuum of developmental systems that produce highly canalized, variability-constraining outcomes on the one side and elaborately complex, richly variable outcomes on the other. It is tempting to think of this continuum as containing Baldwinized (innately under-written) ontogenetic processes on the constrained side, associative learning processes in the middle, and improvisational ontogenetic processes at the opposite end (Baldwin, 1896; White & Smith, 1956).

This continuum of developmental systems is a useful way to organize the contemporary research literature, and this idea has much in common with a popular conceptualization of comparative and/or ontogenetic differences in associative learning ability (Seligman, 1970). However, it is probably a mistake to assume that species differences in song complexity can be explained entirely by the species' positions on the hypothetical continua described here or in Seligman (1970). Two closely related species of wren, both possessing complex song repertoires in adulthood, differ dramatically in ability to learn songs from a tutor tape during their sensitive periods (Kroodsma & Verner, 1978). Male sedge wrens (*Cistothorus platensis*) seem to require social interaction in order to imitate the songs of one another and/or adults. Isolated male marsh wrens (*C. palustris*) readily learn songs presented over a loudspeaker. This difference in requirement for social interaction during the critical period for song learning could make one species appear far more canalized than the other. As a matter of fact, the associative-learning systems of the two species are probably quite similar as are their song repertoires in adulthood. It is an interaction between taxa and a condition of exteroceptive stimulation (social interaction) that causes the divergent behavior vis à vis tutor tapes. Hence, species can differ dramatically in behavior because they are at different points on the "Baldwin-improvization continuum," or because external stimuli interact powerfully with otherwise quite similar ontogenetic processes. Accordingly, overzealous application of continua of the sort here discussed is contraindicated.

The maintenance of local song dialects is another naturally occurring communicative phenomenon that can be understood within the context of mechanisms regulating the timing of signal development. If we presume that populations can become well adapted to local resources, then it is easy to imagine that a female's inclusive fitness will ordinarily be best served by mating only with males from the same locally adapted population. Therefore, song dialects can be conceptualized as a statement by a male regarding the population of which he is a part and the geographic area to which he is best adapted. A female can detect and mate with an appropriate male by paying attention to dialect and by preferring males who sing her natal dialect. Behavioral ecology and sociobiology thus give us good reasons to predict when dialects will evolve. The next question is of course the ontogenetic one: what developmental mechanism s are associated with the appearance and maintenance of geographically structured systems of dialects? The answer is remarkable for its simplicity. Natal philopatry extends through the sensitive period for song learning, so young males are exposed only to proper-dialect models and are thus predisposed to learn the natal dialect (Baker, 1975, 1980; Baker & Mewaldt, 1978; Baker, Sherman, Theimer, & Bradley, in press; Baker, Thompson, Sherman, & Cunningham, 1981). By delaying the occurrence of dispersal movements until after the sensitive period for song learning, the ontogeny of white-crowned sparrows (*Zonotrichia leucophrys*) results in males that sing proper dialects and in females that are properly responsive to the proper dialects (Baker, Spitler-Nabors, & Bradley, 1981). On the other hand, when natal philopatry cannot be assured because of factors such as habitat instability, birds are likely to shift through many local environments and to mix with individuals from diverse genetic backgrounds. In such cases (e.g., sedge wrens, *Cistothorus platensis;* Kroodsma & Verner, 1978) the premium may be for adaptations that facilitate mixing, and under some conditions this may involve an uncoupling of the ontogeny of dispersal from the sensitive period for song learning as well as a neotenous elongation of the ability to learn new songs. Hence, an alteration in the timing of signal development could be the proximate basis for extremely different communicative systems and population structures.

The existence of facultative polyethisms poses another kind of question that should be considered in this section. Male tree frogs (*Hyla cinerea*) exhibit two different mating strategies. A male may call from a territory, or he may be a satellite and lurk around the outskirts of a calling male's territory attempting to intercept females attracted to the calls (Perrill, Gerhardt, & Daniel, 1978). Such sexual parasitism is known in a variety of species (crickets, sunfish, bullfrogs), and is clearly facultative in *H. cinerea*. Individual males can switch from calling status to satellite status during a single night. Accordingly, it is of interest to determine the conditions of stimulation that predispose males to adopt the respective statuses: (1) Is the number of calling males strictly determined by the number of suitable territories? (2) Do satellite males transform to calling status readily, depending upon the availability of a territory? (3) Do younger (smaller) males start out as satellites? (4) Do males undergo regular changes of status during the course of a reproductive season? and (5) Do males undergo regular changes of status during the course of a single night? Specification of stimulus factors responsible for switching males from one status to another constitutes a developmental analysis of communication in that an important temporal variation in male expressive behavior is explained by identifying the adaptive advantages of the two modes as well as the antecedent stimulus conditions controlling their respective probabilities of emergence.

In *H. cinerea* there is little reason to believe that early experience has a formative effect, making some males satellites and others callers (Perrill et al., 1978). Hence, a developmental perspective on this behavioral system need not look retrospectively into the period before the first breeding season. It is *development during that breeding season* that needs to be examined. However, polyethic breeding strategies in males of other species may require a longer retrospective analysis. The bulegill sunfish (*Lepomis macrochirus*) may be an example of a species in which the experience of males during years 1–3 has an influence on subsequent male reproductive strategies (Drager & Chiszar, 1982; but see Dominey, 1980; Gross & Charnov, 1980).

The literature on social, aggressive, and reproductive behaviors, especially in reptiles, is also of interest in the present context. Numerous papers describe repertoires and/or speculate on the adaptive significance of particular responses (e.g., Carpenter, 1967; Carpenter, Badham, & Kimble, 1970; Carpenter, Gillingham, & Murphy, 1976; Gillingham, Carpenter, Brecke, & Murphy, 1977; Murphy & Mitchell, 1974; Murphy & Lamoreaux, 1978a,b; Murphy, Lamoreaux, & Carpenter, 1978; Murphy & Barker, 1980), but little information exists about the temporal sequence in which these responses develop or about the potential fitness value of these behaviors upon their *initial* appearance. This remark is not intended to be disparaging; instead it points once again toward an opportunity for developmental research. Consider, for example, the observation that newborn lizards (*Sceloporous jarrovi*) exhibit push-ups and head-bobs within minutes after birth (Duvall, in press; Duvall & Guillette, in preparation). From the more or less traditional perspective already described we would probably ask if these behaviors represent practice, or are the responses without any immediate or long-range consequences. On the other hand, perhaps newborn lizards have need for a social-signaling repertoire, in which case the neonate's execution of assertive displays is neither practice nor functionless, but rather the responses could represent an expressive system designed to control some subtle resource (Simon & Middendorf, 1980). At least one behavioral ecologist has developed this idea considerably. Stamps (1982) suggested that the value of a territory or any item of biological importance should be reckoned within a prospective framework in which two important assessments must be made: (1) What is the current resource value of the territory? and (2) How long will the animal exploit the territory, and, therefore, what will be its net value summed over the duration of residence or use? The second question represents the behavioral ecologist's version of an ontogenetic perspective, and several interesting ideas emerge immediately. A continuously exploitable patch may have much greater value for an animal that will exploit it for a lengthy period than for a short-term exploiter; and, the former animal should be more willing to defend the patch than the latter.

Stamps observed the lizard *Anolis aeneus,* and she discovered that young juveniles live in clearings while older juveniles (about 30 cm long) move into arboreal adult territories. All young juveniles preferred the same sort of territories, and the duration of territory use was inversely correlated with the animal's age at the start of observation. Measures of aggression (including ritualized displays) revealed that the youngest residents were more reactive to tethered intruders than were older and larger residents nearing the length of 30 cm.

This work not only established the functional significance of aggressive responses in young lizards, but the theoretical notion of prospective resource value (PRV) generated a directional prediction that at first blush seemed counterintuitive (i.e., the present author would never have predicted that younger-smaller juveniles would have been more aggressive than older-larger ones). The PRV concept could become a tool for developmentalists who sometimes become frustrated with the purely descriptive research so often encountered in the literature on animal ontogeny. At the same time, hypotheses based on PRV could be developed in order to generate increasingly specific predictions about time of emergence of signals within many species where the young exhibit systematic transformations in micro-niche during ontogeny. Also, it seems possible to extend this idea from trophic resources to informational resources in that young animals of many species have long been known to exhibit more investigatory behavior than adults (Bronstein, 1972, 1973; Valle, 1971). Perhaps this is related to the probability that new information is acquired per bout of investigation as well as to the probability that such information will be useful in the future. Both of these probabilities would be expected to decrease with age and with the accretion of experience in a relatively constant habitat. Accordingly, natural selection ought to produce differential levels of curiosity during difference phases of life history; and, from the perspective of juveniles (vs. adults) we could predict increased attentiveness to communicative behavior, increased investigation of new food sources and increased experimentation with new food-handling techniques, new shelters, resting postures, or ambushing sites. Of course, change occurs in many factors other than PRV during ontogeny (e.g., growth rate, activity level, familiarity with features of the environment, reproductive status, and diet), and separating the effects of these factors from the effects of PRV will be a necessary and formidable job (see Campbell & Spear, 1972; Vince, 1966). Also, identification of the proximal mechanisms by which animals, particularly young ones, assess PRV is an essential component of this job. In spite of these problems, the idea of PRV is exciting, testable and likely to spawn a new theoretical dimension within the literature concerned with development of animal behavior.

The major point in this section has been that the timing of signal development has probably been influenced by natural selection. Hence analysis of this aspect of communication must consider the ecological context in which development occurs. Moreover, the experiential context (prior history) and the interoceptive context (physiological and morphological substrates) also represent conditions that constrain or canalize ontogeny. Therefore, an understanding of the mechanisms regulating emergence of signals depends upon an examination of contextual effects be they interoceptive, experiential, or ecological.

ADAPTEDNESS OF ONTOGENETIC PROGRAMMING

The previous sections have emphasized that early communicative behaviors are often functional *in the environment and at the time they occur,* whether or not this early experience causes a sharpening of stimulus control or an increase in the semantic value of the displays. Hence, our attention was naturally drawn to the mechanisms responsible for signal emergence in young animals, and we discovered that it is possible to make some interesting predictions about the emergence and the function of signals during ontogeny. As valuable as such analyses may be, they are merely the beginning. Animals have repertoires consisting of many signals, involving multiple sensory channels; and, different signals develop at different rates. Development of communication clearly involves both multimodal and polyphasic processes (Gollin, 1981) which are temporally sequenced in ways that may be adaptive quite apart from the semantic value of the signals themselves.

The development of mother-offspring interactions in many mammals, especially altricial litter-bearing species, involves an initial period that is heavily dependent upon thermotactile cues. Subsequently, chemical cues become increasingly important, and eventually visual-behavior signals take on great importance in regulating many aspects of filial and social behavior. The initial significance of the thermotactile channel is correlated with the value that is then associated with heat as a commodity that can be exchanged between littermates or between pups and mother (Alberts, 1978a, 1978b; Alberts & Brunjes, 1978). Chemical cues associated with thermotactile primary reinforcers then acquire control over filial contact behavior, and the experiential basis for the consequent polysensory integration of the stimulus control of filial behavior is well understood (Alberts, 1981; Alberts & Gubernick, in press; Galef & Kaner, 1980). Is there some advantage associated with slightly delayed development of the chemosensory systems relative to the thermotactile systems (Alberts & May, 1980a, 1980b)? To venture an answer we must consult the literatures on kin recognition and parent-offspring recognition (Beecher, 1981; Holmes & Sherman, 1982; Waldman, 1981, 1982) which have produced a tentative generalization: recognition by association (termed "social learning" by Alexander, 1979) seems to develop among litter-reared mammals or clutch-reared birds just before the neonates become ambulatory or migratory, or just before they emerge from sheltered nests. It is as if earlier learning of sibling-identifying odors, sounds and/or visual cues might be wasteful because some siblings will die before weaning, or it may be that family-signifying cues (i.e., nest odors) might not be well developed early in the litter period. In any case, it seems that the initial appearance of thermotactually guided filial behavior and the subsequent appearance of chemically guided filial behavior represent ontogenetic sequencing that is worthy of study in its own right, over and above the specific signals and/or responses that are acquired in each stage. Perhaps it is appropriate to say that the importance of the signals and/or responses depends in part on the sequence in which they are acquired, and a developmental analysis ought to focus upon these sequential aspects of complex communicative systems as well as upon particular signals. At the very least, we should recognize that delayed development of chemically guided filial behavior is probably not a mechanically necessary consequence of the ontogeny of olfaction. If heat exchange is critically important during the early period, then attention to chemical, auditory, and/or visual stimulation might be distracting or even harmful. One way to focus the neonates upon the thermal dimension is to delay the development of responsiveness to other cues (Schneirla, 1965).

Brown (1982) studied predator avoidance behavior in the developing fry of two species of centrarchid fishes, rock bass (*Ambloplites rupestris*), and large mouth bass *Micropterus salmoides*). The former species exhibits only a brief period of parental care whereas the latter exhibits prolonged parental care. Antipredator behavior, not surprisingly, appears earlier in rock bass fry than in large mouth bass fry. Brown (1982) considers that large mouth bass fry may be generally less attentive to visual cues than rock bass fry, and this differential utilization of the visual channel early in ontogeny may function to keep the large mouth fry near their parents and to focus the rock bass on the sensory information most likely to detect predators at a distance and to permit escape.

In ducks, early communication between prehatchling and mother occurs through the auditory channel (Gottlieb, 1965, 1971; Impekoven & Gold, 1973). Hence, by the time of hatching the ducklings are attuned to the auditory channel, and the maternal assembly call is said to be prepotent. Visual imprinting occurs soon after hatching, and the prepotent maternal assembly call ensures that the ducklings are drawn to the appropriate stimulus source. Furthermore, careful laboratory studies have demonstrated that the assembly call remains prepotent. If a duckling has been imprinted on a mallard decoy and if this object is paired with another (e.g., a red and white box) in a subsequent test, the duckling exhibits clear preference for the decoy. But, if the maternal assembly call issues from the red and white box, the ducklings prefer it instead of the decoy (Johnston & Gottlieb, 1982). This finding has a number of implications that cannot be explored here, but we can recognize one particular point. The earlier utilization of the auditory channel probably has the eventual effects of attuning ducklings to maternal wavelengths and, eventually, to the assembly call. This, in return, creates a powerful device for capturing duckling attention and orienting it to the visual channel during the posthatch period, particularly during the imprinting process itself. Even if ducklings attend to inappropriate objects or stimulus dimensions, at least during the initial part of the sensitive period, the maternal assembly call may be able to countervail by refocusing the duckling on the proper object. This amounts to a built-in safety or compensatory system.

It is also worth mentioning that Johnston & Gottlieb (1982) imprinted ducklings on decoys that issued maternal assembly calls in two ways. For some ducklings the call was emitted contingent upon duckling vocalizations, whereas other ducklings experienced the maternal call an equal number of times but in a sequence that was not contingent upon duckling behavior. Both groups showed clear evidence of imprinting during a test conducted 48 hours after the imprinting session, but the contingent group showed stronger filial attachment during a second test (72 hours after the imprinting session). That ducklings discriminate between contingent and noncontingent maternal calls is evidence for integration of at least two bits of sensory information (duckling call and maternal call). And in all likelihood, a third bit (temporal separation between the two calls) is also a part of this integration. This point is raised to show that newly hatched ducklings are not only attuned to the auditory channel, they are also responding to maternal auditory information in a fairly complex way. The response is not simply a Go-NoGo process, but rather it clearly involves some kind of information processing that treats maternal signals differentially, depending upon the temporal relationship between duckling behavior and maternal assembly call. Thus, the early utilization of the auditory channel involves the simultaneous operation of a temporal discrimination system, and this may have later cognitive effects that have not yet been examined by investigators. For example, early exercise of this system may facilitate later processing of auditory and visual information arising from maternal behavior, peer behavior, and/or predator behavior.

Another aspect of the auditory channel in birds deserves attention; namely, information provided to the *parent* from offspring vocalizations. Johnston & Gottlieb (1982) emphasized this point by suggesting that keeping the brood together is facilitated by duckling vocalizations (e.g., contact calls, lost calls), and this may reduce the energetic costs of maternal behavior. This emphasis on information (and resource) exchange between parents and offspring is becoming increasingly important in ontogenetic theory (Alberts & Gubernick, in press).

It seems reasonable to hypothesize that prehatch vocalizations may be important information for parents in that such stimulation means that the embryos are alive and that continued parental investment is indicated. An observation by Blockstein (1982) is intriguing in this regard. He noticed that the probability of emitting distraction displays (i.e., injury feigning) to threatening stimuli by male and female parent mourning doves (*Zenaida masroura*) increased in frequency just before hatching. Peeping by prehatch chicks was a probable proximate cause of this behavior in that parental emission of distraction displays (an obvious sign of parental investment) increased greatly after the parents heard peeping sounds from their eggs.

In species where parents must decide between continuing to incubate the current clutch versus starting a new one, embryos in the current clutch may experience selective pressure to provide reassurance to the parents. Not only would such reassuring stimulation establish the value for continued parental investment, it could also become a priming or releasing cue for shifting parents to greater levels of investment or to the next stage in the reproductive cycle.

In short, the emergence of signals and the sequential relationships between signals are apt to be adaptive partly because of selective pressures that emphasize temporal factors. This must not be ignored by workers interested in animal or human development.

THE ADAPTATIONIST PROGRAM

In this chapter I have been concerned with the probable adaptiveness of early communication and, hence, with the fitness values of such behaviors. Over and over I have pointed to potential advantages of neonatal signals to the offspring themeselves and/or to parents, and it is easy to expand these suggestions into an attitude that regards all early behaviors as having been evolved to accomplish some important function(s). Gould and Lewontin (1979) criticized such Panglossian thinking, particularly when it atomizes an organism, its behavior, or a complex social system into discrete parts and then regards each part as optimally adapted to its functions. It is necessary, they say, "that organisms must be analyzed as integrated wholes, with Bauplan so constrained by phyletic heritage, pathways of development, and general architecture that the constraints themselves become more interesting and more important in delineating pathways of change than the selective force that may mediate change when it occurs" (p. 581). Although it is reasonable to speculate about the value of traits, it is unreasonable to build a science of "just so stories." Ideas about adaptive value are empirical hypotheses and must eventually be subjected to tests in which they can either be confirmed or disconfirmed. According to Mayr (1983), "Only when all such specific analyses to determine the possible adaptive value of the respective trait have failed, is it time to adopt a more holistic approach and to start thinking about the possible adaptive significance of a larger portion of the phenotype, indeed possibly of the Bauplan as a whole" (p. 329). Therefore, while it is here argued that early behaviors represent specific adaptations more often than has heretofore been acknowledged, it is also intended that assertions about adaptedness be analyzed, accepted, rejected and/or modified according to the ordinary methods of evolutionists (Mayr, 1983) or according to the more challenging methods of Gould and Lewontin (1979).

PHASIC VERSUS TONIC CUES

Throughout the above discussion no distinction has been made between signals based on their duration. Yet, it is obvious that cues differ in temporal extent and that different functions are associated with tonic and phasic cues. By tonic cues, I mean those that signal a relatively long-term state, such as juvenile colors and morphology. Providing such signals is often of critical importance in the elicitation of succorant behavior and/or in the inhibition of adult aggression. Phasic signals include all relatively brief cues that are indicators of transitory states such as fear, hunger, or discomfort.

When cues are of brief duration and it is essential that they be detected and responded to quickly, innate perceptual bases for their recognition are often hypothesized. A fair amount of data exists to confirm this hypothesis for some species (e.g., Burghardt, 1970). On the other hand, tonic cues can acquire at least part of their control over behavior more gradually, and learning is often found to contribute to the establishment of the semantic value of such stimuli (Hailman, 1967).

The emphasis of research has traditionally been on the receivers of tonic and phasic signals, and justifiably so. Yet, examination of emitters may be interesting. For example, juveniles may learn to exploit their state-signaling cues. If such cues inhibit adult aggression and if juveniles thereby gain access to resources, then it seems that an opportunity exists for juveniles to learn to take advantage of this situation (Weldon, 1982). On the other hand, genetic mechanisms may retain juvenile features into adulthood in some species. Accordingly, there is much to be gained by detailed study of the ontogeny of tonic signals and the variables that influence the maintenance of particular signals during various stages of an animal's life history. At the very least, data of this sort are likely to focus our attention upon the contemporaneous roles of juvenile signals as well as upon the extent to which such signals can also be viewed as preadaptations for subsequent modes of social adjustment. Also, it is necessary to avoid hasty conclusions regarding the mechanisms that mediate retention of juvenile signals into adulthood. Surely natural selection can lead to communicative neoteny, but the ontogenetic processes that subserve neoteny are not straightforwardly predictable from the fact of neoteny. For example, the occurrence of infantile begging signals in adult animals probably implies a genetic mechanism that generates the response topography, but this alone is insufficient to account for variation in frequency of begging. The high frequency of this behavior in some captive environments almost certainly depends upon interactions between animals and humans where the latter have delivered reinforcers (not always food, but sometimes contact and/or approval) contingent upon the occurrence of begging signals. Therefore, it is essential to be skeptical of assertions that assign the burden of explanation either to proximate or to ultimate causes. As in all aspects of behavioral ontogeny, neither nature alone nor nurture alone can provide a complete account.

DEPRIVATION EXPERIMENTS

Deprivation experiments have been a standard approach for developmentalists interested in separating the effects of experience from the effects of inheritance. Rearing animals in social isolation involves deprivation of various kinds of stimulation, and it is often difficult to specify what aspect(s) of isolation was responsible for subsequent deficits seen in the animals (Bekoff, 1976b; Bronfenbrenner, 1968). Only when no behavioral deficits occur can relatively clear conclusions be generated (i.e., about lack of effect of deprivation), but even here a need for an epigenetic orientation is usually apparent (Lehrman, 1953; Moltz, 1968).

An especially interesting potential outcome of a deprivation experiment is the case where the isolated animal actually performs *better* than socially reared controls. It is almost always assumed that deprived animals will perform poorly or at best, equally, compared to controls, and that the experiment will reveal that experience is either stimulatory or neutral for the ontogeny of the trait under consideration. Such binary thinking has always been part of research dealing with development, and it is almost always visible in the interpretation of deprivation experiments, even though several generations of writers have cautioned against so simplistic a view. Further testimony to the limitations of this thinking derives from the fact that few researchers have ever anticipated the possibility of superior performance by isolated subjects, and there has been no theory advanced that would predict or accomodate such an outcome. Yet, an open-minded psychobiological-epigenetic approach to animal development cannot logically defend the proposition that all stimulation encountered by young animals should be either excitatory or neutral. It is entirely possible that some early stimulation naturally encountered by developing animals can be inhibitory; hence, removal of such influences via social isolation could logically lead to enhanced performance. There is no a priori reason to eliminate this possibility from our spectrum of predictions about deprivation experiments; it is only the conceptual limitation of traditional binary logic associated with the nature-nurture approach to development that does so. Yet, this limited purview has been reinforced by many studies that show isolated subjects to be deficient in comparison with controls, or that show isolates to be equivalent to controls. There are precious few cases of isolates doing better than controls, and I suspect this situation exists because the binary presuppositions that inspired the work also predisposed investigators to select developmental phenomena and dependent variables that conformed with binary expectations.

A case where isolates did, in fact, perform better than socially reared controls (West, Eastzer, King, & Staddon, 1979; West et al., 1981) is worth careful scrutiny, partially because it is a model of good developmental psychobiology and partially because it may turn out to be a prototype for many studies on the ontogeny of communication. This series of experiments used cowbirds (*Molothrus ater*) as subjects, and the work was inspired by the curious ontogenetic situation created by the cowbirds' way of life. Female cowbirds deposit their eggs in nests of other species of birds (more than 100 species are exploited by cowbirds), and the young cowbirds are called brood parasites. Nestling cowbirds are cared for entirely by their "foster parents," and no adult cowbird makes any contribution whatsoever. Although nestling cowbirds hear and see only heterospecifics during their early ontogeny, the cowbird male is able to sing its species-specific song during his first breeding season and the cowbird female is able to recognize that song during her first breeding season. Such facts readily tempt us to conclude that ontogeny of sexual communication in cowbirds must be genetically underwritten and the ontogenetic program must be closed to exteroceptive stimulation.

Most interesting was the observation that male cowbirds reared in isolation sang songs that were more potent (i.e., more attractive to females) than songs of socially reared males. Male songs were tape-recorded and later played to females. The dependent variable was frequency with which females exhibited the copulatory posture upon hearing the song. Songs of socially reared males elicited the copulatory posture on about 28% of the trials whereas songs of isolates did so on about 60% of the trials. The "isolate song effect" has been replicated several times; hence, it is a reliable finding that at first glance seemed anomalous, puzzling, and counter-intuitive. Subsequent research revealed that in a quasi-normal flock situation, potency of male song was strongly correlated with male dominance, and that both factors were correlated with male reproductive success (i.e., number of copulations). Moreover, subordinate males who attempted to sing potent songs were displaced, attacked, and could even be killed by dominant males. Therefore, we can make two interesting conclusions: (1) quality of song is correlated with male status within a dominance hierarchy, and (2) male song has semantic value to males as well as to females. Although the sexes respond quite differently, both sexes respond systematically as a function of song quality. For males, song quality influences probability of attack (male-male competition); for females, male song quality influences probability of assuming the copulatory posture (female choice).

Now it is possible to explain how isolation enhances the quality of male song. All males are probably capable of singing potent (i.e., dominant) songs; and, the ontogeny of such song occurs according to an innate program. When males encounter each other in flocks, they learn their respective places in the peck order, and songs of subdominant males are correspondingly *degraded*. Isolate males are dominant males in a hierarchy containing a single alpha and no competitors. Hence, isolates are not exposed to social contingencies that result in degraded song. Although additional research is required on this fascinating problem, West et al. (1981) have adduced enough evidence to indicate the plausibility of this argument. They add "that although these particular findings regarding the cowbird might not have been predicted, they should not come as a surprise" (p. 64).

Social isolation is indeed a complex form of deprivation for an individual of a social species, and many forms of stimulation (some excitatory and some inhibitory) are eliminated by such a manipulation. Whether isolation results in behavioral deficits or enhancements will depend as much upon what is measured as upon what has been deprived. Indeed, looking at the results of deprivation experiments through the old binary perspective misses all that is truly important. It is far less useful to make value judgments about the behavior of isolated or otherwise deprived organisms than it is to identify (1) the ontogenetic pathways that give rise to normal development and (2) the developmental options that can be exploited by victims or beneficiaries of particular sources of stimulation.

Social structures not only provide models for effective distribution of resources among individuals differing in status, they also constrain the expressiveness of *most* individuals. It is not surprising, in the light of these findings on the cowbird, that a period of isolation results in dominant-like behavior in animals that would otherwise be subordinants (see also Drager & Chiszar, 1982). Indeed, such a procedure is commonly used to allow individuals to establish residence in test environments so that subsequent assessments of aggressive behavior can be made upon the introduction of an intruder (Chiszar, Ashe, Seixas, & Henderson, 1976; Poulsen, 1977). These studies produced status shifts and enhancements of aggressive behavior that were quite analogous to the "isolate song effect."

Much of the early literature on environmental deprivation (or enrichment) measured dependent variables that were selected to reveal deficits resulting from absence of excitatory stimuli. There is no doubt about the reliability of these findings. But, they have created a one-sided picture that promotes a belief that ontogeny depends upon excitatory input and that behavioral development, like somatic growth, is a matter of accretion and gain. It is likely that behavioral ontogeny is also heavily dependent upon inhibitory shaping, and that differentiation of viable behavioral phenotypes involves a complex control system in which genetic predispositions and multimodal stimulus inputs (some inhibitory and some excitatory) define a *spectrum* of possible outcomes. Hence, assertions about *the* ontogenetic trajectory are more a matter of myopia than of psychobiology.

A MODERN VIEW OF THE INNATE RELEASING MECHANISM: THE WORK OF G.P. BAERENDS

Konrad Lorenz's hydraulic model of instinctive behavior is certain to be familiar to everyone reading this chapter. This model has been and continues to be a useful heuristic device for communicating essential ethological concepts such as key stimulus, innate releasing mechanism, and fixed or modal action pattern. The model probably cannot be improved as a didactic tool for introducing students to (1) the proximate causation of innate behavior and (2) the phylogenetic relativity of perception. On the other hand, the model is not straightforwardly useful for understanding the kinds of adjustments an animal can make as a consequence of experience with motivational states, key stimuli, and/or adaptive action patterns.

A perusal of the history of speculation regarding the innate releasing mechanism reveals that recent conceptualizations have become rather elaborate information processing systems (Lorenz, 1981). Always the original Lorenzian concepts can be seen at the heart of the flow charts, but the elaborations add important flexibilities. Lorenz (1981) has, himself, introduced some modifications into the old psycho-hydraulic model to account for the "additional effect of unspecific readiness-releasing stimuli" (p. 181; see Fig. 7.1).

It is when flow charts are constructed for complex behavioral systems that the need for flexibilities becomes immediately apparent. This is particularly true when the behavioral system being modeled involves reciprocal communication between two or more animals. Fluctuating levels of conflicting drives and shifts in figure-ground relationships lead to dramatic changes in the meaning of signals as well as to equally dramatic changes in responses emitted to those signals (see Smith, 1977, and this volume for detailed treatments of these issues). Likewise, the previous experiences of signaler and responder can exert effects on (1) the particular signal selected for emission, (2) the topography of that signal, (3) the behavioral context in which the signal is embedded, (4) the ability of the recipient to detect the signal (i.e., the selectivity of the recipient's IRM), and (5) the response the recipient selects as an answer to the signal. Accordingly, exchange of information cannot easily be understood without considering both the motivational and ontogenetic antecedents of the communicative episode. Of course, this is not a surprising statement, nor is it a new idea. On the other hand, the history of ethological flow diagrams (and the history of the innate releasing mechanism as an integral component of them) has not contained many systematic attempts to inculcate ontogenetic or contextual variables. This does not mean that ethologists have been insensitive to the need to study ontogeny or context. Quite the opposite is true (Lorenz, 1965, 1981), and an impressive amount of developmental research has accumulated. Nonetheless, the theoretical impact of this work has been felt more in the conceptualization of life history variations and polyethisms (Hamilton, 1978), and in the identification of basic psychobiological mechanisms (see Alberts & Gubernick, in press) than in the construction of increasingly sophisticated views of the innate releasing mechanism and/or its articulation with adaptive behavior.

The most scholarly review (Schleidt, 1962, as cited in Lorenz, 1981) of experiential influences on IRMs reaches the following general conclusion:

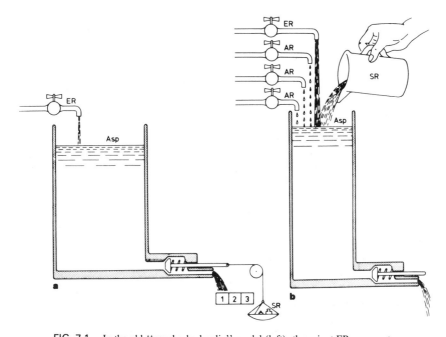

FIG. 7.1.   In the old "psycho-hydraulic" model (left), the spigot ER represents the source of endogenous and automatic generation of energy; the line Asp symbolizes the present level of action-specific potential. The spiral spring at the outlet represents what Roeder called the "stability of the system." The traction exerted by the weights SR stands for the effect of the releasing stimuli. In Fig. 7.1 (right) the additional effect of unspecific readiness-releasing stimuli is represented by the outflow of the spigots AR. This new model is meant to account for the fact that the effect of the specifically releasing key stimulus SR is different from that of the endogenous stimulus ER and that of the additional readiness-increasing stimuli AR only with regard to its time curve. (Energy from ER and AR accumulates slowly; energy arising form SR accumulates rapidly.) The difference in the height of the two reservoirs containing Asp in the two models is meant to suggest that, according to the new hypothesis, the opening of the valve is effected only by the necessary pressure from within the reservoir. The simulation could be brought closer to the real physiological process by adding a few gadgets, for instance, by a mechanism imposing the phenomenon of inertia on the opening and the closing of the valve. (Figure and text from Lorenz, 1981, p. 181)

The filtering effect of the IRM is often enhanced during ontogeny by the learning of additional characteristics or by habituation to stimulus configurations which have been encountered repeatedly. I propose to separate conceptually from the IRM (in a strict sense) those IRM "modified by experience" and to use the acronym IRME. Releasing mechanisms which either have lost the originally existing structure of their IRM, or which have developed without an underlying IRM, can be separated from the previously mentioned types as "acquired releasing mechanisms" (ARM).

If there is no experimental basis for such a classification, or if it is irrelevant whether the linkage between stimulus and response has been established by phylogenetic or ontogenetic adaptation to characteristics of the environment, the term "releasing mechanism" (RM) should be used without an additional specification. (p. 273–274)

To this, Lorenz (1981) adds:

I must repeat that this process of increasing the selectivity of IRMs through learning is extremely common, not to say omnipresent. In fact, IRMs which are not adaptively modified by experience, thereby having achieved a higher degree of selectivity, are not easy to find in higher vertebrates. (p. 274)

Hence, there has been no reluctance by ethological theorists to recognize the role of experience in sharpening the operation of IRMs or in facilitating the teleonomic functions of behaviors under the control of IRMs. Yet, the conception of how an IRM operates (whether an IRM, *sensu stricto,* or an IRME, or an ARM, or an RM) has remained essentially unchanged: If the correct stimulus is detected, then the adaptive response is released. There has been reluctance to give RMs freedom to operate variably or multimodally, except for a tendency to become less selective with disuse. Present data seem to require that RMs be viewed qualitatively and quantitatively as variable filters rather than as fixed or unimodal ones.

If the reader thinks that too much is being made of this issue, consider that the envenomating strike of a cottonmouth (*Agkistrodon piscivorus*) can be innately released by fish, amphibians, reptiles, birds, and small mammals. Should we regard the IRM to be a unitary neural representation of such abstract features of prey as might be common to all of these prey types, or should we regard the IRM as a multimodal device capable of accepting several relatively simple but qualitatively distinct sets of key stimuli? The latter view is most parsimonious and is most in accord with experimental data (Chiszar, Radcliffe, Overstreet, Poole, & Byers, in press; O'Connell, Chiszar, & Smith, 1982). For example, if a specimen has recently been fed only fish, that specimen will frequently refuse a mouse (or the snake will exhibit a long latency to strike the mouse). If the IRM was a representation of abstract features common to all of the prey types normally accepted by cottonmouths, there should be no rejection or hesitation to take a mouse. But, if the IRM is a multimodal filter, then there might be an expectation that a particular mode could be temporarily "locked in" through an inertia-producing consequence of local abundance of prey (see Tinbergen's, 1960, ideas about search images).

The operation of the IRM is influenced constantly by feedback endogenous to itself as well as by feedback arising from consummatory acts. Hence, to construct a model of this releasing mechanism, it is necessary to indicate its multimodal nature and the history of stimulation received by the respective modes.

A formal model has been proposed by Baerends (1982), and it is reproduced here in Fig. 7.2. The goal of this model is to represent the various subtasks that must be performed in order for an animal to execute an action pattern consequent to the presentation of a key stimulus. Note the complexity of this flow diagram relative to the models of Fig. 7.1. Central to Fig. 7.2 are the detectors (D_1-D_9) responsible for recognizing key stimuli and activating adaptive motor patterns. These units, however, are organized like the feature detection systems familiar to cognitive psychologists and we immediately see that several D units must be activated simultaneously in order for object recognition to occur (i.e., for the selector to select the appropriate behavioral response). Additionally, the capacity exists for different combinations of D units to select the same behavior (i.e., multimodality). The selector itself can be primed or sensitized by prevailing motivational conditions, hence a connection is indicated between incubation and selector. Presuming that threatening stimuli are not triggering prepotent escape responses, the selector can send its message (intended motor pattern) to an integrating module that will consider three pieces of information: the selector's message, the prevailing motivational state, and relevant information from memory. Notice that the memory system is directly primed by the motivational state, and note also that stimulus representations retrieved from memory are compared with the actual stimulus situation. Although the animal has an innate feature recognition system, its personal experience with prevailing and/or previous conditions is added, and the total of these two sources of information is stored in memory and can be called ''situation expected.'' The line called ''NS-test'' essentially consists of a comparison of ''situation expected'' with stimulus situation observed; a match results in positive input to the integrator, whereas a mismatch can trigger escape. Finally, when the integrator collects three positive signals and permits an adaptive response appropriate for the prevailing motivational state, notice that a conditioning process is activated. All stimuli detected in the present nest situation are represented in the conditioning module along with the adaptive response currently in progress. Hence, new stimuli can acquire control over the response, and the new S-R links can quickly be stored in memory.

Enough has now been said to indicate that Baerends has not only elaborated the innate releasing mechanism into an information processing system, he has also built into his system a capacity for acquiring and storing new information. Therefore, an animal will make increasingly sophisticated decisions, based in part upon innate recognition processes and in part upon experience with local conditions. (It might even happen that innate detectors could be replaced by acquired ones.) The capacities diagrammed in Fig. 7.2 represent a way for us to conceptualize the ontogeny of communication. The integration of innate predispositions with contextual, historical and motivational information is the critical requirement for any theoretical system designed to model the ontogeny of communication. Increasingly elaborate flow charts will be needed, but Baerends

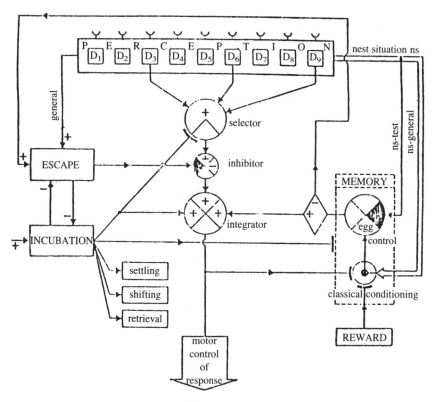

FIG. 7.2. Model (flow diagram) of the information processing mechanism proposed for explaining the results of experiments on egg retrieval by gulls (Baerends, 1970, 1982). Perception is subserved by feature detectors (D_1-D_9), and when a proper combination of detectors is stimulated a behavioral response will be selected. The selector is directly influenced by the prevailing motivational state so that responses appropriate to incubation will normally be readily available for selection. Of course, threatening stimuli could override the system and produce escape at any time. If no threatening cues are detected, the selector will indicate its "intended response" to an integrating unit that simultaneously considers two other pieces of information, prevailing motivational state and information from memory. This last point is especially important because Baerends is explicitly adding memory to his conceptualization of the innate releasing mechanism. Previous experience with similar situations is compared with the situation detected by D_1–D_9. If the comparison results is a match, a positive signal is sent to the integrator, which then releases appropriate innate behavior. Hence, the model allows individual experience to interact with the flow of information; and each activation of the system involves new learning which is assimilated with memory. Such a model is capable of dealing with historical variables, moment-to-moment changes in conflicting drives (e.g., approach, escape), and moment-to-moment changes in the exteroceptive stimulus field. Any attempt to model animal communication must be able to do at least these three things. (figure from Baerends, 1970, p. 301)

has pointed the way. Indeed, it seems reasonable to predict that researchers interested in the ontogeny of proximate causal systems subserving communication will be guided by the questions latent in every arrow of Fig. 7.2.

ACKNOWLEDGMENTS

I would like to thank the many colleagues who kindly provided reprints of their work, and I would like to extend special thanks to the participants of the Winter Animal Behavior Conferences and the national meetings of the Animal Behavior Society. Without the benefit of these excellent meetings, this paper could not have been written. The manuscript was completed while the author was "on loan" to the National Science Foundation, and I thank NSF (Division of Behavioral and Neural Science) for allowing me the time and secretarial support needed to finish this chapter. The financial support of the M. M. Schmidt Foundation is greatefully acknowledged.

Special thanks go to K. Z. Lorenz and to G. P. Baerends for permission to reproduce Figs. 7.1 and 7.2, respectively. Springer-Verlag and E. J. Brill Co., the respective publishers, generously concurred with the authors in granting permission to reproduce these copyrighted figures.

REFERENCES

Alberts, J. R. (1981). Ontogeny of olfaction: Reciprocal roles of sensation and behavior in the development of perception. In R. N. Aslin, J. R. Alberts, & M. R. Petersen (Eds.), *Development of perception: Vol. 1. Psychological perspectives.* New York: Academic Press.

Alberts, J. R. (1978a). Huddling by rat pups: Multisensory control of contact behavior. *Journal of Comparative and Physiological Psychology, 92,* 220–230.

Alberts, J. R. (1978b). Huddling by rat pups: Group behavioral mechanisms of temperature regulation and energy conservation. *Journal of Comparative and Physiological Psychology, 92,* 231–240.

Alberts, J. R., & Brunjes, P. C. (1978). Ontogeny of thermal and olfactory determinants of huddling in the rat. *Journal of Comparative and Physiological Psychology, 92,* 897–909.

Alberts, J. R., & Gubernick, D. J. (in press). Reciprocity and resource exchange: A symbiotic model of parent-offspring relations. In H. Moltz & L. Rosenblum (Eds.), *Symbiosis in parent-young interactions.*

Alberts, J. R., & May, B. (1980b). Development of nasal respiration and sniffing in the rat. *Physiology and Behavior, 24,* 957–963.

Alberts, J. R., & May, B. (1980b). Ontogeny of olfaction: Development of the rats' sensitivity to urine and amyl acetate. *Physiology and Behavior, 24,* 965–970.

Alcock, J. (1979). *Animal behavior: An evolutionary approach.* Sunderland, MA.: Sinauer Associates.

Alexander, R. D. (1979). Darwinism and human affairs. Seattle: University of Washington Press.

Baerends, G. P. (1970). A model of the functional organization of incubation behaviour. In G. P. Baerends & R. H. Drent (Eds.), The herring gull and its egg. *Behaviour,* Supp. 17. 263–312.

Baerends, G. P. (1982). *The "innate releasing mechanism" revisited and revised.* Keynote address, Animal Behavior Society, Duluth, MN.

Baker, M. C. (1975). Song dialects and genetic differences in white-crowned sparrows (*Zonotrichia leucophrys*). *Evolution, 29,* 226–241.

Baker, M. C. (1980). Behavioral adaptations that constrain the gene pool in vertebrates. In H. Markl (Ed.), *Evolution of social behavior: Hypotheses and empirical tests* (p. 59–80). Basel: Verlag Chemie.

Baker, M. C., & Mewaldt, L. R. (1978). Song dialects as barriers to dispersal in white-crowned sparrows, *Zonotrichia leucophrys nuttalli. Evolution, 32,* 712–722.

Baker, M. C., Sherman, G. L., Theimer, T. C., & Bradley, D. C. (in prep.). *Population biology of white-crowned sparrows: Residence time and local movements of juveniles.*

Baker, M. C., Spitler-Nabors, K. J., & Bradley, D. C. (1981a). Early experience determines song dialect responsiveness of female sparrows. *Science, 214,* 819–821.

Baker, M. C., Thompson, D. B., Sherman, G. L., & Cunningham, M. A. (1981b). The role of male vs. male interactions in maintaining population dialect structure. *Behavioral Ecology and Sociobiology, 8,* 65–69.

Baldwin, J. M. (1896). A new factor in evolution. *American Naturalist, 30,* 441–451, 536–553.

Beecher, M. D. (1981). Development of parent-offspring recognition in birds. In R. N. Aslin, J. R. Alberts, and M. R. Petersen (Eds.), *Development of Perception: Vol. 1. Psychological Perspectives,* (pp. 45–65) New York: Academic Press.

Bekoff, M. (1976a). Animal play: Problems and perspectives. *Perspectives in ethology, 2,* 165–188.

Bekoff, M. (1976b). The social deprivation paridigm: Who's being deprived of what? *Developmental Psychobiology, 9,* 499–500.

Bekoff, M., Byers, J. A., & Bekoff, A. (1980). Prenatal motility and postnatal play: Functional continuity. *Developmental Psychobiology, 13,* 225–228.

Blockstein, D. L. (1982). *Changes in distraction display behavior in mourning doves (Zenaida macroura) related to stage of the nesting cycle.* Paper presented at meeting of the Animal Behavior Society, Duluth, MN.

Bronfenbrenner, U. (1968). Early deprivation in mammals: A cross-species analysis. In G. Newton & S. Levine (Eds.), *Early experience and behavior,* (pp. 627–764). Springfield, IL.: C. C. Thomas.

Bronstein, P. M. (1972). The open-field activity of the rat as a function of age: Cross-sectional and longitudinal investigations. *Journal of Comparative and Physiological Psychology, 80,* 335–341.

Bronstein, P. M. (1973). Replication report: Age and open-field activity of rats. *Psychological Reports, 32,* 403–406.

Brown, J. A. (1982, August). *Parental care and the ontogeny of predator-avoidance in two species of centrarchid fish.* Paper presented at meeting of the Animal Behavior Society, Duluth, MN.

Burghardt, G. M. (1970). Chemical perception in reptiles. In J. W. Johnston, D. G. Moulton, & A. Turk (Eds.), *Communication by chemical signals* (pp. 241–308). New York: Appleton-Century-Crofts.

Campbell, B. A., & Spear, N. E. (1972). Ontogeny of memory. *Psychological Review, 79,* 215–236.

Carpenter, C. C. (1967). Aggression and social structure of iguanid lizards. In W. W. Milstead, (Ed.), *Lizard ecology,* Columbia: University of Missouri Press.

Carpenter, C. C., Badham, J. A., & Kimble, B. (1970). Behavior patterns of three species of *Amphibolurus* (Agamidae). *Copeia,* 497–505.

Carpenter, C. C., Gillingham, J. C., & Murphy, J. B. (1976). The combat ritual of the rock rattlesnake (*Crotalus lepidus*). *Copeia,* 764–780.

Chiszar, D., Ashe, V., Seixas, S., & Henderson, D. (1976). Social-aggressive behavior after various intervals of social isolation in bluegill sunfish (*Lepomis macrochirus* Rofinesgne) in different states of reproductive readiness. *Behavioral Biology, 16,* 475–487.

Chiszar, D., Radcliffe, C. W., Overstreet, R., Poole, T., & Byers, T. (in press). Duration of strike-induced chemosensory searching in cottonmouths (*Agkistrodon piscivorus*), and a test of the hypothesis that striking prey creates a specific "search image". *Canadian Journal of Zoology*.

Dominey, W. J. (1980). Female mimicry in male bluegill sunfish—A genetic polymorphism? *Nature, 284*, 546–548.

Drager, B., & Chiszar, D. (1982). Growth rate of bluegill sunfish (*Lepomis macrochirus*) maintained in groups and in isolation. *Bulletin of the Psychonomic Society, 20*, 284–286.

Duvall, D. (in press). A new question of pheromones: Aspects of possible chemical signaling and reception in the mammal-like reptiles. In J. J. Roth, E. C. Roth, N. H. Hotton, & P. D. McLean (Eds.), *The paleobiology of the mammal-like reptiles*, Washington, DC: Smithsonian Institution.

Duvall, D., & Guillette, L. J. (in prep.). Discrimination of and response to conspecific adult markings by naive neonatal Yarrow's spring lizards, *Sceloporus jarrovi*.

Eibl-Eibesfeldt, I. (1981). *Human ethology*. Keynote address at meeting of the Animal Behavior Society, Knoxville, TN.

Fagen, R. (1976). Exercise, play, and physical training in animals. *Perspectives in ethology, 2*, 189–219.

Galef, B. G., Jr., & Kaner, H. C. (1980). Establishment and maintenance of preference for natural and artificial olfactory stimuli in juvenile rats. *Journal of Comparative and Physiological Psychology, 94*, 588–595.

Gillingham, J. C., Carpenter, C. C., Brecke, B. J., & Murphy, J. B. (1977). Courtship and copulatory behavior of the Mexican milk snake, *Lampropeltis triangulum sinaloae* (Colubridae). *The Southwestern Naturalist, 22*, 187–194.

Gollin, E. S. (1981). Development and plasticity. In E. S. Gollin (Ed.) *Developmental plasticity: Behavioral and biological aspects of variations in development*, (pp. 231–251). New York: Academic Press.

Gollin, E. S. (1984). Early experience and developmental plasticity. *Annals of Child Development, 1*, 239–261.

Gottlieb, G. (1965). Prenatal auditory sensitivity in chickens and ducks. *Science, 147*, 1596–1598.

Gottlieb, G. (1971). *Development of species indentification of birds: An inquiry into the prenatal determinants of perception*. Illinois: University of Chicago Press.

Gould, S. J. (1977). *Ontogeny and phylogeny*. Cambridge, MA: Belknap.

Gould, S. J., & Lewontin, R. C. (1979). The spandrels of San Marco and the Panglossian paradigm: A critique of the adaptationist programe. *Proceedings of the Royal Society (London), B205*, 581–598.

Gross, M. R., & Charnov, E. L. (1980). Alternative male life histories in bluegill sunfish. *Proceedings of the National Academy of Sciences, 7A*, 6937–6940.

Hailman, J. P. (1967). The ontogeny of an instinct. *Behaviour supplement, 15*, 1–159.

Hamilton, W. D. (1978, month). *Genetic polyethism: Can it ever be best?* Paper presented at Danz Symposium, Animal Behavior Society, Seattle.

Harper, L. V. (1970). Ontogenetic and phylogenetic functions of the parent-offspring relationship in mammals. *Advances in the Study of Behavior, 3*, 75–119.

Hartshorne, C. (1973). *Born to sing: An interpretation and world survey of bird song*. Bloomington: Indiana University Press.

Heatwole, H., & Dawson, E. (1976). A review of caudal luring in snakes with notes on its occurrence in the saharan sand viper, *Cerastes vipera*. *Herpetologica, 32*, 332–336.

Henderson, R. W. (1970). Caudal luring in a juvenile Russell's viper. *Herpetologica, 26*, 276–277.

Hinde, R. A. (1969). *Bird vocalizations*. Cambridge: Cambridge University Press.

Hinde, R. A. (1974). *Biological bases of human social behavior*. New York: McGraw-Hill.

Holmes, W. G., & Sherman, P. W. (1982). The ontogeny of kin recognition in two species of ground squirrels. *American Zoologist, 22*, 491–517.

Impekoven, M., & Gold, P. S. (1973). Prenatal origins of parent-young interactions in birds: A naturalistic approach (pp. 325–356). In G. Gottlieb (Ed.), *Behavioral embryology* (Vol. 1). New York: Academic Press.

Itani, J. (1958). On the acquisition and propagation of new habit in the natural group of the Japanese monkeys at Takasakiyama. *Primates, 1*, 84–98.

Johnston, T. D., & Gottlieb, G. (1982, August). The role of the maternal assembly call in the formation of visual preferences in neonatal peking ducklings. *Paper presented at meeting of the Animal Behavior Society*, Duluth, MN.

Konishi, M., & Nottebohm, F. (1969). Experimental studies in the ontogeny of avian vocalizations. In R. A. Hinde (Ed.), *Bird vocalizations* (pp. 29–48). Cambridge: Cambridge University Press.

Kroodsma, D. E. (1976). Reproductive development in a female songbird: Differential stimulation by quality of male song. *Science, 192*, 574–575.

Kroodsma, D. E. (1977). A re-evaluation of song development in the song sparrow. *Animal Behavior, 25*, 390–399.

Kroodsma, D. E. (1978). Aspects of learning in the ontogeny of bird song: Where, from whom, when, how much, which, and how accurately? In G. M. Burghardt & M. Bekoff (Eds.), *The development of behavior* (pp. 215–230) New York: Garland.

Kroodsma, D. E., & Pickert, R. (1980). Environmentally dependent sensitive periods for avian vocal learning. *Nature, 288*, 477–479.

Kroodsma, D. E., & Verner, J. (1978). Complex singing behavior among *Cistothorus* wrens. *The Auk, 95*, 703–716.

Lehrman, D. S. (1953). A critique of Konrad Lorenz's theory of instinctive behavior. *Quarterly Review of Biology, 28*, 337–363.

Lorenz, K. (1965). *Evolution and modification of behavior*. Illinois: University of Chicago Press.

Lorenz, K. (1981). *The foundations of ethology*. New York: Springer-Verlag.

Maier, S. F., & Seligman, M. E. P. (1976). Learned helplessness: Theory and evidence. *Journal Experimental Psychology: General, 105*, 3–46.

Marler, P. (1967). Comparative study of song development in sparrows. *Proceedings of the XIV International Ornithological Congress, 231*–244.

Marler, P. (1970). A comparative approach to vocal learning: Song development in white-crowned sparrows. *Journal of Comparative and Physiological Psychology, 71*, 1–25.

Mason, W. A., Davenport, R. J., Jr., & Menzel, E. W., Jr. (1968). Early experience and the social development of rhesus monkeys and chimpanzees. In G. Newton and S. Levine (Eds.), *Early experience and behavior: The psychobiology of development* (pp. 440–480). Springfield, IL: C. C. Thomas.

Mayr, E. (1963). *Animal species and evolution*. Cambridge, MA: Harvard University Press.

Mayr, E. (1983). How to carry out the adaptationist program? *American Naturalist, 121*, 324–334.

Mitchell, R. W. (1982, August). *A typology of deceptive communication*. Paper presented at meetings of the Animal Behavior Society, Duluth, MN.

Moltz, H. (1968). An epigenetic interpretation of the imprinting phenomenon. In G. M. Newton & S. Levine (Eds.), *Early experience and behavior* (pp. 3–41). Springfield, IL: C. C. Thomas.

Moye, T. B., Grau, J. W., Coon, D. J., & Maier, S. F. (1981). Therapy and immunization of long-term analgesia in rats. *Learning and Motivation, 12*, 133–149.

Mulligan, J. A. (1966). Singing behavior and its development in the song sparrow, *Melospiza melodia*. University of California Publications in Zoology, *81*, 1–76.

Murphy, J. B., & Barker, D. G. (1980). Courtship and copulation of the Ottoman viper (*Vipera xanthina*) with special reference to use of the hemipenes. *Herpetologica, 36*, 165–170.

Murphy, J. B., & Lamoreaux, W. E. (1978a). Threatening behavior in Mertens' water monitor, *Varanus mertensi* (Sauria, Varanidae). *Herpetologica, 34*, 202–205.

Murphy, J. B., & Lamoreaux, W. E. (1978b). Mating behavior in three Australian chelid turtles (Testudines: Pleurodira: Chelidae). *Herpetologica, 34*, 398–405.

Murphy, J. B., Lamoreaux, W. E., & Carpenter, C. C. (1978c). Threatening behavior in the angle-headed dragon, *Goniocephalus dilophus* (Reptilia, Lacertilia, Agamidae). *Journal of Herpetology, 12,* 455–460.

Murphy, J. B., & Mitchell, L. A. (1974). Ritualized combat behavior of the pygmy mulga monitor lizard, *Varanus gilleni* (Sauria: Varanidae). *Herpetologica, 30,* 90–97.

Neill, W. T. (1960). The caudal lures of various juvenile snakes. *Quarterly Journal of the Florida Academy of Science, 23,* 173–200.

Newton, G., & Levine, E. (Eds.). (1968). *Early experience and behavior.* Springfield, IL: C. C. Thomas.

Nottebohn, F. (1969). The song of the Chingolo, *Zonotrichia capensis* in Argentina: Description and evalution of a system of dialects. *Condor, 71,* 299–315.

O'Connell, B., Chiszar, D., & Smith, H. M. (1982). Poststrike behavior in cottonmouths (*Agkistrodon piscivorus*) feeding on fish and mice. *Bulletin of the Philadelphia Herpetological Society, 29,* 3–7.

Perrill, S. A., Gerhardt, H. C., & Daniel, R. (1978). Sexual parasitism in the green tree frog (*Hyla cinerea*). *Science, 200,* 1179–1180.

Peters, R. (1980). *Mammalian communication: A behavioral analysis of meaning.* Monterey, CA: Brooks/Cole.

Petrinovich, L., Patterson, T., & Peeke, H. V. S. (1976). Reproductive condition and the response of white-crowned sparrows (*Zonotrichia leucophrys nuttalli*) to song. *Science, 191,* 206–207.

Poulsen, H. R. (1977). Predation, aggression, and activity levels in food-deprived sunfish (*Lepomis mocrochirus* and *L. Gibbosus*): Motivational interactions. *Journal of Comparative and Physiological Psychology, 91,* 611–628.

Radcliffe, C. W., Chiszar, D., & Smith, H. M. (1980). Prey-induced caudal movements in *Boa constrictor* with comments on the evolution of caudal luring. *Bulletin of the Maryland Herpetological Society, 16,* 19–22.

Schleidt, W. M. (1962). Die historische Entwicklung der Begriffe "Angeborenes auslosendes Schema" und "Angeborener Auslosemechanismus". *Zeitschrift fur Tierpsychologie, 19,* 697–722.

Schneirla, T. C. (1965). Aspects of stimulation and organization in approach/withdrawal processes underlying vertebrate behavioral development. In D. S. Lehrman, R. A. Hinde, & F. Shaw (Eds.), *Advances in the study of behavior* (Vol. 1 pp. 1–74). New York: Academic Press.

Scott, J. P. (1958). *Animal behavior.* Illinois: University of Chicago Press.

Sebeok, T. A. (Ed.). (1968). *Animal communication.* Bloomington: University of Indiana Press.

Sebeok, T. A., & Ramsay, A. (1969). *Approaches to animal communication.* Paris: Mouton.

Seligman, M. E. P. (1970). On the generality of the laws of learning. *Psychological Review, 77,* 406–418.

Seligman, M. E. P., Maier, S. F., & Geer, J. (1968). The alleviation of learned helplessness in the dog. *Journal of Abnormal Psychology, 73,* 256–262.

Simon, C. A., & Middendorf, G. A. (1980). Spacing in juvenile lizards (*Sceloporus jarrovi*). *Copeia,* 141–146.

Smith, W. J. (1977). *The behavior of communicating: An ethological approach.* Cambridge, MA: Harvard University Press.

Stamps, J. (1982, August). *Defense of prospective resources by juvenile lizards* (*Anolis aeneus*). Paper presented at meeting of the Animal Behavior Society, Duluth, MN.

Stevenson, H. W., Hess, E. H., & Rheingold, H. L. (Eds.). (1967). *Early behavior: Comparative and developmental approaches.* New York: Wiley.

Thorpe, W. H. (1958). The learning of song patterns by birds, with special reference to the song of the Chaffinch (*Fringilla coelebs*). *Ibis, 100,* 535–570.

Tinbergen, L. (1960). The natural control of insects in pinewoods. 1. Factors influencing the intensity of predation by songbirds. *Archives Neerlandaises de Zoologie, Leydig 13,* 265–343.

Tinbergen, N. (1952). "Derived" activities; their causation, biological significance, origin and emancipation during evolution. *Quarterly Review of Biology, 27,* 1–32.

Trivers, R. L. (1972). Parental investment and sexual selection. In D. Campbell (Ed.), *Sexual selection and the descent of man.* Chicago: Aldine.

Trivers, R. L. (1974). Parent-offspring conflict. *American Zoologist, 14,* 249–264.

Tsumori, A. (1967). Newly acquired behavior and social interactions of Japanese monkeys. In S. A. Altmann (Ed.), *Social communication among primates (pp. 207–219). Illinois: University of Chicago Press.*

Valle, F. P. (1971). Rats' performance on repeated tests in the open field as a function of age. *Psychonomic Science, 23,* 333–335.

Verner, J. (1975). Complex song repertoire of male long-billed marsh wrens in eastern Washington, *Living Bird, 14,* 263–300.

Vince, M. A. (1966). Developmental changes in learning capacity. In W. H. Thorpe & O. L. Zangwill (Eds.), *Current problems in animal behaviour* (pp. 225–247). London: Cambridge University Press.

Waldman, B. (1981). Sibling recognition in toad tadpoles: The role of experience. *Zeitschrift fur Tierpsychologie, 56,* 341–358.

Waldman, B. (1982). Sibling association among schooling toad tadpoles: Field evidence and implications. *Animal Behaviour, 30,* 700–713.

Weldon, P. J. (1982, August). *The guises used by intraspecific mimics.* Paper presented at meetings of the Animal Behavior Society, Duluth, MN.

West, M. (1974). Play in the domestic cat. *American Zoologist, 14,* 427–436.

West, M. J., Eastzer, D. H., King, A. P., & Staddon, J. E. R. (1979). A bioassay of isolate cowbird song. *Journal of Comparative and Physiological Psychology, 93,* 124–133.

West, M. J., King, A. P., & Eastzer, D. H. (1971). The cowbird: Reflections on development from an unlikely source. *American Scientist, 69,* 57–66.

White, F. M., & Smith, H. M. (1956). Some basic concepts pertaining to the Baldwin effect. *Turtox News, 34,* 51–53, 66–68.

8 Processes of Change and the Elaboration of Language

Andrew Lock
University of Lancaster

INTRODUCTION

It is over 100 years since the Linguistic Society in Paris banned papers on language evolution from its meetings, because they were speculative rather than scientific. That ban has not been repealed. Given that data concerning the problem has never been easy to come by, the spectre of speculation still haunts us. Today we may have some more data, but we also face other problems. While no serious voices are raised against the *fact* of evolution, the orthodox neo-Darwinian account of the process is under increasing doubt. That natural selection of small variation occurs is well established; but whether the cumulative effects of this process can be credited with the responsibility for major change—for the Origin of Species—is another question. An affirmative answer has ever eluded biologists, and it is becoming more and more difficult to paper over the discontinuous gaps in the fossil record and maintain the orthodox account. Further, recent spectacular work with nonhuman primates makes it abundantly clear that there is little agreement within the scientific community over what exactly constitutes a language. Hence, the topic of language evolution does not look a very inviting one.

If the problem of data, theory, and definition are not sufficient deterrents to an enquiry, the next may well prove the last straw: recapitulation. In his recent reappraisal of the topic, Gould (1977) writes:

> I tell a colleague that I am writing a book about parallels between ontogeny and phylogeny. He takes me aside, makes sure no one is looking, checks for bugging devices, and admits in markedly lowered voice, "You know just between you, me, and that wall, I think that there really is something to it after all." (p. 1)

His experiences are more fortunate than mine. But, taking these four areas together, I have a suspicion that in putting the problems beyond the pale, we may be throwing away the bath, let alone the baby and the bathwater. It is this suspicion that animates the following discussion.

The field of enquiry presents enough problems for anyone to want to invoke divine or extraterrestrial intervention as the most plausible explanation of "human nature." Even if evolution is a fact, there is no escaping that humans do indulge in ways of life that apparently have few precursors, and that must therefore be regarded as unique. Wallace himself could not come to terms with that aspect of his co-hypothesis with Darwin that implied man's total continuity with the rest of creation. This dissention led to his scientific ostracism and labeling as a mystic. The problematic nature of the field thus necessitates some opening statement of "belief":

1. It is a fact that humans have evolved. Thus their accoutrements—mental and physical—have "ancestors." Current abilities do, though, appear to be different in kind from their predecessors.

2. There is unfortunately something more to language than meets the objective eye. Unfortunate in that one of the canons of science is that it is objective; but not totally damning in that linguistics is able to maintain a claim to scientific status, despite the fact that it dabbles in the realms of semantics and pragmatics, neither of which can be sustained in a truly objective way. Objectively, language is just noise with pattern. In reality, it is a bit more than that. This "bit more" cannot be ignored.

3. It does not seem too difficult to believe that an evolutionary process can throw up systems that appear to have new properties. After all, the ability to be reciprocally altruistic is not something one would expect to be available to a world in which the amoeba or shark were the epitome of life. Yet, it is not a property of living organisms that science finds disturbing. It is a logical extension of what is known of the evolutionary system, even though it may only be able to occur at an entirely different level of organization to that exhibited by these "lower" forms of life. The question of reciprocal altruism constitutes a good place to begin this discussion.

CHARACTERIZING CHANGE OVER TIME

Why Don't Amoebas Indulge in Reciprocal Altruism?

Research into behavior from an evolutionary perspective has reached the point where certain principles can be enunciated. These will be framed here as *descriptive* principles of the evolutionary "game," and discussed in the context of behavioral strategies. It would, however, be equally legitimate to develop this discussion in the context of anatomy, embryology, and so one. First, though, it should be emphasized that an evolutionary approach to behavior is also, of necessity, an ecological one: as Van Valen (1976) notes, "evolution is the control of development by ecology" (p. 180). The lesson to be taken is that organisms adapt to their environments, are part of the environments they adapt to, and also constitute and so define their environments. Further, these environments have temporal as well as spatial extension. Thus a description of an environment cannot limit itself to present actualities, but must also take account of the future possibilities afforded by the environment, and the extent to which the current range of organisms inhabiting that environment appear capable of realizing those possibilities.

The descriptive and axiomatic principles of change in evolving organic systems are:

Survive to breed.

Having done that, attempt to increase the proportional representation of one's genetic material in the population of the next generation; i.e., have as many offspring as possible.

But do not attempt to have more offspring than is possible.

To illustrate these principles, let us play "God" for a moment. "Survive to breed" demands two things: that a means of sustaining organization is found, and that the ability to duplicate that organization is devised. If any organization is to sustain itself in the face of entropy, it has to counterbalance its inherent energy dissipation by capturing some other energy source. Once it has done this, it needs an energy budget, a way of trading its energy utilization to maintain its organization against that which it requires to organize its reproduction. Let us make life easier by assuming that a reproductive ability is a given: what we require is an energy source.

Starting from scratch, the most reliable potential energy sources are natural radiations. It appears in retrospect that it is difficult to organize systems from "world stuff" that can utilize X- or gamma-rays, and a lot of the other things generated by radioactive decay. These things are retrospectively regarded as harmful to life forms. Radiation in the form of light rays seems an adequate source, so we must sit around until we have an operational source (the sun) and an earthly environment that permits light to reach the surface, but can filter out to acceptable levels the radiations that are not needed. When that occurs, exploit the possibility, utilize the available energy that affords sustained reproductive organization. At some point in the natural history of the earth, a "situation" arose that was able to exploit its inherent possibilities. The atmosphere was available to allow the possibility of self-sustaining organization; the primeval soup was available; the possibility was actualized. Call this Stage 1. With the actualization of Stage 1, there is a new potential source of energy: that embodied in the sustained forms of the organizational systems that newly exist. Stage 2 will occur when ways of using this energy to sustain new forms of organization are developed;

that is, when herbivorous animals are invented (alternatively, or additionally, parasites and viruses). Complete Stage 2, and Stage 3 is potentially available, carnivorous predators to utilize the indirectly obtained energy potential of herbivorous organizations. New possibilities thus appear as former possibilities are actualized.

Turning to the further axioms, it will be found that they imply the success of those forms of organization that are the most efficient at obtaining and capturing energy, and at utilizing that energy for the production of new forms. This efficiency can be attained in many ways. An individual whose energy-efficiency is appallingly low can in fact be highly successful if it does not face any serious competition: energy-efficiency has no absolute biological yardstick, but is purely relative to the abilities of the competition. It is not a factor that to begin with can be equated with surviving to breed. However, in an evolving system that is able to exploit potential environmental niches as they occur, the logical distinction between these two processes will become blurred by the complexity of the system, and the maxim of "survival of the fittest" will certainly come to *appear* tautological.

Highly organized forms, such as birds, can be seen to be playing out these further axioms in their behavioral strategies. Consider sexual competition. Suppose a male is able to obtain a clutch of four eggs in consort with a female. If he remains with her, their joint efforts at parental care enable them to raise those four eggs to successful maturity: if he deserts her, she can, on her own, raise two young. Obviously, if on deserting her he can find another mate, and repeat his act of desertion to find yet another mate, and even if he then ceases reproductive activity, he will have obeyed principle 2. Through his behavior he will have produced six offspring, whereas if he had stayed with his first mate he would only have had four. If this perspective is reversed, though, it is also obvious that the female's interests are not being served: because of the male's behavior she has only half the number of offspring she might have. It is therefore in her interests to "pursue" strategies that make it more difficult for the male to desert her. She is unfortunately caught in an evolutionary rut in that she cannot follow the male's preferred strategy due to the larger energy investment she has in their eggs. She can, however, "retaliate" in ways that increase the male's own energy investment in reproduction: only "consenting" to mating if the male has been "forced" to "invest" so much energy that it is almost impossible for him to "risk" losing his "investment." Note that the execution of the dictates of this descriptive principle do not require the positing of any awareness of such "calculations" on the part of the individuals involved, nor even the fact that such "calculations" are actually made. It is a consequence of the descriptive axioms that individuals who act in those ways will come to pass more of their genetic material to the next generation. Such behavioral strategies will distill themselves out of the pinball game of evolution, because that is the way the game is inherently biased. This said, the inverted commas will be dropped.

If principle 3 is now considered, a further view of the implications of the game is afforded. Suppose it is possible to gather enough food to successfully raise four offspring; and that if an individual tried for more, less than four would survive due to that food being spread too thinly among them. In this scenario there is obviously a premium put on getting the number right, since a deviation from this will be less successful. To hit the right number need again not require positing animals with problem-solving abilities; the outcome could be managed, for example, by hormonal responses to food availability and population density. If this is one of the constraints in the game, then there are still further possibilities for the evolution of behavioral strategies. It is doubtless quite difficult to change another individual's perception of the abundance of food, but it is not so difficult to change its perception of the population density. While there is no concrete proof of the existence of a "Beau Geste" strategy, it is certainly a viable possibility in the game. Thus, if an animal can convince its fellows that it is more than one individual, it may be able to lower the number of offspring they attempt to raise, and so present itself with the opportunity for taking up the slack by increasing its own output. A consequence of such a behavioral strategy would be an increase in the proportion of "liars" in a population to the point that they would be disadvantaging themselves, lying themselves into extinction. Hence Maynard-Smith's (1976) formulation of the evolutionary stable strategy is a likely description of the distribution of behavioral strategies within a population. Evolution is a metagame within a metagame within a game of blind seriousness.

What kind of account of behavioral change over time is this leading toward? Its main characteristics are these. That the form of an organism and the nature of its behavioral repertoire are explicit renderings of the implications of its environmental niche. The potentialities of any environment are embodied in the meat or vegetable structure of the organism. Its activities are explications of similar potentialities. Its cognitive abilities are likewise elaborated to the extent that the potentialities it is the living embodiment of require. Further, we are dealing with a system in which the potentialities becoming available for biological explication, *and* the abilities of biological organisms to actualize those possibilities, *and* the very existence of those potentialities occur in a logically fixed order. This does not imply that evolution unfolds according to some master plan, that it is aiming at any predetermined end point through a teleological bias: these ordering factors are inherent properties of the system. To expand:

(1) The order of explication is fixed.

It is not possible to have carnivores appearing before herbivores, and it is not possible to have herbivores before "plants." That much is obvious.

(2) The order in which possibilities can be actualized is fixed by the abilities organisms possess at any given point in time, and those abilities are tied to the current elaboration of the ecoevolutionary system.

"Simple organisms live in simple environments" (von Uexkull, 1957). The level of elaboration in the ecological order that requires an organism to invest energy in the sustenance of complex bodily organizations to conduct elaborate physiological or psychological functions will be a high one. No form of life is going to elaborate its energy-binding load beyond that demanded by the requirements of the ecological niche it is explicating (once it is in a competitive system of energy use). It is thus not surprising that it is only those forms that appear late in the evolutionary record that show, for example, elaborated forms of social life: The dynamics of their ecology imply that they could not sustain such an elaborated and thus precarious ecological level in any other way. Consequently, an amoeba does not fit into a world that requires it to develop individuality, nor the "brains" to go with it. It neither requires the indulgence of reciprocal altruism, nor then, the wherewithal to accomplish it. The ecological elaboration of the higher mammals, however, could not be sustained without them.

(3) The existence of potentialities is a fixed order.

At any point in time possibilities exist for change at four levels: possible possibilities, probable possibilities, actual possibilities, and actualized possibilities. Thus, the *possible possibility* exists for a procaryote to evolve legs, as it doubtless once did if there is an evolutionary continuity, but the time and number of additional approximations of form involved are massive. The *probable possibility* exists for a mud-skipper-like form to construct legs from its fins, and because of the approximation of its form and ecology to the possibility, the likelihood of its doing so is high. *Actual possibilities* are more apparent in ontogeny than phylogeny, and their phylogenetic elaboration will be left until later. *Actualized possibilities* are existent realities. The hierarchical ordering of potentialities can be seen in the Beau Geste effect: it is an actual possible strategy only after the establishment of more basic forms of reproductive balancing. Further examples are discussed below.

The nature of this "fixedness" of the hierarchy has to be considered within the framework of the levels of possibility. The general character of possible possibilities is fixed, but in its specifics admits more free play than a level closer to actualized possibilities. That is, possible possibilities are less specified than actual possibilities: the levels of possibility are at the same time levels of specification. This characteristic of systems in change often leads to accounts of them having a "just so" character, for the predictability of events is a function of their level of possibility. But this should not be held to detract from the usefulness of specifying the formal properties of the system. Theories must do the best they can with nature, rather than vice versa.

THE RELATIVITY OF INDIVIDUAL AND ENVIRONMENT

In a thoroughgoing ecological account, the distinction between individuals and their environments becomes very blurred: the two terms are in a dialectical relationship with each other. For example, if an individual organism exists, then by necessity so does not only *an* environment, but *its* environment. Similarly, supposing and specifying a particular environment posits a particular organism. An environment *cannot* be thought of as a vacuum that presents a myriad of potential niches for the ecological elaboration of the organism's progeny. Those niches are constrained by the very existence of the organism. Statements such as "marsupial animals underwent adaptive radiation to fill the ecological niches presented by the Australian continent" do not make total sense. Australia did not at the outset of its colonization present a niche for the kangaroo. That niche had itself to evolve as a possibility as the organic forms transformed, by their evolving form and function, their environment from one set of possibilities to another. Thus, looking at this ecosystem at time 1, the "Kangaroo niche" may be specified as a possible possibility at time 2, developments within the system may or may not have occurred to have moved that niche to the status of a probable possibility; and so on through actual to actualized possibilities. The evolutionary ecosystem must be treated as the unit of analysis, because it is the unit defined by the existence of levels of possibility. This view is put forcibly by Jantsch (1981):

> The *decisive point* is that self-organizing systems continuously generate their own internal fluctuations, and test their stability, and that it is these internal fluctuations when they become internally reinforced (through autocatalytic and other highly nonlinear mechanisms), that drive the system over an instability threshold to a new structure. There is no stability, period; only meta-stability, or else evolution . . . evolution is *self-transcendent,* that is to say, always ready to reach out beyond the system's own boundaries. (p. 192)

Once the system is defined in terms of its possibilities, however, the option of portioning responsibility for events to one or the other of its components does become viable (but even when the theoretical descent is made to the level of the organism-environment subcomponents of the system, these dichotomies are still subsumed by their embeddedness within the system as a whole). For example, there is a remarkable similarity of form between the placental Wolf and the marsupial Tasmanian Devil. It would be possible to attribute these convergent adaptations to the identity of environmental constraints. But at the same time it is the animals themselves that produced and defined those environmental constraints by their attainment of a certain ecologically elaborate form. That is, the environmental constraints were produced by the organic forms that created the environment in the first place.

In line with this shift from the more traditional perspective, it is useful to move from a vocabulary of constraints to one introduced by Gibson (1979) in his ecologically formulated theory of perception: not *constraints* but *affordances.* It is then possible to talk of the degree to which a system affords its own elaboration. Also, an environment may be said to afford the constitution of certain forms through the opportunities it presents to the organisms comprising it: and those affordances will define the levels of possibility as possible, probable, and actual. Similarly, organisms afford the creation of possible, probable, or actually possible environments.

This gives the view, then, of processes of change in which the system itself affords its own change, in which the changes that this system affords at any one point in time serve to further specify the affordances that will emerge at the next point. Developmental change is then the transformation of a set of actual affordances into an actualized set, a change that brings forward previously probable possibilities to more closely specific actual possibilities; possible possibilities to more closely specified probable possibilities; and introduces some specification into a newly actualized set of possible possibilities. The actualization of form in development is thus accomplished by the tighter and tighter delineation of the implicational hierarchy of possibilities it engenders at any point in time: The tighest delineation occurs at the level of the actualized; the least at the possible.

It is now possible to state the main outline of this account. First, the process of change, as demonstrated by the evolutionary system, *is* a hierarchical one, but that hierarchy is not one that rests on notions of progression or perfection that have previously been difficult to define. It rests on a hierarchy of logically necessary implications. Second, that hierarchy is not a God-given, predetermined plan, but is one that constructs itself out of the constraints of the environment and the raw materials that are available. However, once the first point in a changing system has been determined, the general character of the hierarchy has also been determined. Third, while change-as-evolution is being characterized as a process that accomplishes the explication of this implied hierarchy into some level of biological form—meat structures, social structures, cognitive structures—it says nothing about the means by which such explications occur, and neither does it have to to retain its coherence. Finally, this account is not exclusively concerned with evolution, but more generally with changes over time that occur in natural systems.

Note that nothing is being said about the mechanics of change, only about the nature of change. Further, this account is about change, and evolution is an exemplar of that process: other orders of change—cultural, developmental and perceptual, for example—are not excluded from this characterization. Thus, if the operation of similar explicatory developments can be shown in other spheres, the establishment of relationships between different orders of organization is possible: it becomes possible to shift at the formal level from analogy to homology. For the fact that the "mechanics" and "substrates" of change in two levels are different; that the mode of operation of two disparate phenomena that yet appear to be linked in time are different: such considerations do not preclude the homology of apparently diverse systems at the present level of description.

Implicational Hierarchies and Their Explication in Other Orders

"There are . . . only so many ways to move from simplicity to complexity." (Gould, 1977, p. 144).

Some brief illustrative comments will be made here on changes in two other orders. A fuller discussion may be found in Lock (1981a, 1981b).

Early Nonverbal Communicative Development in the Human Infant.   Let us assume that the neonate is endowed with the ability to discriminate states of comfort from those of discomfort. The evidence there is of neonate abilities in the realm of feeding behavior do not allow a more specific statement (for a review, see Lock, 1980, p. 42–47). An anthropomorphic rendering of the implicational hierarchy that stems from this assumption is as follows. The value of the infant's early crying, *to the infant,* is something like this:

(1) *I DO NOT WANT THIS STATE OF AFFAIRS THAT I AM CURRENTLY EXPERIENCING.*

Because no other innate discriminative ability or knowledge has been assumed, the infant is necessarily oblivious to the implication of (1) that, therefore:

(2) *I DO WANT SOME OTHER STATE OF AFFAIRS.*

Consequently, he is also oblivious to his own lack of resources to attain that state of affairs, and is thus unaware of the implication of (2) that, therefore:

(3) *I WANT YOU TO DO SOMETHING FOR ME.*

This is the general character of the hierarchy of implications that are engendered by his existence. They exist in this order because (1) encompasses (2) which likewise encompasses (3), or put another way, (3) is a more explicit, or specified, rendering of (2), which is a more explicit rendering of (1). To a mother, (1) specifies (3): to the child it under-specifies it. Thus, it may be expected of the child's development that he will move from the stage of under-determination to more specific modes, such that each move will involve a small increment in specification. The move from (1) to (2) involves a smaller increment of specificity than from (1) to (3), and thus (2) will be explicated before (3). This explication will at the same time transform (3) from being a possible possibility to an actual possibility, and so afford future development. When we look for evidence of the actual transition that occurs in development, we find that the general character of the hierarchy undergoes a course of development along the expected lines. That is, the infant first gives evidence of explicatively specifying (2). Piaget (1951) gives an example of this:

Lucienne at 0; 3(12) stops crying when she sees her mother unfastening her dress for the meal. (p. 60)

It is only later that the infant evidences the attainment of (3), by directing his behavior at its goal through the solicitation of another's agency (For a more extensive discussion see Lock, 1980, pp. 8–24, 48–62).

Writing Systems. While the cognitive consequences of literacy are now recognized as tied to social practices (Scribner & Cole, 1981), so that the potentialities of literacy need not be actualized, even though a particular social group has developed a writing system, a general rule of thumb is that given the requisite social conditions, literacy does facilitate the elaboration of abstract thought. Goody (1977, pp. 106, 128), for example, notes Kay's conclusion from a review of color terminology in different cultures:

> Kay comments that it suggests a very general hypothesis about language evolution, namely that "the progress of linguistic evolution may be traced in terms of lexical and syntactic devices that permit or require the *explicit expression of certain universal semantic categories and relations that are present implicitly* (at least) in all languages and all cultures." (1971, pp. 11–12, my emphasis) . . . The process he describes seems to fit the one I [Goody] connect with the introduction and development of graphic systems . . . Writing is critical not simply because it preserves speech over time and space, but because it transforms speech by abstracting its components, by assisting backward scanning, so that communication by eye creates a different cognitive potentiality for human beings than communication by word of mouth.

Given this relationship between literacy and abstraction, it may be predicted that alphabetic writing systems will appear later than nonalphabetic ones in the progressive elaboration of notational modes. This is because the theoretical distillation of a more abstract system can only be accomplished after its earlier and lower levels of explication have taken place (following from the hierarchical principles put forward earlier), and because it required the earlier attempts for the facilitation of the abstract thought necessary to make the explication of the consonant/vowel distinction an actual possibility. The consonant/vowel distinction does not exist in nature; it is not humanly possible to pronounce an isolated consonant. These must always be voiced along with a vowel sound. The distinction exists through a theoretical imposition of human perception. But this abstract perception has to be developed. There is an apparent explicatory leap from the paleolithic notational systems described by Marshack (1972) to those of the alphabetic Greeks, but sandwiched between them are the transitional explications in the cognitive hierarchy of implications that occurred and facilitated subsequent stages: hieroglyphs, logographs, syllabaries, and so on. Both of these areas of change exhibit similar formal properties to those outlined above when using evolutionary change as an example.

DOMAINS OF CHANGE: PHYLOGENY AND ONTOGENY

"The type of analogical thinking which leads to theories that development is based on the recapitulation of ancestral stages or the like no longer seems at all convincing or even very interesting to biologists.'' (Waddington, 1982 p. 203) ''. . . excursions into the realm of fiction.'' (Koffka, 1928, on theories of recapitulation.)

Theories of recapitulation, and especially Haeckel's, have an awe-inspiring sweep and plausibility. They are also incorrect. But it is important to note that they have only been shown to be incorrect in certain ways. Those ways are largely to do with their assertion of the homology between the stages of development in the two domains, and between the mechanisms held responsible for the supposed homologies. There are weaker forms of the view that do not run into these pitfalls: for example, the Theory of Correspondence (Koffka, 1928, p. 48; Claparede, 1911),

> according to which ontogeny seems to parallel phylogeny because external constraints impose a similar order on both processes. There are, for example, only so many ways to move from simplicity to complexity, from homogeneity to heterogeneity, from instinct to consciousness. Phylogeny and ontogeny have no direct influence upon each other (as Haeckelian recapitulation requires); each follows a roughly similar path because it is the only path available. (Mudcracks, basalt pillars, soap bubbles, bee cells, and echinoid plates are all hexagonal because only a few regular forms can fill space completely. The external constraints are identical, but no result has any direct influence upon another). (Gould, 1977, p. 144)

The establishment of analogies between hexagonal structures may not seem very enlightening. However, even though the processes underlying the attainment of these similar forms are very different, the similarities are nonetheless established as more than analogies by the proposed unifying principle of common constraint. Here, with respect to the specific problem of language evolution and development, a similar approach will be adopted. Because recapitulation is such a red rag, it is best to state categorically at the outset what this approach will not claim. It will *not* claim that the infant today recapitulates in his language development the course of language evolution in the species because there is a biogenetic law linking ontogenetic and phylogenetic change. It will *not* claim that the mechanisms of elaboration are the same in each domain. It *will* claim instead that the two processes are independent of each other.

To date, any discussion in this chapter of the ''mechanisms'' of change has been avoided. Rather, a characterization has been offered of that process. This characterization is compatible with any number of accounts of how change is accomplished at the evolutionary level: whether by the accumulation of minor random variations through natural selection; quick catastrophic bursts that punctuate equilibria; or through the inherent playfulness of biological material. Here I will outline the changes that the present approach would put forward as involved in language, and indicate how the periodization of these changes may be picked out in both the ontogenetic *and* phylogenetic fields. The fact that similarities in the elaboration of language may be picked out in the two domains implies nothing about their being linked. Neither should it then be taken that the similarities provide an argument for the media in which these phenomena are manifest. For example, the fact that *infants* pass through one period in which communication is realized in, say, a predominantly manual-visual medium is not in itself grounds for drawing the conclusion that the *species* went through this stage in that mode. Other reasons would have to be invoked to draw that conclusion. Thus it could well prove to be the case that human spoken language has an unbroken evolutionary history, in the vocal medium, even if the present ontogenetic pathways it follows involve other media. But conversely, this would not imply that the characterization of the different manifestations as similar is incorrect.

THE INVENTION OF LANGUAGE

The attainment of language may be approached as a design problem within the context of the characterization of change introduced above. Thus it is not a simple unfolding of a blueprint, but the construction of actualities that afford new possibilities that is the concern here. A basically functional approach will be pursued, the system to be designed being regarded as a communicational one with increasing powers of specificity, and hence an increasing differentiation of its components. There are a number of good reasons for developing this design at an abstract level, and then indicating how the design is realized in different specific contexts, e.g., human ontogeny and phylogeny. The main advantage is that it sidesteps many of the traditional recapitulatory problems. However, an abstract exposition is most cumbersome, so for "clarity" the human infant will be taken as examplar.

The Nonverbal Prelude: Setting the Stage for Language

The earlier brief discussion of the development of nonverbal communication is a useful place to start from, because it already points to a number of salient features. The first is that the infant does not face the problem of constructing a communicative ability *de novo,* for he possesses one by default through his mother's interpretations of his activities. What he does not possess, though, is the ability to *control* his communication, nor to *specify* the message he is perceived as sending.

Control of Communication.   The infant's initial position is one of the best examplars of what Vygotsky (1966) termed the *intermental level* of functioning. That is, the communicative function is not possessed by the infant himself: it exists outside him in his interactions with his social world. Communication is read into him. One of the double-binds of being a part of a cultural world is that it is impossible to be encompassed by one and not communicate: It is impossible not to communicate, even if one has consciously decided not to, for the act of not communicating will eventually communicate that decision. The child's task is to discover how he accomplishes what he does accomplish. He *possesses* the means to influence the cultural beings he is in contact with; he has to *discover* what those means are.

Specification of Communication   There are a number of facets to this problem. First, there is no reason to assume that when a very young infant "communicates" he has any idea what his goal is. The care he is administered has a retroactive character, in the sense that it will provide him with the knowledge of what it was that he wanted all along (Dreyfus: 1967). His present discomforts will thereby be specified after the fact as knowable in terms of their future resolution. Thus, if his early crying is rendered as having the value I DO NOT WANT THIS (WHATEVER THIS IS), then through his mother's reactions he will transform this uncertainty through the socially mediated specification he is afforded. (WHATEVER THIS IS) will be retroactively specified by what the mother does to remove and negate it. This is the beginning of the socially created knowledge on which the child will come to base his control of his activities. Second, because there will often exist a contingency between the child's activities and the specificatory reactions of his mother, the ground will exist for his specifying to himself the means that mediate the effectiveness of his activities. He will be able to work out the means of his success as these themselves become specified in interaction. Third, these occurrences imply that the process of specifying meanings has begun. The above discussion has been concerned with the transition in the specification of early crying from I DO NOT WANT THIS to the actualization of I DO WANT THAT (cf. above on nonverbal development). Note, though, that while crying now specifies this meaning, it does not specify any of the components of that meaning. It in fact specifies them all in concert with its context of occurrence.

None of the elements of such communications are individually marked or differentiated. The child's message is egocentric, and only specific within the context of the mass of presuppositions in which he unbeknowingly operates. But, there is a further specification functionally operative within his communication, and a similar explicatory path to that above is available to him. His crying is socially constituting the components I WANT, and not THAT, which is in fact being specified from two different sources. First, it is being specified contextually, as say DRINK, FOOD, COMFORT, and second, interactively in the sense that this undifferentiated THAT encompasses not only a goal-object or event component, but also a means component, YOU DO SOMETHING.

This means-component does not need marking communicatively, but can be realized in the mode of communication. Thus, if the child later gives evidence of taking into account the fact that communication is only successful through the mediation of another (aiming his communication at the other), he indicates his explication of this means condition. But where social crying specifies I WANT, reaching specifies THAT. It may be postulated that reaching initially conveys an entire undifferentiated message in the same way as crying does, but that since social reaching specifies THAT and leaves the remainder of the meaning to be contextually specified, contra to crying, it will eventually come to specify just that one component of the message. So, sophisticated nonverbal communication could be accomplished by employing crying and pointing together, and aiming them at another.

Sophistication is present in such communicative activities, but the level of specificity within the message itself is still very low. A pointing gesture, for example, can serve in different contexts to specify THAT as SOMETHING I AM INTERESTED IN or SOMETHING I WANT, but it cannot of itself specify that "something" any more specifically. That "something" is still only given greater specification at the cultural levels of communication that the infant has yet to explicate. That level specifies as distinct all the components of the child's "something" that he is as yet incapable of differentiating. We as adults use pronouns on occasions when our cultural systems do not specify the required differentiations, but we are operating in a much more explicated system than the child, whose THAT is all-embracing: implying other agents, their actions, the objects acted on, the change in state or position those objects undergo, and so on, without being able to specify any one of these implications, yet encompassing them all within the contextually obvious THAT. Language development *is* this process of further specification.

EARLY LANGUAGE DEVELOPMENT: FROM ACTION THROUGH GESTURE TO SYMBOL

Because the above discussion has in fact been rather abstract, the following outline of language development will be prefaced by recapping its nonverbal prelude. The outline given here is more fully elaborated elsewhere (e.g., Lock, 1978, 1980, 1982). Note that the use of the concept of "stages" here is more to aid in clarity than to imply their reality as separable periods in development. Figure 8.1 gives a summary view of the developmental schedule up to the two-word stage. Certain aspects of this are given a more detailed treatment in the remainder of this section.

1. Action to Gesture

Neonates and very young infants present us with no evidence of possessing communicative abilities, except by default of their living in an environment that treats their actions as if they were already communicative. Many early actions, e.g., crying and reaching for too-distant objects, are only effective through their

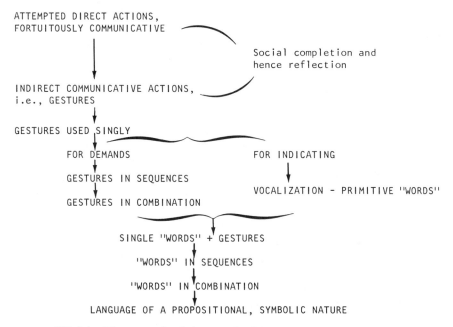

FIG. 8.1.   The course of early language development.

completion by another. Infants give very little evidence of understanding this means-end relationship; however, as a result of this social completion, their effective actions tend to become ritualized and partly vestigial (cf. Piaget's category of secondary circular ractions, 1952, p. 201). By about 9–10 months of age these *stylized actions* appear to have been subjected to means-end analysis, and now function as properly communicative *gestures*. That is, they are not aimed at objects and events per se, but at objects and events *via* another. Where at first they were aimed at obtaining an object, they are now aimed at obtaining assistance. These gestures are used singly. Functionally, they appear to fall into different classes: crying, for example, indicates the child wants something, and requires its context of occurrence to delineate what that something is; pointing, in contrast, indicates a something, and requires its context of occurrence to convey why it is being indicated. Cognitively, however, these different gestures are probably equivalent, conveying from the child's point of view similar undifferentiated holistic messages, anthropomorphically rendered as "gimme that."

2. The Combination of Gestures

Perhaps for functional reasons, to allow more efficient and hence specific communication, gestures move from being used singly to being used in combination

(11–14 months). Thus the child will cry *and* point; cry *and* raise its arms; point *and* lip-smack. Cognitively, there appears little reason to suspect that the individual elements of messages are becoming many more differentiated than they were previously—they are still holistic entities.

3. The Categorization of Gestures

While the normal child appears preadapted to vocalize, the medium in which this present development occurs is not of crucial relevance to us at the moment. Indeed, because we have such a tendency to regard vocal productions that sound to us like adult words as language—with much of what that categorization entails—it is probably best to ignore the medium of production. Suffice it to say that in normal children this next development tends to occur predominantly at the vocal level; in congenitally deaf children at the manual level. Since it is most likely motivated by functional considerations, it is not necessary to become embroiled in questions regarding cognitive change dependent upon the emergence of symbolic language, and so forth. Enough of reservation: the development in question is that of producing gestures of a more specificatory nature than pointing. Thus specific gestures for objects, for example, begin to make an appearance. Rather than merely pointing at all objects, some become indicated by particular gestures: cars, for example, by vocalizations like "brmmm-brmmm," "beep-beep," "car," or actions like manipulating a steering-wheel; trains by "chuff-chuff," or circulatory pumping actions with the arms. This development has generally been termed "naming": It would be preferable at this point to suspend such a judgment, and just call it an increase in functional specification.

4. Symbols: Naming, Reference and Words

(a) Even if reference is made to the above stage without specifically saying "this is naming," such a judgment is implicated, because the ability is very close to what would normally be thought of as naming. This notion of implication is a very important one. The infant's repertoire of communicative strategies contains a number of nonpropositional ways of both making demands of, and comments about, the world and his or her desires and actions in it. These abilities are those of:

1. Making demands, established gesturally: demands for objects (crying plus pointing), demands for changes in state (crying plus arm raising, to initiate being picked up), and the like.
2. Prelinguistic gestural commenting: e.g., indicating an object (of interest?) by pointing at it; perhaps also looking at the mother, laughing, and looking back at the event in question.
3. "Linguistic" gestural commenting, or "naming," in relation to objects: e.g., using different vocalizations when mother points at different pictures in a book.

4. "Linguistic" gestural commenting concerning the child's own movements and experiences (an ability not discussed above): e.g., saying "Up" when being lifted, or "Down" when stepping down from a seat.

Because these abilities are very context-bound they need not be thought of as properly symbolic, or part of a true language system. Certainly, they border on this, but are better regarded as modes of increasing the functional specificatoriness of the infants' communications. Cognitively, there is not yet a referential or representational system comprised of differentiated parts.

The suggestion here, however, is that these early abilities, nonpropositional though they are, are sufficient in combination to allow the propositional level to emerge because *they engender a hierarchy of implications that lead to that level,* and that *they also provide the tools whereby elements of this hierarchy can be explicated.* Bear in mind in the following that the developments being discussed need *not* be about profound changes in the infant's cognitive abilities, the attainment of symbolic language: they may only be reflective of an increasing functional efficiency in communication brought about by his or her living in a more and more complex intersubjective world. The argument about hierarchical explication will be developed *without* recourse to data, so that the principles and processes involved in the proposed developmental sequence may be seen. Data will be considered *afterwards.*

(b) From the starting point provided by the above four abilities, it may be expected that the first extension of "word" usage to occur will be their incorporation within demands: This does not require a new ability, just a "shuffling" of those that already exist. Objects that were previously demanded gesturally are now demanded "linguistically"—a "word" combined with demand gestures. Similarly with action "words," they too come to be used in demanding. Early action "words" probably have a large experiential component in their meaning for the child. But this experiential component has both inner and outer aspects: The child not only experiences the action, but also sees its physical result. When action words are used in demands this physical component is emphasized, and constitutes the rudiments of a conception of changes in physical state: It is, after all, this change that the child is demanding.

Three of the abilities now possessed—those of being able to "name" an object, an action, and make a small distinction between experiential and physical correlates of the effects of action—are sufficient in combination to allow a new development to occur: They imply it, and provide the tools for its explication. Thus, when the infant looks at an object he is acting upon he perceives a situation in which he has some conception of the object's movement, some conception of the objects having a name, and the situation bears a relation to the implied self through the action it performs. Hence both the abilities to "name" an object that is being acted upon *by the* implied self and to "name" an action performed on an object *by the* implied self are made possible.

Given that this possibility is actualized, a new implication is ripe for being made explicit. The child's perception of action is now not only structured around his implied self, but also around the objects he acts upon. This development is sufficient to open up the *new* possibility of action being anchored around objects per se—independently of his involvement with them: sufficient for changes in his conception of action to occur. That possibility is his perceiving both the changes in state and position he experiences *and* those he causes an object to undergo as instances of the same explicit event. In other words, the original ability implies a propositional one—the child's doing something to an object (nonpropositional) implies the object is having something done to it (propositional)—and again provides the tools for its explication. The child may now be expected to begin "naming" objects that are being acted on *irrespective* of the actor, and similarly also the actions of agents (or implicit selves) other than himself.

Having by this path arrived at the propositional ability he may now give explicit form to further features that were originally implicit in the messages of the communicative gestural stage. That is, he may begin to talk about non-self agents, whose actions upon objects he can already comment on: and through coming to do this he will explicate his implied self and give it some objective existence within his conceptualization of the world. The order of developments just outlined, then, is as follows:

1. prelinguistic demands and comments, implying other-self actions
2. "naming" objects
3. "naming" implicit-self actions
4. demanding objects; demanding changes in implicit self-state; implying other-self actions

NON-PROPOSITIONAL

5. (a) "naming" objects acted upon by implicit-self
   (b) "naming" implicit-self actions performed upon these objects
6. (5 (b) is effectively naming the state or change in state of objects)

TRANSITIONAL

7. (a) "naming" objects acted upon by other-self actions, implying other-self agents
   (b) "naming" changes in state of objects irrespective of the actor
   (c) "naming" the actions of other-self agents, implying other-self agents
8. "naming" other-self agents, implying self
9. "naming" self—implicit self becomes objective self.

PROPOSITIONAL

A further development that may be expected is that after each ability is realized it will come to be used as part of a thus extended demand capability.

A Theoretical Example: Changing Uses of "Up" and "Cup"

Some flesh may be put on the above skeleton by a thought experiment, beginning with "words" from (2) "naming" objects and (3) "naming" implicit-self actions. The vocabulary for this exercise is *cup* for (2) and *up* for (3). *Cup* is used initially in the context of seeing a cup: *Up* on being moved, or getting from one place to another—movement in relation to one's "self." It does not require a great change in one's cognitive grasp of the world to begin using these words in new contexts—those of moving the cup by one's own efforts—a situation that is again defined in relation to one's self. Hence there is no great difficulty in saying *cup* when you act on a cup, or alternatively *up*. A necessary implication of saying something with a holistic meanings such as I AM MOVING THE CUP is that THE CUP IS BEING MOVED. Take away one's own arm, and the spectacle of a moving cup is similar whoever moves it. Use either "word" in this situation, not a large jump, and something quite dramatic results: "words" are being applied to a reality beyond one's self. Something is almost being said about cups and their movements not their relation to one's own movements. It is the beginning of a system of categorizing the world objectively—a new organizational framework for cognition. Because of the emergence of this new framework, it is possible to move to the newly possible implication that if the cup moved without any self-action, another acted—for would *up* in this context refer to the movement of the cup, or the action of another? To some extent to both; yet effectively, the propositional realm has been entered.

Evidence?

What evidence is there that this sequence actually occurs in development? Studies of this phase of language growth are not easy to compare as no accepted classification or descriptive systems have yet emerged. If, however, we read between the lines of these studies, then the sequence appears to be valid. It would only be invalidated if such studies as those by Greenfield and Smith (1976), Leonard (1976), Ramer (1975), Nelson (1973), Ingram (1971) provided evidence that the late explications proposed here occurred earlier in the sequence than argued: and they do not. This sequence is in fact supported by proposals by Sinclair-de Zwart (1973), MacNamara (1972), Slobin (1970) and Brown (1973) with regard to the relation between cognitive and linguistic development. Here an attempt has been made to get at the logic that underlies this relationship (see also Lock, 1980, pp. 123–196).

In sum, the two phases of development outlined here, the gestural and the linguistic, are first being seen as essentially continuous, and second, in consequence, as based on the same underlying processes. In the gestural phase a hierarchy of implications, engendered by the child's given relationship to the world, is gradually made determinate by the child through components of his behavior that have been constructed from his social interactions. In the linguistic phase the further reaches of this hierarchy are given an explicit construction through components of his behavior that we term "words." "Words," however, remain part of the gestural system during much of their early appearance. However, even though this development has an essentially continuous character, its poles are in different realms of cognition, and hence discontinuous: reflective, propositional self-consciousness has emerged where it did not exist before.

THE STATUS OF EARLY LANGUAGE

"Words" have been kept in inverted commas above so as not to obscure how closely the developmental sequence is in line with Vygotsky's (1966) dictum that "any function in the child's cultural development appears on the stage twice, on two planes, first on the social plane and then on the psychological, first among people as an intermental category and then within the child as an intramental category" (p. 44). Thus, functionally, the child's language differentiates into apparently differing categories, but when these are used, either as single utterances or as parts of early combinations, they function holistically in combination with their context of utterance. It is only later that they will wreak their cognitive change, establishing themselves as a system in which the different elements have only restricted reference in relation to each other: action words coming to refer to particular actions, differentiated from actors and the objects acted upon; and so on. Prior to this, they are cognitively holistic while functionally differentiated. (This is very much a transitional phase in which cracks in the holistic representational system are being forged—primordial symbolic soup.) The view here is that to begin with, early words help children in discriminating the world, only later allowing them to categorize it in productive ways. Thus, a differentiation in gestural communication produces the bedrock from which symbolic communication of an analytic nature may arise.

What is generally thought of as language thus appears in the child's repertoire much later than might, on the surface, appear to be the case. This discussion has, then, separated the appearance of differentiated vocalizations that, communicatively, are functionally efficient yet of a basically holistic nature, from differentiated vocalizations that are symbolically propositional and facilitate analytic thought and complex communication through their ability to render the world as comprised of differentiable and discrete objective events and categories. This latter stage is consolidated with the emergence of skills around 6 years of age that are often referred to as "metalinguistic" (e.g., Hakes, Evans, & Tumner, 1980).

A SUMMARY OF LANGUAGE DEVELOPMENT

To summarize this outline of the developmental process, we have:

(i) The establishment of a holistic gestural ability from a base in action;
(ii) the functional elaboration of the gestural ability whilst still retaining a holistic elemental base; this occurs
    a) at the non-vocal level;
    b) at the vocal level; and
    c) it also occurs at what is usually termed the "verbal" level—vocalizations that have the form of adult words.
(iii) The functional elaboration of the "verbal" level leads to a functionally differentiable repertoire of what look very much like propositional symbols, but probably remain from the cognitive viewpoint holistic items. Elaboration is at the intermental level, and cognitively is "protosymbolic."
(iv) Finally, these separate holistic items become organized into a structure-dependent network, each now with particular reference: true symbols emerge, and language as a propositional medium replaces the "verbal." Elaboration occurs at the cognitive, intramental level, analytic thought is facilitated, and the stage is set for full-blown cognitive development predicated on symbolic categorization.

This view of language is consonant with the characterization of change developed earlier. Forms—in this case cognitive or mental ones—become explicated from the hierarchy of possibilities that they serve to generate. *Self-transcendence* is clearly demonstrated: the system affords its own development.

ONTOGENY AND PHYLOGENY

I wish to put the view that language development and language evolution follow the same path at the level of the underlying transitions outlined above, because:

(i) they both involve a transition from a non-self-conscious and nonpropositional mode of dealing with the world to a self-conscious, propositional and hence linguistic mode;

(ii) the nature of nonlinguistic awareness and the functional exigencies facing its possessor in the elaboration of a communication system *constrain* the path of the affordance of that transition, so that while different processes may be operative at the ontogenetic and phylogenetic levels, the steps on the path will follow in the same order in each case;

(iii) that while sophisticated and functionally elaborate nonlinguistic communicative systems will be based on holistic modes of knowledge, once they reach a certain level—either ontogenetically or phylogenetically—they will create the possibility of transition to objective, propositional forms, and hence to objective, propositional knowledge.

I have previously put forward the view that language arises through making explicit the implications of our relationships with the physical and social worlds (Lock, 1978, 1980). Thus language emergence is a problem-solving event: how to make explicit what is implicit in earlier abilities: how to objectify and conceptualize the components of those abilities. Solving these problems results in the emergence of the symbolic world. This approach led me to the view that "the *evolution* of language can be seen as the solution of these problems by the invention (the means by which properties are given explicit form) of the conceptual mode . . . the *development* of language needs to be qualified as the *guided reinvention* of a specific conceptual system, predicated on an earlier prelinguistic communicative ability" (Lock, 1978, pg. 14). In language development: "the mother is the guide and the child the inventor" (Lock, 1980, pg. 36).

It is from these considerations that I now put forward the suggestion that the stages in the child's invention of language, as outlined above, may be taken as those by which *any* holistically constituted knowledge system will invent language. Note that this suggestion says nothing about the behavior and methods of invention having any homology in ontogeny and phylogeny. It argues for a recapitulation of stages irrespective of the medium in which they are manifested. Thus, in a very important sense, the Haeckelian, the development of language by the child *does not* recapitulate its evolution in the species. What that development shows are the characteristics of any changing system; so consequently, should its evolution.

LANGUAGE EVOLUTION: SOME RELEVANT DATA

Intellectual Capabilities

In studies of the different tool-technologies in the human evolutionary record, Wynn (1979, 1981) concludes that "essentially modern human intelligence was achieved 300,000 years ago" (1979, p. 371). In claiming this, Wynn used the Piagetian concepts of reversibility and conservation "to assess the spatial concepts used by the hominids who manufactured the artifacts from the Isimilia Prehistoric Site, Tanzania. [He concluded] that these artifacts required the organizational abilities of operational intelligence and that, therefore, the hominid knappers were not significantly less intelligent than modern adults'' (1979, p. 371). The ascription of operational intelligence means that the ability to conduct, among other things, whole-part analyses is present in a quite sophisticated form. Such analyses would obviously be implicated in the construction of a linguistic communicative system (cf. Bates, Benigni, Bretherton, Camaioni, & Voltera, 1979). By contrast, Wynn (1981) summarizes his investigation of earlier tool-traditions thus:

> From the analysis of the geometry of two-million-year-old artifacts from Olduvai Gorge it is concluded that the hominids who made the tools possessed pre-operational intelligence. Pre-operational intelligence employs such organizational features as trial-and-error and control of single variables but lacks such important modern features as true classification and pre-correction of errors. Pre-operational intelligence is also typical of modern pongids (p. 529)

It is possible, then, that differences in the communicative abilities of our ancestral hominids may also be present.

Speech Capabilities

The work of Laitman and his associates (e.g., 1981) appears to yield the best data on this topic. They note that modifications to the structure of the larynx have occurred in humans compared to other primates, and that these modifications are adaptations for speaking (Laitman, Crelin, & Conlogue, 1977; Saski, Levine, Laitman, & Crelin, 1977; Laitman & Crelin, 1980a, 1980b). Further, the only mammal in their samples that did not show a highly placed larynx was man (Crelin, 1976). According to Laitman, "While the position of the larynx affects the mode of respiration and ingestion of food, it also affects the ability to produce sounds (1981, p. 4)." A low larynx is necessary for the production of the full range of speech sounds. Correlated with the position of the larynx are changes in the structure of the base of the cranium (the basicranium): "In animals where the larynx was placed high in the neck such as cats, dogs, monkeys and apes, the basicranium was relatively non-flexed. Only older humans showed a larynx placed absolutely and relatively lower in the neck, and only these individuals exhibited a markedly flexed basicranium" (Laitman, 1981, p. 5). Laitman's subsequent investigation was then on the basis of the following reasoning. Given that the low position of the larynx (that is correlated with full speech ability) is correlated with a particular structural pattern of the basicranium, then measurements of the basicrania of fossil adult hominids will indicate when the larynx attained a position suitable for the production of human speech comparable to that of modern man. The results of this investigation of fossil specimens (Laitman, 1981; Laitman *et al.*, 1977) were:

> The early australopithecines . . . appear to have had basicrania, and by extension upper respiratory systems, closely approximating those of living apes. (Laitman, 1981, pp. 11–12)

> While not exhibiting the marked flexion of modern *sapiens*, *H.* erectus appears to show the first signs of increased basicranial flexion. (Laitman, 1981, p. 12)

> The line leading to modern man, passing through populations represented by hominids such as Sale, Steinheim, Broken Hill and Cro-Magnon, probably acquired an upper respiratory system similar to ours by 300,000 to 400,000 years before the present. The vocal tract anatomy necessary for the production of the full range of human speech sounds was thus probably also present by this period. (Laitman, 1981, p. 13)

Note that the postulated timing of the ability for full speech sounds is comparable to that advanced by Wynn (1979) for the achievement of "essentially modern intelligence."

THE RATE OF TECHNICAL ADVANCE

One of the few points of apparent agreement regarding human evolution is on the pattern shown in the development of preserved artifacts. Tool development, for example, shows a very slow rate of change from its appearance possibly as early as 3 million years BP, until the Acheulian period began in the late lower Paleolithic period of the middle Pleistocene, around 350,000 years BP. There then follows a period of an increased rate of development, through the Mousterian and into the Aurignacian to about 40,000 years BP (roughly, the Middle Paleolithic). Around 40,000 BP, as Krantz (1980) summarizes:

> (a) Tools became more sophisticated, suggesting that more learning was involved in their manufacture. (b) Tool types became more geographically localized, specific techniques being developed for local circumstances. (c) Stone-tipped projectiles became common everywhere. (Earlier "points" are mostly thick-based and are almost impossible to haft). (d) Fire using and cave dwelling became common everywhere, not just in colder climates. (e) Technological changes began to occur more rapidly. (p. 774)

"More rapidly" becomes "most rapidly" as one increasingly approaches the present. Krantz (1980) proposed that this explosive development at (and from) about 40,000 BP (and the contemporary rapid changes in cranial anatomy) occurred as a result of the appearance of spoken language: "This is not to say that the totality of our linguistic behavior dates from this time, but rather that some critical aspect approved then which perfected the system of communication'' (Krantz, 1980, p. 775). Hewes (1980) is in broad agreement with this: "It has long been supposed that the explosive cultural manifestations of the Upper Paleolithic were in some way connected with a surge in cognitive competence, perhaps triggered by linguistic improvements." Both Hewes (1981) and Krantz (1980) similarly agree that the "invention" of the phonemic principle may be the crucial event: "phonemes function . . . very much like the letters of the written alphabet, as meaningless signs from which longer and meaningful sequences can be constructed without paying attention to the original meaning, if any, inherent in the sound of the letter or phoneme" (Hewes, 1981, pp. 6–7). A phonemic organizing principle in language would allow for a more efficient lexical storage and retrieval system, allowing "a dramatic rise in the ability to handle complex, conceptual thought at high speeds" (Hewes, 1981, p. 7). How this change might have come about has been discussed by Foster (1978).

An Account of Language Evolution

Note that while there is a discrepancy in the timing of the above development compared to those reviewed earlier (c. 40,000 years BP compare to c. 300,000 years BP), these timings are not incompatible. Translating the course of language change through the increasing specificity of communication that was outlined earlier into stages, it becomes possible to outline a calendar for language evolution. Table 8.1 presents this information in summary form, the stages being:

STAGE 1 : the development of gestures.

STAGE 2 : the functional elaboration of gestures, predominantly manual.

STAGE 3 : the functional elaboration of gestures in the vocal medium, leading to a functionally differentiated repertoire of holistic elements.

STAGE 4 : a period of transition to the symbolic, propositional mode per se, discovering the referential properties inherent in the functionally differentiated vocal system (e.g., whilst this system is basically context-dependent, it does allow for the possibility of absent objects, and so forth, being referred to).

STAGE 5 : The construction of objective, propositional, and hence functionally analytic, language.

Stage 1

Whilst there are a number of studies of ape language skills under laboratory conditions, there are almost none suggesting anything comparable in the wild. Plooij's report (1978) is a notable exception. His data indicate that feral chim-

TABLE 8.1

A Tentative Timetable for Language Evolution

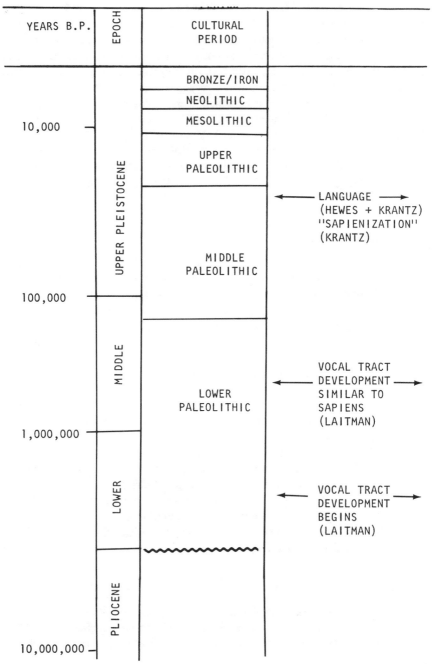

	LANGUAGE STAGES PROPOSED HERE (SEE TEXT)	
AGRICULTURE ETC. + COMPLEXIFICATION OF SOCIAL LIFE UPPER PALEOLITHIC TOOL "EXPLOSION"	STAGE 5	Exploitation of a system of structure-dependent items (language proper). Analytic takes over from wholistic processing. Increase of cognitive power + consequent faster development in cultural traditions.
FASTER DEVELOPMENT OF BASIC STONE ARTIFACTS	STAGE 4	Transitional period following stage 3 in which the functionally elaborate system begins to be exploited for its symbolic + propositional potential beginning of shift from wholistic to analytic units of representation + concommitant sophistication of artifacts (+ labor, symbolic practices-burial).
SLOW DEVELOPMENT IN FORM OF STONE ARTIFACTS	STAGE 3	Transition of stage 2 to the vocal medium, resulting, doubtless, from the usually cited selection pressures.
	STAGE 2	Functional elaboration of gestures: needing the cognitive prerequisites of means-ends analysis + imitation to be established. These implicated in, and sufficient for, simple fabrication + transgeneration transmission of artifacts.
	STAGE 1	Development of communicative intent + gesture, allowing social coordination, but possibly not sufficient for the elaboration of artifacts.

panzees elaborate a proto-symbolic system of communication from more direct actions during their infancy: arm raising to initiate bouts of tickling, for example. Rambaugh and Savage (1977) reported a natural sign language as being used by pygmy chimpanzees living under zoo conditions, and suggest its progressive development as being from direct social action to true communication (Klopfer, 1976). Certainly, these systems are not particularly sophisticated, but they certainly mark a departure from the emotionally laden call systems that might, traditionally, be expected of animals. Given Wynn's (1979, 1981) conclusion from his study of the earliest of "human" artifacts that early man possessed a level of intelligence similar to that of modern pongids, it would seem probable that their communicative systems were at last as elaborate.

If there are any unique human propensities, apart from bodily form, that mark off man from the animals (and the main candidates—language, culture and tool using—no longer seem that viable), then the two that seem the best candidates are using tools for making tools, and teaching. Goodall's research (1964) on feral chimpanzees shows that chimpanzees do fabricate tools, but:

1. tools are fabricated with their "bare hands" and not by the use of a fashioning implement;
2. the skills of toolmaking and tool use are not taught to the young; they are developed through individual imitation and trial and error.

Stage 2

The earliest stone tools were certainly made with more than bare hands: one stone (a protohammer) had to hit another (the eventual tool). There can be no direct evidence that tool traditions were taught: indeed, they could be preserved by imitative trial and error as in pongids. However, the interpolation of an extra step in the tool-making process, the selection of a stone as a means for working on another stone, which was itself a means to another end, does suggest that the communicative system could have been more functionally elaborated and specific. The kind of part-whole analysis that is required to develop a functionally elaborated ability is indicated. For example, congenitally deaf children of deaf parents are able to fashion a functionally specific and elaborate gesture system for themselves: at the same time they possess only fairly rudimentary part-whole analytic skills. Further, if the scavenging-hunting-gathering scenario of human evolution is correct, then an efficient system of diectic communication at least would be put at a premium. Thus, the suggestion for this period is that the tool record evidences sufficient cognitive ability for the elaboration of a more efficient communication system. It is impossible to decide whether cognitive elaboration led to communicative elaboration or vice versa: it is quite possible that both are predicated on the same underlying base. It is difficult to know what evidence could be put forward on the question of whether "deliberate" teaching occurred. That the communicative system was manual rather than vocal is similarly difficult to determine, and can only be decided through the use of arguments that rely on plausibility rather than fact. The one relevant "fact" is that if the system was vocal, it would have been very different from anything we hear today, since the vocal tract anatomy of these beings was not of a modern nature. Hewes (1973, 1976, 1977, 1981) has reviewed the arguments for the earliest manifestations of language precursors being manual. That they were would seem a reasonable conclusion.

Stage 3

Given that evidence of changes toward the modern form of the larynx appear in the fossil record (Laitman, 1981) without change occurring in the basic nature of the human tool-kit, there is little reason to assume anything major in the way of communicative advance was concurrently coming to pass. This suggests that there may exist a remarkable parallel with the present human development of language (this being perhaps the only true "recapitulationary" parallel there is, and perhaps being predicated on similar developments in the anatomy of the vocal tract (Laitman et al., 1977): this parallel should not be taken to be of major significance). There is again no hard data to suggest why this change in medium might have occurred: plausible scenarios can be advanced, however. For example, one cannot "talk" with one's hands full; manual communication requires visual attention to be focused on the communicator, and not the contextually present item or event he is communicating about. The shift in medium fits with the present arguments concerning increasing functional efficiency and specificity, and with the evidence concerning the evolution of the vocal tract. If one accepts that human communication systems were originally manual, then present-day experience argues the shift must have occurred. The fossil record indicates at least the earliest point that shift was likely to have occurred. Beyond that, it is unfortunately all guesswork.

Stage 4

The increasing rate of development in the tool record that is apparent from c. 300,000 BP is not one based on any new ability, but on the recursive embedding of part-whole, means-ends analyses. The distance between initial action and final product is increased continuously: there are more intervening steps between the beginning and end of an activity. This is illustrated in the new Levallosian prepared-core technique of toolmaking. Here the use of a percussive instrument is a means for making a core, which is itself the means for the final tool. Because of the similarity of the operations involved in this and earlier fabricational techniques, it seems likely that no major change in the nature of the toolmakers occurred. Whereas the emerging vocal capability of Stage 3 would require concommitant neuroanatomical change, this present development suggests that brain reorganization is not necessary, but on the principle that "bigger is better," only that more of it was available. There is certainly evidence of an increase in brain size in humans since 300,000 BP; there can unfortunately be little or no evidence of any reorganization since brains do not fossilize. But, if there was no reorganization, then some "cognitive technology" is likely to be required to facilitate the recursive embedding of cognitive operations. A greater elaboration of "language" would be a plausible candidate for this, going hand in hand with the elaboration of skills. This is not to suggest that language determines thought, or that its possession allows new mental operations. Rather, words provide better "counters" within cognitive operations (e.g., "this is very difficult to comprehend because we lack a developed vocabulary"); and facilitate the breaking down of wholes into parts by labeling parts for easy memory retrieval, and so on. The argument here is that the very same stage of increasing functional specificity that contemporary infants exhibit, which necessarily occurs in the creation of any language system, was occurring at this point in human evolution. However, that said, there are still a number of very different stories that could be told about this period:

1. An increasing specification of linguistic units was occurring, attaining a fully propositional form of language. Something dramatic then occurred at c. 40,000 BP, such as phonemization or the invention of syntax;
2. only a transitional-to-proposition stage was established, with or without phonemization and/or syntax;
3. any permutation of these factors.

Stage 5

Something dramatic certainly seems to have occurred about 40,000 BP, allowing the potentiality of a propositional linguistic system to be fully exploited. As the possible scenarios for Stage 4 indicate, it is difficult to know exactly what did occur. However, whatever occurred, it facilitated the further specification of language and hence the use of the latent possibilities of the system. Propositional thought was probably not impossible before this period—being a latent potentiality of the system—but would be greatly facilitated by the invention of either or both syntax or a phonemic organizing principle. The further exploitation of these potentialities is probably circumscribed by the impossibility of getting any more hardware down the human birth canal. Thus extrasomatic devices have been necessary for the full exploitation of the latent possibilities of the linguistic system (cf. Eisenstein, 1979; Goody, 1977; Havelock, 1963; Marshack, 1972; Scribner & Cole, 1981). This scenario allows an answer to the hoary old evolutionary question of how humans appear to possess brains with a greater capability than is often used: The capacity is fully used in the sustenance of tool technologies. The capacity of the systems of communication and representation it uses is far greater than that of the brain itself. By the recursive embedding of its basic operations that is facilitated both intrasomatically and extrasomatically through the explication of the possibilities of a system of its own accidental manufacture, "evolution was self-motivated and self-transcendent."

> Words are thus like the steps of a ladder, by the help of which we climb into higher and higher regions of abstraction; they are also like coins or bank-notes, into which we manage to condense a large amount of that value which we term meaning; or to

use a still closer analogy, they are like the symbols employed by the mathematician, which may contain in an easily manipulated form the results of a long calculation, no part of which could have been conducted but for the use of other symbols of the same kind. (Romanes, 1897, pp. 69–70)

The formal principles of change that were initially outlined in the context of biological change are thus also manifested in the elaboration of language.

REFERENCES

Bates, E., Benigni, L. Bretherton, I., Camaioni, L., & Voltera, V. (1979). *The emergence of symbols: Cognition and communication in infancy.* New York: Academic Press.

Brown, R. (1978). *A first language: The early stages.* Cambridge, MA: Harvard University Press.

Crelin, E. S. (1976). Development of the upper respiratory system. *Ciba Clinical Symposium, 28,* 3–26.

Claparede, E. (1911). *Experimental pedagogy and the psychology of the child.* London: Edward Arnold.

Dreyfus, H. L. (1967). Why computers must have bodies in order to be intelligent. *Revue of Metaphysics, 21,* 13–32.

Einsenstein, E. (1979). *The printing press as an agent of change* (Vols. 1 and 2). Cambridge: Cambridge University Press.

Foster, M. L. (1978). The symbolic structure of the primordial language. In S. L. Washburn & E. R. McCown (Eds.), *Human evolution: Biosocial perspectives.* Menlo Park, CA: Cummings.

Gamble, C. (1980). Information exchange in the Paleolithic. *Nature, 283,* 522–523. (Cited by Hewes, 1980).

Gibson, J. J. (1979). *The ecological approach to visual perception.* New York: Houghton-Mifflin.

Goodall, J. (1964). Tool using and aimed throwing in a community of tree-living chimpanzees. *Nature, 201,* 1264–1266.

Goody, J. (1977). *The domestication of the savage mind.* Cambridge: Cambridge University Press.

Gould, S. J. (1977). *Ontogeny and phylogeny.* Cambridge, MA: Harvard University Press.

Greenfield, P. M., & Smith, J. (1976.) *The structure of communication in early language development.* New York: Academic Press.

Hakes, D. T., Evans, J. S., & Tumner, W. E. (1980). *The development of metalinguistic abilities in children.* New York: Springer-Verlag.

Havelock, E. (1963). *Preface to Plato.* Cambridge, MA: Harvard University Press.

Hewes, G. W. (1973). Primate communication and the gestural origins of language. *Current Anthropology, 14,* 5–24.

Hewes, G. W. (1976). The current status of the gestural theory of language origin. *Annals of the New York Academy of Sciences, 280,* 482–504.

Hewes, G. W. (1980). Comment. *Current anthropology, 21,* 781–782.

Hewes, G. W. (1981, August). The invention of phonemically-based language. *Paper presented at the International Symposium on Glossogenetics,* Paris.

Ingram, D. (1971). Transitivity in child language. *Language, 47,* 888–910.

Jantsch, E. (1982). Cited by Hitching, F. (1981), *The neck of the giraffe* (p. 192). New Haven: Ticknor & Fields.

Kay, P. (1971). *Language, evolution and speech style.* Draft paper. Cited by Goody (1977).

Klopfer, P. H. (1976). Evolution behavior and language. In M. E. Hahn & E. C. Simmel (Eds.), *Communicative behavior and evolution.* New York: Academic Press.

Koffka, K. (1928). *The growth of the mind.* London: Routledge & Kegan Paul.

Krantz, G. X. (1980). Sapienization and speech. *Current Anthropology, 21,* 773–792.

Laitman, J. T. (1981). *The evolution of the hominid upper respiratory system and implications for the origin of speech. Paper given at the Transdisciplinary Symposium on Glossogenetics,* UNESCO, Paris. August

Laitman, J. T., & Crelin, E. S. (1980a). Tantalum markers as an aid in identifying the upper respiratory structures of experimental animals. *Laboratory Animal Science, 30,* 245–248.

Laitman, J. T., & Crelin, E. S. (1980b). Developmental change in the upper respiratory system of human infants. *Perinatology/Neuratology, 4,* 15–22.

Laitman, J. T., Crelin, E. S., & Conlogue, G. J. (1977). The function of the epiglottis in monkey and man. *Yale Journal of Medicine, 50,* 43–49.

Leonard, L. B. (1976). *Meaning in child language.* New York: Grune & Stratton.

Lock, A. J. (1978). The emergence of language. In A. J. Lock (Ed.), *Action, gesture and symbol: The emergence of language.* London: Academic Press.

Lock, A. J. (1980). *The guided reinvention of language.* London: Academic Press.

Lock, A. J. (1981a). Universales in human conception. In P. L. F. Heelas and A. J. Lock (Eds.), *Indigenous psychologies: The anthropology of the self.* London: Academic Press.

Lock, A. J. (1981b). Indigenous psychology and human nature: A psychological perspective. In P. L. F. Heelas & A. J. Lock (Eds.), *Indigenous psychologies: The anthropology of the self.* London: Academic Press.

Lock, A. J. (1982). A note on the ecology of meaning. *Quaderni di Semantica, 3,* 112–117.

MacNamara, J. (1972). Cognitive basis of language learning in infants. *Psychological Review, 79,* 1–13.

Marshack, A. (1972). *The roots of civilisation.* New York: McGraw-Hill.

Maynard-Smith, J. (1976). Evolution and the theory of games. *American Scientist, 64,* 41–45.

Nelson, K. (1973). Structure and strategy in learning to talk. *Monographs of the Society for Research in Child Development, 149, 38,* 1–2.

Piaget, J. (1951). *Play, dreams and imitation in children.* London: Routledge & Kegan Paul.

Piaget, J. (1952). *The origins of intelligence in children.* New York: International Universities Press.

Plooij, F. X. (1978). Some basic traits of language in wild chimpanzees? In A. J. Lock (Ed.), *Action, gesture and symbol: The emergence of language.* London: Academic Press.

Rambaugh, D., & Savage, S. (1977). *Paper presented to the American Association for the Advancement of Science.*

Ramer, A. (1975). *The merging of communicative and categorical functions of language.* Paper presented to the American Speech and Hearing Association, Washington, DC.

Romanes, G. J. (1897). *Essays,* London: Longmans, Green.

Saski, C. T., Levine, P. A., Laitman, J. T., & Crelin, E. S. (1977). Postnatal descent of the epiglottis in man: A preliminary report. *Otolaryngology, 103,* 169–171.

Schribner, S., & Cole, M. (1981). *The psychology of literacy.* Cambridge, MA: Harvard University Press.

Sinclair-de-Zwart, H. (1973). Language acquisition and cognitive development. In T. E. Moore (Ed.), *Cognitive development and the acquisition of language.* New York: Academic Press.

Slobin, D. (1970). Universals of grammatical development in children. In G. B. Flores d'Arcais & W. M. Levelt (Eds.), *Advances in psycholinguistics.* Amsterdam: North Holland.

Van Valen, L. (1976). Energy and evolution. *Evolutionary Theory, 1,* 179–229.

Von Uexkull, J. (1957). A stroll through the world of animals and men. In C. H. Schiles (Ed.), *Instinctive behavior.* London: Methuen.

Vygotsky, L. S. (1966). Development of the higher mental functions. In *Psychological Research in the U.S.S.R.* Moscow: Progress Publishers.

Waddington, C. H. (1982). Cited by Hitching, F. (1982). *The neck of the giraffe* (p. 203). New Haven: Ticknor & Fields.

Wynn, T. (1979). The intelligence of later Acheulean hominids. *Man, 14,* 371–391.

Wynn, T. (1981). The intelligence of Oldowan hominids. *Journal of Human Evolution, 10,* 529–541.

Author Index

Italics indicate pages with complete bibliographic information.

Subject Index